The *Big* Fact Book About
MOUNT RAINIER

*Fascinating Facts, Records, Lists, Topics,
Characters and Stories*

by

Bette Filley

with maps and graphics by

Rachel French

Dunamis House
Issaquah, WA 98027

Dunamis House
P.O.Box 321
Issaquah, WA. 98027
(206) 255-5274
fax (206) 277-8780
E-mail rainier@tcm.nbs.net

Manufactured in the United States of America

Publisher's Cataloging in Publication

(Prepared by Quality Books, Inc.)

Filley, Bette.
   The big fact book about Mount Rainier : fascinating facts, records, lists, topics, characters and stories / by Bette Filley ; with maps and charts by Rachel French.
   p. cm.
   Includes bibliographical references and index.
   ISBN: 1-880405-07-05 (hardcover)
   ISBN: 1-880405-06-07 (softcover)

   1. Rainier, Mount (Wash.)   I. Title
F897.R2F55 1996   917.97'782
                                    QB195-20597

THE RAINIER FACTOR

Old Timers called it "Mountain Fever." It is highly contagious. Most visitors to the Northwest catch it too. One glimpse and you've got it for life. The affliction has drug-like qualities. Rainierophiles regularly drive out of their way to and from work just for a better view. Physical symptoms include moodiness: a sense of well-being if the Mountain is "out", and disappointment if it isn't.

It's a condition afflicting Northwest residents causing them to give up lucrative job offers elsewhere, or if they must leave, renders them incurably homesick for "The" Mountain. Management and labor negotiate over it. Northwest companies are constantly accused of taking advantage of the hapless victims of it by not paying competitive wage rates, because they know employees with the factor don't want to leave the area. It's gender neutral and afflicts men and women alike.

Even the name Rainier is revered. It has labeled beers and banks, two baseball teams, and every product and business in between. (And outraged customers switched banks in droves when Rainier Bank sold out to Security Pacific and changed the name.) It adorns the state's license plates. Countless schools, streets, businesses, apartment buildings, housing developments, and subdivisions share the moniker.

Real estate prices reflect it too. Even a peek-a-boo view of the Mountain is worth real money. People have been known to buy houses they didn't even like because they had a great view of the Mountain.

Ownership of the mountain is claimed by more people than anything else in the Pacific Northwest. "It's MY mountain," people proudly proclaim. Rich and poor alike want a piece of the rock. It's our common denominator.

Like a pilgrimage to Mecca, the faithful flock to the great white shrine annually. As a candle is to a moth, the mountain draws people to itself. The pull is magnetic. There's no use resisting.

Lou Whittaker said it best for all of us, "Nothing is more spectacular than Mount Rainier. Every time I see it when I'm coming home, I get goosebumps. It is the most beautiful mountain in the world."

So to those people who can never get enough of the mountain, this book is dedicated. You're right, by the way. It really IS your mountain.

Thank you

This work, which began as an effort to get my own Mount Rainier files computerized, soon took on a life of its own. I realized that all these wonderful tidbits were too good to keep locked in a computer, and that all my fellow Mount Rainier fans would savor this smorgasbord of information as much as I do. When it came to filling in the gaping holes and missing facts, tracking down the pictures and charts, and myriad of other things in these pages, the following people came along at just the right time, with exactly what I needed. I put a lot of prayer for guidance into this project, and I can't help but believe that many, if not most, of these people were what I call "divine appointments."

My personal thanks to: Carl Allen, Charles and Edna Anderson, Bob Arnold, Marion Ballentine, Mike Banner, Jim and Sandra Brand, Bob Brown, Michael Canney, Evan Cast, Karen Christensen, Karen & Mark Clement, Heath Colvin, Jon Corriveau, Kevin Crowley, Karin Czulik, Mrs. Ome Daiber, Captain Danaker, Andy Dappen, Bill Dengler, George Dunn, Stan and Helen Engle, Phil Ershler, Jack Evans, Carl and Dinni Fabiani, Dick and Phyllis Filley, Laura Filley, Mary Fries, Julie Gangler, Dixie Gatchel, Mary & Paul Gilmore, Larry Hagerness, Joan Hamburg, John Hartl, David Hastings, Brian Holmes, Ken Hopping, Bob Jirsa, Gary Johnson, Brian Kamens, Katherine Kowalski, Gertrude Kruger, Bob Landon, Bob Lanphear, Jack Lawson, Bill Lokey, Anne Malver-Fuller, Caroline Marr, Anne Marshall, Jim Martin-Almy, Carol Masnik, Imbert and Rainier Mathee, Steve McNutt, Joe and Carol McVeigh, Elaine Miller, Seth Moran, Mike Munson, Dan Nelson, Mark Ortman, Don Orton, Robert Pyle, Marion Reed, Gary Reese, Beth Rossow, Mary Schurman, Eric and Kathy Simmonson, Frank Sincock, Ira Spring, Ben Steele, Brad Stracener, Bronka and Ake Sundstrom, Janet Tanaka, Carla Tanner, Dave Tucker, Ken and Helen Voss, Ed Walsh, Jack Ward, Cheryl Wemp, Lou Whittaker, John Zilly.

The back cover photos are the good work of Charles Anderson, Bob Storaasli, and Eric Simonson. Other inside photos are by Ken Hopping, Mike Banner, Jean Trousdale, Ed Walsh and Frank Sincock.

There are also seven people to whom I am especially indebted: my husband Larry, and daughter Kathy for letting me have a year off to write this; to Dee Molenaar, our living Mount Rainier legend, for his reading, corrections, insights, choice comments and facts here and there; to Rachel French for her wonderful maps and charts, and Mike French for his help with photo reproduction, to Jean Trousdale for her wonderful witty way of pointing out my mistakes and catching most of my typos, (although I'm sure we still left a few classics for you to find) and to my son Tom for his computer expertise, and for getting this *out* of the computer in one piece, once it was all done.

To everyone with The Rainier Factor, I hope this enhances your enjoyment, appreciation, and use of our favorite mountain.

Bette Filley

TABLE OF CONTENTS

Early Exploration of the Northwest Coast

Establishing the Territory

But for the grace of God, today our park rangers might all be speaking Spanish, British English, or Russian. Beginning with Balboa's discovery of the Pacific, Spain's flag flew over the Northwest. Spanish names were bestowed on several Pacific Northwest landmarks. Port Angeles, Fidalgo Island, Camano Island and Rosario Strait still bear them. For many years, Spain's sovereign rights went unchallenged.

Then one day in 1579, Francis Drake's "Golden Hind" circled Cape Horn and sailed into the Pacific. To add insult to injury, Drake plundered Spanish treasure ships before sailing north in search of trade winds which he hoped would carry him safely across the Pacific. He claimed to have come as far north as latitude 48° (about parallel with the present city of Everett.) Presuming he did, he was the first European to enter Northwest waters. Drake claimed the land for England.

Next came the Russians who first sailed eastward in 1724. Russian exploration of the North American coast began in earnest in 1742. Eventually they sailed as far south as San Francisco, and once had a post near there which was known as Fort Ross (1812-1841). Somewhere in that hundred year span, Russians landed in Puget Sound. We know this in a very interesting way.

Back in 1910, two brothers, working at a logging camp in Pe Ell felled a large old "school marm", a big Douglas-fir with a cleft top. When they felled the tree, it blew apart and out popped an ancient double musket with the Russian Crown emblem on it. It was still loaded with black powder and a musket ball. The tree had carefully protected the musket. What happened to its owner? Did he rest it in the cleavage of the young tree for a minute and then was not able to find it again in the thick woods? Did an Indian discover the intruder before he could get back to his musket? We will never know his fate, but he left the irrefutable proof that he was here. You can view the old musket for yourself at Brand's Alpine Gallery a couple blocks outside the Park's Nisqually entrance at 37918 SR 706E (that's the Mountain Highway) on the south side of the road.

During this same time frame, the British had a great interest in their colonies on the East coast of America, and wanted to push west to expand their rights. But in 1774 while they became engaged in a little skirmish with some rebellious Colonists, a Spaniard named Juan Perez sailed North from Mexico. The Spanish feared both Russian and English domination and felt they had to reassert their rights.

Four years later, another Englishman named Captain James Cook sailed up the West Coast for the purpose of following up on the discoveries of Sir Francis Drake. One of his young lieutenants, George Vancouver, was to come back several years later and make the discovery this book is all about. Meanwhile the great contention between Spain and England over who got to lay claim to the

North Pacific Coast was resolved without firing a shot. While the two nations negotiated the matter, in 1788 Captain Robert Gray of Boston sailed into the picture. On his second visit to the area in 1792, he crossed the bar of the Columbia River and named the mighty river after his ship. At the same time near the present city of Port Townsend, the well-named Royal English ship "Discovery" was about to be the first to make the same wonderful discovery we have all made.

Captain George Vancouver, now back as a British explorer, stood on the deck of his ship near the present city of Port Townsend, admiring the lush virgin panorama before him. He couldn't help but be impressed by the unmistakable dominant feature on the horizon. The big white mountain captured his imagination and Captain Vancouver was the first man of record to be hooked by the Rainier Factor. He named the landmark after his friend Rear Admiral Peter Rainier.

> "(Tuesday, May 8, 1792) The weather was serene and pleasant, and the country continued to exhibit, between us and the eastern snowy range, the same luxuriant appearance. At its northern extremity, Mount Baker bore by the compass N. 22 E; the round snowy mountain, now forming its southern extremity, and which, after my friend Rear Admiral Rainier, I distinguished by the name of Mount Rainier, bore N. (S.) 42 E."

Sighting of the mountain was recorded again fourteen years later in 1805, by Lewis and Clark, who had reached the Pacific via the overland route. They noted seeing it on their return trip back up the Columbia River.

With the Spanish and Russians out of the sovereignty picture, the struggle over whose land it was now came down to England and the United States. Both countries laid claim to the "Oregon Country".

Early Exploration of the Mountain

In 1808 England dispatched Simon Fraser to explore a great river three hundred miles to the north of the Columbia River, which soon bore his name. The Americans, meanwhile, had a small settlement run by the Astor Company (fur traders) at what is now the site of Astoria, Oregon. It was abandoned to the British in 1813 during the War of 1812. At the end of the war, Astoria was returned to the United States. The fur business, however, continued to operate under the English flag by the Northwest Company. In 1821 the Northwest Company merged with the Hudson's Bay Company.

By 1825 Astoria was abandoned again, and Fort Vancouver (near the present site of Vancouver, Washington), was built as a regional headquarters. A second trading post was founded on the Fraser River in Canada. After an employee was murdered by the Indians during the long trip between the two outposts, it became apparent a mid-way post was needed.

It was not until 1833 that any non-Indian's close approach to Vancouver's 'round snowy mountain' was made. May 30, 1833, the Hudson's Bay Company established Fort Nisqually as the first permanent settlement on Puget Sound. It was, by today's locations, about a mile west of Interstate 5 at the mouth of the Nisqually River. One of the thirteen men at the new fort was a young Scot, Dr. William Fraser Tolmie. He was employed by Hudson's Bay as a physician and surgeon with a side specialty in botany. Plants played an important part in medicine in those days, and it was unknown what medicinal plants might be found in this new area. It was during one of Dr. Tolmie's "botanizing expeditions" as he called them, that he became the first white man to enter the country abutting Mount Rainier.

On August 29, 1833, Dr. Tolmie left Fort Nisqually in the company of five Indians. Their exact route is not known, but it is believed they went up the Puyallup River to the confluence of the Mowich River, then up the Mowich to its junction with Meadow Creek, then up to Meadow Meadows. On September 2, he climbed to the summit of "a snowy peak immediately under Rainier." Some believe that was Tolmie Peak, however Aubrey Haines in *Mountain Fever*, claims Tolmie was at Spray Park. (Haines followed Tolmie's diary closely, and came out on the ridge overlooking Spray Park, between Hessong Rock and Mount Pleasant.)

By 1840, more than one hundred men, women and children (all professing American allegiance) lived in the "Oregon Country."

In 1841 another momentous event occurred. The United States Exploring Expedition, better known as The Wilkes Expedition, arrived at Fort Nisqually, under the command of Commander Charles Wilkes. And explore they did! They made the first calculation of the height of Mount Rainier (establishing it at 12,330 feet, about 2,080 feet lower than it really is), and made the first recorded crossing of the Cascades via Naches Pass to Eastern Washington. The crossing was made by Lieutenant Robert E. Johnson, who also made extensive scientific and geographical studies of the area.

U. S./Canadian Border Established

Finally in 1846, the land dispute between England and America was resolved. The U.S./Canadian boundary line was established at the 49th Parallel, and once and for all, Mount Rainier belonged to the United States.

In 1849, after the formation of the Washington territory, Fort Steilacoom was established and an army garrison stationed there. Settlers were pouring into the region, coming via the Oregon Trail to the Columbia River, then north via the Cowlitz then overland to Puget Sound. The trip was long and laborious and it was evident a more direct route across the Cascades was needed. In 1853, work was begun on the more direct Naches Pass route.

Work was halted when the road builders decided an expected immigrant train was not coming. They were wrong. The pioneers did come and the hardships of that formidable trip could fill a book unto themselves.

The Wagons Rolled West

Aboard the prairie schooners was one man whose name was to forever be linked with a mountain he had never yet seen, - James Longmire. Once reaching his goal of Puget Sound, Longmire loved what he saw. He staked his claim on the Yelm Prairie within sight of the beautiful mountain and like everyone before and since himself, James Longmire fell victim to the Rainier Factor. The big mountain had him by the heartstrings. He wanted to see more of it, but that would have to wait. First he had to clear land, build a home and provide for his family. Finally, in 1861, he hiked from his ranch in Yelm to Bear Prairie, by way of Mishal Mountain.

With the new route west open, immigrants poured into the territory. Towns and settlements sprang up all over Puget Sound. It was "God's Country" and everyone loved it. The Indians, however, thought it was their country, and their resentment erupted in the Indian War of 1855. Many lives were lost before peace was finally restored in 1858.

With the Indian War over, and travel safe once again, A. V. Kautz, a young lieutenant from Fort Steilacoom had his heart set upon reaching Mount Rainier's summit. On July 8, 1857, he took off for The Mountain with Dr. O. R. Craig from the army garrison at Fort Bellingham, four soldiers, and a Nisqually Indian guide by the name of Wapowety. The climb was a lot higher and harder than it looked, and the attempt was unsuccessful.

It was to be another thirteen years before a successful climb was achieved and two men, Hazard Stevens and P. B. VanTrump, stood on the summit. On August 17, 1870, they proved it could be done.

In 1883, P. B. VanTrump climbed the mountain again, this time in the company of James B. Bayley and James Longmire. On the way back down, another momentous event took place.

The Longmire Discovery

Upon returning to their camp along the Nisqually River (nearly across from the campground behind Longmire) they discovered that their horses were gone. The horses had been hobbled, and wandered off while the men undertook their climb. Longmire found the horses in a nearby meadow, but they weren't all he found. The meadow where they were grazing was a natural wilderness spa of warm, bubbling mineral springs. The rest, as they say, is history.

Longmire soon returned to the wonderful spot, and staked his claim to an area of 20 acres. The following year he began the process of securing and developing his claim. He later secured title under the Mineral Act. The first order of business was construction of a building, and te next few years were spent working toward this goal. In 1890, with the help of his sons, grandsons and several Indians, he tackled the last big project: construction of a primitive road (which would not be completed until the following year). The trail out soon became known as the "Yelm Trail." He also built a small hotel. which measured

20 by 30 feet. The lower floor served as a lobby, and upstairs were five guest rooms (the hotel was enlarged about 12 years later.)

He finally opened for business, and the Tacoma newspapers carried glowing ads for "Longmires Medical Springs." Survivors of the rough ride out from the city welcomed the thoughts of a soak in the warm mineral springs, a hot meal and a real bed. The glorious scenic backdrop didn't hurt either. Longmire's springs were on the map, and word of them spread far and wide.

About this same time, on the opposite side of the mountain, the Northern Pacific Railroad was also envisioning the potential of bringing visitors to the park. In 1881-83, under the supervision of their "Assistant Geologist of the Northern Transcontinental Survey," Bailey Willis, a trail (the Bailey Willis or Grindstone Trail) was built from their railway terminus at Wilkeson to the mountain. Although the trail was primarily for the purpose of aiding in the surveying of mineral resources, it also attracted enthralled visitors.

Pre-Park Protection of Mount Rainier

In 1893 President Benjamin Harrison created the Pacific Forest Reserve which encompassed Mount Rainier. On December 12, 1893, Washington Senator Watson Squire submitted Senate Bill 1250, proposing the creation of "Washington National Park." but it was to be another 5-1/4 years before that was to become a reality. Just prior to the establishment of the Park in 1897, President Grover Cleveland changed the name of the area to Mount Rainier Forest Reserve, and P.B. Van Trump was the first government ranger to serve within the present Park region. Little did Ranger Van Trump realize his name would go down in history for an entirely different reason than for rangering.

Mount Rainier National Park is Born

It soon became evident that this magnificent unique asset needed protection and management for the benefit of all the people. People and organizations from all over the United States started calling for the establishment of Mount Rainier as the nation's fifth National Park. (The first four were Yellowstone National Park (1872), Sequoia National Park (1890), General Grant National Park (1890), and Yosemite National Parks (1890). Later, in 1940, General Grant National Park was incorporated into Kings Canyon National Park.) Such organizations as the National Geographic Society, the American Association for the Advancement of Science, the Geographical Society of America, the Sierra Club, The Mountaineers, the Appalachian Mountain Club and others took their requests to Congress.

Then on March 2, 1899, after some minor boundary modifications, the bill passed both houses of Congress. President William McKinley signed it March 12, 1899, and thus was born "Mount Rainier National Park."

March 16, 1901, the Washington State Legislature ceded exclusive jurisdiction over Mount Rainier National Park to the Federal Government. On June 30, 1916, Congress formally accepted it (39th. Stat. 243).

Early Park Administration

The National Park Service did not come into being until 1916, thus even though Mount Rainier was set aside as a national park in 1899, originally there was no organization to look out for its administration, protection or development.

In 1904, the United States Forest Service was put in charge of care of the park. Mr. Grenville Allen, son of O. D. Allen, was supervisor of the Rainier National Forest, which completely surrounded the park. Under Mr. Allen's supervision, the back country was regularly patrolled by forest rangers, who had to add protection of the huge new National Park area to their regular assignments in the National Forest outside the Park.

This overwhelming job fell to just two men. From 1903 to 1907, the Longmire-Paradise region was patrolled by Forest Ranger William McCullough, while Ranger Alfred B. Conrad patrolled the Carbon River-Spray Park region from 1903-1906. The era of U.S. Forest Service management of the Park came to an end on December 31, 1909, probably much to the rangers' relief.

The first park superintendent whose sole job was overseeing Mount Rainier National Park, was Mr. E. S. Hall who took office January 1, 1910. His headquarters was in the log building just south of the Nisqually Entrance Gate.

National Park Service Established

By the time President Woodrow Wilson signed the bill establishing the National Park Service, (August 25, 1916) twelve national parks had been established. There was no uniformity in the management of the parks. Some, like Yosemite, Sequoia and Yellowstone, were administered by the troops of the War Department. Others, like Mount Rainier, were under the care of the U.S. Forest Service.

Priority #1: Roads!

The Puget Sound natives were restless. They wanted access to the mountain! The task of building the roads to get them there was turned over to the Army Engineer Corps, and two men took up the challenge. In 1904, on the east side of the mountain, John Zug surveyed a route to the vicinity of Ohanapecosh. It was rather circuitous, going by way of Bumping Lake, then south of Chinook Pass. His road was never built. It took until 1931 for a road from Eastern Washington to come to the mountain.

Good Engineering, Mr. Ricksecker

At the same time Zug began his survey, Eugene Ricksecker, a young civilian engineer employed by the Army Engineer Corps was commissioned to tackle the survey of a route to the mountain from western Washington. The ultimate plan was to join both roads in a cross state road through the park. Unlike Zug's route, Ricksecker's road was built. So good was his design, it is essentially the same exact route we follow today. Ricksecker was one of the first

6

highway engineers to preserve scenic attractions without sacrificing safety and engineering principles when building roads. Ricksecker Point, on the highway to Paradise, is named in honor of him.

Prior to the new road to Paradise Valley, the only means of getting to the park by road was via the old road built by the Longmires in 1890-91. Automobiles first came to Longmire in 1910, and the first car to make it to Paradise came in August, 1911, bearing Park Superintendent E.S. Hall, Edward Allen and driver, Mr. Lynn Miller. The public wasn't allowed to drive there until 1915. Until then, horses and wagons were the only transportation.

Priority #2 Accommodations

Once the first roads were open, the people came, and with them came the need for accommodations. The little hotel at Longmire was no match for the hordes of people who wanted to see the park up close and personal.

It took two days by horse and wagon over rough washboard roads to make the trip from Tacoma to Longmire Springs. A mid-trip stop was usually made in Eatonville at T. C. Van Eaton's Hotel.

The first accommodations at Paradise were a tent camps, the first known as "Camp of the Clouds", and a few years later, "Reese's Camp." With the opening of the road to auto traffic in 1915, the camp was closed.

The following year, the Rainier National Park Company was founded, and the construction of Paradise Inn was begun.

At Indian Henrys Hunting Ground, from 1908 to 1915 George Hall and his wife, the former Sue Longmire, had a similar tent camp. A government bulletin from 1912 listed prices as $.75 for a bed or a weekly rate of $15.00 for bed and board. You could have your freight hauled up from Longmire for $.02 per pound. This camp, known as the "Wigwam Hotel" rivaled the one at Paradise in popularity, however it was seven miles of hard hiking to get there. It too was abandoned in 1915.

Early settlers in the Cowlitz Valley were attracted to the bubbling hot springs at Ohanapecosh, and a resort complete with cabins and bathhouses was developed in that area.

"Longmire Springs"

Foothills

The First Homesteaders

While James Longmire came to the mountain only in the summertime, by 1885 a man named James B. Kernahan homesteaded in the valley outside what is now the park. He was the first white man to live there year-round. The Indians called the area where he settled So-ho-tash, "the place of the wild raspberry," a name which soon became corrupted to "Succotash Valley". Kernahan built a comfortable log cabin, and brought in all the furnishings for his home by pack horse. The Kernahans lived in their "Palisade Ranch" twenty miles from their closest neighbors.

In 1889 the Kernahans finally got a closer neighbor. Professor O. D. Allen, a retired chemistry professor from Yale University, settled two miles east of them. Professor Allen's home still stands within sight of the mountain highway today.

Professor Allen's House, an Asahel Curtis Photo, courtesy Washington State Historical Society

Early Life Around the Mountain

There was a settlement of 50-100 cabins called "Old Town" just outside the Nisqually Entrance where many of the miners lived. They hiked in to the park each day to work at the Eagle Peak Mine upriver from Longmire. In the same vicinity is where Superintendent Hall's homestead was. (Hall was the first Park Superintendent.) Nisqually Park is developed on his former property. The home burned, but the chimney is still there.

The earliest settlers around the Mountain were a hardy lot. Most were homesteaders, drawn to the area by the free land. They lived and worked under hard, cold, wet, dark circumstances without benefit of electricity, automobiles, or any of the other creature comforts we take for granted today. Light came from kerosene lamps and lanterns which had to be cleaned, trimmed and filled each day. Instead of a TV set, family life generally centered around the stove which gave settlers warmth, fellowship, fresh bread and hot food. Many a marriage came about because a man built a cabin *with a stove*. No stove, no wife. One woman managed to talk her husband and another man into carrying a cast iron stove all the way out from Tacoma, suspended between two poles which they carried on their shoulders.

Some settlers living near the National Mill were lucky. They were supplied with electricity from the mill when the mill's steam plant was running. Regular electricity came into the area in the early 30's.

The Early Schools

Kids living in the hills outside the Park in the early days were a hardy lot, as well. Many had to walk five or more miles each way through the woods to and from school each day, and records are replete with reports of bear, cougar, elk and coyote encounters.

The first school in the area was just past Copper Creek. It had five students. Schools were usually one room buildings, and one teacher taught all grades. The old Alder schoolhouse is on display across from Alexanders on the highway.

The Indian children from Indian Henry's village (and probably a lot of other areas too) attended the Cushman Indian School, located on what is now the Puyallup Reservation in Tacoma. They had to wear uniforms, and a great effort was made to acculturate them into the white man's way of life.

The Depression at the Mountain

Eking out a living in the foothills around the mountain was (and in many cases, still is) difficult, but never moreso than during the Great Depression. Not only the men, but the women and children too had to pitch in to do whatever they could to bring in enough money for the family to keep the wolf from the door. Inside the park, they worked as "mules" and hauled freight. But "regular" jobs were scarce, and most woods-wise settlers turned to nature, harvesting and selling the bounty of the land to anyone with the money to buy.

Common money-making activities were harvesting and selling ferns, berries, mushrooms, bark, boughs, cones, fence posts, shakes and firewood. They also trapped, hunted, tanned hides, sold pelts, venison and fish, and made pies and jams.

Blackberries brought two bits a gallon. (The going rate today is $20.00 per gallon.) The blackberries grew prolifically on sunny recently logged-over land. Settlers also raised chickens, sold eggs, and raised cows for both meat and milk; they dug camas roots and peeled and dried cascara bark to sell, (used in manufacturing laxatives) - at $.04 cents a pound (today's rate - $.28 lb.)

Old Time Celebrations

Without telephones, radio or TV, social events were much anticipated and prepared for. Dances were one popular form of entertainment that brought people out of the hills for miles around. *The Federal Writers' Project* noted there was "wild abandon at Saturday night dances, and fervent evangelistic sermons on Sundays, which gave the region a strong frontier flavor."

The major social event of Packwood was a big Spring dance designed as a memorable send-off for 'the men of the woods': the foresters, fire lookouts, rangers and game wardens, just prior to their departures for a summer in the wilderness. People came from far and wide for this premiere social event of the year. A four-piece orchestra, comprised of a piano, fiddle, bass viola and drum played, punctuated with laughter, yells, "stomping of feet," and "an occasional shot from the pistol of an over-exhuberant 'hillman,' the crowd danced until dawn."

Other fun times were school events, Pentecostal revivals, taffy pulls and box socials. The women would each pack a special lunch for two, decorate the box, and then the boxes were auctioned off for some worthy cause. The buyer got to eat lunch with the preparer of the box. The young men went to great lengths to find out which boxes the single girls had prepared so they didn't end up eating lunch with somebody's grandma.

One report tells that a piano was such a rare commodity, that when one was needed, someone who had one would put it on a sled or wagon and haul it wherever the party was.

Current local celebrations are listed later in this section under each town.

More Treasure in the Hills

Copper Creek was named by James Longmire and Billy Packwood for the green rock which they thought to be copper. They were right. Eventually there was a copper mine complete with an ore crusher behind the Copper Creek Restaurant. Amethyst was also mined there. (Amethyst and copper ore are usually found near each other.) In Ashford there was a coal mine right beside the fire hall. The big tailings mound is still there to see.

In 1895 the National Mill was built, but three years later it burned to the ground and was rebuilt in a new location. One day a young logger who was setting chokers by a spring, filled his pockets with what he thought were good samples of fool's Gold. He put the samples in a jar and kept them for many

years. Finally his friends convinced him they were the real McCoy, and he spent the rest of his life trying to find the spring. The problem, many felt, was that he was looking in the wrong canyon. He should have looked where the original mill had been.

Art in the Hills

The unique natural wood alphabet on the outside wall of Copper Creek Restaurant is one object 'd art familiar to everyone passing by on the Mountain Highway. It was collected by

11

Hank Canty in 1948. Copper Creek is also home to several other unique items. The huge dining room chandelier is a cedar root, completely hand rubbed and polished by Roselea Triggs, the owner in 1955. The high chair is another one-of-a-kind masterpiece made of vine maple and deer horn. It was made by Francais Babcock, also in 1955. The coup d'gras is the beautiful wall mural of the mountain, painted in 1957 by Fred Oldfield. The lunch counter is also worth seeing. It is made of one solid piece of Alaskan yellow cedar. The counter is 25 feet long, 22-1/2 inches wide and 3 inches thick.

In the Still of the Night

Prohibition was adopted in Washington state in 1916, three years before the 18th Amendment made it the law of the land. During prohibition when bootleg whiskey was all the rage, old timers around the mountain had their share of ingeniously hidden stills. One favorite moonshiner haunt was the broad benchland between Elbe and Ashford.

When remodeling the Copper Creek Restaurant in 1955, owners found a still, complete with brick exhaust chimney, hidden in a "solid" wall between the dining room and souvenir room. An occasional owner of an old property in the area still turns up an occasional jug of bootleg booze in a stump or under a porch or floorboard.

Not to be outdone, the old boys of Wilkeson, Carbonado and Fairfax also kept the nights well lit with "moonshine."

The repeal of the Volstead Law cut out the cat and mouse game between the Revenuers and the lowdown upright citizens.

Surrounding Towns

Ashford

Nestled in "Succotash Valley," Ashford was founded by Walter Ashford and his wife, Cora, who homesteaded there in 1888. By 1891, the townsite was established and more settlers moved to the valley, drawn by the prospects of coal and gold. Soon the railroad arrived, with three trains daily, and Ashford became the terminus of the Tacoma Eastern Railroad. It was the hub of activity during early life around the mountain. It had a good school, a fine hotel, stores, tourist facilities and a gas station. Today life still revolves almost exclusively around the tourist industry as most of the Park's nearly 2+ million annual visitors pass through Ashford on their way to the mountain.

Buckley

Originally known as 'Perkins' Landing,' this pretty little settlement became 'White River Siding' when the Northern Pacific Railroad came through the town. In 1888, it changed names for a third time, this time named Buckley in honor of the railroad's division superintendent. Also in 1888 the town became home to one of Pierce County's first newspapers, *The Banner*. Buckley was blessed by an abundance of natural wealth. The town was surrounded by a seemingly endless

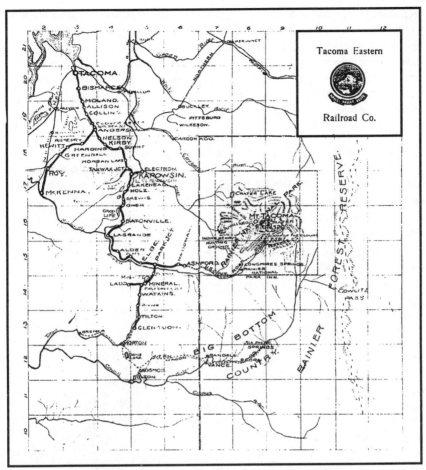

bounty of lumber. Mining spurred the economy as well, and even the rich dirt the town sat on was blessed.

Known as "Buckley Loam" the fertile soil contributed to profitable farming and orcharding operations around the area. One of the prize crops was peaches, which were celebrated annually in the big "Peacherino Festival." The big event now is the annual Logging Rodeo featuring 20 events.

In tiny triangular Buckley Park, there's a tree stump 12-1/2 feet in diameter and 38 feet in circumference. 56,000 board feet of timber were cut from this tree, which was estimated to be 2,000 years old.

Carbonado

This model north-side mining community was ahead of its time. The company, which owned the town, paved the streets, installed a sewer and drain system, provided a large community hall, a school, a store, organized sports teams and fraternal organizations, kept the houses repainted, and rented them to their workers for $14 a month. The old Carbonado mine, which supported this whole operation, closed in late 1920's. When the company closed the mine, it removed the pumps, and the five miles of collieries were flooded. Carbonado today is a barely-alive ghost town. A sad reminder of the town's history can be seen by reading the tombstones in the tiny cemetery. Buried in the back row are the ten of the thirty men who were died in the December 9, 1899 disaster. Each of the gravestones reads, "Killed by Mine Explosion."

Eatonville

Eatonville and Washington state were both founded the same year: 1889. Named for T.C. Van Eaton, Eatonville boasts a rich logging and lumbering past. The old road to the mountain came right through town, and a night in one of the real beds in Van Eaton's Hotel was a much anticipated goal after enduring the ordeal of the terrible road. Another famous resident of the area was Indian Henry, who farmed in the area and whose extended family also lived here.

All visitor services are available here, and there's a nice "self-guided Historic Walking Tour." The big events each year are the *Real American 4th of July* parade and the Annual Eatonville Arts Festival each August.

Elbe

Immigrating from Germany in the 1880's with their seven children, Henry and Clara Lutkens named their new settlement along the Nisqually River after their river back home, the River Elbe. In 1906, the Lutkens donated the land and lumber for the little white Lutheran Church which stands just off the Mountain Highway. Though only 24 feet long and 18 feet wide, the tiny church is topped by a 55-foot steeple and iron cross. The church is a designated National Historic Place and went on the National Register in 1976.

Though Elbe was tiny, it was an important crossroads where loggers, farmers and Indians came together to do business. Just out of town was a big C.C.C. camp, and this same location may soon be home to a large destination resort planned for the area.

The big celebration each year is Hobo Days, held each 4th of July.

Enumclaw

Enumclaw was named by Frank Stevenson, an original settler, for a nearby foothill called by the local Indians, "home of the evil spirits." It is the gateway to Chinook Pass and the north side of the Park, and also to the Ipsut Creek and areas. Early residents worked in logging, farming, and mining (working at the nearby towns of Black Diamond and Carbonado.) Today many farms still operate in the area, as well as many horse, cattle and llama ranches. It is also a bedroom community for those working in Seattle and Tacoma, and is a popular place for airline personnel to live, with over 400 residing in the area.

Fairfax

Just beyond the 218' high O'Farrell Bridge across the Carbon River Gorge lie the remains of Fairfax. In its heyday, Fairfax had a population of 200 and

was a flourishing mining and lumber town. In 1908-1909 a logging railroad was built from Fairfax to the national forest, but stopped just short of the park boundary. During the early logging boom, the Manley/ Moore sawmill there was the largest mill in the state for a time and the Eatonville Lumber Company built a number of homes for all the miners and mill workers.

The railroad had a coal-loading bunker and a depot there, and the town had a fine school. For many years several old logging locomotives stood rusting on the tracks. Out of town, on the east side of the Carbon River, there was Camp Electron, a C.C.C. camp.

Greenwater

At the confluence of the Greenwater and White Rivers on Highway 410, the Longmire pioneer wagon train exited the mountains and was finally on the home stretch of their trip. Nearby Huckleberry Mountain, used to be another favorite Indian haunt for setting up camp and making their winter

Asahel Curtis Photo-Museum of History & Industry

Cedar Tree - 59' 10" circumference

15

supply of pemican. Today Greenwater is but a scattering of a few businesses and several residences.

Mineral

Mineral was headquarters of the West Fork Logging Company's logging operations, carried on over 23,000 acres. In its day, Mineral was a model of the new concept of conservation, as they developed and practiced a method of selective logging which resulted in a minimum destruction of immature trees.

Nearby were deposits of red realgar, from which arsenic is extracted. A surface vein of rich ore was discovered in 1900 and worked until 1922. The mine closed when a smelting process was developed which recovered arsenic as an inexpensive by-product made the operation of the mine unprofitable. Today Mineral has the distinction of having the smallest Post Office in the United States (eight square feet). Mail service began in Mineral in 1892. The big event of the year is the annual Crayfish Festival, held every August.

Morton

Morton had its beginnings as a settlement which was a trading and social center at a footbridge across the Tilton River. By 1885 about 100 homesteaders lived in the surrounding area. The tiny settlement was named after Levi Morton who was elected Vice President in 1888. With the establishment of the Morton depot of the Tacoma Eastern Railroad, the local economy took a decided upturn. Railroad ties, which previously had to be packed out one at a time, could now be shipped in volume by rail. The enterprising settlers set up as many as 100 sawmills, and soon Morton became known as the "Tie Capital of the World. Tie docks stretched from the depot for nearly two miles along the tracks. Morton once shipped nearly 100 railcar loads of logs and (railroad) ties a day to Tacoma and Seattle.

A little ways out of town was the Morton Cinnebar Mine, which in the 1920's was a major producer of mercury. Morton's population today is about 1,200, and it celebrated its 100th anniversary in 1990. The town is famous for its annual Logger's Jubilee held the second weekend each August, and a big Christmas celebration when the world's tallest living Christmas tree (130') is lighted.

National

Exactly one mile west of Ashford, on the south side of SR 706, lies a road to the site of National, a once-thriving lumber town. The heart of the town was the great red sawmill, with its huge rusted stacks which belched black smoke and white steam. Crowded together on planked streets over the ever-present mud, were dozens of identical box-like cottages, all painted the same red as the giant mill. This was a true company town, and the lumber company dominated every facet of the 4,000 employees' lives. They bought their every need: food, clothing and sundries from the company store. The the Mill whistle dictated when they arose in the morning, ate their meals and went to bed. Several of the houses (including Whittaker's Bunkhouse) are still in the area, having been bought and moved when the town died. All that remains of the townsite is a portion of the old mill pond.

Orting

The original name of Orting was Carbon or "Upthascap" in Chinook jargon. The name was changed to Carbon when coal was discovered along the banks of the river in 1876. Orting means "prairie in the woods" or "prairie village." Farming in the early days included vast hop fields and tobacco fields. A tall red barn which was the oldest hop kiln in the valley still stands today at the Red Barn Tree Farm. Today the rich valley soil produces vast quantities of flower bulbs, pumpkins, strawberries, raspberries and rhubarb. It also supports several large dairies and tree farms producing Christmas trees and thousands of apple tree seedlings which are sold to orchards all around the world. Orting is also home to the Washington State Old Soldier's home and cemetery.

Packwood

Back in 1854, two Tumwater settlers, James Longmire and Billy Packwood, and a trio of Nisqually Indian guides set out to locate a low pass to connect Puget Sound with the Oregon Trail. They skirted around south of Mount Rainier and came out upon a vast bottomland bisected by the upper Cowlitz River. The original settlement was called "Sulphur Springs."

Packwood lies 10 miles from the southeast entrance to the park, just a few minutes from Ohanapecosh. It is also the gateway to the Goat Rocks Wilderness Area. One of the community's most historic landmarks is the grand old Hotel Packwood. With its wrap-around porch, dark clapboard siding and rustic design, it looks like part of an old western movie set. President Teddy Roosevelt stayed here when he visited Mount Rainier in 1912.

Randle

Founded in 1902, the Randle Logging Company's mill once had a capacity of 35,000 board feet of lumber. In addition to farming and dairying, many residents of the area regularly supplemented their meager incomes by gathering, drying and selling cascara bark. Today many excellent fishing lakes and campgrounds are in the area. The highlights of the year now are the annual Outhouse Dance, held each April or May, and the 4th of July Big Bottom Blast and fireworks.

Wilkeson

Wilkeson, on the north side of the mountain, was thrice blessed with natural resources. They had timber, coal deposits, and high quality sandstone. The town was named for Samuel Wilkeson, secretary of the Northern Pacific Railroad which built a line to the town in 1876 and began mining coal in 1879. The Wilkeson Coal and Coke Company took over operations of the mine in the early nineties, and ran it until mining ceased. The Wilkeson Mine also had a calamity. A blast on December 13, 1925 caught 32 men in the mine, killing five of them.

The sandstone quarries provided stone for the State Capitol at Olympia. Another sample of Wilkeson sandstone can be seen in the 1913 three-story Wilkeson Grade School, which has the distinction of being one of the oldest schools in the state.

In its heyday Wilkeson boasted 2,200 residents, and had three churches, three public halls, a community hall, two bakeries, two theaters, a newspaper, drug stores, bottling works, a bank, a doctor, a dentist, numerous saloons, several fraternal orders, a paved main street with cement sidewalks, and a cigar factory.

There's a map in the window of the Wilkeson Grocery, which shows those interested in a walking tour of the town, the location of the 1880's ovens used to turn coal into coke for making steel. At one time 180 beehive coke ovens existed. Today the 60 that remain have been placed on the National Historic Register.

For aficionados of zany events, Wilkeson's biggie is the annual Handcar Races, held the third weekend in July. The bleachers and the track are near the arched brick coke ovens along the main street.

South of town on the way to the mountain, the 218' high bridge (formerly called the O'Farrell Bridge) crosses the deep Carbon River gorge.

Museums Containing Mount Rainier Memorabilia:

Buckley Foothills Historical Museum off Highway 410 at River Ave. and Cottage Street in Buckley.

This museum contains an interesting collection of memorabilia of Buckley's pioneer past. There's a replica of a 19th century kitchen, bedroom and playroom, a blacksmith's shop, a bunkhouse and a saw shop and a collection of early medical equipment. Open Sunday and Thursday 1-4. Call first. (360) 829-1289 or 829-1533.

Camp Six (Logging Museum) Point Defiance Park, 5400 North Pearl, Tacoma 98407 (206) 752-0047

Listed in National Register of Historic Places, this 20-acre site in the forest at Point Defiance allows guests to travel back in time to the era of logging in Washington. Designed after an actual logging camp, it is as camps in the foothills looked from the 1880's to the mid-1940's, "when loggers were boss, and steam was king!" Camp 6 is filled with all the basic equipment used in the era of steam power. See an 1887 Dolbeer Donkey and a Lidgerwood Tower skidder weighing 240 tons.

Cowlitz County Historical Museum Kelso. (360) 577-3119

Open Tues - Saturday, 10:30-4:30, Sunday 2-5, closed holidays

Eatonville Library 205 Center St. W, (360) 832-6011 contains displays of local photos and artifacts collected by the South Pierce County Historical Society.

Enumclaw Library 1700 First St., (360) 825-2938 contains a display by the local Historical Society. This interesting little display changes frequently, so check it out each time you go through town.

Fort Nisqually, Tacoma, (206) 591-5339

Established in 1833, it was moved to this site in 1937. The 1843 Granary is the oldest existing building in the state, with The Factor's House (1853) also original. Eight other buildings are reconstructed according to original specifications using handmade hardware and lumber. (free admission)

Lewis County Historical Museum, 599 NW Front, Chehalis, (360) 748-0831 In addition to historical displays, they have a library with historical family records, books, photographs and newspapers documenting Lewis County's early families. Hours are Monday through Friday, 9 a.m. to 5 p.m.

Pioneer Farm Museum and Ohop Indian Village Tours, 7716 Ohop Valley Road, Eatonville, WA 98103 (360) 832-6300.

Three miles north of Eatonville, midway between Highways 7 and 161 is a genuine 1880's pioneer farm. To see what early life around the mountain was like, bring the kids here. (This is also a great place to bring *busloads* of kids.) They'll get to try their hand at milking a cow, churning butter and grinding grain. Hour and a half guided tours begin every 45 minutes.

There's also an 1890's Schoolhouse lesson where pupils learn about Washington Statehood and write lessons on an old fashioned slate board with soap stone. The farm is open daily in summer, (Memorial Day to Labor Day from 11:00 a.m. to 5:00 p.m.) and on weekends in spring and fall. There's a small admission fee. Call for winter hours.

Settler's Museum, Highway 508, Morton. (360) 496-6844 or (360) 496-6881 This museum is in Gust Backstrom Park. It also houses the Eastern Lewis County Museum, and is open by appointment and during Loggers' Jubilee weekend.

Steilacoom Tribal Cultural Center and Museum 1515 Lafayette Street, Steilacoom, 98388, a block south of Bair's. (206) 584-6308

There are two floors of Native American artifacts and displays describing Puget Sound life just before and after the white man arrived. The museum is housed in the former Oberlin Congregational Church. Guided tours and Indian store. For a fun cultural experience, attend the authentic plank salmon dinner held late each August.

Sumner Ryan House Museum 1228 Main., Sumner, 98390 (206) 863-8936 This modest farmhouse built in 1875, is constructed from locally cut cedar. The museum area alternates displays and features one "Old Book Room" which contains historical documents and Northwest history.

Thomas Burke Memorial Washington State Museum, University of Washington Campus, 17th Ave. NE and NE 45th St., Seattle (206) 543-5590. This museum contains probably the best collection of Northwest Indian artifacts most people will ever see, and such interesting items as clothing made of cedar bark and mountain goat wool.

Washington State Historical Museum 315 N. Stadium Way, Tacoma. (206) 593-2830

Exhibits include Washington State History and Native American collections. Research library. (Tues-Sat. also Sunday afternoons)

Western Frontier Museum 2301 23rd Ave. SE, Puyallup (Trails End Ranch) (360) 832-6300.

While this has the distinct feel of being a "cowboy" museum, there were real cowboys in the area in the early days, so we include it here. They have carriages, guns, arrowheads, etc. Open 9 a.m. to 5 p.m. Wednesday through Sunday, or by appointment.

White River Valley Historical Society H Street SE, Auburn, WA.

Open Thurs & Sun afternoons

Yakama Nation Cultural Center, Toppenish (509) 865-2800

Excellent library and museum with early Indian artifacts .

Yesteryear Park, Ashford, WA (360) 569-2946. Antiquities of the area.

The Forests Surrounding The Park

Surrounding National Forests

There are three National Forests surrounding Mount Rainier National Park: Mount Baker National Forest, Snoqualmie National Forest and Gifford Pinchot National Forest, with five separate designated wilderness areas.

▪ **Mount Baker -Snoqualmie National Forest** is on the north and east sides of the Park. The White River District manages lands on the north. These lands are designated for several uses, including Wilderness, trailless recreation, viewshed areas, habitat for various species, recreation, Mather Memorial Parkway, winter recreation (Crystal Mountain Resort), and timber harvest. The designation of Habitat Conservation Areas (HCA) for the Northern Spotted Owl encompasses 90% of the district. (206) 775-9702.

▪ The **Wenatchee National Forest** manages Mount Baker-Snoqualmie forest lands to the east of the park, administered by the Naches Ranger District. Most of the western portion of the Naches District is also designated wilderness. Designations adjacent to the park also include lands for scenic retention, unroaded-non-motorized recreation, wild and scenic river, and Mather Memorial Parkway. The Naches District has not been as affected as widely by the Northern Spotted Owl issues as the other forests surrounding the park although about half of the previously scheduled timber harvests have been cancelled. (503) 326-2877.

• **Gifford Pinchot National Forest** adjacent to the west, south and southeast park boundary is managed mostly as Wilderness. Approximately 84% of the Packwood District has been designated for conservation of the Northern Spotted Owl. (360) 750-5001. *(MRNP Adjacent Lands Report.)*

Surrounding Ranger District Stations

Naches Ranger District, Naches, WA 98937, (509) 653-2205
Packwood Ranger District, Packwood, WA 98361, (360) 494-5515
Mount Adams Ranger District, (509) 395-2501
Oak Creek Habitat Management Area, 16601 Highway 12,
    Naches, Wa 98937, (509) 653-2390
Randle Ranger District, Randle WA 98377, (360) 497-7565
Wind River Ranger District, M.P. 1. 26R Hemlock Rd. Carson, WA
    98610 (509) 427-5645
White River District, 857 Roosevelt E., Enumclaw (360) 825-6585

Surrounding Wilderness Areas

Clearwater Wilderness   Tatoosh Wilderness Area
Glacier View Wilderness Area   William O. Douglas Wilderness Area
Norse Peak Wilderness Area

Surrounding DNR Lands

State Department of Natural Resources lands managed for timber production lie to the southwest of the Park along the Nisqually River.

Forestry outside the Mount Rainier National Park Area

Visitors who take a walk in the woods both inside and outside the National Park will find interesting comparisons. While there are many differences between the preserved forests in the park and the "working" forests on the largely private land around the park, there are also many similarities.

Constant change can be seen in both kinds of forests, though it occurs on a slower pace inside the park. For example, open areas in the forest are produced by fire or windstorm both in and outside the park, and also by harvesting outside. Natural regeneration in the park takes longer than outside, where landowners hand-plant seedlings to begin growth of the new forest more quickly.

Another similarity is that Douglas fir is the tree type that dominates the forests in both areas, as it does in all of western Washington. And all the other tree species found in the park also grow outside, since the wind and animals spread those seeds to areas where one species is planted.

Historic Forest Management

Active forest management has been part of the area around Mount Rainier since the late 1800s, when lumber was needed to house the growing population on the West Coast. Steam-powered "donkey" yarders reeled in logs to marshaling areas near railroads. Specialized locomotives were designed to fit around tight corners and worm up the steep grades required by the geography.

Today, these old railroad grades, even the steeper ones, often make excellent walking paths. (Probably the best-known in the state is the Iron Horse Trail on the old Milwaukee Railroad right-of-way through the Snoqualmie Pass along Interstate 90). Serious woods wanderers sometimes find old grades with collapsed wooden trestles on forest land throughout the state.

Forest Management Today

Since the days of railroad logging, both harvest tools and management thinking have evolved in the working forest outside the park. Trucks eventually replaced railroads as the transportation system. Today's harvesting equipment uses hydraulics rather than muscle, and computers help operators make decisions.

Forest management has steadily evolved as well. In the early years the forest was allowed to regenerate itself after logging. Then foresters began to think more about how to work with nature to promote reforestation. Research and on-site tests led to the start of the Tree Farm movement, formalized with the dedication of the first Tree Farm in June 1941 near Montesano, Washington.

Today, private forest landowners plant more than 35 million tree seedlings every year to ensure rapid reforestation of harvested land. Different tree species are planted on different sites, guided by factors such as altitude and the dominant tree type before harvest. The working forest outside the park is producing a second and third cycle of trees.

Protecting the Resources

Protecting the public resources of water, fish and wildlife on private land is always part of planning for the working forest. Washington is one of 11 states with a Forest Practices Act, which controls forest management activities on private forest land. Washington's regulations are among the strongest in the country, especially after the addition of new rules that took effect in 1993. Private forest landowners helped develop those new rules, which limit the size of harvest areas, so the larger clearcuts of the past won't be seen anymore.

There's also a rule restricting new harvest areas next to old ones, requiring a wait of about five years until the old area has "greened up" with new trees approximately five feet tall. The new rules also require landowners to leave behind a specific number of live and dead trees, and logs for small-animal and bird habitat. Ironically, this has led to some criticism of harvest areas as "messy looking."

Better Forests through Research

Scientific research, with cooperation between private forest landowners and government agencies, is guiding today's forest management. For example, just a few years ago, forestry regulations required logs, even old ones, to be removed from streams because it was believed they impeded fish movement. But research showed that large, woody debris in streams actually is a benefit to fish, forming slower-moving pools for juvenile fish. Now private landowners are *adding* logs to streams in some harvest areas.

Research is also bringing us new views about the role of fire in the forest. While large wildfires are highly destructive, smaller, less intensive fires actually help maintain good forest health. The smaller blazes help clear the forest floor of excess dead limbs and other debris, which produce a catastrophic fire if left to accumulate, and leave almost all established trees undamaged. In the working forest, catastrophic conditions are avoided and forest health maintained by a practice of thinning out some trees coupled with controlled burns.

Looking Better All the Time

Today, private forest landowners are experimenting with new concepts, such as visual management. Foresters are applying landscape architect principles to harvesting and roadbuilding, in order to minimize the visual impact of these activities.

In a two-year experiment guided by the University of Washington, 11 private forest owners used computer graphic simulations to assess the visual impact of several different options for harvesting. The selected option was then carried out and evaluated. A manual was produced, based on the knowledge gained from the experiment, and made available to all forest managers. (This experiment was completed in October, 1995.)

Society needs both the preserved forest of the Park, and the working forest on the land outside the boundaries. Today's forest management, guided by science, is a continuing cycle of growth, harvest and replanting to supply a renewable resource for building materials, paper and other useful products that can be recycled and re-used.

Come See For Yourself

Anyone interested in visiting an outstanding example of NEW forestry, can take a short side trip while traveling Highway 706 toward the Longmire entrance of Mount Rainier National Park. Approximately one mile west of the town of Ashford, turn north on 278th Avenue East and travel north 1.8 miles on the Washington Department of Natural Resources (DNR) No. 8 Road. This is the same road that leads to the Mount Tahoma Ski Trails Snow Park #92.

At 1.8 miles, you will see an informational sign titled "Side Road Timber Sale." This sign gives a brief description of a final timber harvest termed NEW Forestry.

The Department of Natural Resources harvested ninety-seven acres of timber that produced $2,000,000.00 in revenue for the state, Pierce County and taxing districts like the local Fire District. This was accomplished with a two-unit sale divided by a riparian non-harvest area along the upper reaches of Sahara Creek. 1552 mature animal habitat trees were left scattered throughout the harvest units. The Tacoma Aububon Society, in cooperation with the DNR, installed two hundred bird boxes in some of these trees to enhance habitat.

This is just one example of NEW Forestry being conducted in the commercial forest adjacent to Mount Rainier. For more examples of responsible forestry in the area, contact the Washington Forest Protection Association, 711 Capitol Way, Suite 608, Olympia, WA 98501 (360) 352-1500.

Private Timber Companies Bordering the Park

Champion International Corporation (800) 782-1493. Champion owns 200,000 acres of timberland in Washington State, with 100,000 acres of it being the Kapowsin Tree Farm, which is adjacent to the Western boundary of Mount Rainier National Park. Under a fee-for-access program, their land is open to year-round vehicle access to most tree farm roads, seven road management areas, totaling 30,000 acres for non-motorized vehicles, overnight camping with improved campgrounds (with firewood provided at entry point), security staff, garbage disposal at exit point, and general control of poaching.

Champion is also a part of the Mount Tahoma Trail System which is covered on pages 255, 256 and 275

PlumCreek Timber Company (360) 825-5596. PlumCreek's Wilkeson Tree Farm is approximately 25,000 acres located in the South Prairie Creek and Carbon River drainage area. The public is welcome to come to the tree farm to hunt, fish, hike and picnic. There is no charge to enjoy their tree farm. Wood cutting is by permit only. No ORV (Off Road Vehicles) are permitted. Neither is shooting (except while hunting during legal hunting seasons). Please report any prohibited activity to a member of the Plum Creek Forest Patrol (360) 802-9868.

Weyerhaeuser Company (206) 485-0955. The Weyerhaeuser Forest is about 22 miles east of I-5 on Highway 410. Turn onto the Greenwater River Road. You'll see a Weyerhaeuser sign that says "planted 1960." Drive or walk up the road (which is shared by the U.S. Forest Service and Weyerhaeuser), and you'll see lots of variety, including old-growth, intensively managed Weyerhaeuser forests, new clear-cuts, and 20-30 year old second growth forests. Another Weyerhaeuser operation is immediately east of Eatonville (360) 748-1888. Reports of vandalism, gate problems or improper conduct should be reported to the patrolman, or by calling 1-800-458-0274, 24-hours a day.

Mount Rainier People

The Longmires

If any one person left his mark on the mountain, it was James Longmire, and if there was a "Mount Rainier family," it was the Longmires. James' wife, Virinda, ran one of the first known "bed and breakfasts" in the territory when James set up the first hostelry at the mountain. She was a good cook with a wonderful wit. It was she who named "Paradise".

James Longmire led the first Cascade-crossing wagon train over Naches Pass in 1853. He staked his claim in Yelm Prairie within sight of the mountain, and in 1861, blazed a trail to the mountain. In 1870, he packed Hazard Stevens and Philemon Van Trump into the area of Bear Prairie as they prepared to make the first ascent of the mountain. In 1883 he climbed the mountain himself, and it was on the return trip he discovered the mineral springs. He built the first cabin within what is now Park boundaries the following year.

John Muir described Longmire as follows: "We got animals from Longmire, a tall, wiry, enterprising moneymaker, who hewed his way through the woods, and settled here at Yelm Prairie, raised cattle, prospected with an Indian as guide, hunted and claimed springs. He will do anything to earn money. He proclaims his goodwife as a cook, and says: 'Drink at these springs and they will do you good. Everyone's got medicine in 'em. A doctor said so, no matter what ails you.'" James Longmire died in 1897.

With James' death, his son Elcaine and grandson Benjamin took over the Longmire enterprises. Two years later the area surrounding the family claim became Mount Rainier National Park, and their land became a private island surrounded by the Park. There began a certain amount of friction between the family and park officials, however that didn't prevent several Longmire family members from working for the park.

The original Longmire Hotel was destroyed by fire in 1910. The Longmire claim remained in private hands until 1939 when it was finally purchased by the National Park Service for $30,000.

James and Virinda Longmire had four children. Their eldest son, Elcaine (also spelled Elcain and Elkaine) spent most of his life at the mountain. He died at the (Longmire) Springs in 1915. Elcaine and his wife Martha had sons Len & Ben who were also fixtures at the mountain.

Len assisted his parents and grandparents in many projects, and in the 1920's and 30's he was an institution among seasonal park maintenance personnel. Len Longmire later lived in the Yelm area until shortly before he died. Ben named many of the features of the mountain, including Mount Ararat and Martha Falls, which he named after his mother. The Longmires also named Bear Prairie, Devils Dream Creek, Denman Falls, Fishers Hornpipe Creek, Paradise (Glacier, River and Valley), and Pigeon Springs.

Mountain Men

The first man to write about Mount Rainier was **Theodore Winthrop**. In 1853, Winthrop, an employee of the Pacific Mail Steamship Company, made a trip by Indian canoe from Port Townsend to the Hudson's Bay Post at Nisqually. Then he went by horseback over the Cascades to the Dalles, Oregon. He wrote a book, *Canoe and Saddle*, published in 1862 after his death, on his adventures. The book was a best seller of its day, and introduced enthralled readers to the glories of Mount Rainier via vivid word pictures of the author's cross-country adventures.

John Muir was an early naturalist, conservationist and founder of the Sierra Club. In 1894, he demanded the creation of Mount Rainier National Park. In personal letters and a book, he gave vivid impressions of the massive peak. As Aubrey Haines says in his book *Mountain Fever*, Muir's account of his Mount Rainier climb "spread the mountain fever among many who would never dare to climb - he left more eyes turned mountainward than ever before."

Oscar D. Allen, a Yale Professor of Botany, made vast collections of botanical specimens in the upper Nisqually Valley beginning in 1895. Professor Allen is buried on his property about a mile west of the park on the north side of the Nisqually River. His son Grenville Allen was a graduate of the Yale Forestry School, and became supervisor of the Rainier National Forest from 1901 to 1909. His brother, Ethan Allen, was acting supervisor of the park from July 1913 to December 1914.

Hazard Stevens who in 1870 was one of the first two men to climb Mount Rainier. He was the son of the first governor of Washington, and went on to become the Union Army's youngest Civil War General. His name, along with that of **P. B. Van Trump**, his climbing companion, have been generously bestowed on many natural features of the park: Stevens Peak, Stevens Glacier, Van Trump Glacier, and Van Trump Park.

Billy Packwood was a friend of James Longmire, and in 1865 proved a land claim of 326 acres of land along the lower Nisqually River. He operated a ferry across the Nisqually river near Yelm for years. The town of Packwood is named for him.

Mountain Women

In August of 1890, **Fay Fuller** became the first woman to climb Mount Rainier. She later married, became Mrs. Fritz von Briesen and moved to New York.

In 1950 she made her first visit back to the park since 1923. According to a letter to Supt. Tomlinson, written May 4, 1933, she said the "stock" or "staff" she carried was made from a curved shovel handle by a blacksmith in Yelm. Her scrapbooks were given to the Library of the Mazamas in Portland. Her father's newspaper, *"The Tacomian"* is in the Washington State Historical Library in Tacoma.

The second and third ascents by women were the following year. In 1891, Sue Longmire, (age 13) and Miss Edith Corbett, a schoolteacher from Yelm, reached the summit. In 1894, Miss Helen Holmes and two more women made it to the top when they went up in a party of 14.

In 1918 Helene Wilson was hired as a ranger. She filled a position left vacant by a man going into the Army and she was put in charge of the Nisqually entrance.

Also in 1918, Miss Alma Wagen became the first woman hired as a Mount Rainier Guide.

With the advent of World War II, many park wives were "drafted" into jobs as aircraft warning observers. Outside the park, logger's wives went to work in the mills as their men went to war.

In 1943 another woman, Barbara Dickenson, made history by being hired as the first fireguard. Later she and Miss Catherine Barnes were hired as rangers due to the fact that the men were all at war. From after the war until 1974, there were no women rangers.

Mountain Kids

In 1928, no less than Stephen T. Mather, Director of the United States Department of the Interior, and Dr. M. Lyle Spencer, President of the University of Washington, gave their personal recommendations and endorsements of "The Wonderland Camp for Boys." The camp's ornate brochure boasted of "a glorious four weeks in the nation's most beautiful playground." The hefty $250 fee assured parents that each boy was assigned his own horse.

Boy Scouts

Love of the old Mountain has never been the exclusive domain of adults. Early Boy Scouts were among the first to make camp on the Mountain. One early scout camp of note was "Camp Horsefly" in Spray Park in the summer of 1912. For years a wooden post stood in the meadow, with hobnail letters spelling out BSA 19-something. Since then countless thousands of scouts have learned outdoors skills and earned woodsman and outdoor survival badges in the open-air classroom of the wild.

To their great credit, the scouts weren't just there for the fun times, they also were willing workers whenever there was a job to be done. Scouts provided much of the muscle and young-man power to haul the steel and cement up the mountain to build Camp Schurman.

There was a close kinship among mountain devotees in the early days, and each year The Mountaineers selected three Boy Scouts to get three years of free membership.

Many of the northwest's famous climbers learned their love of the mountain, and did their first climbing with the scouts, among them, Jim and Lou Whittaker.

Ptarmigans

In 1937 a number of Seattle Boy Scouts enamored with climbing, parted company with the parent organization (which was getting increasingly nervous about their risky pastime), and formed a new club devoted exclusively to climbing, - the Ptarmigans. The club only stayed together about ten years, but in that time, they made a respectable number of first ascents. In addition to "going where no man had gone before" in the North Cascades, they bestowed their name on the famed Ptarmigan Traverse.

Mazamas

The Oregon Mazamas had perhaps the most unique founding of any alpine club around. They held their organizing meeting on the summit of Mount Hood and only those present on the top were allowed to join. The date for the charter climb was set for July 19, 1894, and surprisingly 250 showed up to make the climb. 155 men and 38 women climbed from the south side, and 22 more climbed from the north. Fay Fuller, the first woman to climb Mount Rainier, was among the founders, and was elected historian while at the summit.

The group immediately started going to other areas to hike and climb, and in 1897 made their first expedition to Mount Rainier. In 1906, they came again for a joint outing with their Seattle branch, which the following year broke away to form their own group, and become the Seattle Mountaineers.

In 1914 the Mazamas returned to Rainier, this time pioneering a new route to the summit over the Winthrop Glacier. A bivouac was made at 9,500 feet between the Carbon and Winthrop Glaciers. After the scouting ascent, a group of 75 made the climb, with 71 making the summit. The highlight of the trip was when one young lady had a snow bridge collapse under her. She was roped between two men who stopped her fall. In 1918 the Mazamas were back again, and this time put 93 out of 150 people on the summit.

The Mountaineers

In the early days of the Park, the names of Mount Rainier and Mountaineers were practically synonymous. From the founding of the organization in 1907, when the Seattleites broke away from the Mazamas to become a separate organization, the mountain was the hub around which many of the club's early activities were centered. With the advent of the automobile, busses and trains, club members were at the mountain at every opportunity, - hiking, climbing, snowshoeing, skiing, exploring and anything else they could think of. Their summer outings were legendary. They traveled complete with pack train, camp cooks and beef on the hoof. Evenings in camp were spent doing skits and harmonious singing. Bedtime was marked by "the Goodnight Song."

For sixteen years, beginning in the mid-twenties, a much-anticipated event was spending the vacation week between Christmas and New Year at Paradise. New Years Eve was celebrated with some of "the boys" hiking across the valley and building a big bonfire in the saddle of Pinnacle. It was a congenial group and zany stunts were the order of the day.

Eventually, Irish Cabin, the club hideaway outside the Carbon River entrance to the Park became the favorite close-in escape from the big city. Since 1935, when they started their renowned "climbing course," thousands of Northwesterners learned how to cross crevasses and do self-arrests on the slopes of Mount Rainier.

Many Mountaineers made first ascents of various Rainier climbing routes, among them a 1934 ascent of Ptarmigan Ridge by Wolf Bauer and Jack Hossack, making them the first to make it up Rainier's forbidding north side. They were followed two weeks later by three Mountaineers (Ome Daiber, Arnie Campbell and Jim Borrow) doing the first ascent of Liberty Ridge. It was twenty years before either of these climbs was repeated.

Park Superintendents (from beginning to present)

Greenville F. Allen	Acting Superintendent	1901 - 1909
Edward S. Hall	First Park Superintendent	1910 - 1913
Ethan Allen	Superintendent	1913 - 1914
John J. Sheehan	Supervisor	1915 - 1915
Dewitt L. Reaburn	Supervisor	1915 - 1919
Alex Sparrow	Acting Superintendent	1919 - 1919
Roger W. Toll	Superintendent	1919 - 1920
H. B. Barnett	Acting Superintendent	1920 - 1920
William H. Peters	Superintendent	1920 - 1922
Clarence L. Nelson	Acting Superintendent	1922 - 1923
Owen A. Tomlinson	Superintendent	1923 - 1941
John C. Preston	Superintendent	1941 - 1951
Preston P. Macy	Superintendent	1951 - 1961
John A. Rutter	Superintendent	1962 - 1966
John A. Townsley	Superintendent	1967 - 1972
Daniel J. Tobin	Superintendent	1972 - 1977
William J. Briggle	Superintendent	1977 - 1984
Neal G Guse, Jr.	Superintendent	1984 - 1991
William J. Briggle	Superintendent	1991 - present

William Briggle, second-term Mount Rainier National Park Superintendent (1977-84 and 1991 to present), is one of the longest tenured park superintendents in the National Park system. He's a 45-year veteran with the Park Service.

Major Owen E. Tomlinson (1923-1941) earned his title as an American officer in the Philippine Constabulary following the Spanish American War.

Early Park Employees

As noted earlier, the first two Forest Rangers were William McCullough, who served at Longmire and Paradise from 1903-1907, and Alfred B. Conrad, who served the Carbon River-Spray Park area from 1903-1906.

In a letter of May 11, 1911, applicant C. E. Phillips of Seattle was told he was recommended to the Secretary of the Interior for the job of Gate Keeper at Mount Rainier National Park for the season of 1911, but the position required that he supply his own uniform costing $15. This consisted of a Norfolk Jacket, wool shirt, riding trousers, leggings, and a felt hat.

The annual salary of one early Superintendent was $3000, but he was required by terms of his commission, to supply and keep his own horse. In appealing for relief, the superintendent wrote, "This I do at the expense of approximately $1.00 a day, though I have not ridden the horse more than 5 miles in 6 months. I maintain an automobile in which I have traveled more than 600 miles on park business, during the month of April. Gasoline costs 30 cents per gallon. I respectfully ask relief from the necessity of maintaining a horse." - *(Supt. Report, April, 1914.)*

Floyd Schmoe was the first Park naturalist at Mount Rainier, and the second naturalist in the entire National Park system. He worked in the Park from 1919 to 1928, and wrote three books about the mountain .

Frank Brockman, the second naturalist, worked at the Park for 14 years, from 1928-1941. "Brock" left to join the faculty at the U.W. School of forestry where he rose to become Professor of College of Forestry Resources. He retired in 1968 and died in 1985. Brockman was a pioneer in inaugurating the interpretive programs we enjoy in the park today. He too was a prolific writer, and left much valuable material about the mountain.

One evening in the 1930's, some campers at the Sunrise campfire program had the surprise opportunity of a lifetime. There was a very special visitor in attendance, one Bailey Willis, back to his beloved Mountain for one last brief visit. Bailey had gone on to become a revered professor of geology at Stanford University. That night at Sunrise, as the campfire crackled, he held his audience spellbound as he reminisced about previous times at Mount Rainier. What a shame that tape recorders hadn't yet been invented.

The C.C.C.

Between the Depression years of 1933 and 1940, thousands of unemployed young men were put to work on public construction projects via Franklin D. Roosevelt's Civilian Conservation Corps. They built roads, trails, and buildings, - many of which we today consider to be our nation's architectural and National Park treasures. About 1,000 men a year were assigned to Mount Rainier. Several hundred of those young chaps must have undergone quite a culture shock as they found themselves transported from life in New York City and to the rigors of year-round life in the backcountry of Mount Rainier. Many of the Manhattan youths had never seen big trees until they arrived at the mountain.

They lived year-round in tent villages in the forest. There were five C.C.C. camps in the park, - Tahoma Creek, Narada Falls, St. Andrews Creek, Carbon River, and White River. New York Troopers C.C.C. Company No. 1231 arrived during a heavy July snowstorm, and first had to clear the land on which their permanent camp was to be built at St. Andrews Creek on the West Side Highway.

Most ranged in age from 18-25. The pay was $30 a month, of which each man got $5 to keep and the remaining $25 was sent directly home. They were trained first by the U.S. Army at Fort Lewis, and once in the Park, were supervised by the National Park Service.

Much of their handiwork is still not only visible, but in use today. In fact, were it not for the C.C.C., the visitor areas and many of the creature comforts at Mount Rainier would have a different look, or perhaps would not be there at all. It also was the C.C.C. working with the WPA (Works Project Administration) which graded the roads to Mowich Lake and the Puyallup River, thus giving access to those areas. The C.C.C. built the many beautiful rock walls along the road edges and lookout points. One such sample of their handiwork is the large masonry wall at the Narada Falls parking area. They also built campgrounds, the nice rock fireplaces in all the campgrounds, shelters, restrooms, water and septic systems, and many a sturdy rock and log structure. In fact it has been said the park contains one of the nation's best examples of a largely intact complex of historic structures in the rustic park architectural style from the C.C.C. era.

Many of the C.C.C.'ers grew to manhood swinging Pulaskis on the trails at Mount Rainier, then left the C.C.C. to go directly into the Army and off to war. The pay was better, but at least in the C.C.C nobody shot at them. When the war was finally over, the "home" they longed to get back to, was no longer the streets of New York City, but the shadows of Mount Rainier.

The Military at the Mountain

As World War II storm clouds gathered over the nation, the value of the training possibilities the mountain offered became evident to our military forces. In November of 1941 a platoon of the 41st Division Military Ski Patrol came to the mountain for a "preliminary instruction exercise." The following month a detachment of the 15th Infantry (the "Can-do" Regiment Ski Patrol) arrived to spend most of the winter of 1941-1942 training in skiing and maneuvers. The high point of their training was a six-day, 55-mile ski trip. Another detachment from the 41st Division came in February 1941 to make training patrols within the park. The first group was housed at Longmire, the latter troops were stationed at a former C.C.C. camp three miles outside the Nisqually Entrance.

In the spring of 1942 a small detachment from the 87th Mountain Infantry Division from the Mountain Training Center, Camp Hale, Colorado, arrived for intensive training at Mount Rainier. The Division made Paradise their base of operations during their time at the mountain. The organization of the 87th Mountain Infantry Regiment, was followed shortly by organization of the 86th then the 85th MIRS. These three regiments became the 10th Mountain Division. Under the hardships of a Mount Rainier winter, they trained in mountain survival, cold weather warfare, and tested equipment, rations, and clothing. These regiments were initially composed of well-known skiers and climbers from across the country, but primarily from the Pacific Northwest, California, Colorado and New England.

The Famous 10th Mountain Division

The 10th Mountain Division was the only unit of its kind in the United States, and later in the war was involved in retaking KISKA in the Aleutians. Later still they led to breaking the German Gothic Line in the mountains of Italy, before pursuing the Nazi troops into the Alps. A bronze memorial plaque dedicated to the 10th Mountain Division is located in the Paradise flower fields .

By the fall of 1943, no fewer than three army units were training on the mountain. In addition to the 10th Mountain Division at Paradise, there were also 150 soldiers there from the 938th Aviation Engineers practicing camouflage training. They were later joined by Camera Unit No. 9, of the U. S. Army Signal Corps Photographic Center of New York City, which made an army training film.

Many of the men who cut their 'mountaineering teeth' in the 10th Mountain Division came back to the Northwest as the world-class climbers of their day (and for many days and decades to come). The Tenth Mountain Division Association membership book shows the names of several fomer Mount Rainier rangers and summit guides. Former rangers who served in the "Old Tenth" are Larry Jensen, Elvin R. "Bob" / "Swede" Johnson, Cornelius M. "K" Molenaar (deceased), Gordon K. "Pat" Patterson (deceased), George R. Senner (also a guide) and Dar Williams (Deceased).

One-time summit guides who served in the Tenth are Jim Crooks (deceased), William "Bil" Dunaway, Bob Jamison, Ed Kennedy, Robert W. "Bob" Parker, George R. Senner (also a ranger), and Gordie Butterfield (deceased).

Mount Rainier Ordnance Depot

Also during World War II, the Army Motor Base between McChord Air Force Base (McChord Army Airfield) and Fort Lewis was designated "Mount Rainier Ordnance Base, Tacoma, Washington (*TNT* 1/4/43). The facility was large enough that special housing (American Lake Gardens) was built by the Tacoma Housing Authority for the workers and their families. The depot repaired vehicles, stored spare parts, and stored excess stocks of military materials from throughout the region. The Ordnance depot finally closed in July 1963, and its facilities and functions were transferred to Fort Lewis. (*TNT* 8/27/63).

Some BIG Navy Rainiers

Not to be outdone by the Army, three ships have borne the proud name of Rainier. The latest USS Rainier (AOE-7) is the U. S. Navy's newest fast combat logistics support ship.

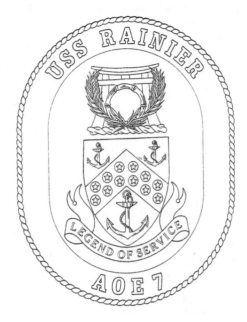

The ship's primary mission is to conduct replenishment operations with other vessels, supplying these ships with fuel, food, munitions and consumables. (Sort of a one-stop shopping center for our floating forces). The Rainier will contribute to the readiness of our naval fleet. The USS Rainier was commissioned in early 1995. Its home port will (appropriately) be Bremerton, Washington.

The first USS Rainier was built in 1917 in Portland, Oregon and throughout World War I was attached to Division two, Pacific Fleet, assigned to the Mexican Patrol. This Rainier was decom- missioned May 28, 1919.

The second USS Rainier was built and commissioned in 1941 and immediately converted for use as an ammunition auxiliary ship. She was decommissioned in 1945 at Port Angeles.

By 1951 the Rainier was recommissioned, operating out of Sasebo, Japan for about a year. After an overhaul in California, she then went back to Korean waters to resupply United Nations Naval Forces in February 1953. In 1964 her focal point was Subic Bay, the Philippines, until the Tonkin Gulf crisis occurred. The Rainier immediately put to sea, steaming to the gulf to rearm aircraft carriers conducting strikes on North Vietnam. Between spring 1965 and January 1966, Rainier transferred at sea almost 12,000 tons of ammunition, 83 tons of freight, and 11,500 pounds of mail.

Overhauled again in 1966, the Rainier resumed her annual deployments in early 1967, providing underway logistics support to the 7th Fleet. September 16, 1968, the date of her last at-sea munitions transfer on that tour, the Rainier had transferred 13,000 tons during 20 underway replenishments. The Rainier received her first Battle "E" (efficiency award given annually to the best ship in the class) for the fiscal year 1968. On November 21, 1968, the Rainier established her best underway replenishment record by transferring 826 tons to USS Camden (AOE 2) in a 5-hour period.

By the end of 1968, the converted World War II cargo ship transferred more than 11,000 tons in support of carriers, escorts, sea-air rescue vessels and coastal surveillance units operating in the Gulf of Tonkin and along the coast of South Vietnam.

In January 1970, following completion of her last tour of duty off Vietnam, the Rainier sailed for home and prepared for inactivation. She was decommissioned and struck from the Navy list, August 7, 1970.

The current Rainier is essentially a floating city. Services onboard include an airport, barber shop, laundry facilities, medical and dental facilities, a post office, ship's store, galley/mess deck (restaurants), utilities (called auxiliaries), and numerous administrative support offices. The ship has a "population" of 579 male and female personnel. It is 753 feet long (or about 2.5 football fields), has a cargo water capacity of 20,000 gallons, 252,000 ft. of pipe (about 50 miles), 19,796 feet of ductwork (4 miles), and 1.6 million ft. of cable (or 303 miles). The ship's generators supply over 12.5 million watts of power (enough to run 25,000 homes, or a city the size of Bremerton). The cargo refrigerators are capable of holding 400 tons of food. Fuel storage/delivery capacity is 6,552,000 gallons, or enough to fill the average automobile 364,000 times (almost every day for 1,000 years) with the fuel in Rainier's tanks.

The big mountain gave her name to a big ship, and this fine ship, as has the previous USS Rainiers, bears it proudly.

Conscientious Objectors at Mount Rainier

Another interesting footnote in the wartime park records involves not the military, but conscientious objectors.

In July of 1942, the superintendent was notified that the Selective Service was considering the establishment of a Civilian Public Service Camp (CPS) for conscientious objectors to be at the former C.C.C. camp at Sunshine Point. However those facilities had already been turned over to the U. S. Navy, so attention then turned to another former C.C.C. camp, this one at Packwood. This time it was concluded that the citizens of Packwood would object to such a camp in their community, so that plan was dropped.

Finally in 1945, Superintendent Preston requested a detail of 12 conscientious objectors to be sent to engage in insect control. The crew arrived in June, but instead of insect control, they undertook snag felling near Klapatche Park. Much to everyone's surprise, the men were such hard workers the superintendent wanted to keep them for the duration, however the director of the camp they had come from insisted they had to be returned because their spiritual needs (Mennonite) could not be met at Mount Rainier.

During the Korean War, there was again discussion of reestablishing a conscientious objector work camp at Mount Rainier. Currently, the Park administration and Fort Lewis have worked together on a number of occasions in search and rescue operations, as well as training exercises.

Celebrity Visitors

Shirley Temple came in 1937 with an entourage of two cars. Other park visitors were Sonja Heine, Tyronne Power, Robert Mitchum, Frances Farmer, Cecil B. DeMille, Audie Murphy (America's most decorated World War II soldier), Charles Laughton, Mary Martin and her daughter "Holiday" (Holly), Bing Crosby, Crown Prince Olav of Norway and Virginia Bruce (star of the Zigfield Follies). Since it isn't necessary to register one's presence, many others have slipped in unannounced and simply enjoyed themselves anonymously.

First Million Visitor Year

By the middle of September, 1958, for the first time in one year, one million visitors had come to visit the park.

The BILLIONTH Visitor

The Park Service's billionth visitor came to Mount Rainier August 22, 1962. The happy World's Fair tourist dubbed, Mr. Billion", was a joking Canadian, Fred Jones from Montreal, who was promptly deluged with gifts from the Park Service. When asked how he felt about being the billionth visitor, he replied, "I suppose this is my first and only one-in-a-billion shot. I rather think I would have preferred to have had it on an Irish Sweepstakes ticket."

Political Visitors

The only three presidents ever to visit the park were President Teddy Roosevelt in 1910, President William Howard Taft, who came in October, 1911, and President Harry S. Truman, on June 22, 1945. President Truman only stayed long enough for lunch, but the poor crew at Paradise had to work around the clock to prepare for the surprise visit of the president and his party of 55.

Over 100 (U.S.) senators and representatives have visited over the years, including those from Washington State currently in office (and who, putting politics aside, all agree Mount Rainier is one of their favorite places on earth!) The influence of the late Senator Henry M. Jackson, who loved the mountain, is still evident today. The visitor center at Paradise bears his name, in fact.

Another prominent lover of the mountain was Supreme Court Justice William O. Douglas, whose home was just a few miles east of the park, in the shadow of the great peak. Though he ruled on the affairs of the nation, the thing he cherished most, was the precious time he got to spend in the wilderness that now bears his name. Countless other judges, congressional committees, bureau chiefs, cabinet secretaries and miscellaneous bureaucrats have also shared the experience of stepping out of their public roles, and standing in awe of the majesty of the mountain, just like everyone else that sees it. James Watt and his wife visited in 1983 when he was Secretary of the Interior.

Most Washington state governors have at least visited the park, a handful have climbed it. Former governor Dan Evans has climbed it and is still an ardent park supporter and deceased ex-governor Dixy Lee Ray was one of the youngest people ever to climb it. Senator Slade Gorton has bicycled around it.

Scientists Who Study Mount Rainier

Those boys and girls in the white coats, khaki jackets and Vibram soles, are (alphabetically): algologists, anthropologists, archaeologists, atmospheric scientists, bacteriologists, biologists, botanists, chemists, ecologists, entomologists, environmental scientists, geologists, geophysicists, glaciologists, glaciospeleologists, hazard management planners, horticulturists, hydrologists (study water), meteorologists, mycologists, naturalists, paleontologists, plant ecologists, seismologists, social psychologists, sociologists, speleologists, soil chemists, stream ecologists, volcanologists and all manner of engineers.

Who's Who of Scientists Who Study Rainier

Rocky Crandell, the geologist who first recognized the mudflow deposits for what they were, and initiated the first volcanic hazards study of the mountain. Now retired, he is still considered a pioneer of Cascades volcano studies, and the father of Cascade volcanic hazards.

Carolyn Driedger, Glaciologist at the USGS Vancouver Volcano, does glaciology studies and outreach activities.

Elliott Endo, USGS, is doing GPS monitoring of ground deformation

Dr. Eugene P. Kiver, Eastern Washington State College, initiated the Summit Steam Caves Project in 1970.

Dr. Steven Malone, University of Washington seismologist, is in charge of the Pacific Northwest Seismology Network.

Seth Moran, University of Washington, Volcano Seismologist

Don Mullineaux, did a study of park pumice and pyroclastic deposits

Pat Pringle, Department of Natural Resources, is a specialist in mapping mudflows.

Kevin Scott, USGS, is doing a major new study on prehistoric mudflows, and is author of a paper on Hazards of Debris Flows..

Donald A. Swanson, former Scientist-in-Charge of Cascades Volcano Observatory, and present Affiliate Professor, University of Washington, led the push to declare Mount Rainier as one of this country's "Decade Volcanoes."

Janet CullenTanaka, pioneer in volcanic hazards management studies, published the first urban and regional planning study of Rainier hazards, using the Puyallup Valley as an example.

The Indians

Until the 1920's, there was a big longhouse near the junction of the Nisqually and Maschel Rivers, where hundreds of Indians from all over the region came to trade. Indian Henry is buried up the hill from the longhouse site.

Loggers in the hills around Mount Rainier report finding many Indian graves, usually on ridge tops, and all marked with rock mounds. Old timers reported occasionally hearing the Indians "keening" from a high place. The keening and lamentation was usually done by a medicine man or woman. It apparently was an unforgettable sound, a high mournful wail, repeated over and over for about three days at evening time.

Old time loggers, miners and woodsmen used to pay Indian women to knit their underwear and socks. The women would mix strands of their long black hair with shredded Western red cedar bark, bear fur, dog hair and mountain goat wool to make a product that was both warm and nearly indestructible. (Although a little itchy!)

Western red cedars were an essential part of Indian life. They used the wood for everything: - canoes, longhouses and various implements and instruments. From the bark they made clothing, baskets, medicines and ointments, rain hats, which like their baskets, never leaked. They also made diapers, towels, capes, headbands, leggings, fishing nets and rope from it. Out of beargrass, which was very plentiful at Mount Rainier, they made very durable baskets. Food was actually boiled in the watertight baskets, with hot stones. Roots were baked over heated rocks.

Foods gathered by the Indians at the mountain were salmon and other fresh-water fish, berries, (huckleberries, salmonberries, serviceberries, salal berries, and wild strawberries, roots (especially camas), seeds, nuts and various medicinal herbs. Hunted for meat, were deer, elk, mountain goat, bear, squirrel, marmots and grouse, and wild fowl. Catches of fish and meat obtained from hunting were divided among all present including strangers.

The Indians taught the early settlers how to pick wild potatoes, onions and wild carrots. They made flour from water lily roots and skunk cabbage roots, which they dried and then pounded into powder. (The skunk cabbage root had to be baked for several days first.)

In addition to camps at Yakima Park, annual huckleberry camps were set up at Indian Henrys, Paradise, Ricksecker Point, Reflection Lakes, Rampart Ridge, Mowich Lake and Sunset Park. Berries were squashed and dried into a sort of huckleberry raisin and also used in pemican. They also made quantities of berry jam. Meat was cured and dried before transporting it home.

In 1906, Cowlitz Indians were still making occasional hunting expeditions up Cowlitz Divide to Indian Bar, Ohanapecosh and Summerland. Many carried their supplies on poles pulled behind their horses. They came from Yakima (and some from as far away as Canada) and in addition to berrying, many went to

Puyallup to work in the hop harvest. By 1920, they were coming to the mountain by car.

A Government Bulletin of 1912 says "Indian Henrys was a favorite resort of a small band of Klickitat Indians. The Cowlitz Divide Trail is the old Indian Trail up the east side. Indian Bar, the gravel deposit on the Ohanapecosh River above Wauhaukaupauken Falls, was another favorite stopping point.

The Indians loved get-togethers and fun times. They had many celebrations and festivals, some of which are still held today. The most common festival among Puget Sound tribes, was the potlatch, a ceremonial feast where valuable gifts were given to friends and neighboring tribesmen. The recipient was then obligated to respond in kind with a potlatch of his own.

Another early big festival was "Treaty Days" complete with games, water sports, dances, native handiwork exhibits, feasting and war canoe races.

Tribes around the Mountain

Tribes either living within sight of, or having some kind of relationship with the mountain, were the Cayuse, Chinook (who lived along the Columbia River), Cowlitz (Coweliskee), Hyada, Klickitat, the Mashel (who lived near Eatonville), Muckleshoot, Nisqually (Squally-o-bish), Puyallup (Puyallup-namish), Salishan, Steilacoom, Taidna-pam and Yakama*

*The Yakama Confederated Tribes have formally corrected the spelling of the name of the tribe from Yakima to Yakama to be consistent with the treaty that formed the confederation of tribes.

The four primary tribes who used the mountain as a hunting ground were the Nisqually and Puyallup tribes from the west, and the Klickitats and Yakamas from east of the Cascades.

Chinook: The Common Language

With trading tribes coming together from as far north as British Columbia and southeastern Alaska to the Umpquah River in Oregon, and from the other side of the mountains, the eastern Washington tribes, and occasionally some from Idaho and Montana, the Chinook jargon developed as a type of trade language. The root language was basic Chinook, with a corruption of words added by each of the other trading tribes. Later the whites made their contributions too. It served as an intertribal communication medium, and the language of exchange and barter. It was learned by most whites who had dealings with the Indians.

The 1855 Indian War

By the mid-1800's the Native Americans were becoming increasingly alarmed as more settlers staked claims and fenced their favorite fields, took over their hunting grounds and fishing places, and paid no respect to their sacred grounds.

We find it humorous to hear that Indians walked through cabins which were built over trails. It didn't matter if you were eating dinner or in bed, through the house he went. It may have been your house, but it was his trail. In reality, the Indians were just exercising what they considered to be their rights.

As tensions escalated, so did the number of attacks on farms. According to *The Evergreen Post, a History of Fort Lewis*, "from 1855 to 1856, 500-600 Native Americans throughout the region revolted. Fayette McMullen, the governor of the Washington Territory, wrote in mid-September 1855, '...a general and simultaneous rising (of the Indians) could annihilate our settlements. They complain that the government of the United States has been giving away and still is selling their lands to settlers without making them any sort of compensation. They don't understand by what right these things are done, and upon what principles of justice the government refuses to ratify their treaties and pay them for the land'..."

It was the Donation Land Law passed by Congress in 1850 which gave the settlers land ownership without fee, however title wasn't given until treaties were made with the Indians. The Eastern Washington Klickitats were particularly militant and resistant to relinquishing any of their lands. They kept trying to incite the Western Washington tribes to fight. Fortunately most Indians did not get involved in the conflict, and in fact many, at great risk to themselves, aided the settlers. There are many touching stories of how friendly Indians warned their white neighbors about impending danger.

Two soldiers were killed October 27, 1855, and the war was on. In what became known as "The White River Massacre," three families were attacked by several bands of Indians. Nine people were murdered, and their homes were burned. The settlers thought the attackers were "blanket Indians," (Klickitats from Eastern Washington).

The war amounted to a few murders, several skirmishes and a number of good scares. Frightened settlers fled to the safety of Fort Steilacoom, and in January 1856, reinforcements were sent in to battle the Indians. By March the uprising was squelched, and peace once again settled on the foothills.

It fell to Governor Isaac Stevens to try to convince the Indians to accept the peace proposals, which included restricting the Indians to life on reservations, and specific provisions for hunting and fishing, as well as a nominal amount of money for their lands

The first Treaty was held on Medicine Creek on the Nisqually Flats (known today as McAllister Creek). Indians from all over Puget Sound met and most accepted the proposal.

The Indian massacre was a tragedy for both the Indians and the settlers.

Indian Henry probably had good reason to hate the white man, but he was level headed, and recognized that there were good and bad men in both races. He didn't want to have any trouble with anyone, so he moved his family to the western slope of Mount Rainier, making camp on what we now know as Indian Henrys Hunting Ground for the duration. He sat out the war up at the Mountain. Henry decided it was safer just to stay away from the white men for a few years while things settled down. Indian Henry was smart.

Mount Rainier the Sanctuary

Like the biblical City of Refuge, where one was safe, even from one's enemies, Mount Rainier was a safe haven for the Indians. Even a murderer was safe from retaliation from his victim's kin, if he could make it to the Mountain. When he crossed its border, the warrior was required to lay down his arms.

Called "the Land of Peace", chiefs also often sent their criminals, wayward, and troublemakers to the mountain to do penance. The Indians had a definite concept of the "boundaries" of the mountain, and it was inside those boundaries that the pursued were safe from their pursuers. The Cascade Crest was the boundary on the east side.

What Sex is Mount Rainier?

Another thing the Indians had definite concepts of, was whether mountains were male or female. The problem came in which tribe you asked and which legend they told.

The Cowlitz, for instance, had two legends regarding the mountain. In one, Mount Rainier was a female, in the other, a male.

Legend one, has Mount Rainier ("Takhoma") and Mount Adams ("Pahto") as the wives of Mount St. Helens ("Seuq"). A terrible quarrel ensued between the wives, and during the course of it, Takhoma stepped on all of Pahto's children and killed them. The two women turned into mountains.

Under the next legend, Mount Rainier and Mount St. Helens were once separated by an inland sea. They had a fierce fight over who would rule the region, and hurled hot rocks at each other, shot flames from their summits and rained ash on the water between them. The birds finally intervened and took Rainier far inland, then peace settled on the land again.

According to the Lummi Indians of northern Puget Sound, Komo Kulshan (Mount Baker) had two wives. One of his wives, "Duh-hwahk," meaning "clear sky" was so jealous of the second wife, she took up all her roots and traveled a few days' journey south. There she made a permanent camp and planted all her roots and seeds. She had to stretch herself very tall to look back on her husband and children. Clear Sky is known today as Mount Rainier.

The Duwamish, Puyallup, Skokomish, and Nisqually, who lived along the shores of southern Puget Sound, had a different legend. According to them, Rainier was one of two wives of Docewollops, who lived on the peninsula west of the Sound. She used to reside beside Mount Constance, the other wife, but both were very jealous, and the wives were always fighting. Mount Rainier became very angry, and gathered a lot of food before starting on a long journey from her home. Before leaving, she tore the breasts from her rival, and threw them to the ground. They can still be seen today as the two rounded points that jut into the water at Jackson Hole near Quilcene. She left most of her children (mountains) to live on the Olympic Peninsula, but she took one little boy when she moved across the sound. As she traveled to her new home, she dropped some of the food she carried. As she passed the Skokomish River, she dropped salmon, which is still there today. On the prairies near Olympia, she dropped camas root, and it too is still grows there. Today we call her Rainier, and her son is known as Little Tahoma. Docewollops' children from his two wives are the Olympic Mountains, still all huddled together.

The Yakamas, east of the mountains, also considered Mount Rainier to be female. She was one of the wives of the Sun.

The Klickitats, however, believed Mounts Rainier, Hood and St. Helens were brothers. They warred against each other, and lopped each others heads off.

Finally in a version written by Henry Sicade, last of the chiefs of the Nisqually, Mount Rainier was a female monster who sucked into her maw, all who came near. Finally the Changer, in the form of a fox, challenged her in a sucking contest, The fox won, and the monster died, with streams of blood running down her side. The Changer declared, "Hereafter, Tacobud shall be harmless. The streams of blood I will change into rivers of water. The waters shall have plenty of fish for the good of all people."

Indian Trails Across the Cascades

Just as many of our trails today follow old Indian trails, so do many of our cross state highways. For centuries the Indians knew the best routes across the mountains. Snoqualmie Pass was a popular crossing, as was Naches Pass, Chinook Pass, Cayuse Pass and White Pass.

These trails got a lot of use, but especially in the fall. In addition to the berrying trips, bands living east of the Cascades looked forward to an annual trip over each year for the salmon runs. While on the west side, they also feasted on shellfish, halibut, cod, sturgeon and fresh-water fish. They especially loved the crabs, oysters and clams. They dried, preserved and hauled home as much as they could carry of their seafood bounty.

Museums Containing Local Indian Artifacts

There are several collections of Indian artifacts around for those who like Native American antiquities.

State Museum, University of Washington Campus, Seattle, WA
State Historical Society Museum, Tacoma, WA
American Museum of Natural History, New York City
Smithsonian Institution, Washington, DC
Yakama Nation Cultural Center, Toppenish, WA

There are several smaller displays owned by various historical societies.

Wilkeson: There is also an authentic Indian Pow Wow with jackpot dancing each year in conjunction with the Wilkeson National Handcar Races. Call (360) 897-8892 for more information.

The Puyallup Pow Wow

Those interested in Indian lore can participate in an authentic Puyallup Tribal Pow Wow early each September in the Cascadian Building on the Puyallup Reservation. Call (206) 597-6200 for dates and times.

The Indians as Climbers

Hazard Stevens and P. B. Van Trump get the credit for being the first to climb Mount Rainier, but there's mounting evidence they may have been the first *white* men, but oral history and legends imply that the Indians were on the summit long before.

CHRONOLOGY OF INDIAN CLIMBS

1855   According to Aubrey Haines in "Mountain Fever", two white men and an Indian guide Saluskin (not to be confused with Sluiskin who guided Stevens and Van Trump) climbed via the Winthrop Glacier. They gave accurate descriptions of the summit crater and steam vents. Dee Molenaar says, "An old Indian (Saluskin) told historians that when he was a youth he led two white men who were surveying the boundaries of the Yakima (now Yakama) Indian Reservation to the eastern base of the mountain in about 1852, and that they then climbed to the summit from there. There's no written record by these unidentified men of their feat."

1857   Wapowety, a Nisqually guide for Lt. A.V. Kautz. He attempted the climb, but turned back after climbing a considerable distance because of snowblindness. Wapowety Cleaver is named for him.

1870   Sluiskin, in his impassioned plea with Stevens and Van Trump, tried to inform the men of the dangers to them if they proceeded with their plans to climb. He said "Many years ago, my grandfather, the greatest and bravest chief of all the Yakima, climbed nearly to the summit. Here he caught sight of the fiery lake and the infernal demon coming to destroy him. He fled down the mountain glad to escape with his life. Where he failed no other Indian dared to make the attempt.

"At first the way is easy and the task seems light. The broad Snowfields, over which I have often hunted the mountain goat, offer an inviting path. But above that you will have to climb over steep rocks overhanging deep gorges where a misstep will hurl you far down -- down to certain death. You must creep over steep snowbanks and cross deep crevasses where a mountain goat would hardly keep his footing. You must climb along steep cliffs where rocks are continually falling to crush you, or knock you off into the bottomless depths.

"And if you should escape these perils and reach the great snowy dome then a bitterly cold and furious tempest will sweep you off intospace like a withered leaf. But if by some miracle you should survive all these perils the mighty demon of Takhoma will surely kill you and throw you into the fiery lake."

It sounds like Sluiskin's grandpa had indeed been at least a good way up on the mountain!

1886   A party of seven or eight Yakima Indians, together with Allison Brown, reached the summit. They climbed via the Cowlitz Divide over the Whitman and Ingraham Glaciers.

Mining

Photo courtesy of Pemco Webster & Stevens Collection, Museum of History & Industry

A typical Mount Rainier Miner's Cabin

Between 1905 and 1908 approximately 300 mining claims were located within the Park, mostly in the west and northeast sections, with countless more claims filed and worked in the hills outside the park. Miners came looking for gold, silver and precious metals, but most found only a little copper. The vast majority of the claims proved to be unprofitable. Few of the miners made serious attempts to extract ore. Old park records state that most claimants stayed long enough each summer to construct unsightly cabins, cut timber indiscriminately, and hunt game freely. Most claims were soon abandoned.

There were several notable exceptions, covered individually below. As for the rest of the claims, when news of the Alaska Gold strike reached the Mount Rainier miners, many dropped their tools where they stood and headed for Alaska. Remains of their mines and digs were evident for many years. There was the Rudolph Creek Mine, the Evans Camp Mine, Rainier Copper Mining Co. Digs, an old miner's cabin near Moraine Park, and a blacksmith shop near Mystic Lake. There were prospecting holes by Hessong Rock and even the tools left up there. There were more mines by the Carbon River entrance, and up by Mowich Lake. Up by Coplay Lake there was the Queen Bee and Copper King, and three or four others.

The problem that soon became evident, was what to do with all the mining claims. In 1908, Congress passed a law (Sundry Civil Act of May 27, 1908)

which prohibited any new mining locations within Mount Rainier National Park (35 Stat. 365) and provided that the Park Service could buy existing claims. A mine could remain viable under two conditions. One, if $500 or more of improvements had been made by claimants since 1908, and two, if evidence was given that there was enough valuable mineral worth extracting.

Some of the Old Mines

Looking at these old mine names now, one wonders what some of them meant, and why the miners chose the names they did. A few are probably names of the owners, and others of their loved ones. Still more express a hope of the contents, but what of the rest?

Adit Tunnel #1 & #2, Adula, Bar, Benny, Bisbee, Buty, Camp Storbo, Cloudy, Copper King, Crater #1 & #2, Dandy. Eagle, Eagle Peak, Evans Camp, Fergus, Flate, Gadge, Gate Claim, Ghost Gold Mine, Golden, Gilt Edge, Good, Hope, Grace, Henning, Hephizibah #1, #2 & #3, Iva Henry #1 & #2, Jenny, Klondike, Lake City, Lodi #1 & Lodi #2, Lorraine Mines #1, #2, #3, Lucky 13, Lucky Boy, Mary, Narada, New Discovery, North Mowich Glacier Mine, Odin, O.I.C., Otter Tail, Orinda, Paradise, Paradise Mine #1, Peach, Pedro, Perth, Pinto Horse Mine, Queen Bee, Raven, Rob Roy, Round Top, Rudolph, Creek, Silver King, Snow Cap, Snowflake, South Side, Starbo, Stronghold #1 & #2, The Clarence J., The Discovery, The Electric, The Mineral, Mountain, The Mary, The Mountain Goat, The Short Canyon Lode, The Walter W, The Throndhjem, Turtle, Washington #1 & #2, and White Glacier #1, #2, #3 & #4.

The Mount Rainier Mining Company (The Starbo Mine)

The Starbo Mine

On the northeast side of the mountain in the big valley below Sunrise, copper fever first struck. By 1898 forty-one claims had been filed in Glacier Basin. Eventually one firm, the Mount Rainier Mining Company acquired all other claims, and merged with the Starbo Mine. Between 1914 and 1930, several tunnels were driven, numerous prospector pits dug, and many buildings, including a large hotel, blacksmith shop, sawmill and power plant, were put up.

As for workings, there were tunnels 700-feet, 300-feet and 240-feet long in addition to a 13-foot deep prospect hole. There was also an aerial tram, 800-feet long, which led from one of the shorter tunnels down to the wagon road. In 1924, patents were granted on eight claims, and the rest were relinquished. The total area under claim was 164.84 acres.

In 1928, stockholders filed complaints against the company for using the mails to defraud in their stock selling operations. This resulted in two men serving time at the Federal Penitentiary on McNeil Island in nearby Puget Sound. In 1932, the claims were sold at Sheriff's sale for $500. Then like

Phoenix, a new Mount Rainier Mining Company again arose, organized and more stock was sold. In 1948 47 tons of ore was shipped off to Tacoma, and again, little money was realized. In 1950, stockholders valued their claims at two and one half million dollars, while the government valued them at between $500 to $6,000. Finally, in 1984, the government purchased the last of the park's inholdings for a total purchase price of $55,800. The transaction marked the final chapter on mining within Mount Rainier National Park.

This old hotel and boarding house measured 36 x 70 feet, had a full basement with stone walls, a dining room that would seat 120, and living capacity for 40.

Mining Claims in the Glacier Basin

(Mt. Rainier Mining Company 1898 - 1966)

1897-98	Many men were prospecting and working claims in Glacier Basin. 41 claims were filed in the Basin.
1905	The original Mount Rainier Mining Company was incorporated.
1908	By act of Congress, mining claims were no longer allowed within the Park. Existing claims were not affected.
1914-30	Several tunnels were driven and numerous prospector pits dug. Several buildings, including a large hotel, were built. A power plant was brought in, and a road built to connect the area with an old road to Enumclaw. Small amounts of ore, containing mostly copper, were taken out.
1924	Patents were granted on 8 claims with a total area of 164.8 acres. The rest of the claims were relinquished.
1928	Stockholders filed complaints against Starbo and the Mount Rainier Mining Company for using the mails to defraud in their stock selling operations. Two men were fined $1,000 each and sentenced to 18 months in the Federal Penitentiary at McNeil Island for fraudulent use of the mails.
1932	The Glacier Basin claims were bought at a Sheriffs Sale for $500.
1944	The mine's owner died.
1946	A new Mount Rainier Mining Company was organized and more stock sold.
1948	47 tons of ore was shipped to American Smelting Company in Tacoma.
1950	Stockholders valued their claims at 2 to 2-1/2 million dollars. The government valued the claims at between $500 to $6,000 maximum.

Lorraine Claims, Winthrop Creek

This group of claims was first worked in 1897 by Fred J. Chamberlain, who staked his claims on the east and west sides of the Winthrop Glacier. The claims on the east side of the glacier were the Lorraine mines #1, #2, #3, #4 and #5, the Walter W. and the Clarence J.

The Electric Claim included Garda Falls near the foot of the Winthrop Glacier, and the claim's name gave a hint of their intentions. They planned

Lorraine Mines Winthrop Creek

45

to install an electric plant there. On the west side of the glacier in the vicinity of Mystic Lake, were the Mineral Mountain and the Mountain Goat mines.

The company's president was ousted by stockholders in 1910 for having neglected to carry out the required annual assessment work. In 1926 the General Land Office annulled the claims on the basis of abandonment.

Eagle Peak Mine

Eagle Peak Mine

The second of the claims to have a great deal of work and money put in to it, was the "Adula Claim" filed in 1903. It was south of the confluence of the Paradise and Nisqually Rivers, on the north side of Eagle Peak. That's almost directly across the river from the Cougar Rock Campground. In 1906 the Paradise Claim was staked beside it, and the two claims totaled 41.32 acres. In 1908, the Eagle Peak Copper Mining Company was formed and acquired both claims. That same year, new mining claims were no longer allowed within the Park by act of Congress, however existing claims were not affected.

Between 1914 and 1930 several tunnels were driven, numerous prospector pits were dug and buildings erected, and an 800-foot flume was built upstream on the Paradise River to a powerhouse at the confluence of the two rivers.

Occasional remains of the old flume can still be seen be taking a short hike up the Wonderland Trail.

Early in the century, once there was enough power to dig through the rock, 1,100 feet of tunnels, drifts and cross-cuts were made inside Eagle Peak. But the work was all for naught. When the ore was shipped to the Tacoma smelter, one load showed a profit of only $7.00. A second shipment of 24 tons of ore realized a $115.00 profit. As late as 1955, the company was still proposing developmental plans and insisting Eagle Rock was a valuable copper claim, but by then, the government wanted no further development in the park. They just wanted the mines closed! But it still took them another 19 years (until 1974) for them to realize this goal and close the final chapter on legal mining in the Park.

Paradise Mining and Milling Company

Also on the lower slopes of Eagle Peak, and adjacent to the Eagle Peak Copper Mining Company holdings, Ike and Sherman Evans staked their copper claims on their Iva Henry claims #1 and 2.

The mine entrance of the Iva Henry #1 is still visible. Stand at the bridge by the Cougar Rock Campground, look up, and you'll see the now

Paradise Mining and Milling Co.

46

Chronology of Eagle Peak

1903 The Adula Claim was located by Mary A. Long. The claim lies south of the confluence of the Paradise and Nisqually Rivers at the base of Eagle Peak.

1906 Paradise Claim #1, adjacent to and east of the Adula Claim was staked. The claims covered 41.32 acres.

1908 Eagle Peak Copper Mining Company was formed. The Paradise and Adula claims were transferred to Eagle.

1908 Mining claims were no longer allowed within the Park by act of Congress. Existing claims were not affected.

1910 The Eagle Peak Company filed an additional claim on their mill site, across the Nisqually from their mining claims. This site was 4.75 acres and lies adjacent to, and just south of the Cougar Rock Campground.

1914 Eagle Peak was given permission to use water from the Paradise River for generating power.

1918 Eagle Peak Mining Company leased the Evans Claim (owned by the Paradise Mining and Milling Company) and obtained permission to set up machinery near that tunnel.

1918-30 An 800-foot flume was built from upstream on the Paradise River to a power house at the confluence of the Paradise and Nisqually Rivers. One thousand one hundred feet of tunnels, drifts and cross-cuts were dug. A bunkhouse, ore mill, compressor house, powder magazine and other makeshift structures were put up on the millsite.

1930 Several shipments of ore were shipped to a Tacoma smelter. One showed only a $9.00 profit, the second a $115 profit.

1950 The government obtained Evans' claims (Paradise Mining and Milling) through condemnation for $6,000.

1955 The company was still proposing development plans including an aerial tram down the east side of the Nisqually to Skate Creek Road (Forest Service Road 52) between Ashford and Packwood. The compressor house, ruins of a log cabin, ruins of the ore mill, the powder magazine and ruins of the power plant still stood on the mill site.

sealed-over mine entrance high on Eagle Peak. There was an ingenious counterbalance system up to the mine utilizing 2 cables and 2 cars. The weight of the rock coming down would pull the second (empty) car back up.

As was the case with nearly all Mount Rainier mines, the owners put more money into their mine than they ever took out. A government assay in 1931 showed no gold, a trace of silver, and 13.47 percent copper.

The mill was on the north side of the river, between the river and the road, in the woods on the downhill side. In the early 1960's the author and her kids used to eat lunch while sitting on the running boards of quaint old trucks which sat amid a jumble of old mining equipment. It was from this point the thick cables crossed the river up to the mine. In 1946 the Evans brothers, then both in their 70's, offered to sell their claims to the government for $5,000. Congress didn't appropriate the money, and it turned out the brothers couldn't produce a clear title. Finally in 1950, condemnation procedures were begun, and the property transferred to the government that same year.

The Tahoma Mining District (below Eagle Cliff)

The Tahoma Mining District

The North Mowich Glacier Mine, at the base of Eagle Cliff, by the headwaters of the Mowich River, was operated by the Washington Cooperative Mining Syndicate, and was one of several claims in the area called the "Mountain View Group" by the owners. The property was vaguely described as running in an easterly direction 3,000 feet on the south fork of the Mowich River and 1,500 feet in a westerly direction across the Mowich River.

It had a half dozen buildings, including a sawmill and blacksmith shop. There were also numerous prospector cabins. Of all the Park's mining operations, this was one of the most ambitious. The remote mine had two tunnels, a railroad, small ore cars and small gauge railroad track. There was a 500-foot flume, a 150-foot water pipe, a power plant, a pump, an air compressor, a machine drill, and heavy iron machinery weighing tons.

The trail to the mining area branched off the old Grindstone Trail. When Ranger O'Farrell went looking for the mine, he reached the end of the Grindstone Trail, then had to climb ladders to reach the mouth of the tunnel. The miners hauled the equipment in from Orting and must have done it by sled in winter because it was too heavy for horses. The North Mowich Glacier Mine was worked for 4 to 5 years, and abandoned around 1908.

Hephizibah Mining Company

Hephizibah Mining Co.

This mining company had at least six mining claims on the south side of the Carbon River just inside the park boundary. They were all on the east side of Sweet Peak about 600 feet west of June Creek. One of the claims, the Hephizibah #3, was 109 feet deep and 4-1/2 x 6 feet in diameter. This one appears to have hit pay dirt. It was believed that this claim contained gold, silver and cobalt ores. Ranger O'Farrell, who investigated the mine in 1908, concluded this was a valid claim, even though there was no road for taking out the ore. However the owners did little or no work on the claim in the succeeding years, and in 1923, it was found to be abandoned. One partner had moved to San Diego, one had died and the third was old and sick in Tacoma. The General Land Office directed proceedings against the claimants, and they did not make any effort to save their claim.

Washington Mining and Milling Company

Washington Mining and Milling Co.

The most extensive mining operation on the Carbon River was that of the Washington Mining and Milling Company who had a total of 38 lode claims within the park. Most were on the south side of the Carbon River and east of the Hephizibah claims. During 1908 and 1909 they employed a year-round crew of 7 to 15 men. In October 1910, the company relinquished 24 of their claims, and by 1913 they relinquished the remaining fourteen.

In 1950, an old miner from Orting who was visiting the park, told District Ranger Aubrey Haines that a notable feature of one of the mines was an incline railroad which lowered the ore from the tunnel to the Carbon River 300 feet below. This piqued Ranger Haines' curiosity, so he set off looking for remains of the mine. About a mile east of today's ranger station he noticed some cut stumps. Climbing the hill, he came to the ruins of four buildings, and one which was still in fair condition and contained furniture. A ways further on, he came to the mine tunnel, a six foot square opening, neatly cut into the rock. He could see inside about 50 feet, where the tunnel made a right-hand turn. Because there was about a foot of standing water on the floor, he didn't enter it, but he did note the ore car tracks were still in place. Further investigation showed that the track had extended from the tunnel and over a draw by means of a trestle. On the other side of the ravine, the incline railway ran downhill on large logs set end to end with notches for cross ties. The large logs were still in place, but the cross ties had rotted away.

The End of the Mining Era

Eventually all but two claims were bought out by the government. The last two were the Eagle Peak Mine, which was finally acquired in 1974 and the Starbo Mine whose owners refused to sell until 1984. Of that claim of 165 acres, rusted machinery and abandoned tunnels are all that's left.

The Last of the Old Remains

There are still folks around, friends or relatives of some of the old pioneers, who know the whereabouts of the old mines, and the old locations of what we consider 'famous' happenings. Those are the people we attempted to contact in compiling this book.

One such person is Carl Fabiani, now foreman of all trail maintenance in the park. Carl had some benefits few of us have had. For one, he had the opportunity to sit at the knee of an uncle who was one of the original C.C.C.

workers who worked on many of the early projects around the park. Secondly, Carl had the good fortune to grow up in Wilkeson with the great park as his back yard. His youth was spent exploring the historic remains in the hills around his home. What is now rotting and overgrown remains were still standing buildings and in some cases, left just as they were when their inhabitants left.

When Carl was a young explorer, he combed the remains of the North Mowich Glacier Mine, the little mining town at the base of the Eagle Cliff.

There was a lot of 12" diameter pipe, small gauge rail track and ore cars still there. They were partially buried, and nature was taking over, but parts were still sticking out of the ground. When last explored by Carl in 1970 or 71, the buildings had rotted away, and the area was overgrown with brush, however he found many old tools, a saw, wrenches, remains of an oak desk, little brass hinges and hooks, and a number of old bottles. Today there is no longer any sign of a trail going in except for an occasional blaze high in the trees.

He explored other mines at the west end of the Northern Crags, near the snout of the Carbon Glacier and still others both just inside and just outside the Park. One that still gets an occasional visitor is an old Copper Mine near the Ipsut Creek Entrance. Known as the "old Mine Trail," or the "old Copper Mine trail", the trail is unmarked, but the now boarded-over mine tunnel is still there as are some rails.

Not all remains are from mines. Souvenirs of old camps remain in Seattle Park. It's unknown whether they were from Boy Scout or C.C.C. camps, (they're about 1/4-1/2 mile off the trail) but they contained bottles, stovepipe, horseshoes and nails in logs. Other finds are old time graffiti, a name in a cedar log, a large Alaska Cedar, with a large blaze and a name and the date 1890. About 30 feet of heavy wire was found about 6000 ft. up a ridge between the North and South Mowich Glaciers. That old telephone line turns up in strange places.

One final note regarding all old mines. There is virtually nothing left to see, and it is unwise to go exploring, since open shafts may still exist. The Park Service would prefer that you left these old bygones be gonebys.

Coal Mining

In mining, the driving hope was always that something valuable would be found. But the only find with any real commercial value turned out to be what the prospectors jokingly called "black diamonds" -- coal.

Coal was in the mountains all around Mount Rainier: at Carbonado, Wilkeson, and Black Diamond on the north. Coal was first commercially mined at Wilkeson, so much so, that the railroad ran a line there from Tacoma in 1876. One of the state's first major disasters was an 1899 Carbonado mine explosion which killed 30 men, most of whom were Welsh immigrants. (Most of these men had come to American in the big Welsh migration of the 1890's.

Not far from Ashford, the mine at Mineral was the biggest coal mine in the state. This mine too, met with disaster. A fire in the mine burned for months, eventually resulting in the mine being permanently sealed. Fortunately, no lives were lost. There was a smaller mine in Ashford behind the fire hall. The tailings can still be seen behind Jasmer's Bed and Breakfast. There are still extensive coal leases just north of town. In the early days, much of the local coal was made into coke, then shipped to Tacoma for smelting iron ore. Coal mined on the North side went back east for use as pencil lead.

There was also an arsenic mine up Mineral Creek. It operated from 1900 to 1922.

Coal Deposits Around Mt. Rainier

Mount Rainier

Park Facilities

The Nisqually Park Portal

In 1910, superintendent Edward S. Hall envisioned a splendid entry to his stupendous park. In a letter to his Washington, D.C. bosses, he requested the funds for "an archway of rustic design at the entrance to the park." Soon Richard A. Ballinger, then Secretary of the Interior, came to see the park for himself. After traveling three days from Seattle to get there, he agreed with Hall that the great park indeed needed an impressive log entry.

Upon his return east, he issued orders for the log portal to be built immediately. It was to be a symbol to the arriving visitor that he was formally entering a great national park. The new portal was built of large cedar logs, and stood 24 feet high by 22 feet wide. It was built in 1911.

By 1972, time had taken its toll. The old portal was deteriorating. Park officials feared one of the heavy logs would fall on someone. The challenge was to make a new portal that retained the rustic look the public loved. Crews cruised the nearby Gifford Pinchot National Forest in search of the perfect logs. With the Forest Service's permission, they cut six trees, each 160 feet long. The longer they worked on the reconstruction, the more impressed they were with the original job the old timers had done!

When the portal was finally finished, a few sound sections of the old original logs were carved into mementos to be presented to departing and retiring park personnel.

Nisqually Entrance Buildings

The first ranger cabin in the park (built in 1908), lies just a few feet inside the boundary line on the south side of the entrance. Known locally as the Oscar Brown cabin, it is presently used by Superintendent Briggle when he is staying in the park. (This is the same Oscar Brown who raised the flagpole on the summit in 1891.) Brown built the cabin by himself, aided only by a horse to skid the logs and raise them. The rustic cabin also once served as the park's administrative office. The gable with its unique fan-like logwork is distinctive.

Up on the rise to the left, north of the entrance as you enter the park, is the old Superintendent's residence, constructed in 1915 by Supt. Dewitt L. Reaburn. Beside it, is another residence which was the quarters of the Chief Ranger. Although the interiors of these buildings have been remodeled over the years, the exterior appearances remain as they were originally.

As more motor vehicles ventured to the park, the checking in and out of visitors necessitated a building for that purpose. The little L-shaped entrance station at Nisqually was constructed in 1925, and contained a registration room and quarters for three bachelor rangers in the main building. The "port-cochere" (porch-overhang) was not added until 1937. It was short lived, however, and was removed in 1946 by a bus that didn't quite fit under it. In 1962, a new check-in station large enough for busses and motor homes was built for the rangers in an island in the middle of the road.

The entrance arch, superintendent's house, ranger residence, Oscar Brown cabin and entrance station are on the List of Classified Structures (page 135).

Longmire - General

Longmire is located six miles inside the Nisqually entrance on the southwest side of the park. It is usually the first stop for park visitors. It is famous for the Hot Springs, Longmire Inn, and being the in-park administration hub. Many employees live here, as do seasonal volunteers who live in the campground across the river. Longmire is bounded by Rampart Ridge on the north, and the Nisqually River on the south. Being at a lower elevation (2951'), it is generally open and accessible year round.

Longmire National Historic District

The Rustic Style was the predominant architectural style used in western parks by the National Park Service in the 1920's and 30's, but the complete Rustic architecture period ran from 1908 to 1944. The objective was that structures should harmonize with their natural surroundings. At Mount Rainier, this meant incorporating natural raw materials and color schemes found in the surrounding landscape into the design of the buildings by using log framing, cedar shakes or shingle roofs, glacial boulder foundations and stone chimneys.

The collection of these historic and architecturally significant structures was recognized as a historic district and listed in the National Register of Historic

Places in 1991. In 1987 the U.S. Secretary of the Interior designated three buildings within the historic district as Historic Landmarks because of their distinct architectural qualities which reflected the Rustic Style. These are the Longmire Administration Building, the Community Building, and the Service Station. National Historic Landmark status is the highest designation a building can receive and guarantees that the structure will be maintained so they will retain their historic character.

Longmire (Family) Chronology

1853	(October) James Longmire came over Naches Pass in first immigrant train and settled in Yelm
1861	James Longmire built trail from Yelm to Bear Prairie (along the Skate Creek Road just south of Longmire)
1883	Longmire discovered mineral springs by the Nisqually River on his return from the third successful climb of the mountain.
1884	The first trail was constructed to Longmire Springs by the Longmires. Longmire began development of his claim and constructed first building.
1885	Mrs. Elcaine Longmire named Paradise on her first trip to the area.
1888	Elcaine Longmire built his homestead cabin at Longmire.
1890	Construction of the first road was begun and a small hotel was constructed. Len Longmire was guide on first successful climb by a woman, Fay Fuller.
1891	The road to Longmire was completed.
1895	James Longmire improved claim at springs with additional buildings, and built trail to Paradise Valley.
1935	National Park Service purchased Longmire property at Longmire.

National Park Inn - Longmire

The original Longmire Inn was described as "a fine looking place on the right hand side of the road, three stories high. The top story had ten dormer windows, a porch all the way around, and the whole building was covered with cedar shingles. There was a fire escape at both ends." The opening of the Inn in 1918 was marked by a grand dinner and formal ball in honor of General H.A. Greene, the Commanding officer of "Camp Lewis." The Inn continued to be the center of elegant entertaining. Military brass came there to entertain and be entertained, as did the state's governors, congressional delegations, heads of governmental agencies, and captains of industry.

The original National Park Inn's beautiful old massive furniture was hand wrought from Silver Forest cedar logs by Swiss-German Hans Grussion during the winter of 1916-17. He hand hewed Alaska cedar tables, rustic benches, and high-back seats. Unfortunately the old Inn burned in June of 1922.

Construction of the second inn was begun almost immediately.

The recently remodeled National Park Inn has 25 rooms, and is managed under a concession contract with Mount Rainier Guest Services, Inc. It offers fine dining facilities and an attached gift shop and convenience store.

The Inn is open daily, year round. For reservations call Mount Rainier Guest Services at (360) 569-2275. Lodging desk summer hours are 8 a.m. to 10 p.m. Summer dining room hours are 7 a.m. to 8 p.m. The General Store hours are 8 a.m. to 8 p.m. All winter hours are shorter.

The Post Office (behind the hotel front desk) is open weekdays 8:30 a.m. to noon and 1 p.m. to 5 p.m.

The Longmire Museum

This popular museum houses exhibits of natural history, animal specimens, geology, early park exploration and Northwest Indian artifacts.

Built in 1916, this modest little building was the first park headquarters. Twelve years later in 1928, a new headquarters building was constructed, and this one was to be torn down. Park Naturalist Frank Brockman made the case to save the little structure for use as a museum and naturalist's office. Permission was granted, and he spent the next few years designing and constructing many of the same exhibits which are in it today. Brockman built the original shelves and exhibit cases from wood he scavenged in the Longmire area. The exhibit cases were later rebuilt in the early 1930's by a C.C.C. work crew.

56

Brockman also convinced the University of Washington to donate surplus materials to help with the mounted animal exhibits. Most of the animal specimens were prepared and mounted in the 1930's. William Brockman, son of Frank, prepared some of the birds. Seasonal Naturalist Ottmar F. von Fuehrer, a Hungarian artist and taxidermist who lived at Paradise, prepared many of the mammals. Most of the animals were found dead in the wild or on the road. The porcupine was found in Stevens Canyon. The beaver came from the Tipsoo Lake area.

Charlie the cougar, the primary exhibit, was shot on Forest Service land just outside the park. He was stuffed by another early naturalist, Floyd Schmoe in Floyd's first and last attempt at taxidermy. (We're happy to report Mr. Schmoe celebrated his 100th birthday in July 1995, and is working on a new book.)

The Indian baskets date back to 1899, and represent the handiwork of the Skokomish, Klickitat and Thompson River tribes. The baskets were woven from cedar wood and root, and used cherry bark and black mineral dye to create the colors and patterns. These beautiful artifacts are on loan from the Thomas Burke Memorial Museum at the University of Washington.

The building has an upstairs loft which served as a naturalist's office. It also included a darkroom. Some of the photos still on display in the museum were developed in this darkroom in the 1930's by Brockman. A vent was finally installed after he passed out one day from lack of ventilation while smoking a cigar during a film developing session. *(Pierce/Brockman)*

Like most old buildings, this one could tell many other interesting tales. Like about the early rangers who worked to the tap..tap..tap of the pileated woodpeckers as they methodically worked the putty out from around the window panes, or the cold day when the snowblower blew out all the windows.

A ranger is usually on duty daily from 9 a.m. to 4:30 p.m. to answer questions. The books, maps and videos are offered for sale by Northwest Interpretive Association.

The Longmire Hiker Information Center

Situated beside the flag pole, this wonderful old log and boulder masonry building has served a number of functions over the years It now houses the Hiker Information Center in the lobby, and in-Park administrative offices in the remainder of the building. The building was constructed in 1928-1929.

Here backcountry hikers can get up-to-date trail conditions, ask questions and get their trail camp assignments and backcountry permits. The Center houses maps, computer contact with all other hiker centers in the Park, and one of the famed "models of the Mountain" discussed on page 99. Summer hours are 8 a.m. to 6 p.m.

This Hiker Information Center closes September 30, and hiker services (issuance of permits, information on backcountry conditions, etc.) moves across the road to the Longmire Museum.

The Longmire Gas Station

The old gas station, (originally called an "oil station"), was built by the Standard Oil Company, and modeled after the one in Yosemite National Park. There was "a small bachelor quarters in the loft." The gas station you see today was built in 1929 adjacent to the National Park Inn, and is the third building in the area to exhibit rustic architecture. It is the oldest existing gas station in the National Park System having rustic architecture. (The comfort station next door was built in 1929, but has been remodeled so often, it no longer has any architectural integrity.)

As of 1994, gasoline was no longer available anywhere within the Park. The reason is that the old underground storage tanks needed replacement, and the cost couldn't be justified by marginal visitor gasoline sales.

Fuel and tire chains can be obtained in Ashford, Elbe, Greenwater, Packwood, American River and other gateway communities near the various park entrances. Be prepared. Fill up before coming into the Park. Remember, if circling the Park southwest to northeast, it's a long way from the gas station at Ashford to the next closest ones at Packwood, or at Greenwater.

The Longmire Hot Springs

The Longmire Springs are curious.

There once were 49 soda, sulfur, mineral and iron springs around Longmire. Most of the spring water is high in iron and leaves a rust-colored deposit. The springs range in temperature from 50° to 85°F.

One pair of Longmire Springs have an especially interesting phenomenon. Although only 18" apart, the two springs maintain very different uniform temperatures. One is 80°, while the other is 50°. The warmer one is a sulphur spring with yellowish water, and the cold spring flows bluish iron water.

In 1920 two of the soda and iron springs were enclosed by masonry walls, and walkways led visitors around the meadow. These are the same walled springs we see today: Soda Spring (No. 19), and Iron Mike Spring (No 46).

An early century chemical analysis of the waters from the Longmire springs showed they were "highly mineralized, alkaline, saline water; characterized by its content of calcium and magnesium bicarbonates (limestone salts), and sodium chloride (common table salt)."

It is a *hard* water.

Warm Springs #35 & 38 (known as Pigeon Springs) had temperatures of 80°F and 83°F respectively. They had a chemical analysis of being highly mineralized, alkaline, saline water, the chief constituents being magnesium and calcium bicarbonate (limestone salts), sodium chloride (common salt), and sodium bicarbonate (common bread soda). Both had hard water. These springs were so named, because the Longmires noted that there were frequently pigeons drinking from them.

The best known of the springs was "Iron Mike", which was a moderately mineralized, alkaline, saline water, with the chief constituents being magnesium and calcium chloride (common salt). This was another hard water spring.

Spring #49 had potassium nitrate, sodium chloride, magnesium chloride, magnesium sulfate, magnesium bicarbonate, silica dioxide, oxide of aluminum, manganese bicarbonate, calcium phosphate, potassium bromide, traces of ammonia boric acid, strontium, arsenic, and lithium. The heavy sediment contained iron oxide and calcium carbonate.

Trail of the Shadows

Many of the "soda and iron springs of great variety" which James Longmire discovered in 1883 are still bubbling away today. The springs can viewed in an easy .7 mile self-guided hike around the "Trail of the Shadows" which takes about half an hour. It passes the site of the former Longmire Springs Hotel and Elcaine Longmire's restored cabin that was part of the original Longmire settlement, and is now the oldest structure in the park. The trail starts across the road from the Hiker Center and loops the meadow, passing most of the springs.

One word of caution: Do NOT drink the water from the Hot Springs. They are not medicinal, and they are not safe to drink. Those who have not heeded this advice have experienced minor volcanic eruptions of their own, (in their tummies, --calling it "Tahoma's revenge.")

Elcaine Longmire's Cabin

In 1888 or 1889, Elcaine built his cabin just outside his father's claim on a tract of land he had hoped to claim for himself. The cabin was cedar log and measured 14 x 16 feet. It had a floor, a door, and a window. About 100 feet west of the cabin, he built a meat or "cache" house, which straddled a small stream. Restoration was done on Elcaine's cabin by the C.C.C. in 1934 and again by the

Photo Washington State Historical Society

59

Park Service in more recent times. Elcaine's cabin is the oldest structure in the Park.

The Giant Log Cross-Section

This giant wooden "time-piece's" life spanned nearly seven centuries. The 8-foot diameter giant was just a Douglas fir seedling in the Snoqualmie National Forest in 1293, and was already 199 years old when Columbus arrived in the New World in 1492, it saw 1620 when the pilgrims landed, 1776 when the Declaration of Independence was signed, and 1889 when Washington became the 42nd state in the Union. Finally in 1963, at the age of 670, it was cut into five cross sections which were donated to the park by St. Regis Paper Company. The tree was cut near the headwaters of the Nisqually River, adjacent to the park.

Longmire of Yesteryear

In 1907 a permit was given to George B. Hall (Elcaine Longmire's son-in-law) to build a livery stable at Longmire. The large stables housed 60 saddle horses and 7 pack animals, 13 driving horses, 3 buggies, 1 stage and 2 freight wagons. The horses were used to transport tourists and supplies to Hall's tent camp at Indian Henrys Hunting Ground. They were also used to haul ice from the Nisqually Glacier. Huge blocks of ice were chopped from the glacier and hauled in wagons back to Longmire, where it was stored in sawdust for later use as refrigeration, in cold drinks, and for making ice cream. By 1911 there was a barbershop, a new club house, an ice and electric plant, a new veranda, 50 new tent-covered sleeping quarters used in conjunction with the Inn, a new store, photo gallery, stage stables, bath pool, and 2 garages.

Winter snowpack at Longmire was usually 5-10 feet, good news to the early snow bunnies. In the 1920's Longmire had a toboggan run and small ski jump. It was 6-1/2 miles by snowshoe to Paradise and that trail was well traveled too.

The first word about the Longmire Campground shows up in the park superintendent's annual report of 1918. The big Longmire Community Center on the south side of the Nisqually was the heart of the close-knit little community. It was in constant use for social events, pot-lucks, church services, lectures, speakers, educational events, weddings, dances, and anything else that needed a good big dry room. It's still there, just closed to public use except for an occasional wedding.

In 1923, a tennis court went in at Longmire, and that same year the laundry facilities and ice cream plant moved from Longmire to Paradise.

Moving out of Longmire

In 1941, Frank Mattson, the Park's landscape architect, proposed moving the housing and shops out of Longmire to a lower elevation outside the Park. He feared a flash flood at Longmire, and also wanted to get out of the problem of winter snow.

That move finally came about in 1977 when housing for year-round employees was moved to Tahoma Woods, about 12 miles down the Mountain Highway from the Park.

Paradise

Credit for naming Paradise goes to Mrs. Elcaine Longmire, who, on her first visit to the area in 1885 exclaimed, "Oh, it looks just like Paradise!" Paradise already had an equally appropriate Chinook name, "Saghalie Illahe" meaning "land of peace." It is the peace and beauty of Paradise which makes it the most visited area of the park. For the most "peaceful" Paradise experience, go mid-week, when there are far fewer people.

From Paradise, one views the Nisqually, Kautz, Pyramid, Success, Paradise and Stevens glaciers, and for even closer glacier views, good safe trails lead to lookouts or even better viewpoints.

Poor Old Paradise

Looking at the pristine flower fields of Paradise today, one imagines what they must have looked like before the necessity of blacktopped pathways, vast parking lots, and obvious signs of civilization. It's hard to believe it used to look **worse**, instead of better.

In 1923, the laundry and ice cream plant moved from Longmire to Paradise. In 1927, the Rainier Park Boat Company had a boat rental concession and general store at Reflection Lakes. By 1931, 275 cabins and a golf course covered the present flower fields at Paradise. There was also a tent city, and snowshoe rental facility, the guide house, photo shop, a horse rental corral and barn, and the "Tatoosh Club." In summer there were also boys camps.

In the winter, there was a snow carnival, "sliding" wearing "coasting trousers", and rope tows which hauled skiers up the slopes. The lifts were put up in fall and taken down in spring. There also used to be old ski lift buildings.

Other commercial winter endeavors at Paradise included dog sled rides. Teams of malamutes and Siberian huskies were brought down from Point Barrow, Alaska, along with their sleds, paraphernalia and drivers. The dogs were shown all around Puget Sound in an effort to promote the rides. The hungry canines, however, could eat their weight in cracklings every day, and they ate up all the profits. When summer came and there was no income, the hapless concessionaire went broke.

The Early Tent Camps

In addition to the conventional inns at Longmire and Paradise, two tent camps also offered accommodations to the hoards of early park visitors. The largest was Reese's Camp of the Clouds at Paradise. The other was the "Wigwam Hotel" (the term hotel apparently was used loosely in the early days), run by George Hall and his wife Sue Longmire (daughter of Elcaine Longmire). Their camp was on the north side of Squaw Lake at Indian Henrys, on the flat between the lake and Iron Mountain. They operated the camp from 1907 to 1916.

That same year, the newly formed Rainier National Park Company took over operation of the Wigwam Hotel, and Reese's Camp at Paradise. They ran the Wigwam Hotel until 1918, at which time they abandoned it, allowing the landscape to revert to nature.

CAMP REESE MT. RAINIER

Washington State Historical Society photo

> Wide and Narrow Horses
>
> Tall and Short Horses
>
> We fit the Horse
>
> to the Individual
>
> Skyline Trail Saddle Horse Trip brochure.

In 1922, under the auspices of the Tacoma Motorcycle Club, hill climbing contests were held with over 300 motorcycles tearing up the flower fields at Paradise.

Other promotions in the early days were Indians putting on demonstrations, and an enterprising photographer who met each guided tour group. He took their pictures, then raced back and got the prints ready by the time the tour returned.

Another entrepreneur decided the road to success should have sleigh rides on it. But the big horse-drawn sleighs had problems of their own. Though they only hauled the people up the road and back a short distance, one lady sagely observed the sleighs sure could have used windshields, because there was more than snow flying behind the horses.

In the 1960's it was proposed to run a tram to Camp Muir.

With the exception of Paradise Inn, with its lodging, restaurant and gift shop, the guide service and limited equipment rental, which is still available at Paradise, 1973 was the last year the tow ropes ran, and thus marked the end of uncontrolled commercial development at Paradise.

Paradise Flowers

It has been said, "a trip to Paradise is going to heaven *before* you die." John Muir described Mount Rainier's superb subalpine garden as the greatest he had ever found. It hasn't changed. The phenomenon of the flower fields at Mount Rainier has to be seen to be believed. The tenacious little glacier and avalanche lilies are too impatient even to wait for the snow to melt from over them. They pop through the retreating snowbanks, then chase the snow up the hill. The vast carpet of riotous floral color, contrasted against the close-enough-to-touch backdrop of white snow is about as striking as beauty can get. Even beauty-saturated Alps-imbued Europeans have to admit, Mount Rainier is in a class by itself!

In size, the Paradise meadows are about 960 acres, and extend from 5,400' to 7,400' in elevation. The meadow is primarily within the subalpine parkland zone with a small portion of it above treeline. It is dominated by alpine vegetation. The picturesque tree clumps are interspersed with herbaceous meadows. The tree clumps are comprised of mountain hemlock (Tsuga mertensiana) and subalpine fir (Abies lasiocarpa).

Sixteen trails network the Paradise meadows. Those in the lower meadows are asphalt surfaced. ***Please stay on the trails!***

Paradise Inn - Paradise

Looking every bit like one would expect a high mountain inn to look, this historic 129-room rustic lodge was built in 1916-17. Reminiscent of the grand lodges of the 1920's, it features a cavernous timbered lounge with tall cathedral ceilings, two huge stone fireplaces (50 and 60 feet high), a large formal dining room with good hearty food, the Glacier lounge, a gift shop, snack bar, and million dollar views of Mount Rainier and the Tatoosh Range. The frame of the building is made entirely of weathered Alaska cedar, felled from the Silver Forest when the road to Paradise was being built. The big timbers are needed to support the roof when the heavy snows build up. The logs are exposed all the way to the ridge pole in the large lounge, which measures 50' x 112'. The vast dining room is about the same size and has a huge fireplace similar to those in the lobby. The Inn was built at a cost of $100,000.

By 1979, the old Inn was starting to show it's age, and an extensive a 2-year, $1.5 million rehabilitation and upgrading project was undertaken. The decades of severe winters piling thirty feet of snow on the roof had taken a toll on the structure, pushing it this way and that. The huge cedar posts developed great cracks, and the great building needed more than a temporary patch. A new permanent support system was put in place, giving it up-to-date structural integrity, while retaining the rustic charm. A fire suppression system adding automatic sprinklers brought it up to current fire codes, and modifications were made to provide greater access for handicapped persons.

As is also true at Mount Rainier Guest Service's companion lodging at Longmire, prices to dine or stay there are surprisingly reasonable, thus making a few days at the mountain popular with those seeking a nearby escape from city stress or a great honeymoon hideaway. Paradise Inn usually opens prior to Memorial Day, and closes for winter in early October. Phone (360) 569-2275 for reservations. The hotel front desk is open 24 hours during the season. The dining room is open through September, 7 a.m. - 9 a.m. for breakfast; 11 a.m. - 2:30 p.m. for lunch and 5:30 p.m. - 8:30 p.m. for dinner. The Glacier Room is open from noon - 11 p.m. daily.

photo loaned courtesy of Jim Brand

The Old Paradise Lodge under construction

The Paradise Inn Furniture

An elderly German carpenter, Hans Fraehnke, was hired to carve the woodwork in the lobby. It was Fraehnke who built the rustic hand-hewn Alaska cedar 13-foot grandfather clock and upright piano and bench. This is the same piano which was played by President Harry Truman when he visited the park years later. Fraehnke also built the two huge Alaska cedar tables, the 6 writing tables, the registration desk, and the big chairs. All the cedar came from the Silver Forest.

Henry M. Jackson Visitor Center

Commonly known as "the Flying Saucer," the Henry M. Jackson Visitor Center is best known for it's 360 degree covered observation deck and spectacular panoramic views. At the time of its construction, people suspected the designer was influenced by the reports of UFO sightings over the mountain.

Fast food service, a book store and gift shop are available daily in summer from 9:00 a.m. to 7:00 p.m. Winter operations are limited to Saturdays, Sundays and holidays. This facility features interpretive exhibits, films and slide programs on the animals, glaciers, geology, wildflowers and natural features of the park. Programs are shown in the visitor center every half hour. Building hours are from 10:00 a.m. to 5:00 p.m.

Snowshoe walks are offered in the winter, usually until about Easter. Snow sliding, (inner tubes) is permitted only in specified areas. It is not permitted anywhere at Mount Rainier other than on the established runs. (This does not apply to skiers.) Inner tube runs at Paradise usually close when the snow level is under 4 feet deep. Snow camping is permitted in the vicinity of Paradise. Check with rangers for regulations in effect, allowable areas, etc. (Usually the same as designated summer camping sites.) Construction of snow caves is not permitted except by special permission to organized classes.

Public bathrooms are located in the Center, as well as public pay showers (on the lower level), - always a wonderful surprise for weary hikers and climbers. Scrub fast, it's $.25 for 2-1/2 minutes.

Annual Visitor Center usage runs about 195,000 persons per year.

Paradise Guide Hut

Built in 1920, this rustic four-story building still serves as headquarters for the climbing service. It serves as both the takeoff point for climbers, and as a dormitory for RMI and concession employees. The dormitory portion has 23 rooms containing 43 beds. The dimensions of the building are 75 by 32 feet.

It also serves as an equipment rental headquarters and guide service office.

Nisqually Vista Self-Guided Trail

This easy 1.2 mile trail has everything you go to Mount Rainier for: knock-out views of the Mountain, acres of fragrant flower meadows, a close-up view of the Nisqually Glacier and the possible sighting of an animal or two.

Paradise Picnic Area

This former campsite is located a quarter mile below the Jackson Visitor Center. *Picnicking is **not** permitted on the fragile flower fields around Paradise.*

Skyline Trail

When fog or clouds sock in the valleys, it's often possible to hike the Skyline Trail to Panorama Point and look above the soft white sea to see Mounts Adams, St. Helens, Hood and Jefferson poking up like islands. Early Park Naturalist Frank Brockman once wrote an autobiography entitled *The Sun is Shining at Panorama Point.* The 2.5 mile hike to Panorama Point takes about three hours and has as 1,050' elevation gain.

One of the most photogenic views of Mount Rainier, is seen from across the Paradise valley on the Pinnacle Peak saddle. The mountain rises nearly 10,000 feet, from the base of Mazama Ridge to the summit in one grand dramatic sweep. This magnificent panoramic view is reached via a 1.5 mile hike from the trail which begins at the road across from Reflection Lake.

The (Former) Paradise Ice Caves

For decades, (from 1908 to 1991) the most visited attraction at the Park was the Paradise Ice Caves. The Paradise Glacier terminus was about half a mile from Sluiskin Falls, and an easy walk from Paradise. Visitors loved the "blue-light" beauty and interest of the cave system itself. Charles H. Anderson, Jr., the world's foremost glaciospeleologist, called the Paradise Ice Caves the largest known glacier cave system in the world. During 310 trips into the caves, Anderson mapped 8.23 miles of passages within the glacier. Between 1971 and 1982 he was joined by fellow glaciospeleologist Mark Vining who had 168 cave trips. They did yearly surveys of cave passages by mapping and documentary with photography.

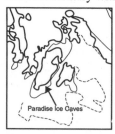

Paradise Ice Caves

Charles Anderson, Jr., who give the features such names as "Suicide Passage" and "Paradise Lost," suffered a grave loss himself. In Feb. 1968, Anderson, his wife and another man

Photo by Charles H. Anderson, Jr.

Charles Anderson, Jr. photo

were returning from the caves, when they were caught in a whiteout. Anderson's wife, Edith Anderson, 22, died of hypothermia.

A second tragedy struck the same year. A mother and her two children died July 16, 1968, after they slipped down a snow-covered gully. They were returning from an outing to the ice caves when the accident occurred. They decided to take a short cut down to the road, slipped and fell over a waterfall, and the mother and two small daughters were swept underneath an ice pack covering the stream. Another son suffered a skull fracture. *(TNT 7/19/68)*.

Then as if that weren't enough, that autumn a man suffered a heart attack at the ice caves. He was evacuated by helicopter and survived.

As the decades rolled by, however, the glacier began to retreat up-valley, and then separated into an upper and lower section. The lower section received considerably less snowfall than it previously had, and soon became an isolated stagnant ice mass. The thinning glacier continued its retreat, and the ice caves shrank into small unstable crawl spaces. By 1993, the lower Paradise Glacier no longer existed.

The Paradise Ice Caves closed to the public in 1971. They were simply too dangerous to allow

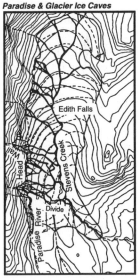

Paradise & Glacier Ice Caves

Paradise and Stevens Glacier Caves, C. Anderson map

67

people to enter. Huge chunks of ice fell without warning. Finally in the fall of 1991, the ceiling of the last cave collapsed completely. Within six months after the collapse of the Ice Caves, seven kinds of plants took up residence on the newly exposed rock. They were an algae, a lichen, two mosses, horsetail, sedge, grass and monkeyflower.

Sunrise

At 6,400 feet, Sunrise is the highest point reached by paved road within Washington. Sunrise is a favorite spot for many people for several reasons. Far fewer people go there, so it isn't as overcrowded as Paradise. Another reason is that when Paradise is "socked in" as it often is, being on the ocean side of the mountain, Sunrise has its own sheltered weather, and is often bathed in brilliant sunshine. The spectacular close-up Sunrise view of the mountain, and the awesome Emmons, the largest glacier in the United States outside Alaska, is spellbinding. Sunrise is also the jumping off point for many good hiking trails and day trips.

In fact one of the early proposals for Sunrise was to make it the home of a dude ranch, with day trips to nearby attractions. Such trips were to go to Sheepskull Gap (where 2,000 sheep were supposed to have died in a snow storm) or Devil's Hole (where rustlers supposedly once hid out). Another day trip was to go to Ghost Gold Mine (apparently one of the mines in Glacier Basin). Guides at the ranch were to be real rodeo stars from Ellensburg. This plan never got beyond the discussion stage, and the dead sheep and rustler stories are not verified in the archives.

Until 1931, The name of this area was Yakima Park or "Me-yah-ah-Pah" (meaning 'place of the chief), as it was known by the Indians. This was a particularly important place to the Indians. They believed it had been created and arranged for their benefit by the mighty and wise Speel-yo (Coyote). This big meadow provided abundant grazing for their great herds of horses as well as feasts of berries and game for the people. They had horse races here, where some of the fastest horses in the Northwest were pitted against each other. Mock battles were held where young warriors honed their skills, and there were games of all sorts, -wrestling, foot races, spear tosses, and other games of skill. When not gathering and preserving food, there was time for celebrating, dancing, wooing, religious ceremonies and keening for the dead. Their annual trip to Me-yah-ah Pah was a favorite time of year.

Development at Sunrise

1908	The access trail from outside the Park came up the White River to Silver Creek, then paralleled the creek.
1915	A ranger cabin was constructed, and a telephone line was strung to the White River.
1919	The White River Road was out due to washouts and slides.

1921   The White River Camp was located 6.7 miles inside the Park entrance, and a hotel was operated, similar to the one at Paradise.

1923   The White River Camp had piped water, a comfort station, 18 camp stoves, 12 tables and a grocery store.

1925   Guide Service was begun at the White River Camp.

1929   A log cabin check station, garage and equipment shed was built at the White River Entrance. A water system for Sunrise was put in from Frozen Lake. A dam was built and 7,000 feet of 6" pipe was laid.

1930   Sunrise was developed and a picnic ground and campground built. 1,000 tons of materials were brought in from great distances. The Rainier National Park Company built the cafeteria building and 200 cabins. They also proposed a miniature golf course for Sunrise. Rock for the blockhouse was obtained a mile away in a slide. A road was built to "the quarry." Logs for the blockhouse were obtained on the old White River Road from a stand of white pine and hauled 12 miles to Sunrise. Shakes for the roof were made in the Carbon River District and hauled 80 miles to the site. Blockhouses were built to resemble frontier architecture.

1931   Yakima Park opened with blockhouses, comfort stations, sewers, reservoirs, campgrounds, roads, trails and trail guides. Bear problems were handled with tear gas, bird shot and ammonia.

1932   The first C.C.C. camp in the park opened at White River. The entire crew of 1,000 was from New York City. A C.C.C. crew was at White River until 1939.

1935   A landslide of unprecedented proportion devastated the White River Road near the intersection of the Naches Highway.

The C.C.C. mounted a major forest protection effort against bugs. There was an infestation of White Pine beetles and White Pine Blister Rust. (It was not a good year for White Pines). The young men also worked at fire hazard reduction, landscaping and restoration of old trails.

1936   The roads to Sunrise and White River were resurfaced.

1940   C.C.C. made the log trailside exhibit at Sunrise

1942   A massive slide occurred about 1-1/2 miles above the White River "Y". The slide was about 400 feet long.

1943-44 The cabins at Sunrise were sold to folks in the Puget Sound area for government defense housing as part of the war effort.

1944   A second blockhouse was completed at Sunrise.

1963   Campground and picnic equipment were put in at the White River Campground.

The Sunrise Visitor Center

30-minute guided walks are conducted daily from the visitor center, and a glacier walk is led once a week. Check with rangers for the current schedule. Campfire programs are conducted Thursday, Friday and Saturday evenings at the White River Campfire Circle. Rangers from Sunrise also journey to Sunrise Point, and the Sourdough Ridge/Frozen Lake area to answer visitor questions and give directions.

The Sunrise Historic District

Five structures, the two blockhouses, the community building, the stockade and the comfort station comprise the Sunrise Historic District. The quaint little gasoline station was already on the List of Classified Structures.

Sunrise Lodge

The Sunrise Lodge was built in 1931 by the Rainier National Park Company and acquired by the National Park Service in the mid-1950's. The frame two-story building, measuring 51 by 137 feet, was originally intended to be a wing of a much larger (proposed) hotel. The main floor contained a dining room, kitchen and toilet facilities. Dormitories for seasonal personnel were on the 2nd floor. Concrete was poured for the foundation of the next wing which was to be built east of the present building, however it was never constructed, and eventually the concrete was all removed. When viewed from the ridge above the lodge, the scar is still visible. The Lodge is listed on the National Register of Historic Places as part of the Sunrise Historic District, however the administration has said they are going ahead with their plans to demolish it as soon as funds become available.

In 1926 the park's landscape architect wrote that the soil at Sunrise was a very light pumice, and although it was well covered with bunch grass, even limited public use would ruin it in a very short time. "On the other hand," he further observed, "Yakima Park would make one of the most wonderful golf courses in the world if irrigated."

Mount Rainier at Sunrise

She lifts her head, shakes off her veils
the Mountain that was God is free!
No longer draped with clouds of fog,
the heights appear for all to see.
                              Author unknown

Sunrise is traditionally the last of the Park's visitor facilities to open each summer and offers no lodging. It has only light food service and a gift shop. Sunrise is normally snowed in until late June, although the maintenance crews always make a Herculean effort to have it open by the 4th of July. Also traditionally, it is the first of the Park's facilities to close down at the end of summer, usually Labor Day or shortly thereafter. Call the park (360) 569-2211 for exact date.

The Visitor Center houses interpretive exhibits and a good assortment of books.

Public bathrooms are located in a small building by the parking lot midway between the Visitor Center and the Lodge.

The Blockhouse Architecture Debate

Also located at Sunrise is the Yakima Park Stockade Group, four log structures that have also been designated as National Historic Landmarks because of their architectural significance. Early this century a big bureaucratic debate took place over the reason for the blockhouse architecture. Asahel Curtis thought it was a replica of the British Fur Trading Posts, while Park Supt. Thomlinson thought they were designed to resemble American Pioneer blockhouses.

The first blockhouse was built around 1930, the second wasn't completed until 1943. The vertical-log palisade enclosing the yard at the rear of the community building was built in 1930.

The Old Sunrise Cabins

At about the same time guest cabins sat in the flower fields at Paradise, there were also cabins at Sunrise, - 215 of them, in fact. By the end of World War II, the last of the cabins was gone. Most went on to a new life as war worker homes in Puget Sound and picker's cottages on eastern Washington farms.

Sunrise Point

For connoisseurs of good views, stop at Sunrise Point (6,100') for views north to Mount Baker and Glacier Peak, and south to Mount Adams, Mount Hood, and Mount St. Helens.

White River

The oldest structure in the White River area today is the little patrol cabin adjacent to the Wonderland Trail in the White River Campground near Loop D.

The White River entrance station was constructed in 1929, and is another good example of rustic architecture. The former C.C.C. mess hall-dormitory at the White River Entrance is now the ranger office and Hiker Center.

Ohanapecosh

If you like beautiful forests of western hemlock and western red cedar, you'll love Ohanapecosh on the southeast side of the mountain. A lot of people have. As with Longmire, the hot springs had a devoted following.

In 1912, when the area was still outside the Park boundaries, Mrs. Eva O'Neill set up a tent camp at the hot springs. In those days, visitors came in via trail on foot or horseback from "Lewis" (known today as Packwood).

For three decades, from the 1920's thru the 1950's, the Ohanapecosh Hot Springs Resort was a destination resort. In 1921, N.D. Tower of Morton built a hotel and bath facilities at the springs. Three years later, he formed a partnership with Tacoma physician, Dr. A. W. Bridge, and they built a small hotel and two bathhouses. Soon Dr. Bridge enlarged the resort, and renamed it the "Bridge Clinic." When the road opened between Packwood and Ohanapecosh in 1933, the popularity increased. The hotel and bathhouse were enlarged, and 30 guest cabins were added. A swimming pool was begun but never finished.

In 1947 Dr. Bridge sold the operation to Martin Killian of Eatonville, who ran the springs until 1960, when his concession contract was terminated. Finally in 1965, the Park Service purchased the resort, and by 1967, removed the buildings and soon the springs returned to their natural state.

Today two hundred campsites are nestled amid ancient forest and nearby there are lots of interesting things to do. The old hot springs area is still interesting to explore, even though most people are disappointed to see it's now just boggy seeps of historical interest only. Follow the signs to the Hot Springs Nature Trail.

Another a good trail leads to Silver Falls just one mile north from the campground. There's trout fishing along the river, and unlike many other rivers around the park, the Ohanapecosh flows from a "dead" (inactive) glacier, thus the water is crystal clear instead of the usual chocolate milk brown.

Be careful around the fast moving Ohanapecosh River. It has claimed lives.

Ohanapecosh also has a visitor center with an interesting forestry exhibit, and fun campfire programs at night. This is a good place to camp if wanting to be midway between Sunrise and Paradise. Sunrise is 32 miles distant, Paradise is 23 miles.

The Ohanapecosh Hot Springs

"What springs?" you might wonder, as you look at the less than attractive burping remnants. These springs once were as active as their counterparts at Longmire, and equally as popular. These springs supported the large Ohanapecosh Hot Springs Lodge here, which catered to the throngs who came for the famous mineral baths. The springs once ranged in temperature from approximately 85 to 120 degrees Fahrenheit.

And what were these medical miracles that bubbled out of the earth? According to the chemical analysis of the day, they were sodium, silica, iron, calcium, potassium an eleven other minerals. In 1992 the hot springs at Ohanapecosh Campground were closed due to nude bathing and high coliform counts in the water.

The Ohanapecosh Visitor Center

This rustic Center is usually open from early June through mid-October. The hours are 9:00 a.m. to 6:00 p.m. Guided walks are offered to Silver Falls

(Monday and Saturday mornings) and to the Grove of the Patriarchs (Sunday and Thursday mornings). There are longer Explorer walks to the Grove and Silver Falls on Fridays, and to the Naches Peak Loop Trail at Chinook Pass on weekends. Campfire programs are presented at the Ohanapecosh Amphitheater weekends early and late in the season, and seven nights a week during the peak season. They also present occasional children's programs. Ask the ranger for details. (Funny footnote: at least once each season, a tourist asks the way to the *Grave* of the Patriarchs.)

Development at Ohanapecosh

1912   A log ranger cabin was built at Ohanapecosh at a cost of $347.30.

1916   Access to Ohanapecosh was via a 13 mile trail from Lewis (now known as Packwood) or via a 15-mile trail from Narada Falls. Ohanapecosh was on National Forest land just outside Mount Rainier National Park.

1923   750 visitors ventured to the Ohanapecosh Campground, which was one cleared acre in size.

1925   A crude road was opened to Ohanapecosh, and 1,800 visitors soon followed.

1931   The boundaries of Mount Rainier National Park were enlarged to include Ohanapecosh.

1933   The Bridge Clinic, which had operated the Ohanapecosh Lodge prior to the area being a part of the National Park, was granted a franchise to continue offering accommodations there.

1934   The C.C.C. came to Ohanapecosh, and built a ranger and 'checking' station, a log cabin at the Park entrance, and many miles of trails. This was all done at a cost of $3,570 Depression dollars.

1940   A forestry exhibit was built at Ohanapecosh, including the popular log cross-section.

1943   A winter storm at Ohanapecosh left a vast swath of blowdown. The timber all was put to good use in the war program.

1965   The Ohanapecosh Visitor Center opened.

Ohanapecosh Boundary Ranger

In 1913, a small patrol cabin was built at the southeast corner of the original park boundary. It was 1/4 mile north of the hot springs on the Silver Falls Trail. Then in 1931, Congress changed the park boundary, moving it south of the hot springs and east to the crest of the Cascades. The District Ranger was responsible for patrolling the park boundary to the north and west. The little cabin was finally removed in 1965. In the 1930's the C.C.C. had a summer work camp at Ohanapecosh, and it was they who built the original campground. The old "Forest House" museum was constructed from two C.C.C. buildings (under the direction of Park Naturalist C. Frank Brockman), and served as the visitor center until 1963.

Carbon River/Ipsut Creek Campground

The Carbon River area is one of the Park's best kept secrets. At less than two hours from Seattle, it's close enough to run down for a picnic supper by the river on a hot summer night.

The Carbon River lies in the northwest corner of the park, and is the closest point to the Puget Sound metropolitan areas. Access is via local roads to Buckley and Wilkeson. Only .25 mile of the road in the Carbon Valley is paved. The remainder of the road to Ipsut Creek Campground and the road to Mowich Lake are gravelled.

A gradual trail from the campground provides a close-up view of the snout of the mighty Carbon Glacier. A road used to go all the way up to the glacier, but the river changed course one winter and took out the 3-mile road once and for all. During summer weekends there may be a ranger at the glacier snout to give information and answer questions. On Friday and Saturday nights during July and August there are usually campfire programs at the Ipsut Creek Campground Amphitheater.

The Ipsut Creek Campground, at the end of the present road, has 29 individual sites and 2 group sites. Only the group sites can be reserved. Individual sites are on a first-come, first-served basis.

Picnic tables are located at Falls Creek, 2 miles from the entrance, and in the Ipsut Creek Campground.

The first ranger cabin at Carbon River was built in 1911, however it was destroyed by fire in 1962.

A C.C.C. camp was located on the Carbon River in 1933. Their first project was the construction of a large log entrance arch which is no longer there. They also built a ranger cabin near the mouth of Ipsut Creek. It was so well built, and the logs fit so tightly that no chinking was required. The cabin is still in excellent condition today. In 1958 the Carbon River Road was improved as a part of Mission 66.

This small station is unlike the larger centers which have exhibits. This one sells a few books, and usually has someone to collect fees, issue hiker permits, and answer questions.

Carbon River Rain Forest

What makes this corner of the park special is the abundant moisture and mild climate which combine to produce the only true inland rain forest in the park. The 20 minute .3 mile self-guiding "Carbon River Rain Forest Trail" at the Carbon Entrance is easy, fun and educational.

This forest has a dual claim to fame. It is also an old growth forest. This stand contains giant true firs, Douglas firs and cedars, all centuries old. Nestled in the Carbon River valley just inside the Park boundary, moisture brought in by prevailing winds is trapped. To that is added an annual rainfall of between 180-210 inches per year. The unique feature of this forest is the storybook quality of seeing everything enshrouded in lush green velvety sphagnum moss, and trees bedecked with epiphytic fungi, lichens and ferns. The canopy height varies, with tree tops stretching to different levels, depending on their differing ages and species. The luxuriant understory consists of new germinating trees, yew, salmonberry and vine and big-leaf maple, both gnarled and contorted by winds and snow loads. As the closest point of the park to Seattle, this delightful place is one of the best kept secrets of the park.

Tipsoo Lake - Chinook Pass

The only structure in this area of the park with historical and architectural significance, is the entrance arch. The stone columns were suggested by Superintendent Tomlinson, and the resulting structure is a classic example of rustic architecture. The most unusual feature of the arch is the flagstone horse trail across the top. The Pacific Crest Trail crosses over the highway at this point. The arch was completed in 1936.

Backcountry Ranger Stations

The first patrol cabins in the northwest portion of the park were abandoned miners' cabins, none of which remain standing today.

The oldest patrol cabin built by the Park Service is the one at Indian Henrys Hunting Ground which was built in 1915. When Roger Toll became superintendent (1919-1920) he envisioned a ring of patrol cabins for rangers and shelter cabins for hikers. In 1921, the first one built was a patrol cabin at Lake George. (This cabin was replaced in 1934-35 by a new C.C.C. model, which is still there.) In 1922 patrol cabins were built at St. Andrews Creek, Mowich Lake and Sunset Park (Golden Lakes).

All the cabins have one or two rooms, some with sleeping lofts, and all except the Lake George cabin are made of logs. (It has a log frame and board walls.) All are of the rustic architecture which was indicative of the National Park Service "look" prior to World War II.

The back country ranger stations still in existence today are: Mystic Camp, Lake James, Three Lakes, Camp Muir, Indian Henrys, Lake George, St. Andrews Creek and Golden Lakes. (Most backcountry rangers today camp out.)

The Indian Henrys and St. Andrews Patrol Cabins are both on the List of Classified Structures.

Frontcountry Ranger Stations

Today there are front country ranger stations at Nisqually Entrance, Mowich Lake, Carbon River Entrance, Ipsut Creek, Sunrise, White River

Entrance, White River Campground, Ohanapecosh, Paradise, Henry M. Jackson Memorial Visitor Center, and Longmire.

Other Staffed Locations

During July and August, Rangers are usually assigned to Tipsoo Lake, Backbone Ridge and Box Canyon on weekends to answer visitor's questions, give directions and provide assistance.

Public Telephones

Public Telephones are located at the Cougar Rock at Ranger Station, Sunrise, Longmire, Ohanapecosh, Paradise, Carbon River entrance, White River Campground and White River entrance.

Facilities Infrastructure

There are a total of 221 buildings within the park, of which 123 are only used seasonally. 98 of the buildings are historic. There are three visitor centers, two overnight lodges, and 228 bedrooms for employee housing.

Rest Rooms

There are 41 picnic area restroom buildings, plus 20 campground restrooms, and 12 pit toilets in the Frontcountry campgrounds and picnic areas. In the non-wilderness backcountry, there is a pit toilet at the Sunrise Trailside Camp, 1 pit toilet and 1 solar-assisted toilet at Camp Muir, and 1 pit toilet at Camp Schurman. In the Wilderness areas there are 45 pit toilets and 2 experimental compost toilets. 47 septic tanks and three wastewater treatment plants complete the rest of the picture.

Administration

The Creation of the Park

Mount Rainier National Park was created by Act of Congress, approved March 2, 1899. (30 Stat. 993). Exclusive jurisdiction of the territory contained within the Park was ceded to the United States by act of the Washington State Legislature on March 19, 1901. Exclusive jurisdiction of the reservation was accepted by act of Congress approved June 30, 1916.

Alphabet Soup

So many of the programs and entities at/or associated with the park have long names, that most go by acronyms instead. The most commonly used are:

CCDP: Conservation Career Development Program
DEM: Digital Elevation Model
EIS: Environmental Impact Statement
FOIA: Freedom of Information Act
FY: Federal Year
GAO: General Accounting Office
GIS: Geographic Information System
GMP: General Management Plan
GSA: General Services Administration
GSI: Guest Services, Inc
HCA: Habitat Conservation Areas
IPM: Integrated Pest Management
MMP: Mather Memorial Parkway
MORA: Mount Rainier National Park
NBS: National Biological Service
NOCA: North Cascades National Park
NPS: National Park Service
NWIA: Northwest Interpretive Association
OLYN: Olympic National Park
PNR Pacific Northwest Region: (now Cascade Cluster)
RMI: Rainier Mountaineering, Inc.
SAR: Search and Rescue
SCA: Student Conservation Association
USFS: United States Forest Service
USGS: United States Geological Survey
VIP: Volunteers-In-Park
VTS: Visitor Transportation System
WASO: Washington Office

Bouquets and Brickbats

If you have a wonderful visit, put your satisfaction in writing, and send it to Superintendent Briggle. Heaven forbid that anyone would find anything to complain about at this beautiful place, but should that occur, put the problem in writing and send that to him as well.

> William Briggle, Superintendent
> Mount Rainier National Park
> Tahoma Woods
> Ashford, WA 98304

Budget

It cost roughly $8.2 million to run the park in 1994. Operating funds are appropriated yearly by Congress, and in spite of increases in the amount, budget increases are often for mandated projects related to the environment, safety, etc. These items are not as highly visible as would be more rangers, naturalists, trail crews, and public programs. Also, congress often gives a cost of living wage increase, but then doesn't give the extra funds to cover the increase. That sum then has to paid out of the annual appropriation.

This also doesn't take into account extra expenses for such unscheduled events as mudflows, major storm damage, search and rescue expenditures and other assorted emergencies. Worst of all is inflation which annually nibbles away at the budget.

Even though Mount Rainier National Park is one of the top ten National Parks in the US in fee collecting, the monies paid as entry fees are not retained by the park for operating purposes, but instead are treated as general U.S. Government revenue. All fees collected are deposited under miscellaneous receipts of the U.S. Treasury. The combined total of all entrance and campground fees collected annually amounts to a little more than 1.4 million, or about twenty percent of the amount it takes to operate the park for a year.

Communications

Several mediums fulfill the Park's need to communicate with the public. Summer visitors are offered a copy of *Tahoma*, a 12-page tabloid newspaper which gives a general overview of park features, rules, activities, maps, trails, environmental concerns, visitor safety, old growth forest, animals, sub-alpine meadow resources preservation, and occasional historic pictures. The paper is printed on recycled newsprint using biodegradable ink. About 150,000 copies are distributed each year. The winter newspaper, *Snowdrift* is an 8-page format and has a press run of 45,000 copies. It covers winter safety issues. The Spring and Fall issues are similar to the summer format, and about 50,000 copies of each are printed. These are all produced using in-house computer typesetting.

100,000 copies of "The Bigfoot Lurks in the Meadows" (a meadow preservation message) are handed out each year. These are printed in English and eight other languages. About 100,000 maps are also distributed. A 4-page booklet for younger visitors is also provided as part of the "Junior Ranger" program. Foreign language information sheets in Japanese, German and Korean (15,000 copies of each), and 5,000 copies each of Russian and Vietnamese are also given out.

Roughly 30 other handouts on various topics are also available with more copied in-house as the need arises.

200,000 copies of appealing "Visiting Mount Rainier" "rack cards" are distributed to travel clubs, tourist information racks and state travel booths.

The park also issues press releases periodically.

Concessions

All lodging at Paradise Inn and Longmire Inn, the gift shops, snack bars and ski touring, are concessions operated by Mount Rainier Guest Services, a Fairfax, Virginia firm. It has been reported that Guest Services takes in revenue in the area of $5 million per year. Surveys show that 51 percent of Guest Services' business comes from Western Washington residents who never tire of the mountain. In fact, multitudes of them come stay at the mountain two or three times a year. In 1994, the two lodges hosted 43,555 visitors.

RMI, (Rainier Mountaineering, Inc.) has the climbing service concession.

Northwest Interpretive Association, a non-profit corporation, has the concession which sells the books and videos at the Museum and Visitor Centers.

Emergencies and Medical Aid

Within park boundaries, call 911 for medical aid, to report accidents or injuries or to request ranger assistance. First Aid facilities are available at visitor centers, ranger stations and park headquarters. The nearest hospitals are in Morton (30 miles south) and Puyallup (60 miles northwest).

Frontcountry/Backcountry

There's been a reorganization at the park in responsibilities and terminology. The wilderness areas, known by most as "the backcountry" are now called 'the Muir group.' The "frontcountry" (areas you can reach by car) are now known as 'the Mather group'. The reorganization affects interpretive and ranger staffs as well as the trail crews.

Law and Order

In the early days, outside the Park, each county had a sheriff. However by the time he got the word that he was needed, it might take several more days for him to arrive. Constables lived here and there around the area and were a closer source of law enforcement.

Inside the Park, the rangers were in charge, and they would go to any lengths to bring offenders to justice. In 1927 three men were fined for leaving campfires burning. They were brought before the U.S. Commissioner, and convicted. Ranger Oscar Sedergren of Mowich Lake walked 32 miles through the snow to appear against them. Each was fined $10.

Today maintaining law and order inside the park is still a primary priority. In 1993, 737 violation notices were issued for speeding and traffic violations alone, plus another 309 "tickets" for such things as no vehicle insurance, no vehicle registration, alcohol/drug violations, weapons, vandalism, disorderly conduct and even domestic violence disputes. Violators will find themselves facing the U.S. Attorney in the Western District Federal Court in Tacoma.

There were 250 motor vehicle accidents with four fatalities between 1992 and 1994. In 1994, 64 violation notices were issued for drug and alcohol related incidents. Sickness and injury incidents represent 25% of all park incidents responded to.

Are Park Police Real Cops?

You bet! They get their authority from a 1976 Congressional action called the General Authorities Act (16 U.S.C. 1a-6) which delegated to the National Park Service a clear assignment of law enforcement responsibility and specific authority to enforce all applicable laws and regulations.

At Mount Rainier there are "Commissioned" rangers, who may or may not be armed. They are authorized to "carry firearms and make arrests without warrant for any offense against the United States committed in their presence, or for any felony cognizable under the laws of the United States if they have reasonable grounds to believe that the person to be arrested has committed or is committing such felony, provided such arrests occur within that system or the person to be arrested is fleeing therefrom to avoid arrest."

They are also authorized to execute warrants and conduct investigations. Commit a crime within the Park, and you'll probably find it was a federal offense and you will be tried in a federal court. If it's serious enough, you may find yourself in a federal prison instead of the local hoosegow.

Crime in and around the Park

Inside the Park, the most prevalent crimes are vandalism, theft and car break-ins. In the old days, you could leave your gear unattended for days. Now you can't leave it for 5 minutes. Thieves enjoy coming to the mountain too. 1993 saw 71 such incidents, with nearly $19,000 in losses.

1995 even saw a bomb scare at Paradise Inn. A Spanaway man who claimed to have a bomb, burst into the Inn dining room, tried to abduct a park visitor, then led police on a car chase that included him commandeering a Washington State Patrol trooper's car. After police shot out three of the patrol car's tires, the man decided to stop.

Outside the Park is another matter. On the north side, Highway 410 is a long stretch of mostly uninhabited forested corridor with only logging roads and Forest Service roads cutting off here and there. Evil minds must think alike, for the road has the unfortunate distinction of being the repository of a disproportionate number of victims of foul play. The infamous Green River Killer left several of his victims there. So have an assortment of lesser known killers and rapists.

In 1987 the body of an unidentified individual who had been shot in an execution style murder was found on the east side of the park. Both the park and the FBI who co-investigated the incident felt it was drug related, and tied in with drug dealers in the Yakima Valley.

Lost and Found

Check for lost items and turn in all found items at the nearest ranger station or visitor center.

Mount Rainier, North Cascades and Olympic Fund

Senator Scoop Jackson once stood at a spot where both Mount Rainier and the Olympics were visible, and shared with Superintendent William Briggle his vision of a joint Mount Rainier and Olympic National Park alliance. After "Scoop's" death Supt. Briggle worked closely with Olympic National Park Superintendent Maureen Finnery to bring "Scoop's" dream into reality.

Kicked off with a grant from the National Parks Foundation, the two superintendents launched a joint effort to establish a "Friends of" organization with the strategic objective of preparing both parks to enter the year 2000, and to assist Mount Rainier National Park in inaugurating it's second century beginning March 2, 1999.

Prominent corporate sponsors came on board, lending key personnel and kicking off the fund with preliminary financial donations. Two of the original appointees to the board are Lou Whittaker and former Governor Dan Evans. Former Senator Evans helped produce a video for use at both parks, and at other events and locations outside the parks. Other board members are Forrest (Bud) Coffee (Boeing), John McMahon (Weyerhaeuser), Ron Sims (King County Councilman), Skip Yowell (Jansport), Helen Engle (Tacoma Audubon Society), and Glenn Yarbrough. President of the Board is David Thorud, U.W., and V.P. is William Pope, McDonald & Quackenbush.

The present objective of the project is work with foundations, organizations, businesses and individuals to secure financial and other contributions needed to undertake specific projects within the parks. The fund's Board of Directors will annually select key needed projects which would not otherwise be funded by government sources.

Among the first corporate contributors to the park are Microsoft and JanSport who are underwriting $13,000 in repairs for four lookout towers. The park is also currently pursuing funding from the Mount Rainier and Olympic Fund to expand their controversial fish "elimination" project. *(MRNP Project Statement N-17, N-008)*. In 1994 the fund raised $144,000 and contributed to eight projects in the two parks. On March 21, 1995, the organization expanded its mission and efforts to include the North Cascades National Park.

The fund has 501(c) (3) not-for-profit, tax exempt status from the Internal Revenue Service, and has been approved to receive payroll donations from the Combined Federal Campaign of Pierce-Thurston Counties, and through United Way of King County. Donation boxes are at the Henry M. Jackson Memorial Visitor Center at Paradise and at the Hurricane Ridge Visitor Center in Olympic National Park. Those wanting to mail donations can send them to: Mount Rainier, North Cascades and Olympic Fund % Kim M. Evans, Executive Director, The Mount Rainier, North Cascades & Olympic Fund, 1221 Second Avenue, Suite 350, Seattle, WA 98101.

Taxes

As federal property, Mount Rainier National Park is exempt from paying property taxes of any kind. If the property was to be placed on the tax rolls, it likely would be classified as Open Space Timber and Open Space. In that case, the 1995 Pierce County valuation is $340 per acre, with the tax being $13 per $1000.00, or $2.94 per acre. With the park having 241,992 acres, the tax would be $711,456.48 for the year. This does not include the value of the buildings or any improvements.

The Washington State Sales Tax rate within the Park is .076%

Trash Collection

Today's Park trash disposal is a far cry from the original system of the bears at the garbage pits. Food and waste is to be disposed of in the brown garbage cans distributed throughout the Park..

Four hundred tons of trash are generated by park visitors each year, a little mountain unto itself which must be hauled off to the Hidden Valley Landfill in Pierce County at a cost of $42.00 per ton. There are no dumps still within the park, but there are collection sites with dumpsters at Carbon River, Ohanapecosh and Kautz Creek. The war on waste goes on annually at the park. Do your part to keep it pristine. Use the litter bag you were given when entering the Park.

Recycling

In 1991 the first recycling containers were placed at Mount Rainier making it one of the first six national parks to have a recycling program. Green bins with the familiar triangular recycling symbol are located throughout the park at campgrounds, roadside turnouts, picnic areas and parking lots.

Visitors can put glass, aluminum and plastic (numbers 1, 2 and 6) in the same recycling bin. Be sure bottles are empty and lids are removed.

Roughly 48,000 pounds of park debris is now being recycled per year. To date 59 tons of recyclables have been recovered.

The recycling program is co-sponsored by Dow Chemical and Huntsman Chemical Corporation. Dow and Huntsman plan to return some of the recycled plastics to the park in the form of picnic tables, park benches, sign posts, guard rails, car stops and other outdoor products.

Sewage Disposal

30,000 lbs. of waste from the temporary toilets at Camp Muir and Camp Schurman is flown out each fall by helicopters. The 55 gallon drums are taken down and transferred to trucks, then hauled to a waste treatment plant in Tacoma. There are a total of three wastewater treatment plants in the park, 47 septic tanks and 13 domestic water treatment plants.

In 1970 a small helicopter was bringing a knocked-down outhouse to Camp Muir, when it began losing power. It jettisoned the structure onto the Cowlitz Glacier before crashing and burning.

The open air comfort station at Indian Bar
photo by Jean Trousdale

Value of the Park

The net worth of the park: - what's it worth on the government books? First figure the value of the real estate, the mineral rights, the recreational value and tourism income, (revenue generation), the water, and value of the power the water generates, the animals and the fish. With just one old growth tree having a minimum value of at least $5.00 per board foot as finished lumber, it would take a complete tree inventory to figure just the lumber value.

We couldn't come up with a figure, but one thing's for sure, it's priceless!

Personnel

In 1907 there were two temporary rangers. By 1932 there were nineteen men.

The year round staff is now about 115 permanent employees, with about another 160 seasonal workers added to help handle the summer crowds. The summer staff consists primarily of seasonal park rangers and maintenance workers. Many "seasonals" are teachers and other dedicated regulars who come back year after year to work in the Park.

Want to Work at the Mountain?

"The sooner the better" is the rule in applying for seasonal positions at the mountain. Applications are taken starting in January. Seasonal positions are for rangers, interpreters, and trail crewmen. Seasonal park ranger positions are usually filled by students or teachers who majored in communications, a natural science or a related field. Seasonal rangers are also under Civil Service. Call (360) 220-4053, (then press 1), for vacancies at Mount Rainier and to ask for an application and particulars on available jobs.

Like other government positions, park ranger jobs are governed by Civil Service. Permanent rangers must be graduates of an accredited college in a field related to park work, or have qualifying experience.

If money isn't a concern, consider volunteering your services. You'll get good work experience, as well as spending some glorious time in the next best place to heaven. Often food and housing and/or a small stipend are provided for volunteers.

Volunteers

As the Park Service cuts back more and more on "ground troops", the need for volunteers and local outdoor organizations to step in and take up the slack on unfunded or under-funded projects increases. Outdoor volunteer work varies from moderate to strenuous, and projects range from building retaining walls and turnpikes, to planting trees, revegetating meadows, brushing and trail work.

The job may last a few hours, a week or two, or the whole summer. Imagine your descendants knowing that you worked at Mount Rainier. If you're interested in volunteering, check with the following organizations to see if any are planning work parties to help out at the Mountain.

American Hiking Society Volunteer Vacations - (703) 255-9304
The Mountaineers Trail Maintenance Committee - (206) 859-2443
Mount Rainier National Park Associates - (206) 282-1064
Washington Trails Association - Volunteer Hotline (206) 517-7032
Volunteers for Outdoor Washington - (206) 545-4868. For those who seriously want to learn about trail maintenance, for a modest fee, Volunteers for Outdoor Washington sponsors a series of spring and summer workshops. Contact them at VOW, 4516 University Way NE, Seattle, WA 98105 (206) 545-4868

Sierra Club also sends up work crews. For instance in 1995, they had a group spend two weeks working on the Wonderland Trail.

Many companies also send in work parties. Target Stores, through their Good Neighbors Program, send in two busloads of volunteers to help ready Sunrise for the season's opening. They dug through 10 feet of snow to expose all fire hydrants, then cleared a trail to the comfort station. When that was done, they moved around the mountain and helped open the Cougar Rock Campground.

Microsoft employees have an "adopt-a-trail" team who volunteers at the Park, as does Boeing, through the Boeing Bluebells.

V. I. P.'s

Individual volunteers are also welcome to apply directly to the park to fill a variety of other needs. In 1994, 465 V.I.P.'s (Volunteers in Parks) contributed 32,473 hours of work. Volunteers bring to the park experience, skills, and time that may not be available to the park staff.

Volunteers ranged in age from 7 to 78, and they represented 15 of the 50 United States. Volunteers came from as far away as Tokyo, Japan and Hosena, Germany. Of the volunteers, 64% were male, and 36 % were female.

Volunteers wear a khaki uniform, a green baseball cap, a badge and a gold name plate. Many, though definitely not all, are retired couples who contribute their valuable talents in appreciation for all the enjoyment the old mountain has given them over the years. Others, like the students who came all the way from Waseda University in Japan to make Cougar Rock Campground Handicapped Accessible, and a civil engineer who came from France to work with park engineers, make a wonderful gift of their time and talent to America.

The program started so that the National Park could utilize help from the public. Virtually anyone can volunteer. Volunteers under the age of 18 must be with either parents or a youth group, and must fill out a Parental Approval Form. Don't let the paperwork discourage you though. Last year, 16% of the volunteers were 18 and younger.

There are also openings for the physically limited, and more information can be had from the volunteer coordinators.

Each volunteer is covered for on-the-job injuries and tort liability. There is no training necessary since everything will be learned on the job. It is also required that each volunteer maintain an accurate time log, since the government is keeping track of all this free labor.

Volunteer Coordinators, and particularly noteworthy volunteers themselves are Dixie and Clay Gatchel, who have donated 8,000 hours over an 11 year period, Also worthy of big gold stars, are Dave Irvine, Jr., of Tacoma, who has worked on the Carbon River side for 25 years, and Jeannie Friend, a volunteer ranger since 1983.

Volunteer opportunities include:

Administration: Assist with office duties, typing, filing, computer data entry and general office skills.

Campground Host: This job requires a 4-8 week commitment (mid-June to Mid-September) and a self contained living vehicle. Job entails being campground resident host, answering questions, collecting fees, litter collection and light maintenance.

Library Archives: Have a library background? Assist with the daily operation of the park's reference library and help keep it OPEN for authorized use.

Interpretation: Got a good knowledge of the Park? Assist with operation of visitor centers, museum and hiker information center, answer questions, sell books, maps & publications.

Maintenance: Got experience in carpentry, electrical, plumbing and automotive repair? Help is always needed in cleaning, repairing and maintaining the buildings, equipment and facilities. Persons are also needed to help with cleaning restrooms and buildings, collecting trash, and picking up litter.

Meadow: Replant social trails and repair damaged meadows or work as a Meadow Rover and meet and greet visitors at Paradise and Sunrise.

Resources: Assist with research projects such as: bear, elk, fisheries, Management mountain goats, owls, and air and water quality studies. Persons are also needed to help operate a greenhouse and conduct vegetation studies. A knowledge of biological or wildlife studies is helpful.

Rehabilitation: Work will be out of doors in all weather at elevations of 4,000 to 7,000 feet. Workers will use hand tools and carry heavy loads short distances.

Trail Work: Work with the park trail crew or independently on the repair and maintenance of the park's trails.

Housing: Housing is limited, and will be shared apartment or bunkhouse. Housing will be provided at no cost. Persons will need to provide their own cooking utensils and bedding.

Training: Training and orientation to the park and job will be provided along with the park staff.

Uniform: Persons working in contact with the public will be provided with a uniform shirt, cap, VIP patches and a name bar. Any additional items needed for the work will be provided or reimbursed.

Applications are accepted year round and kept on file for one year. You may use the Volunteer Application for Natural Resource Agencies, or submit a listing of your available dates, skills and knowledge, and work interests, along with your name, address and phone number. Send this application/information to: **Dixie and Clay Gatchel, Volunteer Coordinators,** Mount Rainier National Park, 11516 - 155th Avenue S.E., Renton, WA 98059. Telephone (360) 569-2211, ext. 3389

The Mountain

Mount Rainier, the grande dame of the Cascade range, sits suspended in the sky as an almost disproportionately large backdrop for Seattle, Tacoma, Olympia, Yakima and several dozen other smaller towns. Unseen from the cities, is the National Park spread beneath the summit. It's no wonder the Mountain can be seen from so many points in the state. Mount Rainier is the largest volcano in the Cascade Range, which extends from Mount Garibaldi in southwest British Columbia to Lassen Peak in northern California.

The land mass of the Park is one-third the size of Rhode Island, but it is the vertical measure of Mount Rainier, nearly three miles high that gives the park it's larger than life proportion. It has aptly been described as "an Arctic island in a temperate sea." The summit at 14,411'1" is more than 2-1/2 miles higher than the lowest point in the park, (1,600') along the boundary.

Mount Rainier's Location

The summit is at 46 degrees 51 minutes 18 seconds north, and 121 degrees 46 minutes 15 seconds west. The northwest corner boundary is at 46 degrees 53 minutes north of Longitude 121 degrees, 45 minutes west.

It is bounded on the north and west by Pierce County and on the south by Lewis County (at Packwood), and Yakima County on the East. The Pierce County line follows the route of the White River about 8-9 miles north of the Park Boundary.

The Many Faces of Mount Rainier

As one encircles the mountain, it becomes like playing hide and seek with a small child who pops out to surprise you when least expected, and each time shows a different face. The road darts in and out, close and far, up and down, teasing the traveler with small tastes of the smorgasbord of Rainier delights.

The Carbon River view is tough and rugged. Avalanches rain off 4,500' high Willis Wall day and night, but the road never takes you quite close enough to see them. Taking the washboard Mowich Lake Fork will give your car a new experience and you'll learn how good your shock absorbers are, but one or two of the views are worth it, particularly the final one from the hairpin turn just prior to coming to the lake. (There are no views from the lake, as it is behind a ridge and in the forest.)

Highway 410, on the north, passes through a corridor of lush old growth forest. The White River churns seaward the full length of the highway on the south side of the road. Once inside the Park, the road to Sunrise sometimes yields the first sight of the mountain to those who came from the "wet" to the "dry" side of the peak. It can be glorious and sunny at Sunrise while it's drizzly and dreary at Longmire. Sunrise is the highest point reached by road in the state (6,403'), and the white snows change hues from rosy-peach at dawn to pale blue or lavender at dusk.

The mountain dominates the field of vision of the east side. When it's "out", there's little else to see. The inviting glaciers are deceptively farther away than they appear, but it's almost as if the clean pure air magnifies the view. The mountain is so big, and so close, and so beautiful, it literally takes your breath away. Be careful when driving, and wait for a viewpoint pullout to take a good look. (It's a l-o-o-o-n-g way down!) One can't help but be impressed by the sight of the Emmons Glacier, donned in white, from it's head at the summit, to its foot 5-1/2 miles below, at the White River. Take a few minutes to drive to mile-high Chinook Pass for one of the most awe inspiring views you will ever see.

From Sunrise or Chinook Pass, you could almost coast down to Ohanapecosh. No mountain views here, just virgin forest and hot springs, but as picturesque a campground as you could ever hope to find.

The Stevens Canyon Highway again teases the traveler with nary a glimpse, but then puts on a good show at Reflection Lakes and goes hog-wild at Paradise! The process works in reverse on the way down to Longmire. Once in the lowlands, one is reminded of the adage about not being able to see the forest for the trees, except here you can't see the mountain for the foothills and lower ridges.

If continuing to encircle the mountain, the road to Eatonville will yield two or three nice views, and several miles beyond town, as the road nears Graham, one begins to envy the cows on those farms with million-dollar views.

For those with the luxury of going to the mountain whenever they choose, sometime try a wider-ranging loop. From Ohanapecosh, continue south to Packwood, and circle back to the Mountain Highway (SR 706) on Highway 52 or Skate Creek Road east of Packwood. Or continue on to Morton and see the south side views which are hidden when doing the closer-in Paradise Road loop.

The amazing part of the whole trip around the mountain, is how in one day, the mountain changes from squat and fat to rugged and daring, to majestic and awe-inspiring and back again. Each glacier has its own look and its own personality, and even casual car tourists can't help but be impressed by the incredible diversity of Washington state's Grande Dame.

Park Area

(Original size: 18 miles square, 207,360 acres)

Current: 241,781.09 federal acres + 210.91 non-federal acres = 241,992.0 gross

The Park contains the land equivalent of about ten and a half townships. (A township is 36 square miles.) It contains 378 square miles, (980 square kilometers), and 241,992 acres.

With the construction of a road (the early stages of the Mather Memorial Highway) through Chinook Pass, private development began to spring up at Tipsoo Lake below Chinook Pass. As a result, the Park Service approached the Forest Service about extending the Park's boundaries eastward and southward.

(They were also concerned about development around Ohanapecosh Springs.) Fifty-three and one-tenth square miles (34,000 acres) were added when the eastern boundary was extended to the summit of the Cascades by act of Congress, January 31, 1931. The Park was originally a near-perfect square, the sides of which were each 18 miles in length.

Acreage's by County

Total: 235,612.5 acres

Pierce County   196,168.5 acres

Lewis County   39,444 acres

Wilderness 228,480 acres

(Plus adjustments: 1986 Crystal Mountain (adjusted -31.5) acres, 1986 Backbone Ridge adjustment (+210 acres), 1986 Klapatche Point (+30 acres)

Acreage's by Zone (Land Classification)

Wilderness Acreage: 228,480 (97% of total park acreage)

Trail Zone   60,317 acres

Cross-country Zone   127,249 acres

Alpine Zone   47,147 acres

Non-Wilderness Acreage: 7,132 acres.

This includes the frontcountry areas of Nisqually, Longmire, Paradise, Ohanapecosh, White River, Sunrise, Carbon River, and road corridors.

Boundaries Changed

March 2, 1899. Boundary originally set at 18 miles x 18 miles

May 28, 1926. Natural boundary lines were substituted for artificial straight line boundaries.

June 31, 1931. Eastern boundary extended to the summit of the Cascades.

1939. Longmire claim of 18.2 acres purchased by federal government for $30,000.

June 27, 1960. Property acquired at Ashford for relocation of Park Headquarters. This is now called Tahoma Woods.

Boundary Mileages

Miles of boundary with U.S. Forest Service: 76.4 miles

Miles of boundary with Wilderness   29.0 miles

Miles of boundary with private property   9.5 miles

Miles of boundary with (now greening) clear-cuts   15.5 miles

U.S. Forest Service   6.75 miles

Private   8.75 miles

Total miles of boundary: 85.9 miles

County Boundaries

County Boundaries

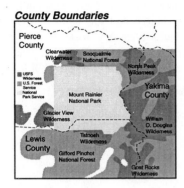

Most of the park lies within Pierce County, with a portion on the southern section lying in Lewis County.

Yakima County abuts the eastern boundary line, and runs about half way up the park.

"Accurate" Heights of the Mountain

One would think from these figures that the height of the mountain has fluctuated considerably and frequently over the years, but the problem was in attempting to get an accurate measurement, not with the mountain. Even to this day, the actual figure is in dispute, as U.S.G.S. does not accept the new Centennial measurement of 14,411'.1".

Methods used to determine the altitude have included "actual leveling", long-distance angulation, (triangulation), vertical-angle measurements, trigonometric determination, barometric readings, and now the latest 'high-tech' Global Positioning System measurement.

1841 -	12,330'	Cdr. Charles Wilkes, triangulation method
1870 -	14,444	Emmons & Wilson - thermometer in boiling water
1873 -	12,360'	Asher and Adams Washington Territory Map
1894 -	15,500'	Major E. S. Ingraham
1895 -	14,532'	S. S. Gannett, U.S.G.S.
1896 -	14,519'	George S. Hyde. U.S.G.S., triangulation method
1897 -	14,528'	Professor Edgar McClure fig. used until 1914
1902 -	14,363	U. S. Geological Survey "final figure"
1905 -	14,326	Department of Interior Map
1907 -	14,526	Government map
1914 -	14,408'	U. S. Geological Survey "final figure"
1956 -	14,410'	U. S. Geological Survey "final figure"
1989 -	14,411.1	Washington's Centennial satellite measurement

How The Latest Measurement was Done

In 1988 in preparation for the State Centennial Celebration, the first high-tech measurement of the mountain was made by the Land Surveyors Association of Washington. Two teams of climbers and surveyors installed state-of-the-art Global Positioning System satellite receivers at six different locations around the peak, including the summit. Seven satellites circling 12,500 miles above the Earth beamed down sound waves to the receivers which recorded how long it took the signals to travel. The satellite measurements were then plugged into computer programs designed to account for such factors as gravity, the curvature of the earth and atmospheric conditions. The computer also calculated relating the mountain to the center of the earth as well as the distance from sea level to the earth's center.

The effort paid off, when the computer spit out the new height and the mountain gained another 13 inches! It went from 14,410' to 14,411.1'

Other Key Elevations

Anvil Rock	9,584 feet
Camp Muir	10,062 feet
Carbon River Entrance	1,760 feet
Cayuse Pass	4,630 feet
Chinook Pass	5,440 feet
Indian Henrys	5,300 feet
Little Tahoma	11,138 feet
Longmire	2,761 feet
Narada Falls	4,572 feet
Nisqually Entrance	2,003 feet
Nisqually Bridge	3,908 feet
Ohanapecosh Ranger Station	1,925 feet
Paradise	5,557 feet
Rampart Ridge	4,080 feet
Sunrise	6,400 feet
White River Entrance (Park Boundary)	2,725 feet
White River Ranger Station	3,500 feet

Rainier - King of the Mountains, ... five times removed

In the 1890's, Mount Rainier was considered America's summit. "Columbia's Crest", the highest of the three summits, was thought to be the high point in the United States. Then in 1914, California's Mount Whitney came in with a new measurement of 14,495' and dethroned the king. Before Washingtonians could adjust to that slight, some upstarts from the young Geological Survey got to rummaging around in the Rockies, and found not one, but *fifty* peaks over 14,000 feet! Three of the interlopers squeezed themselves ahead of Mount Rainier. Mount Elbert measured in at 14,431 feet, thus capturing the number two slot. Mount Massive, at 14,420 then took number over as number three, and then in turn was kicked back to #4 by Mount Harvard at 14,421. Harvard was one foot higher than Massive and twelve feet higher than Mount Rainier. Mount Rainier was relegated to fifth highest peak in the U.S. In sixth place, right behind Rainier, is California's Mount Williamson, at 14,375 feet.

Then came that ominous demotion day, January 3, 1959, when Alaska entered the Union with it's 20,320-foot Mount McKinley and an assortment of other peaks surpassing Mount Whitney. Our noble Rainier slips to 33rd place in the national standings if Alaskan peaks are included.

Let's Talk Base to Summit

One other factor that needs to be taken into consideration when one talks height, is where do we start the count. Mount Rainier not only rises 8,000 feet above its neighbors, it rises 11,000 feet, from base to summit, in seven miles.

Mapping the Park

The first attempt at mapping the park was made by geologists Samuel F Emmons and A. D Wilson in October 1870 while working on the Geological Survey of the Fortieth Parallel. After getting to the east side of the mountain by a rather circuitous route, they surveyed and laid out a base line for future topographic mapping. The region was not thoroughly mapped until 1895, when Henry A. Sarvent, for whom the Sarvent Glaciers were named, drew the first comprehensive map.

In 1894, the Northern Pacific Railroad sent Olin D. Wheeler, editor of their magazine *"Wonderland"*, and a railroad photographer to climb the mountain. The two produced a three-color map which was the best to date, and was to remain so until Eugene Ricksecker made his topographical map for the U. S. Corps of Engineers in 1906.

In 1910, a Geological Survey party again came to the mountain with the two-fold purpose of preparing an accurate topographic map of the park, and to ascertain the exact elevation of the mountain. The project stretched into four years. Initially F.E. Matthes and his party mapped a large portion of the park, and made a preliminary determination of the height of the mountain.

Their map contained hundreds of points and was made in a most interesting manner. They used a "plane table", which means the map was made on a large drafting board mounted on a tripod.

The survey was completed in 1913 under the direction of C. H. Birdseye. In spite of encountering a terrific blizzard while working at the summit, and having to take shelter in the steam caves, the men established the official height of the mountain as 14,408 feet, a figure which stood for 42 years.

Maps

A map is a drawing of terrain at a moment in time. Like books, most maps are probably obsolete by the time the ink is dry.

U.S. Geological Survey 7.5 Minute Series Maps. These are the standard U.S. One inch equals 2,000 feet.

Mount Rainier's most famous cartographer, Dee Molenaar comes by that skill with the talent of an artist, and the eye of a geologist, the accuracy of a mountain guide, and a researcher's love of detail. He is all those things and more. His Mount Rainier depiction is a work of art as well as an accurate map. It belongs the library, or on the wall of, every Mount Rainier fan. (Order your copy from the catalog in the back of this book.)

U.S.G.S. Maps Covering Mount Rainier

Golden Lakes	(1971)	7-1/2 minute
Mount Rainier West	(1971)	7-1/2 minute
Mowich Lake	(1971)	7-1/2 minute
Sunrise	(1971)	7-1/2 minute
Mount Rainier East	(1971)	7-1/2 minute
Chinook Pass (photo-revised	(1987)	7-1/2 minute
Ohanapecosh Hot Springs	(1971)	7-1/2 minute
Tatoosh Lakes	(1971)	7-1/2 minute
Packwood	(1971)	7-1/2 minute
Randle	(1971)	7-1/2 minute
Mount Wow	(1971)	7-1/2 minute
Enumclaw	(1971)	7-1/2 minute
Greenwater	(1971)	7-1/2 minute

There is also a U.S.G.S. map covering the entire park.

Learning More

Pacific Northwest Field Seminars

When your interest in the mountain grows beyond the evening campground program, and you want to delve into the dynamics of a glacier, the intricacies of an old growth forest, or one of the other sciences of the mountain, take a seminar. Topics cover a wide variety of interests ranging from volcanoes to wildflowers, butterflies to elk. Outdoor skills and themes such as photography, astronomy, nature studies and sketching, are taught by authorities on each subject. Several day-long seminars for the physically handicapped are also offered. The classes are offered on location at Mount Rainier.

The seminars are available annually through Pacific Northwest Field Seminars, 909 First Ave., Suite 630, Seattle, WA 98104, (206) 220-4121. Write or call for a catalog describing the seminars, faculty, fees, dates and college credits.

Pacific Northwest Field Seminars is a non-profit program sponsored by the Northwest Interpretive Association in cooperative with the National Park Service.

Other Classes

Two of the best courses around are Bob Arnold's "Natural History of the West Side (of the mountain)," and "East Side Ecology" courses, offered through City University of Tacoma's Quest program. 1-800-422-4898.

The Metropolitan Park District of Tacoma offers one-day 4-6 hour programs with a Park Naturalist at a cost of $15 per person. Call (360) 569-2211 x 3313 for a list of topics and/or registration.

Other worthwhile educational opportunities, outdoor trips, and seminars at the mountain are offered periodically by various schools, clubs and organizations. Most of these are announced in local newspapers and outdoor newsletters such as *Signpost* and *Pack and Paddle*.

Some of the larger outdoor equipment stores also offer clinics, classes and field trips. Those to check with are REI, Swallow's Nest and Wilderness Sports in Seattle, and Backpacker Supply in Tacoma.

Classic Art of the Mountain

Mountains have always been a favorite subject of artists, and few offer more beauty or pose more serenely than Mount Rainier.

The "because it's there" answer seems to apply to the 'why do you do what you do' question asked of both climbers and painters. Some of the first works to achieve national distinction were painted by Tacoma artist A. H. Barnes, who did companion works of the mountain from Paradise valley, and looking toward the Tatoosh Range from Paradise. The Chambers of Commerce of both Seattle and Tacoma clamored to buy the paintings, but first they traveled the country and were used in promotional pieces touting the glories of the mountain.

In 1936 and 37, a world renowned painter, Pieter van Veen painted twelve oil paintings of the mountain and related subjects. The oils were first displayed at Paradise Inn for two months before moving on to exhibitions in The National Gallery in Washington, D.C., The Chicago Art Institute, The Toronto Museum, and several other prominent galleries. Mr. Van Veen's work was said to resemble that of Rembrandt in his love for accuracy and his use of color. The paintings were eventually sold to Eastern collectors.

Some other marvelous renditions of the mountain were in the paintings which were commissioned by Rainier Brewery for the backdrops of their ads in the 1950's and early 60's.

Each year dozens of equally appreciative artists try their hand at capturing the mountain's beauty, and their efforts grace countless mantelpieces.

Classic Mountain Photography

The first Mount Rainier color photograph of record taken from as far away as Tacoma, was taken June 20, 1895 by A. C. Carpenter. According to the *Tacoma News Tribune*, photos prior to that had the mountain "faked" in. The system Carpenter used was to coat his plates with an "eriside of silver coat or emulsion." Using a 30-second exposure and screen or filter between the lens and the negative, he got a "genuine" photograph of the mountain, which he promptly copyrighted. *(Tacoma News Tribune 2/25/22)*.

Classic Books about the Mountain

While many good books have been written about the mountain, these belong on the shelves of every Mount Rainier fan.

The Challenge of Rainier. This classic by Dee Molenaar chronicles the climbing history, plus a wealth of anecdotes and valuable information about the mountain.

Fire Mountains of the West: The Cascade and Mono Lake Volcanoes, and *Fire and Ice* by Steven Harris, two books which belong on every volcanophile's bookshelf.

Our Greatest Mountain and *Winter in Paradise* by Floyd Schmoe,

50 Hikes in Mt. Rainier National Park by Ira Spring and Harvey Manning published by Mountaineers

Wildflowers of Mount Rainier and the Cascades, by Mary A. Fries

101 Wildflowers of Mount Rainier National Park by Grant and Wenonah Sharpe.

Mountain Fever, by Aubrey Haines. This is a meticulously researched work covering the record of explorations and ascents through 1899, prior to the National Park. It was published by the Oregon Historical Society.

Mt. Rainier, A Record of Exploration by Edmund S. Meany, an old classic.

Murder on the Mount by Sandy Dengler, wife of chief naturalist Bill Dengler, is a thrill-a-minute mystery which takes place at Mount Rainier. The vivid accurate location descriptions transport readers to the mountain and brings this hilarious story to life.

Researching Mount Rainier

Bellevue Library - Bellevue, WA (206) 455-6889. Has the *Seattle Times* on CD Rom thus giving instant computer access to all Mount Rainier news mentions from 1990 on. Also good assortment of books, maps, clippings.

Federal Archives and Records Center 6125 Sand Point Way NE, Seattle, WA 98115. (206) 442-4500. Early pioneer census records on microfilm. No Mount Rainier archival material yet, but some coming.

Federal Way Library 848 S. 320th, Federal Way (206) 839-0257.
Good Mount Rainier book section.

Lewis County Historical Museum - 599 NW Front, Chehalis, (360) 748-0831 Pioneer records, good Longmire and Packwood records, good vertical file on early exploration and climbing.

Mazamas Library, 909 NW 19th, Portland, OR 97209. (503) 227-2345. This library contains Faye Fuller's scrapbooks.

McChord Air Museum - McChord AFB, Tacoma (206) 984-2485. Primarily photos of aircraft and the mountain. Historian has only McChord aircraft accident records, not accidents of planes flying in & out of McChord.

Mount Rainier Archives, Tahoma Woods. Not yet in shape for public access. The Park Service has just now gotten a professional archivist and will be cataloging their collection in the near future. A genuine historian has also come on staff.

Mount Rainier Library, Longmire. An excellent little library that's a gold mine of information. The only problem is coordinating your visit with the ranger who serves as librarian, and isn't in the library often, or the regular summer volunteer who arbitrarily allows only a two-hour visit.

Mountaineers Library (206) 284-6310. Old Mountaineer bulletins, annuals and small book collection

Museum of History and Industry Library, 2161 East Hamlin St., Seattle 98112. (206) 324-1125. Photos, books, clippings and Mountaineer Annuals.

National Archives and Records Administration, Wash. D.C. 20408. General National Park files.

Oregon History Center, 1200 SW Park Ave., Portland, OR (503) 222-1741. Museum, film archives, oral histories, manuscripts

Pierce County Library System 6300 Wildaire Rd. SW, Tacoma, (800) 346-0995. Many local libraries with much Mount Rainier material.

Puyallup Library excellent collection of historic pioneer and Pierce County books with much data on Rainier area.

Renton Public Library 100 Mill St., Renton, (206) 235-2610. Excellent Mount Rainier and early history book section.

Seattle Public Library 1000 4th Ave., Seattle, WA (206) 386-4636

Tacoma Public Library Northwest Room 1102 S. Tacoma Ave., Tacoma (206) 591-5622. Incredibly comprehensive old newspaper clipping files, note files, Alfred Smith manuscript collection, books, old photos including glass plates.

University of Washington Archives (N. wing of Allen Library) U.W. Campus, Seattle (206) 543-6509. Special collections (Photographs, Pacific Northwest materials, ephemera)

University of Washington Forest Resources Library 60 Bloedel Hall, AQ-15, U.W. Campus (206) 543-2758. Forestry and wildlife management, soil science, fire management including Mount Rainier references.

University of Washington Suzzalo and Allen Libraries Pacific Northwest Collection U.W. Campus, Seattle 98195 (206) 543-1929. Newspaper and periodical articles, pamphlets and collections of manuscripts. Also historical photography collection, map collection and graphics collection. Excellent source of Mount Rainier material.

Washington State Archives - 1120 Washington Street SE, Olympia, WA 98504 (360) 753-5485. Has Washington State Department of Transportation Rainier National Park Highway records, plus legislative and Governors' Papers related to establishing the park.

Washington State Historical Society Library 315 North Stadium Way, Tacoma (206) 593-2830. Many Asahel Curtis photos of Mount Rainier, plus some old Seattle Post-Intelligencer photos, and newspaper clipping files, manuscripts.

Washington State Library Northwest Room Olympia (360) 753-4024. Special collection of old newspapers on microfilm.

Washington State University Special Collections Division, Pullman, WA

Whitman College, Penrose Memorial Library, Walla Walla, WA Historic photos

Mountain Mysteries, Curiosities and Neat Things

The Little Seal

A little carved ivory seal was found right outside the park entrance by a local woman working in her garden. How did it get there? This mystery is probably answerable by logic. The Nisqually River was a trade route, traveled by Indians going over the mountains. Since there was a Potlatch site at the confluence of the Nisqually and Mashal Rivers, the little seal was probably traded to an Eastern Washington Indian who lost it on the trip home.

The Deer Head

"Mowich" is the Chinook name for "deer", and oddly enough, a prominent collection of rock bands and snow fields on the upper left section of Mowich face or the northwest face of Mount Rainier, create a naturally-occurring deer's head, neck and antlers. John H. Williams, author of *The Mountain that was God*

(1911) mentions the deer head, and points out that the Mowich rivers were so named by the Indians because just below the summit, in the great rocks of the northwest side of the peak, they saw the face of the Mowich. The large head is visible even from Puget Sound, once one knows where to look. Depending on the amount of snowfall each winter, the head ranges from very distinct to sketchy.

The Ice Indian

The Indians have another legendary "face on the mountain", a rock and ice likeness of an Indian, graven by nature on the north slope of the mountain. To date our research hasn't turned up where to look.

Noah's Ark

Ben Longmire was a young man with a vivid and colorful imagination, witness some of the names he bestowed on landmarks. One of his better ones was that his claim to have found pieces of petrified wood and a tree stump encircled by an iron ring on the flanks of a 5,996 peak which he named Mount Ararat.

Natural Bridge

This ten-foot wide, 200 foot high arch, spans a gulf of about 150 feet, and is the eroded remnant of an old andesite lava flow. It is located in a remote area on the north side of the Mountain off the rugged Northern Loop Trail about the 5,400' level. It is one of the natural wonders of the State of Washington. The bridge was discovered in 1913 by a government survey crew.

Mount Rainier Bouillabaisse

There are crayfish galore at Mowich Lake, but even more unusual are the tiny clams in Mystic Lake and the tarns at Elysian Fields, Windy Gap and Mist Park.

The Elusive Wild Rainiers

Rainier Brewery once had a zany ad campaign featuring "Wild Rainiers". These little guys ran around the foothills trying to evade people, sort of like beer bottle sasquatch.

Models of the Mountain

For years, millions of park visitors have admired the large relief models of the mountain at the various visitor centers. Equally interesting is who built them, and how. In 1935 naturalist Frank Brockman undertook the project. He made the master by cutting cardboard in the shape of each 100 foot elevation contour. Modeling clay was then added to create the minute details of topography. In

Photo from Pemco, Webster & Stevens Collection, Museum of History & Industry

addition to the great volumes of plaster to make the mold, other supplies were requisitioned from various scrap piles around the park. The total cost was about $200 excluding salary.

The model was made in the basement of the Administration Building and then cut in half. Part of the floor was removed and the pieces were taken out and reassembled in a nearby equipment shed. The negative was cast and 3 display models (positives) were cast from the original master. Those models (plus a couple more which were made later) were located at Longmire, Sunrise, Paradise, Ohanapecosh and the Rainier Brewery Mountain Room.

One visitor wryly observed, "I suppose you call it a relief model because it was such a relief when the job was done."

Finally in 1977 the aging plaster relief models at Longmire, Paradise, Sunrise and Ohanapecosh were replaced with models made of fiberglass. The new models were made by Rauda Scale Models of Seattle. One of the old plaster models was put on long term loan to the Recreational Equipment, Inc. store in Seattle.

Another meticulous model of the mountain was made by a Washington State University mathematics student, Dennis Carlson who spent approximately 1,000 hours on his Mount Rainier. His model was constructed by individually placing 128 layers of 1/16th inch "pepperboard," with each layer representing 100 feet of elevation. This superlative model has been displayed at the Puyallup Fair several times.

The Biggest Model of All

The newest and largest model is 200-feet high, two dimensional and is an entrance to the SuperMall of the Great Northwest in Auburn, Washington in sight of the mountain and, in fact, faces Mount Rainier. The mall owners had better not be prophetic! They celebrated the 1995 grand opening of their gigantic mall by having their mountain *erupt*. They had better hope they don't inspire Ms. Rainier to follow suit. Their mall is sitting on top of remains of the Osceola mudflow whose source was at her summit, from where it flowed down the White River valley and across the lowland, including Auburn.

A Real Live Little Rainier

Imbert Matthee, a business reporter at the *Seattle PI* and executive editor of *The Mountaineer Bulletin* liked the mountain so much, he named his only son after it. Young Master Rainier is now 6 years old. Dad's looking forward to the day they climb Little R's namesake together.

And a Still Smaller Rainier

While Mount Rainier may be a feast for the eyes, it can also be a feast for the tummy. One of the renowned Black Diamond Bakery's specialties is their Mount Rainier loaf, a crusty mammoth four-pound mound of bread shaped roughly like the mountain, and baked in their famed old wood-fired brick oven. (Black Diamond Bakery & Deli, 32805 Railroad Avenue, Black Diamond, WA 98010. (206) 886-2741. Closed Monday.)

And Smaller Still

While not exact replicas of the mountain, the Brown & Haley Candy Company of Tacoma has, for several decades, produced millions of "Mountain Bars," little mountains of chocolate, with the "lava cavity" filled with creamy fondant.

More Sweet Little Rainiers

In 1956, a different Rainier topped Mount Rainier as a newsmaker. It was the story-book wedding of Grace Kelly to Prince Rainier of Monaco. A northwest candy company felt Mount Rainier had to be represented at the big event, so they had a paper-mache model of the mountain made. They filled the two foot high by three foot diameter mountain with their regionally popular mints.

The Rainier Symphony

Yes, all the senses can experience the mountain, and in 1971, a symphony entitled *"Rainier"* was written and performed by the Tacoma Symphony Orchestra, with later performances by the Vancouver, B.C., Spokane and Portland symphonies.

The work was commissioned by Seattle industrialist Ben Erlichman, and was based on a poem *"Rainier - the Epic of the Mountain,"* written in the 1940's by the late Dan Ward Gibson. Four months in the writing, the score was composed by Dr. Leroy Ostransky and interpreted by conductor Edward Seferian.

The symphony opened with the narrator reading the first stanzas of the poem, depicting daybreak on the mountain with the orchestra flowing into its introduction. The second section portrayed the mood of the mountain at sunset, and the final movement reflected the birth of the mountain millions of years ago.

Perhaps it will be performed again for the Park's Centennial.

Rainiers in Motion

"Rainiers" has been a popular name for baseball teams. The first team bearing the name was the old Seattle Rainiers, owned by Emil Sick, owner of the Rainier Brewery. Sick purchased the team, known as the Indians, and renamed them "The Rainiers" in 1937. The team won five pennants (1939, '40, '41, '51 and '55.) In 1960, he sold the team to the Boston Red Sox.

In 1995, perhaps in a final act of acknowledgment of the legitimacy of the name Rainier, Tacoma officially named their baseball team the Tacoma Rainiers. The team is an AAA affiliate to the Seattle Mariners, and plays each summer at Cheney Stadium in Tacoma. They are a part of the Pacific Coast League.

Post Offices

The first U.S. Post Office in the area was at Elbe. In the early days the mail was delivered on horseback, and post offices were frequently in homes. When necessary an extra horse was sent along to carry Christmas presents. The first post office at Longmire was established August 1, 1908. The tiny Longmire post office today is located in the National Park Inn. The Longmire zip code is 98397. The year round post office hours are 8:30 a.m. to 5 p.m., Monday through Friday. Another (temporary) post office is located in the Paradise Inn, same hours as above.

The mailing address for Mount Rainier National Park Administrative offices is Mount Rainier National Park, Tahoma Woods, Ashford, WA 98304.

The Ashford Post Office was established November 16, 1894. Mrs. Cora J. Ashford, the wife of the founder of the town of Ashford, served as postmistress from its inception until December 1938. For many years the mail was carried by horseback between Elbe and Ashford, then later by horse and buggy.

One youthful mail carrier was 11-year old Jess McCrea, who carried the mail by foot from Ashford to Paradise, a distance of twenty four miles. His pay was $1.00 a trip plus his dinner. Legend has it that he always tried to make the trip up with the mail and back to the kitchen at Longmire by lunchtime. His mother was going through hard times, and the big meal meant as much to the lad as the dollar.

Mount Rainier Commemorative Stamps

The United States has issued three postage stamps featuring Mount Rainier: 1934, 1953 and 1989. The commemorative stamp released August 3, 1934 was part of a series in honor of National Parks Year. It featured a view of the mountain from Mirror Lake. The green and black stamp has a current value of 15 cents.

The 1953 stamp commemorates Washington Territory's Centennial. The stamp shows the mountain rising above Puget Sound, and is also currently valued at 15 cents. The 1989 stamp is the only multi-color stamp of the three. The official description in Scott's catalog states this is a view of the mountain from Reflection Lake, however it is actually from Tipsoo Lake at Chinook Pass, with the Cowlitz Chimneys in the middle ground. The current value of the stamp in mint condition is 45 cents, or 15 cents if used.

There are stamp collectors who specialize in the narrow philatelistic category of collecting only stamps having to do with volcanoes. There are about 150 members of the Earth's Physical Features Study Unit of the American Topical Association who collect only "volcanoes on stamps". Their membership includes university professors, interested amateurs and USGS scientists. The study unit publishes a checklist of volcano topical stamps, and updates it periodically in their newsletter, *Earth's Wonders*.

Want the Post Office were to issue another special stamp for Mount Rainier's 100-year anniversary in 1999? If you do, write to the U.S. Postal Service Advisory Committee, Room 4474E, 475 L'Enfant Plaza SW, Wash., DC 20260-2437. That's the group which decides on new stamp designs.

The Passport Stamp

In 1986, the Park Service began an innovative program of encouraging visitation to multiple National Parks through issuing a collector's "Passport" and offering colorful stamps for the various parks. The stamps are only sold at the location on the face of the stamp, so actual attendance is required to buy

one. In addition to the adventure of seeing the beautiful parks, vacationers have the passport as an attractive souvenir. The stamps are available at the Longmire Museum and all book outlets in the park.

Water

Water. Clean, cool water. Pure water. Everybody needs it, and Mount Rainier National Park has more water stored on it, and in use within it's confines, than few other places on earth. Mount Rainier's water is evident wherever you look in every conceivable form: rain, dew, mist, fog, firn, hail, snow, sleet, steam, clouds, whiteouts, ice, glaciers, waterfalls, streams, rivers, creeks, lakes, ponds, and condensation.

The value of that water has been placed at more than $50,000 per acre annually, if people had to pay for it. Once Rainier's water leaves the park, it grows trees, irrigates farms, powers cities and commerce, and is a major contributor to our state's fishing, recreation and tourism industries. It is an incredibly valuable resource.

The same water may be recycled several times over before finally reaching the sea, just to repeat the process all over again. Rain or snow falls on the mountain, and eventually comes down a river, where it waters things, evaporates, and becomes rain again. etc.

Washington Symbols

The following "official" symbols are present at Mount Rainier:

Washington's state bird is Willow Goldfinch (yes)

Washington's state tree is the western hemlock (yes)

Washington's state animal is Roosevelt Elk (yes)

Unofficial symbols present in the Park are:

Washington Critter: Giant banana slug (yes)

Steelhead trout (once were present)

Washington gem is petrified wood (yes)

Washington flower is Coast Rhododendron (not present in Park)

Awards and Rewards

5-Major Peaks Pin

Aside from the personal satisfaction of reaching the summit of Washington state's major peaks, the achievement also gets you one-fifth of the way toward winning a *"5-Major Peaks Pin"* from Seattle Mountaineers. Winning the pin requires reaching the summits of Mounts Olympus, Adams, Glacier, Baker and Rainier. (This award is for Mountaineer members only.) It used to be a 6-Major Peaks Pin before Mount St Helens turned a major into a minor.

Tacoma Irish Cabin Peaks Pins

The Tacoma Branch of Mountaineers offers four more Mount Rainier Pins. The first are the two Irish Cabin Peaks Pins, which each require climbing 12 peaks in the Irish Cabin area (just outside the Carbon River entrance).

The ***First Twelve Irish Cabin pin*** peaks are: Baldy, Bearhead, Castle, East Bearhead, Fay, First Mother, Florence, Gove, Hessong Rock, Pitcher, Pleasant and Tolmie. A climber must have been awarded the *First Twelve Pin* before he can receive the *Second Twelve Pin*.

The ***Second Twelve Irish Cabin pin*** peaks are: Arthur, Crescent, Echo Rock, Mineral, Observation Rock, Old Desolate, Redstone, Second Mother, Sluiskin Chief, Sluiskin Squaw, Third Mother and Tyee.

The two ***Tahoma Peaks Pins*** require bagging 24 additional peaks within the Park. This series of peaks extends from the Indian Henrys area on the southwest side, down through the Tatoosh Range, across the south side, and up the entire east side to the Sourdough Mountains. They are separated into eight

---

The Tacoma Peaks Pins Climbs

Group I

Mt. Wow 6040+'	Mt. Ararat 6010'
Pyramid Peak 6937'	Tokaloo Rock 7684'

Group II

*Eagle Peak 5958'	Wahpenayo Peak 6231'
Chutla Peak 6000+'	Lane Peak 6012'

Group III

Plummer Peak 6370+ '	Pinnacle Peak 6562'
The Castle 6440+'	Bench Peak (Foss Peak) 6524'

Group IV

*Unicorn Peak 6917'	Stevens Peak 6510'
Dixon Mountain 5134'	Tatoosh Lookout Peak 6310'

Group V

Shriner Peak 5834'	Naches Peak 6452'
*Dewey Peak 6710'	Silver King 6998'

Group VI

*Governors Ridge 6600+'	Tamanos Peak 6790'
Barrier Peak 6521'	Goat Island Mountain 7288'

Group VII

Banshee Peak 7400+'	Ctrl. Cowlitz Chimney 7421'
*Main Cowlitz Chimney 7605'	Double Peak 6199'

Group VIII

Third Burroughs Mtn. 7828'	Palisades Peak 7040'
Marcus Peak 6962'	Slide Mountain 6620'

---

groups of four peaks, of which three in each group must be done for credit for that group. Any four groups may be completed for the first pin, and all eight must be completed for the add-on second half of the peak pin. The two pins join together to form one united pin.

Peaks are grouped by geographic areas. Each group contains a combination of hikes, scrambles and, at most, one basic level climb. An * means the peak's only known routes are climbs.

"Fourteeners" - The Thin-air Devotees

Another award of which Mount Rainier is a part, is the coveted **"Fourteeners."** This is for those who have climbed all 14,000-foot high peaks in the conterminous United States. There are 67 such peaks, with most of those (53) being in the Colorado Rockies and the balance (other than Mount Rainier) being in the Sierras. Mount Rainier is the 19th highest of the 67.

"Highpointers" - The Well-traveled Climbers

There are also those who have the distinction of reaching the highest point in each of the fifty states. They're called the **"Highpointers."** As if that isn't enough of a challenge, competitors now do it as fast as possible. The current **"Fifty Peaks"** record is 101 days. In 1994 a team of three physically challenged climbers and seven support personnel attempted to break the record.

The Highpointers do help Mount Rainier go up in national height standings, in that they move Mount Rainier back up from fifth to fourth place among high peaks. How? Easy. According to Highpointer rules, each state just gets to count *one* mountain, thus Alaska claims Mount McKinley at 20,320', California has Mount Whitney at 14,495', Colorado has Mount Elbert at 14,431', and our beautiful high point comes in at 14,411.1' Thanks, Highpointers.

"Wonderlanders"- One in a Million Hikers

Those completing the 92.2 mile Wonderland Trail (whether doing it all at once, or in segments) are eligible for either a colorful personalized completion certificate and the right to wear a patch which signifies the wearer has done the trail. (The latter two items may be ordered in the back of this book.)

One pin which anyone can get is the "Don't Be A Meadow Stomper" button. Another, which is now a collector's item, is the Mount Rainier 90th Anniversary lapel pin which was sold in 1989. Hundreds are now hiding in jewelry boxes of Mount Rainier fans.

Other Awards and Commendations

The first citation for heroism ever issued by the Department of the Interior, went to ranger Charlie Brown for his part in a rescue. The (Greathouse) accident in question caused two deaths and left four others seriously injured. Brown happened to be at Camp Muir at the time, and upon hearing of the accident, he took off alone into a blizzard, even descending into a deep crevasse, not knowing the two men in it were already dead. He later led the search party back and descended 140 feet into a crevasse to bring out a body. *(TNT 7/25/29).*

A year later, another award was given for heroism in the same accident. This award was given by the Order of DeMolay to Robert Strobel, an assistant guide on the ill-fated climb. As a victim of the fall, and severely injured himself, he crawled from the crevasse and struggled alone through a blizzard for help. He had to climb back up an icy cliff in order to find the route back to Camp Muir. It was he who alerted Charlie Brown (above). The medal given Strobel was only the 12th ever awarded in the nation. Strobel was the only living person ever to receive DeMolay's Heroism honor. *(TNT 5/12/30).*

Two given citations for heroic conduct were Frank "Swede" Willard and William Butler who helped recover the body of a climber who fell to his death near the summit. Both were summer rangers, however Butler went on to have a career with the Park Service, and receive another commendation seventeen years later. *(TNT 9/23/31).*

For his discovery of the Marine transport plane that carried 32 men to their deaths on Mount Rainier in 1946, now Assistant Chief Ranger William J. Butler was awarded the Interior Department's highest award, the Distinguished Service Medal. Butler was also awarded the Navy's highest civilian award, the Distinguished Public Service certificate. Butler refused to accept a $5,000 reward offered by relatives of the victims. *(TNT 10/4/48).*

Butler found the wreckage on one of his days off and was therefore legally entitled to accept the reward. Secretary of the Interior J. A. Krug was so impressed by Butler's refusal to accept the reward that he gave him a promotion and a pay raise of $126 a year.

In 1980, another Interior Department award, this one a Valor Award, went to Park Ranger Garry Olson and ex-ranger Jean-Paul de St. Croix. The two rangers were lowered at nightfall some 70 feet from a wind-buffeted Army helicopter to knife-edged Liberty Ridge to rescue a critically injured climber, Dr. John Donlou of Palos Verdes, CA. A slip on the 60-degree slope would have sent the rescuers careening down to the glacier 3,500 feet below. *(TNT 10/30/80).*

Names

Tahoma

"Great mountain, who once to a pagan race wert God,
   Make us to realize our shame:
That, failing to sing praises to thy Wondrous form,
   We stoop to squabble o'er a name!"

By Miss MacKenzie

The Name "Rainier"

May 8, 1792, the day after his first sighting of "the round snowy mountain", Captain Vancouver named it after his friend, Rear Admiral Peter Rainier.

Rainier was a British Naval officer who never saw the mountain which was to bear his name. He was the son of Peter Rainier of Sandwich, England and the grandson of Huguenot refugees. His French name (Regniere) was anglicized in pronunciation to "Rainy-er" and 'Americanized" to "Ray-neer". He served in the British Navy from age 15, and gained notoriety for capturing an American privateer in the Revolutionary War.

British history tells the battle story as follows: "On the 8th of July (1778), the 14-gun ship Ostrich, Commander Peter Rainier, on the Jamaica station, in company with the 10-gun armed brig Lowestoffe's Prize, chased a large brig. After a long run, the Ostrich brought the brig, which was the American privateer Polly, to action, and, after an engagement of three hours duration (by which time the Lowestoffe's Prize had arrived up and taken part in the contest) compelled her to surrender. Captain Rainier was wounded by a musketball through the left breast; he could not, however, be prevailed upon to go below, but remained on the deck till the close of action. He was posted, and appointed to command the 64-gun ship Burford." *(Battles of the British Navy Vol I., London, 1872)*

But for that musket ball, our mountain might well bear a different name. The fact that the namesake of their mountain had fought against American colonists did not sit well with the early pioneers, and they were quite vocal in saying so.

Then along came another name struggle, this one from the south. One Hall J. Kelley thought all the West Coast volcanoes should be named after former U.S. presidents, and that the range name should be changed to the "President's Range." T. J. Farnham, in 1843 picked up on this idea, modified the plan to change the name of Mount Baker to Mount Tyler, and Mount Rainier to Mount William Henry Harrison. This plan never got far, due to lack of maps and confusion over all the other mountains and their names. Along a similar vein, members of the Grand Army of the Republic wanted to call it Mount Lincoln.

The debate over the name of the great Mountain raged on for over fifty years. In Seattle it was called Mount Rainier, and in Tacoma, the Northern Pacific Railroad was behind the drive to change the name to (Mount) Tacoma, or as many people spelled it, "Takhoma." It was a bitter battle that went all the way to the U. S. Congress.

In 1894, a man named Kirk Munroe suggested a compromise. Perhaps, he suggested, it could be called "Taconier" or "Raicoma." In 1924, the Thurston County Pioneer and Historical Society published a book called *The Great Myth - Mount Tacoma* in which they make a convincing case that "Tacoma" is *not* an Indian word.

A Rainier Comes to the Mountain

Our mountain's namesake, Peter Rainier, never even set foot in America, let alone on the mountain. But July 21, 1935 one of his relatives finally did make it to Peter's moniker bearer. John Loudon Rainier, 74, "the great grandson of Old Peter's brother" stood at Paradise, and declared the majestic peak "magnificent beyond words!" He explained the he was about the best the Rainier family could deliver, since old Peter had never married, and thus left no descendents. He did point out one apropos fact that got lost in history. He stressed that his surname should be pronounced "Rain-i-e-r, as in rainy-er weather."

The Name Nisqually

If Tacoma/Tahoma and its variant spellings were the most common names a hundred years ago, Nisqually and its variants had to be a close second. The name derived from the Nisqually Indians and the region bordering the Nisqually River. Variations of the name included Nasqually, Naskwalli, N'skwali, Nesqually, Nesquallie, Nisqualli, Askwalli, Squally-o-bish, Squalliamish, Si-qwal-it-chie and Qualliamish. Squalli was the name of the prairie grass that grew along the lower river banks. Rather than grass, some Indians (of the Nisqually Tribe) said the word referred specifically to the tops and flowers of the roots and herbs which grew quite thick, and moved in a wavy motion when the wind blew. Still another old manuscript said the name is Sqwalia'bsh, the people of the Tu sqwa'le, meaning "tops of wild carrots." The early settlers solved the name problem by calling the glacier, river, and tribe - "Nisqually".

Names of the Mountain

Each local tribe had a slightly different designation for the mountain. Among their titles were: "breast of milk-white waters," "mother of waters," "snow- covered mountain," "great white mountain," or "near the sky," There were many variations in spelling of Tacoma, among them: Tah-ho-mah, Tacoman, Ta-Y-Ma, Tahoma, Tahobah, Tahome, Takhoma, Tak-ho'ma, Takhobah, or Ta-ho'ma, Takoma, Tacob, Tacobe, Tacobud, Takob, Takobet, Takobed, Takkobad, Tahkobed, Takom, T'koma, Tkomma, Takober, Tacope,

T'kope, Tkohph (white), Tacopa, Takeman, Tu-Ah-Ku, Tuwouk, Tah-Ho-Mah, Kobah, Dahkobeed, Duk-hwahk, Duhhwahk, Puak-coke and Takhoma Wynatchie. Dr. William Tolmie said that one tribe called it "Puskehouse," while another said it was "Tiswauk." In 1881, twenty elderly Indians were invited to the Tacoma office of Elwood Evan, a historian and writer, for the purpose of gleaning their knowledge of the name of the mountain and its meanings. The number two Indian gave him the same combination of syllables to describe the mountain, but no two of the others agreed on the pronunciation (thus all the variant spellings). To the Puyallups it was "Takkobad", to the Nisquallys - "Tacobud", "Tahoma" to the Klickitats, "Takbobah" to the Samish, and "Duh-Hwahk" to the Lummis. They did however, all agree that the mountain was the source of nourishment from the many streams coming from the slopes. *(TNT 3/14/79)*.

Among settlers, there was little agreement on what to call the big peak too. Old history books show it referred to as Mount Wynatchie, Mount Seattle, Mount Tahoma, Mount Tacoma, Mount Puyallup, Mount Orting, "The Mountain that was God," "Old He," Mount "Big Snow," "The Great Snow," Snow Peak, "Mountain in the air" and "the Great Pyramid of the United States." Old S. F. Emmons, second to climb the peak, called it "Tachoma." For years, the only point of agreement, was that to everyone, it was "THE Mountain!"

Mount Rainier Namesakes

Not only are countless Washington businesses and real estate entities named for Mount Rainier, the mountain also has a town named after it. The tiny hamlet of Rainier is situated in Thurston County on the Tenalquot Prairie on the south side of the Fort Lewis Military Reservation. It's a former sawmill town that was given its name in 1884 by the Northern Pacific Railroad. (The town) Rainier's zip code is 98576, but if you want your letter to be delivered at Mount Rainier, (Longmire) better mark it 98397.

A section of the U.S. Military Reservation at Fort Lewis is called the "Rainier Training Area." It was established during World War II and named for Mount Rainier, and has an eye-popping view of its namesake from the area.

Two areas in south Seattle also bear the name. The former Rainier Avenue (now Martin Luther King Way) runs the length of Rainier Valley through the Rainier District to Rainier Beach. All of the above have knockout views of their namesake. Back when telephone prefixes had letters instead of numbers, the prefix for this area was RA for Rainier. Interestingly, the former Rainier Avenue sits atop a major earthquake fault.

Giant-volcano envying Oregonians also named a town Rainier. It sits just across the Columbia River from Longview, Washington. Minnesota wanted one too, but misspelled theirs, and it came out Ranier. California didn't want to be accused of copying, so they named their town Tahoma. We can forgive Hawaii for naming a town Volcano, since they have one of their own.

Mount Tahoma Namesakes

As Seattleites of old were busy naming everything in sight after Mount Rainier, Tacomans were just as busy naming everything Mount Tahoma. Mount Tahoma is a Tacoma neighborhood which lies south of South Tacoma Way, and east of Orchard Street (between South 56th and South 64th Streets. Mount Tahoma High School, which is part of the Tacoma School District, lies within the area. The name Tahoma/Tacoma graces dozens of Tacoma businesses, churches and buildings, as does "Mountain View" and Alta Vista and even an occasional "Rainier View."

Choosing Mount Rainier Place Names

By the time the white man came to the Mountain, the many features around the mountain had been known to the Indians by name for centuries. Bailey Willis was the first non-Indian to bestow names on features of the mountain as he explored the northwest corner of what is now the Park. He named Crescent Creek, Crescent Lake, Crescent Mountain, Crater Creek, Crater (Mowich) Lake, Liberty Cap, Meadow Creek, Mountain Meadows and Tolmie Lake. In 1916 U. W. history professor Edmund S. Meany began a massive effort to record all known area place names. Seven years later he produced the classic *"Origin of Washington Geographic Names"*.

In 1919 Park Superintendent Roger Toll made the first effort to standardize and organize the matter of park names. He wrote: "The Park Service is interested in having names applied to the various scenic points that are now unnamed. The most desirable names are the original Indian names, or if these are too long or unpronounceable, their English equivalents are often very good.

"If no original name can be found, and a name is to be supplied, the Indian names may be drawn upon with advantage, but this should be done by an expert. Descriptive names are very good. The only thing most difficult to avoid is the indiscriminate naming of scenic features after persons."

By 1932, the United States Geographic Board was publishing name decisions. *(#29 MRNP, WA, June 30, 1932)*. The state name board is the State Board of Geographic Names, Dept. of Natural Resources, Olympia, WA 98504.

Place Names

Many of the early explorers left their names or names of their choosing on features of the mountain. Stevens Canyon was named after Hazard Stevens, the son of the first territorial governor of Washington. He and P.B. Van Trump named a number of features around the mountain: Cowlitz Glacier, Crater Peak (Columbia Crest), Glacier Creek (Paradise River), Little Nisqually Glacier (Paradise Glacier), Nisqually Glacier, Peak Success and Sluiskin Falls.

J. B. Flett (after whom Flett glacier was named) was an early ranger from 1913 to 1921. He was a biology teacher in Tacoma Public Schools. He in turn named Basaltic Falls, Mystic Lake and Ptarmigan Ridge.

Lakes James, Eleanor, Marjorie, Oliver and Adelaide were named for the children of Thomas O'Farrell, one of the first rangers in the Park. They lived in Buckley. Lake Tom was named for O'Farrell himself. He in turn named Klickitat Creek and Knapsack Pass. Mount Ruth was named for Ruth Knapp. Her father was a prospector up on Mt. Ruth.

Mount Beljica, just outside the Nisqually Entrance, was named by James Longmire, using the first letter of the names of each of his kids.

Fryingpan Glacier, Ingraham Glacier, Moraine Park, Steamboat Prow and The Wedge were all named by geologist Israel C. Russell before the turn of the century. Jules Stampfler, early day guide, named Cowlitz Rocks, Edith Creek and Myrtle Falls.

Mazama Ridge. Mazama is the Spanish word for "mountain goat." It is also the name of the climbing club in Portland.

The name "Cascades" derives from the Great Falls of the Columbia, which have long since been drowned by Bonneville Dam. The Cascade Range runs from northern California to southern Canada. (*Reader's Digest,* May 1967).

Our Glaciers by any other Name

"Seven Great Glaciers Wiped Off Map, In Name, By Ignorant Government Clerks," read the 1910 Tacoma headline. Students of Mount Rainier geography had a collective case of apoplexy when a shipment of new government maps showed up with the glaciers renamed. Engineer Ricksecker's data was ignored in producing the new map, and the Winthrop Glacier had become the "White" Glacier. Other changes were:

North Mowich Glacier was changed to "Willis."

South Mowich Glacier was changed to "Edmunds."

White River Glacier was changed to "Emmons."

North Tahoma Glacier was changed to "Tahoma."

South Tahoma Glacier was changed to "Wilson."

Little Cowlitz Glacier was changed to "Williwakas."

Park engineers Chittenden and Ricksecker were rightfully upset over the changes, which they attributed to the "arbitrary action" of clerks in Washington. Charges also surfaced that in one or two instances, the clerks had used their own names with the intention of giving themselves a fame that was otherwise unattainable. The guilty clerk never was identified, but eventually most of the name changes were reversed, and the proper names restored. (*News, 8/6/10*).

"Fan" Names

What are Mount Rainier fans to be called? Can't call them Mountaineers, that great name is already taken. How about Rainierites, Rainierologists, Rainierophiles, or ...Rainieraholics?

Name Pronunciations

There's an old homily in Washington that once newcomers learn to pronounce Puyallup without stumbling, they're entitled to call themselves Washingtonians. (It's Pew-al-up).

> Cayuse (Ky-use) Nisqually (Nis-kwally)
> Chinook (Shin-nook)
> Steilacoom (Still-a-come)
> Mowich (Mow-witch)
> Tatoosh (Tat-two-sh)

Places named by The Mountaineers

The early users of the Park also left a legacy of names. Among names the Seattle club left are Avalanche Camp, Camp Curtis, (in honor of early photographer Asahel Curtis), Camp Hazard (in honor of Joe Hazard, chief guide early this century), Denman Peak, Denman Falls, Flett Glacier, Lake Ethel, Lake James, Meany Crest, Russell Cliff, Van Horn Creek and Weer Rock.

Critter Place Names Within the Park

Antler Peak, Bear Park, Bear Prairie, Bee Flat, Beehive Rock, Buck Creek, Cayuse (Chinook for "horse") Pass, Cougar Falls, Cougar Rock, Crow Creek, Deer Creek, Doe Creek, Eagle Peak, Eagle Cliff, Eagle's Roost, Fawn Ridge, Fish Creek, Frog Heaven, Goat Creek, Goat Island, Goat Lake, Goat Mountain, Henskin Pass, Horse Creek, Marmot Creek, Mosquito Flat, Panther Creek, Pigeon Peak, Ptarmigan Ridge, Sheep Lake, Sheepskull Gap, Unicorn Peak.

Mineral Names Around the Mountain

The prospectors also named features for minerals they found and hoped to find: Basalt Creek, Basaltic Falls, Carbon Glacier, Carbon River, Carbonado, Copper Creek, Copper Mountain, Crystal Mountain, Crystal Peak, Emerald Ridge, Gold Hill, Golden Lakes, Iron Mountain, Nickel Creek, Pearl Falls, Silver Creek, Silver Falls, and Silver Forest.

Mining Names Around the Mountain

The old prospectors also left us some intangible souvenirs in the names they bestowed on features around the mountain. Among them Anvil Rock, Copper Mountain, Fryingpan Glacier, Grindstone Trail, Iron Mountain, Knapsack Pass, Lodi Creek, Lodi Valley, Mineral Mountain, Packtrain Ridge, Panhandle Gap, Pickhandle Point (outside the Park), Prospector Creek, Sourdough Mountains and Starbo Camp.

Indian Place Names

One Indian legacy left at Mount Rainier is the names of many of the prominent places.

> Alki (soon, by and by) Crest.
> Cayuse (name derived from a war-like Indian Tribe inhabiting the

Inland Empire) Pass

Chenius (thought to be an Indian tribal leader chin-chin-no-wah)

Chinook (distortion of the original name of the Indian tribe 'Chenoke' who lived by the mouth of the Columbia River.)

Chutla (Nisqually Indian term meaning "rock") Peak

Cowlitz (originally 'Coweliskee' an ancestor of Chief Seattle, also an Indian Tribe.)

Eagle Peak was renamed from 'Simlayshe' Peak (meaning "eagle".)

Indian Bar - hunting place of Indian Henrys Hunting Ground (named for a Cowlitz Indian goat hunter whose real name was "Satulick")

Ipsut ("hidden place") Creek & Pass. The Indians pronounced it "Ipsoot."

Klapatche (a beloved Puyallup Chief) Park

Klickitat ("beyond" - for the tribe that lived beyond the mountains)

Mount Wow ("wow" was the Indian name for mountain goat and Wow had lots of them.)

Mowich ("deer") Lake

Nahunta (means "tall trees or timber". Name is from the Tuscanora Indians of North Carolina)

Nisqually (Indian tribe name)

Olallie ("little or berries - referring specifically to the salmonberry" The name was originally from the Bellebella language.) Creek

Ohanapecosh ("look down on something beautiful")

Owyhigh Lakes ("Owhi" - the name of a famous Yakama Chief and outstanding fighter.

Puyallup ("generous people, or people who added more") Glacier and River

Satulick Mountain ("a hunter")

Seattle Park (a chief on Puget Sound)

Sluiskin (Guide to Stevens and Van Trump) Falls and Mountain

Spunkwash/Spukwash ("many small streams") Creek

Squaw Lake at Indian Henrys (where Henry's wife camped while he hunted.)

Taidnapam ("people of the Upper Cowlitz")

Tamanos ("spirit or evil spirits, taboo") Mountain

Tatoosh ("nourishing breast") Range

Tenas ("little) Creek

Tillicum ("people") Point

Tipsoo ("grassy") Lake

Tumtum ("heart") Peak

Tyee ("chief, head man") Peak

Upthascap (the Carbon River)

Wahpenayo Peak (one of Indian Henry's father in laws)

Wapowety Cleaver: (Kautz's Guide)

Wauhaukaupauken ("spouting water") Falls

Whulge (the salt water of lower Puget Sound)

Yelm (from the Salish chelm or schelm) ("heat waves") It referred specifically to the radiations seen when looking across a flat surface. To the Indians, this was a visible manifestation of the Invisible Power (Great Spirit) in the sky.

Another fun day at Mount Rainier

Ken Hopping photo

Glaciers

"The life of a glacier is one eternal grind." -John Muir

Mount Rainier has one of the largest glacial systems in the world radiating from any single peak (roughly 35 square miles or 90 square kilometers.) These icy tentacles amount to about nine percent of the total park area, and a volume of about two cubic miles. There are 27 glaciers currently classified as such by the Park Service, plus about 50 small nameless glaciers and permanent snowfields on the mountain. There are a combined total of 22,747.9 acres of Glaciers and snow patches. *(USGS, Driedger and Kennard, 1984)*.

According to USGS, "the snow and glacier mantle is greater in volume than that of all other Cascade Range volcanoes combined." During the last glacial period, the great glaciers of Mount Rainier extended 15 to 40 miles from the mountain.

Scientists estimate it takes no more than 50 years for ice to travel from the top of the mountain to the terminus.

Aside from their beauty and recreational value, the glaciers are important for an economic reason as well. They are immense water banks. The U.S. Geological Survey says the glaciers contain as much fresh water as that in all the state's lakes, rivers and reservoirs combined.

Named Glaciers (starting at Northwest corner of the Park)

North Mowich Glacier (Tyler or Willis Glacier) is the northernmost of the west side glaciers. It is nearly 2 miles long, considerably shorter than when it was mapped in 1913 at 3-3/4 miles.

Flett Glacier, named in honor of botany Professor J. B. Flett, is situated to the west of Russell Glacier, separated from it by a cleaver which descends from Observation Rock. It is less than a mile in length and is one of the smallest named glaciers in the park.

Liberty Cap Glacier this "hanging glacier" is 300-foot thick ice-falls which forms the upper part of Liberty Wall.

Russell Glacier, above Spray Park, is named in honor of Professor Israel C. Russell, who was the first scientist to study thoroughly the mountain's glaciers. Russell is one of the larger interglaciers, and has two promontories, Observation Rock (8,364 feet) and Echo Rock (7,862 feet) which stand above it.

Carbon Glacier is over 4-1/2 miles long and contains the mountain's thickest ice (700 feet thick at the 6,200 foot level). The Carbon Glacier reaches the lowest elevation of any glacier in the lower 48 states (3,000 feet). It is so-named because of its black uncharacteristic appearance. It is the protective mantle of this dark rock debris which protects this low-elevation glacier from retreating more than it has. The Carbon Glacier terminus moves very little, but the terminus has changed in size.

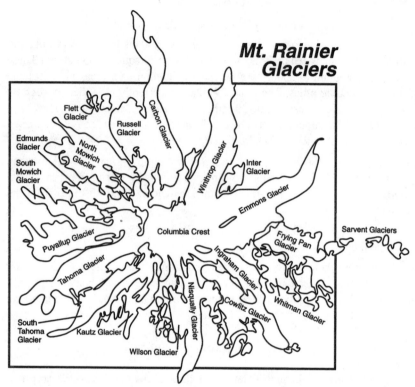

Mt. Rainier Glaciers

Winthrop Glacier (White Glacier) on the northeast side, is named for Theodore Winthrop who passed by the area in 1853 and recorded his observations in his book entitled *The Canoe and the Saddle*. Originating at about the 10,000 foot level, it remains relatively unchanged in terminus point. The noteworthy things about the Winthrop are the spectacular ice cascades, and 50-60-foot high domes. These phenomenon are attributed to a very uneven bedrock base which causes the glacier to stress and convolute as it passes over the rough underlayment. Another peculiar phenomenon are the rock tables which resemble giant toadstools.

Emmons Glacier (Blaine or White River Glacier) named for Samuel Franklin Emmons, geologist, explorer and second (with A. D. Wilson) to climb Rainier in 1870. The Emmons Glacier is 6 miles long, 2 miles wide and covers an area of eight square miles. It is the most impressive and expansive of all the glaciers. It blankets the entire northeast flank of the mountain.

InterGlacier (The Wedge) Between the Winthrop and Emmons Glaciers, this typical InterGlacier slopes northwest off Steamboat Prow. It was named by Prof. I.C. Russell and his party in 1896.

Fryingpan Glacier is an interglacier which covers about 1-1/2 square miles of the northern half of the Little Tahoma wedge. Contrary to the name, it is not fryingpan shaped, but instead is triangular. Whereas the waters of the Ohanapecosh Glacier right next to it flow to the south and eventually into the Columbia River, these waters flow north into the Fryingpan Creek, a branch of the White River, which flows into Puget Sound.

Ohanapecosh Glacier (Serviss Glacier) faces east. It's wider than it is long. It sits in an amphitheater it once filled, but now is a shrunken stagnant ice mass.

The stream issuing from it is the headwaters of the Ohanapecosh River which in turn, turn into the true head of the Cowlitz River. Pumice is present on moraines older than 148 years, but not on moraines younger than 114 years.

Ken Hopping photo

Sarvent Glaciers, two glaciers named in honor of H.M. Sarvent, the engineer who made the first detailed map of the mountain. These glaciers lie at the end of a backbone roughly 5 miles long that runs from Little Tahoma to the Cowlitz Chimneys. They are of special interest because they are the most distant glaciers from the peak of Rainier, and because they originate well below 7,000 feet. They prove that the Mount Rainier winter snows are sufficient to maintain independent ice bodies on ridges of only moderate altitude.

Whitman Glacier (The Wedge) On the eastern slope of the mountain below Little Tahoma. The Whitman is south-sloping and takes a lot of afternoon sun. It terminates at about 7,100 feet and below it lie several detached ice fields which used to be connected. The Whitman used to be considerably larger than it is today. It was named in honor of missionary Dr. Marcus Whitman, who, with his wife and twelve others, were murdered by the Indians near Walla Walla in 1847.

Ingraham Glacier is named after Major E. S. Ingraham. It is a long narrow glacier which flows down the southeast side of the mountain between Little Tahoma and Disappointment Cleaver on the northeast, and Gibraltar Rock and Cathedral Rocks on the southwest. At 6 miles long, it is one of the longest glaciers on the mountain. The Ingraham was known briefly as the Serviss Glacier.

Cowlitz Glacier adjoins the Paradise Glacier, to the west, and the Ingraham Glacier to the east. The glacier originates beneath Gibralter Rock and receives its sustenance from direct precipitation and wind drifting. It culminates in the Muddy Fork of the Cowlitz River, and its waters ultimately flow to the Columbia River, not Puget Sound.

Stevens Glacier was a branch of the Paradise Glacier, and fed Stevens Creek. Today it has all but disappeared.

Paradise Glacier (Little Nisqually Glacier) is one of the lower glaciers, starting at an elevation of only 9,000 feet. It is an interglacier, located between the Nisqually to the west, and the Cowlitz to the northeast. An 1896 map shows the Paradise Glacier about one-half mile from Sluiskin Falls and an easy walk from Paradise. As the century progressed, the glacier retreated up the mountain, and separated into upper and lower sections. The once vast ice caves shrunk into unstable crawl spaces, and finally in 1991, the ceiling of the last cave collapsed.

Photo courtesy Pemco, Webster& Stevens Collection, Museum of History & Industry

The Nisqually Glacier used to come to where the bridge is now

Nisqually Glacier is the best known, most viewed, and most studied glacier in the nation, though by no means the largest. It is 5 miles long, and at Paradise Valley is half a mile wide. It originates at the summit, where it is white and fairly smooth, though by the time it reaches the lower reaches, it is crevassed and dirty with dust, pollution and broken rock. It drops almost 10,000 feet in a little more than four miles and is a relatively steep glacier.

Six of Mount Rainier's glaciers are larger than the Nisqually, and cover about 1.8 square miles. The Nisqually Glacier has one of the longest and most complete study records in the western hemisphere, both in terminus position observations, and ice-surface altitude measurements. A significant thinning of ice has occurred since the mid-1980's.

Wilson Glacier is located to the west of the Nisqually Glacier and east of the Van Trump. It is named after Doctor A.D. Wilson of the U.S. Geological Survey who made the second climb of the mountain. The Wilson is fed by ice flowing east and avalanching onto it from a divide on the upper Kautz Glacier at about the 11,600 elevation.

Van Trump Glacier named after P. B. Van Trump, this interglacier is situated on the south side of the mountain behind the Kautz and Nisqually Glaciers. In glacial times, this glacier had at least six lobes, most of which extended into the region known as Van Trump Park. The Van Trump is now a stagnant body.

Williwakas (Little Cowlitz) Glacier has melted away. It was on the southeastern slope of the mountain, flowing from the Paradise Glacier. The little stream emanating from it was known as Williwakas Creek. The name was shortened from the Indian name for the glacier which was Williwilliwakus.

Muir Snowfield is the vast snowfield between Camp Muir and upper Paradise. Few people think of this as a glacier, but a number of people have died in crevasses on this "snowfield." Glaciologists warn Muir-bound hikers to anticipate increased crevassing. This is not a new phenomenon. In the 1940's or 50's a horse or mule fell in one and died. The Muir snowfield crevasses have been known to be 35 to 40 feet deep, can be 2-3 feet across, and frequently have running water at the bottom. The crevassing has worsened in recent years, and is especially bad in especially "hot" summers.

Kautz Glacier is immediately southwest of the Nisqually Glacier, and has about one quarter of its area. The Kautz has retreated over a mile since first mapped in 1913. It was the source of the October 1947 Jokulhaups which occurred after several days of intense rainfall.

Success Glacier heads in a south-facing cirque below Point Success. This small glacier supplies about 1/3 of the bulk of the Kautz Glacier.

Pyramid Glacier is so named because it is triangular. It is a small inter-glacier which lies north of Pyramid Peak and to the east of the South Tahoma Glacier.

Tahoma (North Tahoma) Glacier is a voluminous ice cascade coming from the summit rim joined by a flow from the Sunset Amphitheater to form the Tahoma Glacier. It has been called the most majestic glacier of the southwest side. More than a mile wide in places, it is distinguished by countless ice falls.

South Tahoma Glacier (Wilson) is another cirque-born glacier (at about the 10,800 foot level), although it is fed and replenished by direct snowfall. At nearly 4 miles in length, near the terminus, it tapers into a slender finger of stagnating ice.

Puyallup Glacier originates in a high cirque in the Sunset Amphitheater above the 12,000 foot level. Near its origin, the Puyallup Glacier first descends a narrow chute. It then expands to nearly 3/4 mile wide and a portion of its volume splits off to the South Mowich Glacier.

South Mowich Glacier is the shortest glacier on the west side.

Edmunds Glacier is named in honor of Senator George F. Edmunds of Vermont. When it was much larger, it had three long parallel lobes.

Mount Rainier Glacier Facts

The Eleven Primary Glaciers:

The Nisqually, Ingraham, Emmons, Winthrop, Tahoma, Kautz, Carbon, North Mowich, South Mowich, Puyallup and South Tahoma

The Secondary Glaciers:

Inter Glacier, Cowlitz, Paradise, Ohanapecosh, Fryingpan, Russell, Flett, Edmunds, Pyramid and Van Trump

Glaciers Which Originate at the Summit

The six are the Nisqually, Ingraham, Emmons, Winthrop, Tahoma & Kautz.

Natural Amphitheaters (Cirque-borne Glaciers)

Eight glaciers originate at cirques. They are:
> Nisqually Cirque (Nisqually Ice Cliff)
> North Puyallup Amphitheater
> South Mowich
> South Tahoma Glacier Headwall
> Success Glacier Couloir
> Sunset Amphitheater
> Willis Wall - Carbon Glacier
> Wilson Headwall Cirque

Four Glaciers Over Four Miles Long:

Ingraham	Winthrop
Carbon	Tahoma

How a Glacier Moves

Though glaciers appear to be static and unmoving, exactly the opposite is true. Geologists cringe at the term "rivers of ice," but to most "civilians," that is a good description of a glacier.

Geologically, glacial ice is classified as rock, rather than liquid. Thickness of the glaciers ranges between fifty feet to many hundreds of feet thick. They deform and flow continuously, influenced by shape of the bedrock on which they lie. Maximum speeds occur near the surface, and along the center line of the glacier. Flow rates are faster in summer than in winter. The Nisqually Glacier set a "speed record" in 1970, when it was measured at 29 inches per day. Annual measurements of the Nisqually's terminus position were begun in 1918, by Park Service personnel, and are now maintained by the (USGS) Geological Survey

Recent Glacial Advancing/Retreating

Glaciers are sensitive indicators of climactic changes. Over years, the terminus or snout, advances or retreats in relation to the amount of snowfall or melt. If snowfall exceeds the melt, the terminus advances whereas if the melt exceeds snowfall, the terminus retreats. Most glaciers have been retreating in the last 100 years. More rapid retreating began in the 1920's. The layers of snowfall can be measured much like tree rings.

Nisqually

The Nisqually Glacier has retreated and advanced three times between 1965 and 1992. The most recent period of retreat took place between 1985 and 1992. During this time, the glacier thinned by 52 feet in the area immediately west of Glacier Vista. Geologists believe that the retreat which has been occurring since the late 1980's may be slowing. The best place to view the terminus of the Nisqually Glacier is from Nisqually Vista, a short distance from the Paradise Visitor Center.

Cowlitz-Ingraham

More than 35,000 years ago, at its greatest reach, the Cowlitz extended approximately 65 miles downstream of the mountain,

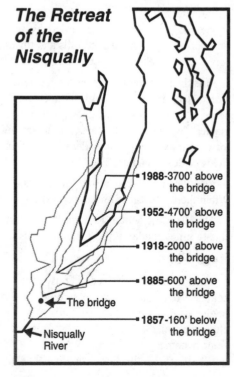

The Retreat of the Nisqually

1988-3700' above the bridge

1952-4700' above the bridge

1918-2000' above the bridge

1885-600' above the bridge

The bridge

1857-160' below the bridge

Nisqually River

nearly to the town of Mossyrock. In the mid-70's the Cowlitz-Ingraham made a notable advance which continued slowly into the mid-1980's. It is currently thinning and retreating.

Emmons Glacier

Since 1963, rock debris from the Tahoma Peak rockfall has insulated the glacier ice from melting. In the 1980's as a result of the decreased melting, the glacier advanced rapidly. That advance continues today, but at a slower rate. The ice beneath the rock debris is melting irregularly and forming a vast hummocky area.

Carbon Glacier

Of all the mountain's glaciers, the Carbon has the greatest measured thickness (700 feet) and volume (0.2 cubic miles) of any glacier in the contiguous United States. The Carbon has retreated less than 0.6 miles since the Little Ice Age. In the 1970's the Carbon began an advance which gave hikers the sight of watching vegetation being crushed by rocks rolling off the advancing terminus. The advance was brief, however, and the glacier is again undergoing a minor retreat. (C.L. Driedger, USGS, 1993)

Anatomy of a Glacier

In the Glaciers

Glaciers, like rivers of water, move more rapidly at the top and center than at the sides. Its speed is retarded by the friction of the sides. The resulting stresses create crevasses, ice falls and towering seracs. A bergschrund is the first crevasse or crack at the top of a glacier.

Inside a crevasse, the color ice ranges from white and granular to deep violet-black in the seemingly-bottomless depths. Crevasses can be 150-200 feet deep. In the summer, a glacier can move as much as 18" per day. A "dead glacier" is one which does not have enough gradient or slope to promote forward movement. Both Paradise and Ohanapecosh Glaciers are stagnant ice fields or dead glaciers. The Ohanapecosh has a clear "limpid" appearance.

How can a glacier move forward and yet become shorter at the same time? When there is less coming in (or on) than is going out at the bottom.

In 1913, the Mount Rainier glacier system encompassed a surface area of 40 square miles. Today it is 35 square miles.

Rock Flour

Inside the glaciers, rock is pulverized into grit and powder as boulders grind against each other under incredible pressure. At the terminus, as the icy river begins its race toward the sea, this rock flour is carried along, giving the water a chocolate milk or grayish color. It is not good to drink. Once deposited, rock flour becomes clay. The only Mount Rainier glacier-originated rivers which are not "milky" are the Paradise and Ohanapecosh, since they originate at "dead" glaciers. Since there is no movement within the glacier, the suspended boulders and rocks are not being ground up, and the resulting melt water is clear. Melt from snowfields also produces clear water.

Ice Worms and Watermelon Algae

Even the glaciers and snowfields sustain life. Watermelon algae is a microscopic plant (*Prococcus nivalis*) which lives its entire life above snowline, gives the snow a pinkish or rose-colored cast, and gives off the odor of ripe watermelon. Each patch embodies a colony comprised of billions of individuals. If there was a "Tough Critter" award, it would have to go to two tiny creatures who spend their entire lives in glacial ice and snowfields. The first are little black threadlike ice worms, (Mesenchytraeus solifugus var. rainierensis), and the second are ice springtails, (Thysanura), a low order flealike insect which can leap an inch or two. Conveniently, the one food they both eat is watermelon algae, the only other life form on the glacier.

On the Glaciers

Travel on a glacier should not be attempted by anyone who is not trained and equipped to navigate the giant deep-freezes. Invisible yawning crevasses hundreds of feet deep may lie beneath a thin snow cover. It may take several people to haul someone up out of a crevasse, and that's *IF* the victim survives the fall, is not injured, and *IF* the right equipment is available. Victims lose body heat and freeze to death quickly in a glacier. Mount Rainier glaciers have claimed many victims over the years. Don't become one of them. Unless trained and equipped, stay off the glaciers.

Stay away from the snouts too. They are particularly dangerous places for two reasons. First, rock and ice chunks continually rain down off the snout. Also, what you are standing on may not be dirt, but may instead be rock covered ice, which could collapse under you. Remember too, the river coming off the glacier is ice water.

Beside the Glaciers

Just as rivers of water strew their banks with logs and floating debris, glaciers deposit rocks. These side accumulations are called lateral moraines. Where two glaciers meet, lateral moraines combine to form a medial moraine toward the center, which is then the center of the now enlarged glacier.

Moraines are also indicators of glacier movement. Dating the age of the trees growing on moraines tells when the glacier last moved through. Measuring lichen growing on rocks on the moraines tells the same thing.

Below the Glaciers

Glacier snouts are particularly dangerous area. Rocks continually rain off them, and slabs of ice regularly break away. The rocks which are carried 'midstream' to the end of the glacier and dropped when the ice melts, form the terminal moraine. The terminus ("termini") below the snout of the glacier, is rock.

Old terminal moraines found down valley from glaciers, can help glaciologists determine the extent of glaciers at various times through history.

The "toe" of the glacier is really slowly advancing ice which is melting at roughly the same rate at which it advances. This, of course, is affected by climatic changes, temperature and snowfall. It is the climatic changes over the years that determine whether the glacier advances or retreats.

Extent of the Glaciers

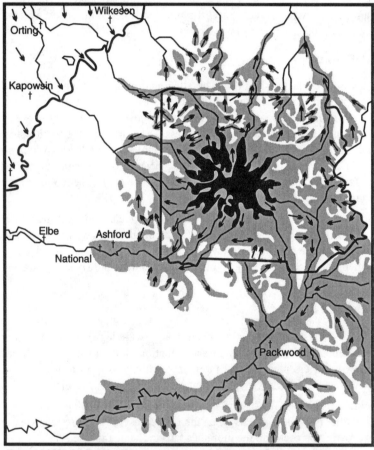

Extent of Mount Rainier Glacier between 15,000 and 25,000 years ago. Arrows indicate the direction of ice movement; solid black represents modern glaciers on Mount Rainier.

Beyond the Glaciers

During the last major glaciation (which ended about 10,000 years ago), the valley glaciers extended as much as 40 miles long, far beyond the present Park boundaries. The Nisqually, for instance, extended 30 miles from the mountain to the site of Alder Lake Dam. As hard as it is to envision, the ice was more than 1,600 feet thick over what is now the town of Elbe. (Driedger, USGS)

As the climate warmed, between 8,000 and 4,000 years ago, the glaciers became even smaller than they are today. Then about 3,500 years ago, in what is called the beginning of the Little Ice Age, a small expansion of the glaciers began again. We are still in the Little Ice Age, although the glaciers are now considerably smaller than they were 80 years ago. (Crandell & Mullineaux)

Striations

Striations are glacier-carved stripe-like scratches caused by the filing action of coarse rocks carried forward by the glacier. Some of the best examples are seen at Box Canyon and Panhandle Gap. Others are on the Skyline Trail near Panorama Point, the Van Trump Trail and on the Paradise Glacier Trail. In contrast, the action of fine-grained debris polishes the bedrock to a glassy smooth lustrous finish called glacial polish.

Tragically, some of the first thoughtless visitors to Box Canyon after the Stevens Canyon Road was opened in 1958 felt compelled to carve their names and other graffiti in the classic examples of striated glacial rock there. By 1965 the park had to conduct a variety of experiments in how to remove the inscriptions without ruining the natural glacial polish. Sandblasting left the rock looking unnatural. The job was finally accomplished by hand-rubbing the gouged names with pumice and Carborundum stones.

Also interesting to note, is that in the 1940's striated rocks were called "slickensides."

Avalanches

Avalanches in Washington and Oregon kill more people than any other natural hazard. Even small ones can be deadly. Many are triggered by their victims. A snowy slope can avalanche at any time of year. Spring avalanches are just as deadly as the winter variety. At Rainier watch for slab avalanches on south facing slopes on sunny days. Avalanches cannot be outrun since they can travel at up to 80 mph. The avalanche forecast system has four levels.

The First Glacier Study at Mount Rainier

In 1905, Professor J. N. LeConte of the University of California, measured the rate of movement of the Nisqually Glacier by means of a row of stakes and surveying instruments. He found that in summer it moved 16.2 inches per day at the center, while the margins, slowed by friction, moved more slowly. His measurements were taken by running a line from one lateral moraine to the other with a transit, then setting stakes across the glacier at short intervals, and measuring their daily advance.

Places

Amphitheaters (Natural)

Nisqually Cirque

Nisqually Ice Cliff

North Puyallup Amphitheater

South Tahoma Glacier Headwall

Success Glacier Couloir

Sunset Amphitheater

Willis Wall

Wilson Headwall Cirque

Archaeological Sites

In 1939 three Tacoma Eagle Scouts found an arrowhead 100 feet from the second of the Cowlitz Chimneys. The rangers at the time said this was only the third arrowhead to be found in the Park. *(TNT 8/6/32).*

Fryingpan Rockshelter is a small overhanging shelter on the southwest flanks of Goat Island Mountain near Summerland. At an elevation of 5,300 feet, it is the highest archaeological site in Washington State, and the only archaeological site excavated in Mount Rainier National Park. The rockshelter itself is one of the few cave-like formations on the mountain. It measures 35 feet long, 20 feet wide, and 15 feet deep. At least four layers of volcanic pumice and ash had fallen on the area.

The carbon-14 age determined for artifacts and faunal remains, was 300 to 1,000 years. (Faunal remains are tiny fragments of teeth and bones, many of which were charred by fire.) Bone knives and scrapers, and flakes of chalcedony, opal and jasper were also found buried at the site. The location was discovered by David R. Rice and Charles N. Nelson of Washington State University during a brief archaeological survey in August of 1963. It was excavated in 1965.

One of the most recent finds of Indian relics came in 1978 when John Dalle Molle, a ranger at Sunrise did some 'off the beaten track' exploration and found stone tools and Indian arrowheads in the Windy Gap area. He also found some in Elysian Fields and Vernal Park. Interestingly, the arrowheads were made from material not native to Mt. Rainier, but that isn't unusual, because it was common for the Indians to trade materials and carry the necessary core material.

The only other known archaeological find in the park was a projectile point about six thousand years old which was found in an exposed roadcut on the Stevens Canyon Road a short distance east of Louise Lake.

The Archaeological Resources Protection Act prohibits the removal, damage, alteration, defacing, or trafficking of archaeological resources on federal land.

Backcountry Suspension Bridges

Tahoma Creek (206' long) completed 1994

Carbon River (206' long) completed 1984

Ohanapecosh River to Grove of the Patriarchs

Bars

Indian Bar   Nisqually River Bar

Basins

Cataract Basin (Mist Park) on the shoulder of Mother Mountain
Cold (Gold) Basin (just south of Grand Park)
Edith Creek Basin (east of Alta Vista)
Goat Lick Basin. Fairy Falls is in this basin below Stevens Glacier
Glacier Basin 6000' at the base of Inter Glacier
Huckleberry Basin (N of Sunrise) on the other side of
    Sourdough Ridge
Kautz Basin. The area below Kautz Glacier.
"Upper Wycash Basin" is in the SE corner of the park *(TNT - 1913)*

Benches

"The Bench" is a natural rock bench 1-1/2 miles SE of Reflection Lakes, located between the Tatoosh Range and Stevens Canyon.

Bench Marks

A benchmark is a surveyor's starting point. They are used to establish elevations, then proceed measuring to the next one, and establish that one. The benchmarks are round brass caps 2"-3" in diameter, which are cemented to prominent rocks.

There are over 50 benchmarks within Mount Rainier National Park. (Different maps show different benchmarks. Over the years, some old one may have been removed, been moved, grown over, knocked loose, etc.)

On the Southwest side they are at the Nisqually entrance (2003'), Nisqually Road at the base of Tumtum Peak (2274'), Nisqually Road at the bend across from Bear Prairie Point (2488'), Narada Falls (4572'), Longmire (2761'), Carter Falls (3159') Nahunta Falls (3908'), Paradise (5557'), McClure Rock (7384'), Inspiration Point (4844') and Pinnacle Peak (6562').

On the southeast side, look for them at Reflection Lakes (4867'), Bench Lake (4336'), Stevens Creek (4015'), Martha Falls (4336'), Stevens Canyon (3392'), and Stevens Canyon Picnic Area (3067'), the Cowlitz Divide (5572'), Double Peak (6200'), and Sheepskull Gap. (5213'). Along the road between Box Canyon and the Park entrance there are several: Cougar Falls (2932'), (2815'), (2887'), (3034'), (3332'), (3295'), (3096'), and (2908'). There's one at the Park Boundary at (1715') and another by the Ohanapecosh Campground at (1928').The East Side Highway has several at (2093') above Ohanapecosh, (2208) above Silver Falls, (2307'), (2666'), (3232) and (3502') by Deer Creek. In the Northeast quadrant, they're at Cayuse Pass (4694'), south of the pass at (4487') and at Chinook Pass (5432'), Dege Peak (7006'). Between Cayuse Pass and the Park Boundary, they're at (4211'), (3920), (3686'), (3047') and (2749').

In the Northwest corner, they're at Tyee Peak (6030'), Tolmie Peak (5939'), Old Desolate (6995'), Observation Rock (8364') and the Colonnade (6995'). There's also one at 6,965 feet, above Sunset Park on the cleaver between the Puyallup and South Mowich Glaciers.

Bends

Horseshoe Bend (overlooking Narada Falls) Round Point.

Biblical Allusions

Ararat, (Frog) Heaven, Paradise, St. Andrews, St. Elmos, St. Pauls

Bridges

There are 31 bridges within the park of which 24 are historic road bridges. The most recently reconstructed bridges are the Laughingwater Creek Bridge on Highway 123 north of Ohanapecosh and the Deadwood Creek Bridge on SR 410 between White River Road Junction and Cayuse Pass, both rebuilt during the summers of 1994 - 1995. There are 577 front and backcountry trail bridges. There is also the Natural Bridge off the Lake James Trail.

Canyons

Edith Canyon	Muddy Fork (Cowlitz) Box Canyon
Kautz Box Canyon	Lost Trail Canyon
Paradise River Canyon (below Narada Falls)	
Stevens Canyon	Van Trump Canyon

Cascades

Canyon Rim	Paradise Cascades
Stevens Cascades	Stevens Ice Cascades
Washington Cascades	

Caves

There are three kinds of caves at Mount Rainier.

- Fluvial glacial caves, such as the old Paradise Ice Caves, which were caused by melt water and air currents
- Thermal steam caves on the summit, caused by the mountain's volcanic heat
- Natural caves in the earth

There are numerous shallow natural caves around the mountain, the largest is on Mother Mountain between the 4,000 to 6,000' level. There are also many old mine tunnels, which might be mistaken for caves (although most are boarded over or sealed in some manner.)

The closest cave outside the Park is Boulder Cave, 24 miles distant.

Washington Cascades

Chimneys

Cowlitz Chimneys

Chutes and Gullies

There are only three named chutes: Gibralter Chute, "the Chutes" and Kautz Chute. Wilson Gully is the only named gully.

Cleavers

Cowlitz Cleaver
Disappointment Cleaver
Kautz Cleaver
Liberty Ridge
Nisqually Cleaver
Puyallup Cleaver
Pyramid Cleaver
Steamboat Prow

Success Cleaver
Tahoma Cleaver
The Wedge
Van Trump Cleaver
Wapowety Cleaver
Whitman Crest
Wilson Cleaver

Cliffs

Andesite Cliff
Basalt Cliff
Colonnade Cliff
Eagle Cliff
Echo Cliffs
Faraway Rock
Mowich Face

Northern Crags
The Palisades
The Ramparts
Russell Cliff
Steamboat Prow (The Wedge)
Willis Wall
Yellowstone Cliffs

Creeks

The many turbulent streams and creeks emanating from snow fields, ice fields or glaciers, become swollen at midday and afternoon and are conspicuous in their beauty and fury. Others originate from springs, swamps and lakes. They radiate from the mountain in all directions, and rush headlong down the mountain toward the river which will carry their waters off to the sea.

Ada Creek
Basalt Creek
Berry Creek
Boulder Creek
Boundary Creek
Buck Creek
Butter Creek
Cataract Creek
Chenius Creek
Chinook Creek
Cougar Creek
Crater Creek
Crescent Creek
Crystal Creek
Dead Horse Creek
Deadwood Creek
Deep Creek
Deer Creek
Devil's Dream Creek

Kotsuck Creek
Laughingwater Creek
Lee Creek
Limpid Creek
Lodi Creek
Lost Creek
Maple Creek
Marmot Creek
Meadow Creek
Meany Creek
Moraine Creek
Mule Creek
Needle Creek (2)
Nickel Creek
Olallie Creek
Panther Creek
Paradise Creek
Pearl Creek
Pebble Creek

131

Dewey Creek	Pigeon Creek
Dick Creek	Prospector Creek
Doe Creek	Pyramid Creek
Edith Creek	Ranger Creek
Eleanor Creek	Rushingwater Creek
Evans Creek	Shaw Creek
Falls Creek	Spunkwash Creek
Fire Creek	Spray Creek
Fish Creek	St. Andrews Creek
Fishers Hornpipe Creek	Stevens Creek
Fryingpan Creek	Sunbeam Creek
Glacier Creek	Sunrise Creek
Goat Creek	Swift Creek
Granite Creek	Tahoma (Rainy) Creek
Grant Creek	Tatoosh (Clear) Creek
Hank Creek	Tenas Creek
Hayden Creek	Tolmie Creek
Huckleberry Creek	Twin Falls Creek
Inter Fork	Unicorn Creek
Ipsut (Ipsoot) Creek	Van Horn Creek
Irish Creek	Van Trump Creek
Jim Creek	Viola Creek
Joe Creek	Whittier Creek
Josephine Creek	Williwakas (Little Cowlitz) Creek
June Creek	Winthrop Creek
Kautz Creek	Wright Creek
Klickitat Creek	Yakima Creek

Drainages

There are five major drainages on Mount Rainier:

- The White River on the northeast (flows to Puget Sound)
- The Nisqually River on the south (flows to Puget Sound)
- The Puyallup River on the west (flows to Puget Sound)
- The Carbon River on the north (flows to Puget Sound)
- The Cowlitz River on the southeast (drains to the Pacific Ocean by way of the Columbia River)

Three of the river systems (White, Puyallup, and Carbon) join downstream.

Erratics

Erratics are boulders which are carried along and then deposited by glaciers. There are many within Mount Rainier National Park.

Flats

Barn Flats - south of Paradise, west of Narada Falls
Bear Flat - NE corner of park facing Crystal Mountain

Flats (continued)

> **Bee Flat** - just south of Chenius Mountain
>
> **Cedar Flat** - between 2 branches of Ohanapecosh River, 1-1/2 mile N of Hot Springs. This area now is known as "Grove of the Patriarchs."
>
> **Grand Park** - Northern portion of Park NW of Sunrise
>
> **Mosquito Flat** - near Lakes James and Ethel

Drainage Divides

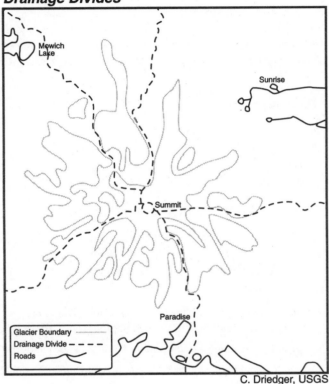

C. Driedger, USGS

Gaps, Passes and Divides (O = Out of Park)

Barnes Pass	**McClellan (Naches) Pass** (O)
Bear Gap (O)	**Martinson Gap** (O)
Cadaver Gap	**Naches Pass** (O)
Cayuse Pass	**Pacific Point**
Chinook Pass	**Packwood Pass**
Corral Pass (O)	**Panhandle Gap**
Cowlitz Pass (or Cowlitz Divide)	**Round (Halls) Pass**
Goat (s) Pass	**Saint Elmos Pass**
Ipsut (Ipsoot) Pass ("Saddle")	**Sheepskull Gap** (O)
Kirkland Pass	**Success Divide**
Knapsack Pass	**Windy Gap**

Grove of the Patriarchs

1/4 mile inside the Stevens Canyon entrance, an easy 2-mile round trip hike leads to the Grove of the Patriarchs. This magnificent old-growth grove contains 36 trees over 25 feet in circumference, some over 300 feet tall, and all estimated to be between 800 to 1,000 years old. The stand contains Western hemlock, Western red cedar and Douglas firs. Some hemlocks stand as if on tippy-toe, on giant fork-like roots with the nurse logs that nourished them having decayed out from under them centuries ago. Somehow, fires that repeatedly ravished the forests all around the area, skipped this island stand in the middle of the Ohanapecosh River. Black scars on the bark of some of the giants show how close the flames came though. An earlier name for the area was "Red Cedar Grove".

Historic Districts

There are six historic districts in the park.

1. Nisqually
2. Longmire
3. Paradise
4. Sunrise
5. Camp Muir
6. White River

Historic Landmarks & Places in & around the Park

There are 103 historic structures in the park, including fire lookouts, trail shelters, patrol cabins, bridges, comfort stations, park entrances, administrative buildings, quarters and a chlorination house at Edith Creek.

National Historic Landmarks are:

Longmire, Longmire Buildings (Administration Building, Community Building and Service Station) [NHL 05/28/87]

Paradise, Paradise Inn, Mount Rainier National Park [NHL 05/28/87]

Sunrise, Yakima Park Stockade Group, Mount Rainier National Park [NHL 05/28/87]

National Register of Historic Places are:

Ashford Vicinity, Ashford Mansion, Mount Tacoma Canyon Road, West of Echo 1 [NR 08/30/84]

Eatonville, John Galbraith House, 140 Oak Street East [NR 03/19/82]

Elbe, Elbe Evangelical Lutheran Church, [NR 10/08/76]

Longmire, Longmire Buildings (Administration Building, Community Building and Service Station*), Mount Rainier National Park [NR 05/28/87]

Melmont, Fairfax (O'Farrell) Bridge, Spans Carbon River south of Wilkeson [NR 10/13/87]

Paradise, Paradise Inn, Mount Rainier National Park [NR 05/28/87]

Sunrise, Yakima Park Stockade Group, Mount Rainier National Park [NR 07/28/87]

Wilkeson vicinity, Walker Cut Stone Company, East of Wilkeson [NR 06/07/78]

Determined Eligible for National Register

Longmire, Longmire Cabin, Mount Rainier National Park [Elig. 11/17/78]

State Register of Historic Places

Carbonado vicinity, Upper Fairfax Historic District, Upper Fairfax-Carbon Glacier Road [SR 05/21/82]

Greenwater vicinity, Naches Pass Wagon Road, East of Tacoma off WA 410 [SR 02/13/70]

Puyallup vicinity, Indian Cemetery (Leschi's Grave), 45-PI-100H, off WA 99 northwest of Puyallup [SR 02/13/70]

*The Old Gas Station (originally called "the Oil Station") was constructed at Longmire by Standard Oil Co. It is a copy of a station in Yosemite National Park.

List of Classified Structures

Mount Rainier National Park [1976] Historic Preservation Div., NPS.

Patrol Cabin at Indian Henrys,* built 1916.

*In 1978, under the direction of Willi Unsoeld, 300 lb. footings were hauled in to the Indian Henry cabin, and set in place to stabilize the cabin.

Historic Places Outside the Park

Alder Lake is the lake formed behind Alder Dam.

Bear Prairie, 3 miles south of Longmire

National Townsite, (near Ashford) between the late 1800's and early 1900's was the site of a large sawmill and home to 4,000 people. All that remains is a small portion of the old mill pond.

Information Centers

- **Longmire** Longmire Museum
- **Paradise** Henry M. Jackson Memorial Visitor Center
- **Ohanapecosh** Ohanapecosh Visitor Center
- **Sunrise** Sunrise Visitor Center
- **Carbon River** Carbon River Ranger Station

Irish Cabin

In 1926, a group of Tacoma Mountaineers discovered an abandoned miner's cabin about one-fourth of a mile outside the Carbon River Entrance. It was called Irish Cabin in honor of the miner of that name who worked the mines on the mountainside behind the cabin and built the cabin in the late 1890's. It took until 1926 for the group to get permission from the Manley-Moor Lumber Company, the then-owners, to use the premises.

In 1937 the cabin and its 18 acres of land were purchased by the Tacoma Mountaineers for $300. To the original building, the club added a kitchen, recreation room and men's dormitory. For several decades, the cabin was home base for all the Mountaineer's activities on the north side of the mountain. It was the base for climbing and hiking in and around the northwest corner of Mount Rainier. The climbers identified 24 peaks and established routes to the "Irish Cabin Peaks."

From after World War II until the early 1970's, Irish Cabin was the site of an annual Thanksgiving Dinner served to over 100 diners. In the winter of 1955, the Carbon River's annual flooding ravaged the road, surging onto Irish Cabin property, moving tons of boulders and debris through the underpinnings of the cabin. Miraculously, when the river returned to its former braided channels, the cabin still stood. Unfortunately, it couldn't withstand the vandalism, break-ins and thefts of gear and supplies which were to come in the following decades. The effort and expense of surveillance, and having constantly to carry back and forth all valuables (generators, tableware, lamps, etc.) soon became too burdensome for a volunteer organization.

Sadly, use of Irish Cabin was finally abandoned and the cabin was demolished in 1980. All that's left of it now is the land, and the name, which lives on in the "Irish Cabin Peaks Pins." *(Mountaineer Bulletin)*

Islands within the Park

Glacier Island, on the southwestern slope of the mountain, actually was an island as late as 1940. this former island lies between the lower parts of the Tahoma and South Tahoma Glaciers.

Goat Island Mountain a round topped 7,301' peak bounded by the White River, Fryingpan Creek, the Fryingpan Glacier and the Emmons Glacier.

Goat Island Rock This is in the lower portion of the Carbon Glacier, in the northwestern area of the Park.

Grove of the Patriarchs, A magnificent virgin grove of Douglas Fir, Western Red Cedar and Western Hemlock located on a small island in the Ohanapecosh River. Some trees in this grove are 1,100 years old.

Silvan Island, so-named by Professor J. B. Flett, is on the south side of the Emmons Glacier.

Lakes

There are 292 permanent and 84 seasonal lakes within Mount Rainier National Park. These lakes have 663.378 (permanent) acres of water, and 18.498 acres intermittent. (These latter figures are a 1990 GIS calculation.) Of the total 376, only thirty were stocked with trout, until 1972 when stocking was discontinued. Lake and stream water is naturally somewhat acidic, but its pH is not at dangerous levels for fish.

The largest and deepest lake in the park is Mowich Lake, at 57 feet deep, and 122.6 acres in size. It is exceptionally clear, and one can see to the bottom with a Secchi disk. Fish are Cutthroat, Eastern Brook and Rainbow Trout. Mowich Lake is at an elevation of 4929'.

Other large lakes are Crescent Lake (20 acres) and Mystic Lake (9 acres). On the Northern Loop Trail there's Lake James (11 acres), Lake Ethel (21 acres), Marjorie Lake (11 acres), Oliver Lake (20 acres), and Adelaide Lake (8 acres).

Golden Lakes are 15 or more small lakes, comprising the headwaters of Rushingwater Creek. They were so named because of their resplendent golden sunset displays.

A tarn is a small shallow lake in a glacier-carved basin. Shadow Lake at Sunrise is an example of a tarn. The most photographed lake is Reflection Lake.

Lakes

Adelaide Lake	Lake of the Clouds
Aurora Lake	Lake Tom
Bear Park Lake	Louise Lake (Balch Lake)
Bench Lake	Lower Crystal Lake
Blue Lake	Lower Palisades Lake
Burnt Park Lake	Marjorie Lakes
Chenius Lakes	Marsh Lakes
Christine Lake	Mirror Lakes
Cliff Lake	Moraine Park Lake
Clover Lakes	Mowich Lake (Crater Lake)
Coplay Lake	Mule Lake
Crescent Lake	Mystic Lake
Croquet Lake	Oliver Lake
Crystal Lake	Owyhigh Lakes
Deadwood Lakes	Pan Lake
Dewey Lake	Princess Lake
Dicks Lake	Reflection Lakes
Elbow Lake	Shadow Lake
Elysian Fields Lakes	Sheep Lake
Eunice Lake (Tolmie Lake)	Shriner Lake
Fan Lake	Snipe Lakes

Fir Lake	Snow Lake
Forest Lake	Squaw Lake
Frozen Lake	St Andrews Park Lake
Goat Lake	St Jacobs Lake
Ghost Lake	Sunrise Lake
Golden Lakes	Sunset Lake
Green Lake	Three Lakes
Harry Lake	Tipsoo Lake
Hidden Lake	The Fan
Klapatche Lake	Tolmie Lake
Lake Allen (Lake O. D. Allen)	Tom Lake
Lake Eleanor	Upper Crystal Lake
Lake Ethel	Upper Johnsonl Lake
Lake George	Upper Palisades Lake
Lake James	

Little Tahoma

If 11,138-foot high Little Tahoma were an independent peak, it would be the third highest mountain in the state. Viewed alone, it resembles the Matterhorn. In reality, the jagged spire is an erosional remnant of the older higher Mount Rainier. It is also the high point of the wedge that separates the Ingraham from the Emmons glaciers.

As every mountain climber knows, "Little T" is notoriously "rotten rock." It's loose, unstable and has a nasty tendency of breaking off in your hands and disintegrating under your feet when attempting to climb it.

In 1963 it gave a graphic demonstration of its instability when four billion cubic yards of rock broke loose and avalanched down the Emmons Glacier for four and a half miles, stopping just 2000 feet short of the White River Campground. Rocks the size of boxcars and houses were carried on a cushion of compressed air at speeds estimated at between 100-125 miles per hour. One gargantuan rock measures 60 by 130 by 160 feet and weighs approximately 50,000 tons. The monstrous rock avalanche sailed 30' high over a stream-gauging station and left it untouched.

Long-lost Locations

Reading the old maps and journals reveals names of places which sometime are familiar, and other times are a mystery. Some places bear new names, and some names don't give a clue as to the location of the feature .

Here are some samples:

Olson's Cabin, a patrol cabin 7.0 miles from the Carbon River Entrance, 0.9 miles below Cataract Creek, at the 2,900' level.

Mesler's Ranch, -1 mile west of the Nisqually entrance, was a place where visiting scientists stayed.

Meadows

Elysian Fields   Mountain Meadows
Longmire Meadows

Mineral Marker

Back in 1951, in anticipation of acquiring the lands and in-park assets of Mount Rainier Mining Company in Glacier Basin, the National Park Service made appraisals of all structures and mines. The old U.S. Mineral Marker was a large rock marked "USMM #1148" located in the meadow near the old Glacier Basin Hotel. It was a starting point for the survey and appraisal.

Monuments and Memorials

Camp Schurman - Originally known as the Camp Schurman Memorial Shelter, there is a bronze plaque commemorating Clark E. Schurman, a beloved chief guide at the mountain.

Elevation Commemorative Plaque - Following the verification of the 1989 Satellite measurement of the mountain, a plaque with the new height of 14,411.1" was placed in Paradise Inn.

Marine Memorial - Commemorating the December 10, 1946 loss of a Marine Transport plane carrying 32 U.S. Marines which crashed on the upper slopes of the South Tahoma Glacier. There were no survivors and the Marine's bodies remain entombed in the glacial ice of Mt. Rainier. The plaque is at Round Point. Relatives of the victims meet at the mountain each year and place flowers on the plaque. *(TNT 6/19/82).*

Mather Memorial - by the Administration Building at Longmire.

The Mather Bronze Plaque reads:

Stephen Tyng Mather

July 4, 1867 - January 22, 1930

"He laid the foundation of the National Park Service defining and establishing the policies under which its areas shall be developed and conserved unimpaired for future generations. There will never come an end to the good he has done."

This plaque was unveiled July 2, 1932 at Chinook Pass, under the direction of Asahel Curtis, Chairman of the Rainier National Park Advisory Board, Governor Roland Hartley, and Doctor Edmund S. Meany of the University of Washington.

Washington State Historical Society photo

McClure Monument - "The Turtle" monument on Burroughs Mountain.

Meany Memorial - On Burroughs Mountain out of Sunrise, this memorial stone bench was erected and dedicated in 1936 to honor historian and Mountaineers president Edmund S. Meany, who died in 1935.

Mountain Troops Memorial - This plaque honoring the 10th Mountain Division is in the Paradise Flower Fields (on "Theosophy Ridge" beside the trail to Alta Vista,) where the troops held maneuvers in 1942.

Professor Russell Cairn - by the former terminus of the North Mowich Glacier near Division Rock. The glacier has receded a mile back since this marker was put in.

Stevens-Van Trump Historical Monument - a stone and concrete bench near Sluiskin Falls 1.5 miles NE of Paradise at an elevation of 5,900 feet, on the Skyline Trail to the old Paradise Ice Caves. Constructed in 1920 on the fiftieth anniversary of the pioneer's climb, this is also called "the 1870 Climbing Memorial," "The Monument" and "The Sluiskin Monument" which a 1920's Guide lists as the place where Chief Sluiskin waited for the return of the first summit climbers. It was co-built by the Mountaineers and the Mazamas.

T-33 Accident Memorial - A plaque dedicated to the memory of two McChord pilots killed in an aircraft accident on the mountain. It read: In memory of Col. Wilfred B. Crutchfield and Major Ivan E. O'Dell, USAF, April 15, 1968." It was placed on the East Wall of Paradise Inn

Tolmie Monument - near Mowich entrance, commemorated the 1833 arrival here of Dr. William Tolmie, the first white man to explore the area. This monument was dedicated September 2, 1933, 100 years after he came to the area, in the presence of Tolmie's son, Simon Fraser Tolmie, then Prime Minister of British Columbia. The small bronze plaque was mounted on a pylon of logs. It is now gone.

1981 Climbing Disaster Memorial - A plaque on the wall of the Paradise Visitor Center memorializes the eleven climbers who were killed in the 1981 icefall. A beautiful picture of the mountain on the plaque was made from film found in the camera of one of the dead climbers, Jonathan Laitone, 27, of Ann Arbor, MI. (TNT June 26, 1982).

World War II Memorial - An unusual Memorial Day observance was held in 1948 when a contingent of 10th Mountain Division veterans and friends made an early season climb to place a wreath on the summit in memory of all mountaineers killed in World War II. The party also used the event to spearhead a drive by the Mountain Cabin Memorial Association, led by Ome Daiber, to build cabins throughout the state as memorials to mountaineer servicemen. (TNT 5/26/48).

Wright Memorial. This plaque is on Aurora Peak near Klapatche Park. It is a bronze plate in memory of George E. Wright, and was dedicated by Mountaineers President Edmond Meany. The plaque reads "George E. Wright, 1867 - 1923, Citizen Mountaineer Friend Climbed Here On His Last Visit To the Hills. This Memorial Placed By The Mountaineers 1924.

Mount Rainier Parks

"The Parks encircle Mount Rainier like a wreath." - John Muir

Between the everlasting snows and timberline, lie large alpine meadows called parks. Tree islands are interspersed amid a sea of flowers to create a photographer's paradise. As if that weren't enough, this feast for the eyes is cast against the backdrop of shimmering white glaciers punctuated with contrasting dark rock outcroppings and ridges. Coming off the mountain like spokes on a wheel, the high parks are all separated by deep glacial valleys. Mount Rainier's parks are:

Aurora Park	Mountain Meadows
Bear Park	No Name Park
Berkeley Park	North Park
Burnt Park	Ohanapecosh Park
Chenuis Park	Paradise Valley
Cold Basin	Pyramid Park
Cowlitz Park	Sluiskin Park
Elysian Fields	St. Andrews Park
Glacier Basin	Seattle Park
Grand Park	Spray Park

Green Park   Summer Land
Huckleberry Park   Sunset Park
Indian Bar   Tatoosh Park
Indian Henrys Hunting Ground   Tipsoo Park
Klapatche Park   Van Trump Park
Lodi Valley   Vernal Park
Mist (Cataract Basin) Park   White River Park
Moraine Park   Yakima Park (Sunrise Park)

Other Mountain Ranges within the Park

Sourdough Range   Tatoosh Range
Sluiskin Range   The Palisades

Peaks Surrounding Mount Rainier

We denigrate these peaks by calling them "foothills", while the fact is that were they anyplace but where they are, they would be impressive mountains in their own right. The problem is that compared to the colossus beside them, the surrounding peaks are dwarfed. Most rise 3,000 to 4,000 feet above the valleys which divide them, but viewed from Puget Sound, Mountain Rainier seems to rise from sea level, and the surrounding peaks appear as insignificant.

Alki Crest 5200'   Mineral Mountain 6500'
Antler Peak   7017'   (First) Mother Mountain 6 480'
Arthur Peak 5465'   (Second) Mother Mountain 6387'
Aurora Peak   (Third) Mother Mountain 5804'
August Peak 4542'   Mount Ararat 6010'
Banshee Peak 7431'   Mount Fremont 7300'
Barrier Peak 6521'   Mount Pleasant 6454'
Beljica 5500'   Mount Rose
Bench Peak (Foss Peak) 6424'   Mount Ruth   8700'
Berry Peak 5112'   Mount Wow (Goat Mt.) 6040'
Boundary Peak 6700'   Muir Peak (unknown location)
Brown Peak 6322'   Naches Peak 6452'
Buell Peak 5933'   North Peak (Liberty Cap) 14,112'
Burnt Mountain   Observation Rock 8364'
(Third) Burroughs Mt. 8328'   Old Baldy Mountain 5795'
Castle Peak (near Mowich) 6116'   Old Desolate 7137'
Central Cowlitz Chimney 7421'   Palisades Peak 7040'
Chenius Mountain 5800'   Paul Peak 4809'
Chutla Peak 6000'   Peak Success (Pt. Success) 14,150'
Colonnade Peak 6965'   Pigeon Peak 3035'
Columbia Crest (Crater Pk) 14,411.1'   Pinnacle Peak 6562'
Copper Mountain 6303'   Pitcher Peak 5933'
Cowlitz Chimneys 7607'   Plummer Peak 6370'
Crescent Mountain 6715'   Poch Peak
Crystal Mountain 6306'   Pyramid Peak 6937'

Crystal Peak 6615'
Cushman Crest 5513'
Dege Peak 7006'
Denman ("That Mt") Peak 6006'
Dewey Peak 6710'
Dixon Mountain 5134
Eagle (Simlayshe) Peak 5,995'
Echo Rock 7870'
Fay Peak 6492'
Florence Peak 5508'
Goat Island Mt (Goats' Pk) 7288'
Gobbler's Knob 5,485'
Gove Peak 5310'
Governors Ridge 6600'
Governor's Needle 6500'
Hessong Rock 6385'
High Rock 5683'
Howard Peak 5720'
Iron Mountain 6200'
Jeannette Heights 7667'
K's Spire 8849
Lane Peak 6012'
Liberty Cap 14,112'
Little Tahoma 11,117'
Main Cowlitz Chimney 7605'
Marcus Peak 6962'
Marriage Peak 6,477'
Martin Peak 5000'
McNeeley Peak 6786'
Meany (Crest) Peak 7200'

Redstone Peak 5680'
Sand Mountain
Satulick Mountain 5574'
Scarface 6100'
Seymour Peak 6337'
Silver King 6998'
Skyscraper Mountain 7065'
Slide Mountain 6620'
Sluiskin Chief 7026'
Sluiskin Squaw 6960'
Sourdough Mountain 6900'
Stevens Peak 6510'
Sunrise Point 6100'
Sweet Peak 4500'
Tahoma Pk (Liberty Cap) 14,112'
Tamanos Peak 6790'
Tatoosh Lookout Peak 6310'
The Castle (Tatoosh Range) 6500'
Tillicum Peak 6654'
Tirzah Peak 5212'
Tokoloo Spire 7684'
Tolmie Peak 5920'
Tumtum Peak 4678'
Tyee Peak 6030'
Unicorn Peak 6917'
Virginia Peak 4934'
Wahpenayo Peak 6234'
Wallace Peak 6800'
Whitman Crest 9364'
Yakima Peak 6231'

Points, Vistas and Viewpoints

Alta Vista
Bear Prairie Point
Baker Point
Crown Point
Emmons Vista
Glacier Vista
Klapatche Point
Inspiration Point
Marmot Point
Mildred Point
Nisqually Vista
Observation Point

Oh My Point
Pacific Point
Panorama Point
Point Success
Rock Crusher Point
Ricksecker Point (Gap Point)
Sotolick (or Satulick) Point
Sunrise Point
Tahoma Vista
Tillicum Point
White River Junction

Prairies

Bear Prairie was the swampy area about a mile south of Longmire along the Nisqually River. James Longmire's trail from Yelm ended at Bear Prairie.

Goose Prairie is due east of the mountain on the Bumping Lake Road.

Mashel Prairie is due west of La Grande, just north of the Nisqually River. This was Indian Henrys stomping ground.

Smith Prairie is south of McKenna, and south of the Nisqually River.

South Prairie is northwest of Wilkeson and Carbonado.

Yelm Prairie is the large plain just east of the Fort Lewis Military Reservation. This is where James Longmire settled.

Ridges

Alki Crest	Mazama Ridge
Backbone Ridge	Meany Crest
Chenius Mountain	Moon Rocks
Colonnade Ridge	Mother Mountain
Cowlitz Chimneys	Packtrain Ridge
Cowlitz Divide	Ptarmigan Ridge
Curtis Ridge	Rampart Ridge
Cushman Crest	Ranger Ridge
Elizabeth Ridge	Rust (Rush) Ridge
Emerald Ridge	Sourdough Ridge
Fawn Ridge	Stevens Ridge
Governor's Ridge	Sunset Ridge
Independence Ridge	The Palisades
Ipsut Saddle	Theosophy Ridge
Klapatche Ridge	Whitman Crest
Liberty Ridge	

Rivers

A 1966 "official" GIS count, showed 470 rivers and streams within the park, with a combined total of 595.608 miles, plus 61.493 intermittent miles. Within these pages, we list every named river, stream and creek we could find, but try as we might, we didn't come up with anywhere near 470 watercourses. Mount Rainier's glacier-born rivers take on lives of their own once released from their icy wombs. The same river that's a shallow easy crossing in the morning, can be a raging, boulder-bouncing killer by late afternoon. Park visitors can readily see the power of water at several places around the mountain, but probably nowhere better than Box Canyon, where deceptively "small" Muddy Fork - Cowlitz River carved its channel 180 feet deep through solid bedrock.

The White River, descending from its point of departure high on the north side of Mount Rainier, once flowed north to Puget Sound through the Kent valley. In 1906 it jumped to a new channel during massive flooding, and now flows west into the Puyallup River. Construction eventually made the change 'permanent', but any major flow coming off the mountain could reroute it again into the low-lying Kent-Auburn valley leading north toward Puget Sound.

Between Enumclaw and Buckley, a side channel of the White River feeds Lake Tapps. From there it runs to the Deringer Power House, then through another channel back into the White River. Many call it the Stuck River, at that point, having gotten stuck with the channel.

The Carbon, flowing off the west side of Mount Rainier, has important runs of salmon and steelhead (outside the park) and flows through one of the most beautiful canyons in the state.

Rivers Originating at the Mountain

(Starting at northwest corner of the mountain, going clockwise)

South Mowich River flows from the South Mowich Glacier to join the North Mowich River in the northwest corner of the park.

North Mowich River originates at the North Mowich Glacier, flows three miles west and joins the South Mowich River.

Mowich River the combined stream of the North and South Mowich Rivers which connect just inside the park.

Carbon (Upthascap) River heads in the Carbon Glacier and also drains Russell Glacier through Cataract Creek. The Carbon ultimately flows into the Puyallup River.

West Fork White River rises at the foot of Winthrop Glacier on the north slope of the mountain.

InterFork White River rises at the terminus of InterGlacier on the northeast slope of Mount Rainier and flows through Glacier Basin.

White River the combined two forks meet and merge outside park boundaries.

Ohanapecosh River originates from the Ohanapecosh glacier and flows south and southeast into the Cowlitz River.

Muddy Fork Cowlitz River empties into the Columbia River below Portland 100 miles to the Southwest of the mountain.

Paradise River is a clear water river which originates at the Paradise Glacier and (former Ice Caves), and merges with the Nisqually River above Longmire. It was formerly known as Glacier Creek.

Nisqually River flows south and west 82 miles to Puget Sound. It is the boundary between Pierce and Thurston Counties.

South Puyallup River flows from the Tahoma Glacier

North Puyallup River flows from the Puyallup Glacier. These latter two rivers combine to form the Puyallup River, which is the main flow off the mountain.

Rocks

Anvil Rock 9584'	Goat Island Rock 5,300'
Bald Rock 5411'	Hessong Rock 6149'
Beehive Pinnacle 11,033'	K's Spire 8849'
Castle Rock 6116'	Little Africa* 8,695'
Cathedral Rocks 8,262'	McClure Rock (The Sphinx) 7384'
Cougar Rock 3180'	Monument 5,900'
Cowlitz Rocks 7457'	Moon Rocks 9480'
Division Rock 4,900'	Needle Rock 7575'
Echo Rock (Seattle Rock) 7862'	Observation Rock 8364'
Elephant Rock	Register Rock 14,350'
Fallen Rock	St. Andrews Rock 11,562'
(off TumTum Peak) 2,270'	Steamboat Prow (Wedge) 9702'
Faraway Rock 5,300'	Sugarloaf
Fuhrer Finger 11,200'	Thumb Rock 10,500'
Fuhrer Thumb	Tokoloo Rock 7675'
Gibralter Rock 12,679'	Weer Rock
Glacier Island 7651'	

*The large rock above Paradise at 9584' level was named for its anvil shape. The rock outcroppings just below it are named Moon Rocks and Little Africa

Slides

"Landslide," an area on the northwest side of Slide Mountain (east of Grand Park)

1963 Slide off Little Tahoma. A steam-explosion oriented rockfall which carried 4-billion cubic feet of rock avalanche debris from high on Little Tahoma 4-1/2 miles down the Emmons Glacier.

"Devil's Slide" off north end of Mother Mountain. This one was so big, it was heard at Fairfax in 1906! Another slide occurred in the same area in 1968.

The White River Road near the intersection of the Naches Highway. A 1935 landslide of unprecedented proportion devastated this area.

Above the White River "Y". A massive 1942 slide about 400 feet long occurred about 1-1/2 miles above the Y.

Willis Wall Slide. The remains of the massive slide that "made bare the face of the wall" in 1911 can still be seen covering the Carbon Glacier today.

Winthrop Glacier. This massive August 16, 1989 rockslide was the first such slide to be detected 100 miles away at the University of Washington geophysics lab.

Soda Springs

Three of the named springs at Longmire are Soda Spring, Pigeon Springs and Iron Mike Spring. Pigeon Springs was one of the warm springs at Longmire. They were so named because of the abundant game and birds (especially band-tailed pigeons) that drank from those springs. Pigeon Springs were on the far side of the meadow and at the north end of the toboggan slide.

The closest bigger soda springs are *outside* the park not too far from Ohanapecosh. From Ohanapecosh go south on State Route 123 to Highway 12. Turn left and watch for the first Forest Service road on the left. Follow FR 4510 past Summit Creek Campground, then past Fish Ladder Falls to Soda Springs Campground.

More springs east of the Mountain are at the Soda Springs Campground on the Bumping Lake Road off Highway 410. As the crow flies, they are about 24 miles from Cayuse Pass, about twice that if driving.

South of the Park, directly north of Packwood in the Tatoosh Wilderness Area, is Bum Springs. It can only be reached via Forest roads and hiking.

Springs - Other

There are numerous springs all around the mountain besides those at Longmire, but one which is significant is Lodi Spring in Berkeley Park. This spring formerly provided water to the facilities at Sunrise. The spring was covered by a picturesque pumphouse, which itself became a source of controversy. Some thought the tiny pumphouse was too sophisticated for the backcountry, and should have been designed to resemble an abandoned trapper's cabin. For many years now water for Sunrise has come from Frozen Lake.

Named fresh water springs are "Gallatin Spring" in Spray Park, and "Gorton Spring" at Mystic Lake. There are other unnamed springs at Glacier Basin and Sunrise Camp.

Swamps

The only true swamps in the park are limited areas around Longmire Springs, Reflection Lakes, and in Mountain Meadows. There are also swampy tracts along some of the watercourses in the park, including Tahoma Creek, the Ohanapecosh River and White River. There is also a marshy flat known as "Frog Heaven" one mile below Narada Falls in the Paradise River drainage.

Tunnels

Tunnel at Box Canyon   Stevens Canyon Tunnel
(East Side) Seymour Peak 512-foot tunnel (completed in 1938)

Pearl Falls

Valleys

Twenty eight valleys originate on the mountain. Among them are Carbon River Valley, Lodi Valley, Nisqually Valley, Paradise Valley, White River Valley.

Waterfalls

There are 122 waterfalls within the park, several of which are spectacular. Those viewable either from the road, or within a short walk are Narada, Silver, Christine, and Box Canyon.

Bear in mind waterfalls are gorgeous but dangerous places. The spray means that trails, roots, rocks and other surroundings are wet and slippery. Several people are killed each year in Washington State either by falling over, into or under falls, or by slipping into the swift churning waters at the base. Even strong swimmers have succumbed. Supervise children closely around all rivers, streams and waterfalls.

Several of the falls are either near the road or within sight of it. One, unfortunately, which is not, is Fairy Falls at the head of Stevens Canyon, which plummets 700 feet in 2 major drops." World Almanac listed this as the fifth highest waterfall in the United States. (Although those who have seen it in recent years dispute this.) The most spectacular waterfalls in the park are Comet Falls.

Comet Falls is on the west fork of Van Trump Creek . It was so named "because of the resemblance of the spreading 'tail' of a comet." The upper and lower falls have a combined fall of two hundred fifty feet.

Pearl Falls is on Pearl Creek in the southwest corner of the park. The falls and creek were so named by A. H. Barnes in 1912, because "droplets from the cascade resemble pearls under proper light conditions." Pearl Creek flows south into Kautz Creek.

Probably the most viewed, is Narada Falls on the way to Paradise. The Paradise River drops 168 feet over the falls into the Paradise River Canyon. There are several viewpoints along the stairway which leads from top to bottom.

Waterfalls *by* Name

It is claimed there are 168 waterfalls within the park. The named falls are:

Those marked with * are adjacent to the Wonderland Trail.)

Affi Falls	Martha Falls*
Alice Falls	Mary Belle Falls*
Basaltic Falls	Myrtle Falls
Bloucher Falls	Nahunta Falls
Boulder Creek Falls	Narada Falls*
Carter Falls*	Pearl Falls
Cataract Falls*	Phoebe Falls

Chenuis Falls	Ranger Creek Falls
Christine Falls	Ruby Falls
Comet Falls	Silver Falls
Cougar Falls	Sluiskin Falls
Cress Falls	Spray Falls*
Denman Falls	St. Johns Falls
Ethania Falls	Stafford Falls
Fairy Falls	Stevens Water Cascades
Falls of St. Andrews	Sunbeam Falls
Garda Falls	Sydney Falls*
Giant Falls	Sylvia Falls*
Horseshoe Falls	Tato Falls
Ipsut Falls	Tomlinson Falls
Kotsuck Creek Falls	Trixie Falls
Larrapin Falls	Twin Falls
Madcap Falls	Van Horn Falls
Maple Falls*	Washington Cascades
Margaret Falls	Wauhaukaupauken Falls*
Marie Falls	Williwakas Falls

Watersheds

There are nine watersheds within the park.

Carbon 25,884 acres	West Fork - White 17,281 acres
Huckleberry 13,741 acres	White 38,997 acres
Ohanapecosh 41,396 acres	Cowlitz 27,644 acres
Nisqually 37,791 acres	Puyallup 13,320 acres
Mowich 19,350 acres	

Wayside Exhibits

Wayside exhibits are at Box Canyon, Comet Falls, Inspiration Point, Ipsut Creek, Kautz Creek, Mowich Lake, Narada Falls, Reflection Lakes and Shriner Peak. Thirty new porcelain enamel signs for Trail of the Shadows and Grove of the Patriarchs were funded by Northwest Interpretive Association.

The Witness Tree

This historic Western red cedar tree at Longmire has the section, range and township inscribed on it, put there in 1870. The location is not public knowledge.

Mount Rainier Statistics

Mount Rainier's Location
  - The National Park covers an area of 378 square miles or 235,612 acres
  - The Park constitutes 1/180th of the land mass of Washington State
  - is 12 miles west of the crest of the Cascade Range
  - lies primarily in Pierce County, partially in Lewis County
  - is 54 air miles from Tacoma City Hall to the summit
  - is in the Pacific Time Zone
  - offers world-class climbing opportunities that have tested the skills of climbers for more than a century.

Mount Rainier is...
  - a stratovolcano
  - the largest U.S. stratovolcano south of Alaska that contains an active thermal system.
  - the largest volcano in the Cascade Range
  - the highest volcano in the Cascade Range
  - mantled by more ice (35 square miles) and snow than all other Cascade volcanoes combined
  - one of five volcanoes in the State of Washington that are currently between eruptions: Mounts Rainier, Adams, Baker, St. Helens and Glacier Peak.
  - the highest point in Pierce County
  - the highest point in Washington state
  - the Northwest's highest mountain
  - visible for a distance of 150 miles on a clear day
  - a part of the Pacific Rim of Fire
  - the 5th highest peak in the lower 48 states

Mount Rainier has/had...
  - the world's highest lake in its crater
  - the largest single peak glacial system in the contiguous United States
  - the largest mass at higher altitude
  - the largest mass of any Cascade volcano
  - the US record for average snowfall: (an average of 575" per year)
  - the record for the greatest snowfall ever recorded in U.S. history (1971-72.93 feet at Paradise.)
  - the first U.S. glacier ever discovered (the Nisqually)
  - had the first road in America to reach a glacier (the Nisqually)
  - the best documented glacier in the Western Hemisphere (the Nisqually)
  - the world's largest mudflow, - the Osceola
  - a higher rise above its base than any other mountain in the lower 48 states (nearly 10,000 feet)
  - a volume of ice and snow (156 billion cubic feet) which is the equivalent to nearly two century's worth of Seattle water use.

Scintillating Statistics
about Mountain Features

. **Sunrise:** The most amazing place on the continent you can drive to
. **Highest waterfall:** Fairy Falls (5th highest in US)
. **Fastest moving glacier:** the Nisqually (16 inches per day in summer)
. **Worst access road:** Mowich Lake's washboard road
. **Best flower meadows:** Paradise, Summerland, Indian Henrys, Klapatche, Sunrise
. **Deepest canyon:** Box Canyon
. **Lowest glacier in the United States:** The Carbon Glacier (3,500')
. **Lowest Point within the Park:** the 1,700 Carbon River entrance
. **Largest lake:** Mowich Lake (122.6 acres)
. **The Deepest lake:** Mowich Lake (57 feet deep)
. **The Deepest gorge:** Box Canyon (180' deep)
. **The Highest cliffs:** Yellowstone Cliffs
. **The Tightest highway turn:** Hairpin turn on Mowich Lake Road
. **The steepest pitch of road:** Sunrise Road
. **The highest tree growing on Mount Rainier** is at about 6,000 feet
. **The Lowest entry points** are The Park boundary south of Ohanapecosh (1715'), with Ipsut Creek just a few feet higher at (1744'). The elevation of the Nisqually entrance is 2003'.
. **Bear-proof garbage cans with concrete slabs:** 191

Biggest and Best

The Biggest
. **The biggest glacier:** the Emmons
. **The biggest waterfall:** Comet Falls
. **The biggest Alaska cedar tree:** enroute to Ipsut Pass on the Wonderland
. **The biggest Douglas fir tree:** in the Grove of the Patriarchs

The Best
. **Reflection of the Mountain:** Reflection Lakes or Mirror Lake (at Indian Henrys)
. **Fall Color:** on the East Side between Chinook Pass and Sunrise
. **Flower fields:** Paradise & Spray Park
. **Fishing:** Golden Lakes
. **"Outhouse" view:** Indian Bar

Mount Rainier Famous Firsts

1948	The Mountain Rescue movement was born here
1891	The first dog to climb the mountain. A deerhound belonging to Dr. Warren Riley, who accompanied P.B. Van Trump and Alfred Drewry, on the first ascent of the Tahoma Glacier.
1897	First recorded death at the Mountain: Professor Edgar McClure
1939	First ski ascent made by Sigurd Hall

The Best Places to view the Mountain

Breathtaking views of the Mountain

From Ashford: Copper Creek Road (Forest Svc. Rd. 59) west of Ashford

From Bonney Lake: from the hill just outside of town

From Chinook Pass: approaching from Yakima via Highway. 410, the first expansive view of the mountain comes at 5,432 ft. Chinook Pass on the eastern boundary of the park.

From Crystal Mountain: from the summit or Summit House restaurant

From Eatonville: from the Pioneer Historical Marker on Highway 161 just past Northwest Trek
from Glacier View Park

From Enumclaw: peekaboo views from north end of town high points

From Fort Lewis: from the parade grounds

From Gig Harbor: Sunrise Beach (the shore of the West Passage)

From Graham: Graham Hill (922' elevation)

From Ipsut Creek Road: several great views along the road

From McKenna: a few miles south of McKenna off the Vail Loop Road

From Mowich Lake Road: just prior to entering the park

From Ohop Valley: a magnificent close-up view

From Olympia: from the crest of 4th Avenue hill on Olympia's west side traveling east toward downtown.
looking east from the crest of Highway 101 hill as it descends toward the junction of I-5.
driving east on Pacific Avenue toward Lacey.

From Orting: from the Mountain View pulloff on the Orting Highway

From Parkland: Along old Highway 7

From Puyallup: from the Thun Field Restaurant

From Rochester: across the natural prairie just east of town

From Seattle: from the Space Needle
from either Floating Bridge
from a Washington State Ferry and from most of Puget Sound
from Seward Park and numerous places on Lake Washington
from SeaTac Airport and from Boeing Field
I-5 southbound from SouthCenter Hill
from the University of Washington campus

From Spanaway: Along old Highway 7

From Tacoma: from American Lake
from Snake Lake
from Custer Road and Bridgeport Way
from 108th and Pacific Avenue
from S. J St. near S. 19th and St. Joseph's Hospital
from S. 23rd St., west of Union Ave. near Bellarmine High School
from Inspiration Point by the Cliff House Restaurant
just N. of Tacoma C.C. on S. 12th St. near Mildred or 6th near. Mildred
from Stadium Way immediately north of downtown, - about 4th Street

From Thurston County: Luhr Beach at the mouth of McAllister Creek on the Thurston County side of Nisqually Delta

From Yelm: the new mall parking lot, also many places along the Yelm Highway

Best Views From within the Park

Dege Peak: Trail starts between Sunshine Point and the Sunrise Parking area. This 1-mile trail climbs 7,006 Dege Peak in the Sourdough Mountains.

Inspiration Point: Another great view of the Mountain, its southern glaciers and Narada Falls.

Tolmie Peak Lookout: From Mowich Lake, Follow the Wonderland Trail north 1.4 miles to the Tolmie Peak Trail Junction. Tolmie is 1.8 miles farther.

Pinnacle Peak Trail: Start at the Reflection Lake parking area (SE of Paradise) on Stevens Canyon Road. Hike about 1-1/2 miles to the saddle between Pinnacle and Plummer Peaks.

Reflection Lake: Love the mountain twice as much. If conditions are right, you'll get a mirror image of the big beauty in the lake.

Ricksecker Point: right on the road up to Paradise

Shriner Peak: This 8-mile round trip trail starts on Hwy. 123, 3-1/2 miles N of the Stevens Canyon entrance, or 7-1/2 miles S of Cayuse Pass. Park on the W side of the road about 1/2 mile from the Panther Creek bridge. Little shade.

Tipsoo Lake: A short ways from the junctions of Highways 410 and 123, Tipsoo is another site for spectacular photos.

Mount Rainier *DOES* Have

. poisonous mushrooms
. four rivers that carry which carry the drainage to salt water (the White, Puyallup, Nisqually and Cowlitz rivers)

Mount Rainier Does *NOT* Have

. poisonous snakes
. quicksand
. grizzly Bears
. geysers

The Perfect Trip to the Mountain

The perfect trip to the Mountain begins with an attitude of anticipation of one of life's momentous adventures. In other words, immerse yourself in the wonder of Mount Rainier. Don't just go to *look* at the mountain, but make the effort to get to *know* it as well. It's like the difference between admiring an attractive person, and really getting to know them as a friend.

As gorgeous as it all is, look beyond the beauty. Make friends with the mountain. Savor the sounds, the smells, the tastes and the feel of it. Touch the rough bark of a tree, listen to the birds and the wind in the trees, taste the berries. Walk a short ways on a trail. Look for the little things: bugs, mushrooms, pumice, lichen, a delicate spider web with diamonds of dew. Hundreds of little worlds coexist at Mount Rainier. Few people will ever see them all, and most people will never see more than a few. But with desire, and a little time and effort, even the handicapped can enjoy a Mount Rainier experience far beyond the beauty.

If you haven't packed a picnic, top off your day with a good meal at one of the fine restaurants at and just outside the Park. After all that fresh air and exercise, savor a fresh trout, some hot homemade bread and a piece of that fantastic wild blackberry pie!

The Wonderland Trail

. **Hardest hiking day:** The second day out of Longmire
. **Highest point:** Panhandle Gap (6800')
. **Lowest point:** Ipsut Creek Camp (1800')
. **Best sunrise:** Summerland or Indian Bar
. **Best sunset:** Golden Lakes
. **Most likely places to see goats:** Panhandle Gap, Goat Island Mountain, Indian Bar, Summerland, Skyscraper Pass, Emerald Ridge
. **Most likely place to see elk:** Indian Bar to Backbone Ridge
. **Biggest adrenalin rush:** Crossing either the Tahoma Creek or Carbon River Suspension Bridge (double the rush if it's a windy, raining day!)
. **Most breathtaking view on trail:** Crest of Emerald Ridge
. **Fastest meal inhaled on trail:** the cheeseburger at Sunrise
. **Steepest, hardest climb:** Carbon River to Lake James
. **Second Steepest, hardest climb:** Carbon River to Mystic Lake
. **Best fishing:** Golden Lakes
. **Best swimming:** Mowich Lake
. **Best layover day:** Golden Lakes or Indian Bar
. **Second best layover day:** Mystic Lake - it's the halfway point from Longmire
. **Most snow to cross:** over Panhandle Gap or Spray to Seattle Parks
. **Most mosquitos and bugs:** Mystic Lake
. **Biggest mosquitos and bugs:** Mystic Lake
. **Hungriest Bugs:** Stevens Canyon

Events

Accidents

A certain amount of risk is inevitable in the wilderness, and visitors to Mount Rainier increase those odds with the activities they pursue while there. In 1993, thirty-one search and rescue operations took place involving hikers, backcountry campers and climbers. That same year, eighty automobile accidents occurred in the park, most of them preventable. Two died in a tragic bus/motorcycle accident. Two more died from heart attacks, one while skiing, and the other while hiking, and one died while climbing. In 1993, there were 146 people injured. Injuries included sprains, strains, dislocations, cuts, abrasions, contusions, fractures, head and neck and back injuries, respiratory and circulatory problems, fainting, seizures and burns.

Alpenglow

If at all possible, position yourself somewhere on the west or southwest side to see the sun setting on the mountain for a wild profusion subtle pinks, peaches, and lavenders. The Sunset Amphitheater near the summit will burn pastel pink, and levitate over a blue or purple haze. It's as if God cleans out his paint pots each evening, and splashes the muted colors against the mountain.

Births/Deaths

The first known life lost at the mountain was that of a young man named E. H. Hudson, who walked out from Tacoma via the Yelm Trail with his two sons to camp at "Iron Creek" where the National Park Inn now stands in Longmire. In the morning, as Hudson bent over to put out his campfire, his derringer pistol fell from a vest pocket and discharged as it struck the ground, severing the carotid artery in his neck. The Longmire women, doing chores nearby, ran to his aid with bandages and medicine, but his wound was too serious and he died within the hour.

Lacking a coffin, his body was placed in one of the large cedar bathtubs used at the springs, and he was buried that afternoon beside the trail, a quarter mile below the meadow. A low, rock-bordered mossy mound marked the grave of the first visitor to die at Mount Rainier.

The next fatality was Professor McClure of the University of Oregon, who died July 27, 1897, while trying to measure accurately the height of the mountain. McClure Rock, where he died, is named in his honor.

The first recorded human birth at the mountain, as well as one of the early deaths, was a baby daughter of Naturalist and Mrs. Floyd Schmoe, when a doctor couldn't make it to the mountain in time to save the newborn infant's life.

Unfortunately deaths far outnumber births. Each year several people die in a variety of circumstances and accidents.

Within Sight of the Mountain

David Michael Hilemon, the young 29-year old Army officer shot down over North Korea in December, 1994, when his helicopter strayed into enemy airspace, got his final wish. He wanted to be buried within sight of Mount Rainier. He was, at a Gig Harbor cemetery.

Cemetery owners around Puget Sound say this is the most common request. Plots with Mount Rainier views are the most desirable burial sites.

Some want an even closer view, which is why countless urns of ashes are strewn about favorite spots around the park.

Canoeing Down the Cowlitz

In June 1978, a "float" of the Columbia River and all its tributaries was sponsored to show the benefits derived from the mighty river and tributaries. Permission was granted for removal of a chunk of ice from the upper Cowlitz Glacier to be carried by park employees on a canoe trip down the Cowlitz to the rendezvous.

The river run began at the Cowlitz Trout Hatchery, approximately 60 miles from the Cowlitz Glacier. The first rest stop was at Mile 6.5, at the site of the first white settlement in the northwest, the Cowlitz Mission, established in 1834. Cowlitz Landing, (now the town of Toledo), was passed at mile 10. (This was the terminus of the old stern· wheel river boat which used to travel up the Cowlitz. From here, travel to Puget Sound resumed overland.)

Camp was made near the fairgrounds across from the early 1870's settlement of Castle Rock. The second day they traveled 8.5 river miles before taking out at Lexington, leaving about 8 miles of river to the Columbia River. They drove the last leg due to heavy industrial use, slack water and lack of time.

Conservation Activities

Encouraging Park visitors to stay on the trails is a never-ending job for both the staff and a small army of volunteers. Under the banner of "the Meadow Stompers Program," 100,000 copies per year of "Bigfoot Lurks in the Meadows" cards in eight languages are distributed to park visitors, encouraging them to not go off-trail, and educating the public to the fragile nature of the subalpine meadows.

The Meadow Stompers Program is now entering its seventh year. The trained volunteers each donate an average of 20 hours per week "meadow roving" (on the trails, of course) retrieving and educating wayward tourists. In spite of more staff and volunteers working the problem, non-compliance continues to be a problem. Spread the basic conservation gospel, **"Please, please, please, stay on the trail!"**

Restoration and revegetation of sites damaged by human impact, particularly in the Paradise meadows is an on-going project. Social trails must be stabilized, filled and replanted or seeded. Fourteen thousand native plants were grown in the park's greenhouse for use in revegetation projects at Paradise and Tipsoo Lake. Volunteers from the Washington Native Plant Society, led by long-time Mountaineer stalwart Mary Fries of Tacoma, collected seeds for their eleventh year in the park.

Conventions

In today's parlance we would say that in the early days, somebody at the Park really went after the convention business. Large groups came from all over the country to hold their meetings and conventions at the mountain. In just July and August of 1919, the following groups stayed at the mountain: Order of Eastern Star (500 in party), West Coast Lumbermen's Association (250) Association of Western Confectioners (87), Knights of Pythias (300), Brooklyn Daily Eagle (125), National Editorial Association (300+), Washington State Bankers' Association (450) The Massachusetts Forestry Association (78) and the Association of Western Confectioners (87). When the crowds threatened to overwhelm the available facilities, the Park administration just arranged for the loan of several hundred army blankets from "Camp Lewis."

Not to be outdone, the Navy also came to the mountain. In 1922, the Pacific Fleet's Admiral's Ball was held at Paradise Inn, with officers coming to the event from the Seven Seas. The largest group to hold their convention at the mountain this same year was the American Institute of Banking, which brought 648 people to stay at Paradise.

Mission 66

Following the Second World War, the number of visitors to Mount Rainier (as well as all other national parks), dramatically increased. In 1956 President Eisenhower approved the National Park Service's plan for a 10-year development program for the parks. The program, called Mission 66, was to be completed by 1966, the fiftieth anniversary of the National Park Service.

As implemented at Mount Rainier, the $10 million plan called for removal of some of the older structures (the Lodge at Paradise, for one), the improvement of others (Paradise Inn), and construction of new ones. (the Henry M. Jackson Visitor Center). Also at this time the decision was made to relocate the park headquarters outside the park, at Tahoma Woods.

Natural Events

Fires

The Indians often burned forests to provide better hunting conditions and to produce more berries. Following a fire, Western red cedar, Douglas fir, hemlock, alder, cottonwood and willow are among the first trees to reestablish themselves rapidly in burned areas. This is because of their frequent seed crops.

One of the oldest known fires was documented by a layer of forest fire debris found in the Kautz Creek exposure upstream from the Wonderland Trail bridge. Wood from this layer yielded a date of 1,625 years.

Fire swept Backbone Ridge and the adjacent Canyon of Cowlitz Ridge around 1800. (The Indians said it was between 1810-1820). The extent of it was so vast, the area still bears the name "the Burn". Another old big one was the lightning-started Stevens Canyon Burn, which burned Cowlitz and Box Canyons, and burned clear up to the glaciers. "Great burns" were experienced in the upper Cowlitz Valley in 1841 and 1856 and again between 1886 - 1889.

The Bear Prairie area on the road between Ashford and Packwood burned in the late 1860's. *(Forests of Mount Rainier, Wm Noir).*

The old original hotel built by the Longmires was destroyed by fire in 1910. Its replacement, the main National Park Inn at Longmire was destroyed by fire in 1926.

A 1920 lightning fire on Cougar Creek (also known as Panther Creek) burned 50-60 acres. The Louise Lake area was denuded in 1929, as far over as Bench and Snow Lakes. Also in 1929 the first of the Shriner Burns scorched 2000 acres. It was caused by lightning. In 1934, 633 acres of it burned again. Outside the Park, there was a big fire in the 30's which burned all the way from Eatonville over the hills to National. All Wonderland Trail backpackers are familiar with the Silver Forest prior to Sunset Park. This happened in 1930 when a debris fire got away from a work crew.

A fire study conducted between 1931 and 1967, tracked 160 fires within the park, of which 103 were caused by lightning, and 57 by man. 1421 acres were affected. Major visible fire scars in the back country include Round Pass, Spray Park and Hessong Rock, the 1930's Sunset Burn and the 1963 Grand Park fire. A lightning-caused fire July 7, 1965 burned 203 acres on Pigeon Peak. The latter two were the last of the big fires in the Park.

a Grand Park Fire in the mid 1960's   Larry Penberthy photo

During the Summer of 1978 there were 25 fires of various size. All the forests of the Park have burned in the past, and they will all burn again. It is a natural part of the forest life. (*Fuel and Fire Behavior Predictions in Subalpine Forests of Pacific Northwest National Parks, National Park Service, College of Forest Resources, U.W. Summer, 1989.*)

Recent Fire Statistics

In 1992 there were six small lightning-ignited fires within the park. In 1991 eight small fires occurred, seven of which were started by lightning. 1990 had 29 wildfires, all started by lightning during two storms in July. The largest was two acres in size. 1989 was a good year. There were only three fires.

Fire Fighting

Today's changes in fire fighting include use of helicopters with 300-500 gallon buckets. The big choppers can be at the park within an hour and then at the fire scene in 30 minutes. Lightweight gas-operated pumps can make use of available lake or river water, and other improvements are fire retardant clothing and portable radios which provide 2-way communication to headquarters. Previously, getting to the fire by foot or on horseback was slow, and the fires had a good head start.

Before the advent of chain-saws, crosscut saws (called 'Misery whips') were used by the fire crews. They were hard on the body, and take a painful toll on the stomach muscles. Pulaskis and shovels are still the basic equipment.

Original job requirements were "anyone under 45 years of age who can breathe."

National Park Service Fire Policy

Since 1968, the National Park Service has recognized fire as one of the natural processes important in maintaining the parks in a primeval condition, and adopted a "let it burn" policy which started a major conflagration of its own. In 1988, everyone watched in horror as nearly one-third of Yellowstone National Park went up in flames. That's one bit of history very few would want to see repeated at Mount Rainier.

Fortunately, in the Pacific Northwest, all parks operate under a total fire suppression policy until they completely revise the fire management plan. The new planing process for fire involves several steps: (1) Determining the natural role of fire in the various ecosystems of the park. (2) Evaluating the natural role of fire in relation to social, economic, legal and cultural values, and the current state of the ecosystem. (3) Consideration of all environmental impacts inside and outside the park's boundaries.

It's especially important to follow Smokey the Bear's advice and prevent forest fires. Since Mount Rainier is never logged, it has a full "fuel load," and is a literal tinder keg.

Fire Lookouts

At 9,584', Anvil Rock lookout, built in 1916, was the state's highest fire lookout, and the person who manned it was Washington state's highest resident. It was also the *only* fire lookout in the park for about a decade. Then under Superintendent Tomlinson's watch, six additional lookouts were built. All that remains of Anvil Rock today is a level spot and a stone outhouse with one of the most unique views in the state -- straight down through the two holes to the Cowlitz Glacier several hundred feet below.

Four historic fire lookouts still in existence at the Park today are at Mt. Fremont (built in 1934), Gobblers Knob (west of Lake George), 1932, Shriner Peak (southeast area) also built in 1932, Tolmie Peak (northwest area) also built in 1932. There's also one at Tatoosh Peak (just outside Park) and High Rock, on the south side of the park. They are usually staffed from about July 1 to September 15 each year. Former lookouts used to be on the Colonnade, Windy Knoll, Anvil, Echo and Observations Rocks. The Gobbler's Knob lookout was a prototype of the new construction. It measured 14 by 14 feet, had two stories, and an exterior stairway which led to a balcony that ran around the second floor.

During the spring of 1937, one old Spanish American war veteran who worked at Anvil Rock as a fire spotter reported having to sit on "the rubber chair" (for protection against electrocution) for 36 hours during the worst electrical storm he had ever seen. It so stirred up his rheumatism, that he had to spend two weeks soaking at Ohanapecosh Hot Springs "to get the poison boiled out of his system." It must have worked. He said it never bothered him again.

Today, supplementing the old visual "after-the-fact" fire lookout system, is the more precise system of judging how dry the forest is by taking fuel moisture readings. The Fire Weather Station which does this daily analysis is at Longmire. They also rely on aerial detection.

Backcountry Fire Safety

- ❑ Fires usually travel faster uphill than downhill.
- ❑ Fires travel fastest in the same direction as the wind.
- ❑ Be alert for changes in the direction of the wind.
- ❑ Keep a sharp eye for burning debris, such as logs and cones rolling downhill, and for falling trees.
- ❑ Keep together. Do not panic. Think of your safest route out and away from the fire.

Possible "Safety Zones" are:

- ❑ large open meadows located downhill and upwind from a fire.
- ❑ rocky outcroppings
- ❑ lakes and large streams
- ❑ within the burned areas

Floods

The Cowlitz River has had a few notable rampages. One of the first that made the news was in 1891 when it carried off the tiny Fulton post office, many miles downstream from the Mountain.

The Carbon River had two notable early floods. In 1906, six houses on the banks of the Carbon were swept away in distant little Orting. In 1933 Carbon floods struck again in Orting, and all bridges were either lost or condemned, and acres and acres of land were lost, along with many homes, outbuildings and livestock.

A wild summer storm in 1973 turned cold and snowed, then turned again and the temperatures rose. The Carbon River swelled to 3 or 4 times normal size. Big chunks of ice from the glacier were found miles downstream. Within the Park, heavy rains in October, 1986, washed out a mile of the Carbon Glacier Trail.

The October 2, 1947 flood (mudflow) down Kautz Creek wiped out the bridge and one-half mile of road. It took until 1958 for new approaches and a new bridge to be completed.

The Nisqually River has had several notable floods. In 1932 a 20-foot high wall of water washed out the concrete Nisqually bridge, and caught a family that was picnicking on the shore who barely escaped with their lives. Guests are Paradise Inn were marooned, and while workmen tried to put in a temporary bridge, two more torrents came down.

A great flood in October 1955 took out the huge "new" Nisqually Glacier bridge. A new still-higher bridge was begun in 1958, and completed in 1961. This flood also inundated all nearby campgrounds and did extensive damage outside the park. As a result of this flood, Congress appropriated money to begin channeling the Nisqually by building dikes and river revetments.

In December 1977 bad floods on the Nisqually took out 1,500 feet of dike put in to protect what was left of the Sunshine Point Campground and the area behind the Gateway Inn outside the park. Over 40 inches of rain fell in a 35-day period starting in late November. More than 7 inches fell on the first of December alone, and it was more than the streams could handle.

At one time, all roads leading to the Park were under water. The Sunshine Point Campground lost all but 5 or 6 campsites. The Ipsut Bridge washed away, as did the road to the sewage treatment plant at Ohanapecosh.

Almost a mile of power lines came down between Nisqually and Longmire, and trees fell on the shop and trail quarters at the Carbon River. The Mountain Highway washed out at Goat Creek, and Highway 410 went out at Greenwater. Skate Creek and Randle were also isolated.

This is when the cabins at "Lost Town" just outside the Nisqually entrance were finally lost.

The most recent floods were in November of 1990. Between November 21 and 25th, the park recorded a total of 14.38 inches of rain at the Paradise weather station with a 24-hour high reading of 5.27 inches taken on the morning of November 24.

Wind

One of the first records of major wind damage, was of a wind-throw in 1931 which mowed down 400 acres of timber in the park. Supt. Tomlinson told the Tacoma press that over 300 trees barricaded the highway between Bear Prairie and Longmire, a distance of about a mile and a quarter. The wind uprooted trees more than four feet in diameter and tossed them great distances as if they were jackstraws. *(Ledger 4/27/31).*

That same wind blew the brand new Fremont Lookout tower over the ridge the first or second day it was up. Lookout Number 2 was anchored a little better. Then a hurricane took the roof off the Tolmie Lookout in 1937. The famed "Columbus Day Storm" of 1962 wreaked an incredible amount of havoc. A 1983-84 winter windstorm (much like a tornado) swept down the Highway 410 corridor doing massive damage in the forests. It left the town of Enumclaw devastated and at the mountain it left 200 acres of old growth forest blowdown in Cataract Creek valley. It completely buried one mile of trail with a jackstraw pile of beautiful old growth trees. Old timers from Enumclaw and Buckley attribute the increased incidence of high winds in recent years to all the old-growth clear-cutting along the Highway 410 corridor.

Earthquakes

Major Western Washington earthquakes occurred in 1949 (magnitude 7.1), and 1965 (magnitude 6.5). According to the University of Washington, Mount Rainier registers an average of 30-40 small earthquakes per year.

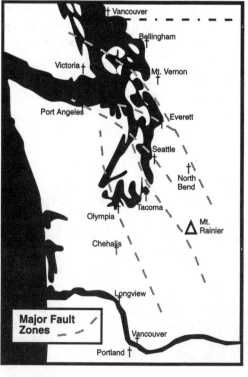

Puget Sound Faults

Mount Tacoma, The Western White House

In July 1913, in Washington, D.C. as the halls of congress reached a humid 98°, the subject of a cooler summer capital was again brought up by the sweltering congressmen. When Representative Borland of Missouri proposed putting it in the Blue Ridge Mountains, Congressman Albert Johnson of Tacoma responded with an impassioned plea to instead place "Washington West" in

Paradise Valley. "With (Washington's) free rough-hewn timber, the United States can build a summer capital for one-half the sum the Missouri congressman would spend," Johnson argued.

"Then, no longer will the chambers of the Senate and House have to be chilled with drafts blown across blocks of artificial ice, for in our summer capital on Mount Tacoma we will be surrounded by glacial peaks of solid ice, topped by the master peaks of the western world."

Fortunately, this plan never went anywhere. *(TNT 7/14/13).*

Movies Made at the Mountain

The first mention of Hollywood and a Mount Rainier connection comes from a surprising source. Zina Ashford, one of the daughters of homesteaders Walter and Cora Ashford, married a man named W. S. Van Dyke, who was to become MGM's leading movie director in the 1920's and 30's. Van Dyke was responsible for many of the early epic pictures, including, *Marie Antoinette, Trader Horn,* and all the Jeanette MacDonald & Nelson Eddy productions which still occasionally show up as late-night re-runs.

The Mountain connection? It was with money earned putting up Mount Rainier visitors, and driving them to Longmire in his horse and buggy, that Mr. Ashford financed his daughter and son-in-law's move to Hollywood in 1914, and made it possible for the bright young man to launch his illustrious movie career.

That same year, (1914), movie cameras were grinding on top of the mountain for the first time, when a party of six men hauled a massive amount of camera equipment around the mountain in search of an avalanche. They made a documentary of the mountain, but went home without a prize calamity on film.

The next summit film crew had more success. First a rock avalanche hurled down beside them, then a lady in their party fell face first down the mountain, managing to stop herself just two feet short of a crevasse "several hundred feet deep." *(News 8/14/17).*

It was 1921 when Mount Rainier put on her best dress for her movie debut with actors. The first movie, "Raw Country" starring Russell Simpson and Anne Cornwall was filmed by the H.C. Weaver Company. *(Tacoma Ledger 5/21/21).*

In August, 1924, "Frivolous Sal," a musical melodrama starring Mae Busch, Ben Alexander and Eugene O'Brien was made at the mountain. Viewers sat on the edges of their seats when the villain got dumped out of an ore bucket crossing the Nisqually and plunged hundreds of feet to his death in the treetops. *(TNT 8/24).*

In October of that same year, Cecil B. DeMille lost $22,000 worth of cameras, lights and equipment on the Nisqually Glacier when a sudden storm caught the crew unexpectedly while filming "The Golden Bed." The cast and crew had to be rescued, and the star, Miss Lillian Rich, had to be carried to safety. DeMille chalked it up as a cost of doing business, and said, "There is no place else in the U.S. or Canada with scenery to compare with Mount Tahoma, except in Switzerland itself." *(TNT 10/28/24)*.

A third 1924 film, "Wife No. 2" directed by J.K. McDonald was made in November, 1924. *(TNT 11/8/24)*.

1925 saw two films made at Mount Rainier. The first, made in March by Principal Pictures, was "The Race to Nome," which duplicated the story of "Balto" the famous Nome dog who broke all speed records in getting to Nome with diphtheria anti-toxin serum. The crew had to wait a few days for just the right snow storm. *(TNT 3/27/25)*

In June, another crew was back at the mountain. This time it was to do a William Fox play, "When the Door Opened." The only part of this film not made at Mount Rainier was a scene where a river had to be dammed, the dam bursts and a house washes away. The Skykomish River near Index was picked to do the honors, much to the relief of those living downriver from Mount Rainier. *(TNT 4/9/25)*.

1926 saw an epic production made at the mountain. MGM made a film of Robert W. Service's book "The Trail of '98". Two thousand extras were needed to portray the trek of gold hunters climbing over Chilkoot Pass to the gold fields in Alaska. They wanted to show miners struggling and suffering in the snow, and the 2,000 extras obliged without even trying. *(TNT 9 4/26/26)*.

A second film was also shot at Mount Rainier this same year. It was a Fox film, "Wings of the Storm" starring Virginia Brown, William Russell, and the dog stars including "Thunder the Wonder Dog". Logging camp scenes were shot at Faraway Rock near Sluiskin Falls, and a Ranger's cabin was built at Glacier Vista for the film. The dog stole the show. *(TNT 7/30/26)*.

MGM opened the 1927 filming season with Reginald Barker's production "The Branding Iron," featuring Aileen Pringle, Ralph Forbes and Lionel Barrymore. A call for extras went out for two mountain climbers, 22 men skiers, and a dark complexioned, 135 lb. expert girl skier who was 5' 5" tall. *(Tacoma Ledger, 1/13/27)*.

In September, 1927 a German crew from the Doring Film Works of Hanover Germany came to film the mountain for inclusion in their film "Greatest Beauty Spots of North America." Mount Rainier got Dietrich W. Dryer (the owner's) vote. Said he, "This is by far *the* most beautiful place we have seen anywhere in our travels!"

The First Talkie Made in the Northwest

"The Girl Who Wasn't Wanted" starring Helen Chandler and George O'Brien was the first 'talkie' made with a Pacific Northwest locale. It was filmed in January, 1930, by Wm. Fox Studios at Longmire and at the West Fork Logging Company's camp near Mineral. Filmed with a cast of 55, it was a story of life in a logging camp. Dog team scenes were shot across the Nisqually behind Longmire Inn. It was noted that Paradise Inn resembled a cross between a Siberian bus station and the lobby of a bachelor's hotel. *(TNT 1/30/30)*

In 1937 Twentieth Century Fox film was back with Sonja Henie and Tyrone Power to make "Thin Ice." Nineteen local kids were hired to haul freight and gear up and down the mountain, including a 1,000 lb. portable generator. But the weather got progressively worse, and the cast and crew of 30 cooled their heels (at $10,000 a day,) waiting for a break in the storm. After 9 days, they got one clear day, and when the weather closed in again, the director sent everyone except a handful of cameramen back to Hollywood to duplicate shots they would have done at the mountain. The final film showed the stars pushing each other around in cornflakes instead of genuine Paradise snow.

Otto Lang, who went on to become a renowned producer-director, donned a blonde wig and doubled for Sonja Henie in skiing sequences. At the time Lang was in reality a ski school instructor at Paradise.

The only other side note is that Sonja Henie's father, mother and brother accompanied her, and Mrs. Henie got ptomaine poisoning at Paradise Inn. *(TNT 4/9/37)*.

The first color film made at the mountain was a short ski film made by 20th Century Fox in 1944. They hired a dozen Northwest skiers who all took brief vacations from their essential war work in the "Ski Troops" to show their stuff on the silver screen. *(Tacoma Ledger 1/23/44)*.

A 1950's movie was "Track of the Cat," produced by Warner Brothers and starring Robert Mitchum. *(LA Times, 9/26/54)*.

In 1961, "Out to Ski" documented the first ski descent of Mount Rainier. Roger C. Brown and John C. Ahern produced the film about the big event which featured eight men: Jim and Lou Whittaker, Brown and Ahern, Squaw Valley Ski School Director Joe Marillac, Sierra Club instructor Roger Paris, Sugar Bowl instructor Bill Briggs and Gordon Butterfield, Western Sales Rep. for Head Ski Company. *(TNT 10/15/61)*.

In 1989 there was a hilarious HBO comedy starring Shirley McLaine, called "Waiting for the Light" about a Bed and Breakfast just outside the Park..

There also were shots of the mountain in a couple of Jeff Bridges movies, "The Vanishing" and "American Heart," also "To Hell and Back" starring Audie Murphy. There was a glimpse or two in "It Happened at the World's Fair" starring none other than Elvis. There's also a great mountain shot in the movie, "Disclosure" featuring Demi Moore, Michael Douglas, Jr., and Donald Sutherland.

A few years back, someone rummaging in the park archives discovered a treasure trove of old movies. It seems in the 1930's and 40's the Park Service had their own movie production crew who documented everything in sight. Subjects found included the park in general, animal life, winter recreation, "behind the scenes," C.C.C. crews, interpretive activities, skiing and climbing.

Mother Rainier, the Matchmaker

Like an old Yiddish Yenta, portly old Momma Rainier brought together many a couple. Within the Park, matches have been made between park employees, old Rainier National Park Co. employees, and hikers and climbers who met on the mountain. Heath Colvin, who managed all the acommodations for the old Rainier National Park Company, said the young men he used to hire, annually begged him to "bring back the best looking girls you can find." He did, and it worked. Several unions came out of those summer jobs. (One of them was the Molenaars. They met when Dee was a ranger, and Colleen, his wife-to-be, ran the gift shop.)

Not only did couples meet there, they got engaged there, married there, honeymooned there, and keep coming back to celebrate anniversaries there.

Many more couples have selected either the Park or the summit for their big event, including the author's son and daughter-in-law, Dick and Phyllis Filley who married at Longmire in 1979. Another couple a few years back married at Alta Vista then walked under crossed ice axes. One innovative couple in 1994 "walked on water" to their wedding spot. They were married in winter in the middle of frozen Reflection Lake. Mount Rainier is a great honeymoon spot too. Countless couples have celebrated their honeymoon at Paradise and Longmire Inns and each year some still come back 50 or more years later, to relive fond memories.

Also along the line of nuptials, the old Rainier National Park News noted that the staff at Sunrise used to have fun naming the many unnamed peaks and ridges visible from the Lodge. The closest peak to the Lodge was named "Antler Peak" because many of the burnt snares on its slopes look like antlers. Another peak close by, was named "Marriage Peak" because it was smooth on one side and rough and rocky on the other.

Nuptials

The first wedding in the Park took place July 2, 1921. Mr. Henry Doerman, a school principal from Hampton, Virginia, married Miss Alice Humphrey of Seattle. The ceremony took place on the trail between Longmire and Paradise. On September 7 that same year the first wedding on the summit took place when Climbing Guide Edward J. Hamilton of Buckley took the chilly hand of Miss Lenora Allain of Auburn, a cashier at Paradise Inn. The wedding party of sixteen all made it up to the wedding. Maid of Honor was Mrs. Horace Whitaker, (maiden name Alma Wagen), the first woman climbing guide. Music was provided by Swiss guide Hans Fuhrer and his mouth organ.

The second summit wedding wasn't until 15 years later when Dr. Joseph Griggs of Sumner married Miss Jeanette Spieden of Washington, D.C., on August 8, 1936. The newspaper report of the event said "a glacial summit gale roared approval and blew up swirls of snow for a bridal veil." It also noted that in place of a bouquet, the bride carried a stalwart Swiss Ice-axe. *(Ledger & Times 8/10/36).*

Then 34 more years went by (1970) before another wedding party (of 13) trudged up the l-o-o-o-ong aisle for the ceremony. Scott Rush and his betrothed, Carol Hiltner, waited until the minute the mother of the bride made her appearance before saying their "I do's" and then all racing down to the reception at Paradise.

Most marriages are supposed to take the participants from the "misery" of being single to the Paradise of marriage. One couple in 1935 did it in reverse. They went from Paradise to Misery to be married, Camp Misery, that is. With Mount Rainier as the great Cathedral of the Outdoors, and the sunrise hour as the time, Miss Eloise Wood and Mr. Lyle Paul were united in marriage July 18, 1935 at Camp Misery at 4:18 in the morning. After the ceremony, the bride and groom stayed at Misery, and the rest of the party climbed to the 13,000 foot level. The record doesn't say what then went on at Misery, but it does say they all ended up in Paradise. The reverse has also apparently been true. There's a rumor of a couple who got married at the summit, and wanted a divorce by the time they struggled back to Paradise.

Another couple to walk up the long white aisle was a New Jersey couple who tied the knot at the summit on July 23, 1982. Glen Soroka and Debra Strous met in a mountain climbing supply store and discovered that not only did they both share the dream of climbing Mount Rainier, so did the minister who married them, so up they all went.

Another really appropriate ceremony took place at Camp Muir in 1987 when a JanSport sales rep, Larry Harrison, and his fiance, Carol, tied the knot in the thin air. They then walked between a column of guides and climbers forming an arch of crossed ice axes.

And then there's that bizarre little bunch who celebrate their arrival at the summit with a very cold, out-of-breath tryst. These celebrants are members of what's unofficially known as the "Rim Club." The members of this rather select little body hold their impromptu meetings right up there in front of God, everybody in Puget Sound and all inbound and outbound flights to Sea-Tac.

Peace Rock

In October, 1935, an act of friendship between the United States and Japan was consummated by the presentation of a rock from the summit of Mount Rainier to be placed in a shrine on Mount Fuji in Japan. The rock was presented to the Japanese consul from Seattle by Park Superintendent O. A. Tomlinson.

Photography Firsts

The first photographs of the summit were taken in 1888 when photographer Arthur Churchill Warner accompanied the Muir expedition to the top. His famous photos were shown worldwide.

Washington Centennial Volksmarch

In 1989, to celebrate Washington State's Centennial, the National Park Service was a host and co-sponsor of a giant Volksmarch at the Park. The event was held in July and involved 2,400 participants. The primary organizer was the Pierce County Department of Parks, Recreation and Community Services. Other sponsors included Washington National Guard, a number of Volksmarch clubs, and several private businesses.

Chronology of (non-climbing) Events

1792	On May 8 Captain George Vancouver was the first white man to sight Mount Rainier, and named it in honor of his friend Rear Admiral Peter Rainier.
1833	September 2. Dr. William Tolmie, a Hudson's Bay physician entered the northwest corner of what is now the park. He was the first white man to enter this region.
1848	Oregon Territory, including all of present Washington, was created.
1853	Washington Territory was created.
1883	James Longmire discovered the springs which bear his name.
1893	December 12. Hon. Watson C. Squire, United States Senator, introduced a bill for the creation of "Washington National Park." The name was later modified to Mount Rainier National Park.
1893-1915	The Park had 2 regular and 3 temporary rangers.
1899	Mount Rainier National Park was created by Congress and approved by President McKinley. It became the 5th national park in the United States.
1904	The first daily stage operated between Ashford and Longmire.
1915	Wonderland Trail completed enabling encirclement of the mountain. The Park had over 30,000 visitors this year.
1916	The inception of the National Park Service, and inclusion of Mount Rainier National Park under its jurisdiction.
1917	Paradise Inn formally opened to the public.
1918	A permit was issued to graze 500 head of cattle in the White River District and was reissued in 1920 as increased food production was needed for the (1st World War) effort.
1920	A lightning fire on Cougar Creek burned 50-60 acres. This was also known as the Panther Creek fire. It was on the SE edge of the park.
1920	The first airplane flights are made around the Mountain.
1923	Elk were seen at Longmire. This was the first recorded elk sighting.
1926	It was concluded there were ten timber wolves in the Park.
1929	80 acres burned along the eastern boundary of the Park.
1931	The eastern Park boundary was extended to the summit of the Cascades, thus increasing Park holdings by another 53 square miles. This same year, Yakima Park first opened to the public.
1932	Ranger reports noted doubts any wolves remained.
1933	Celebration of one hundredth anniversary of visit of first white man, Dr. Wm. Fraser Tolmie. The Mowich entrance to the Park opened. A timber wolf was positively identified below Muir.

1934 The first Silver Skis championships were sponsored by the Seattle Post Intelligencer. Many elk sighted by the West Side Lookouts. A plan was formulated to eliminate all elk. The Shriner Peak Burn occurred. 2,500 man days were required to suppress it. 630 acres were burned. The probable cause was attributed to a careless smoker.

1935 230 miles of telephone line were maintained and improved.

Olympic Trials, the National Downhill, and Slalom Championships were all held at Paradise.

Three more wolves were sighted.

1937 Fire at Summerland burned 140 sq. ft. A report of elk tracks in the vicinity of Indian Bar caused quite a stir. "This animal is not common in the Park," said the ranger's report. Shirley Temple visited the Park.

1938 There were wolf sightings near the 3-Lakes Cabin. Elk were seen in the same area.

1940 The Tacoma Chamber of Commerce finally agrees to accept "Mount Rainier" as the proper name, after 56 years of name controversy.

1941 Ski Detachments of the 15th Infantry were camped at Longmire, and used the facilities at Paradise for training.

1942 War had been declared and a manpower shortage hit the park. The C.C.C. was disbanded.The 87th Mountain Infantry trained at Paradise.

1943 Gas rationing slowed down visitation. Women were hired as rangers and lookouts.

1945 President Truman visited the Park, the first president to visit since President Taft in 1912. Due to the manpower shortage, young boys were employed in the fight against the Blister Rust epidemic.

1946 With the war over, travel in the Park skyrocketed.

1947 The Kautz Creek Mudflow

1949 An exceptionally hard winter caused heavy forest damage.

1950 Visitor facilities at Paradise and Longmire were closed for the winter, due to the Rainier National Park Company losing money. The back country telephone lines were all downed by heavy snows.

1954 The popularity of skiing continues. Two rope tows were installed at Cayuse Pass. Plans for use of Cayuse as a Winter playground were bandied about and a tramway was proposed for Paradise. Rope tows also went in at Canyon Rim, below Narada Falls.

1957 The summit height was re-determined to be 14,410', not 14,408' as had previously been believed.

1958 The one millionth visitor came to the park in September.

1960 A geological mapping of the park was undertaken.

1962 The major rockfall off Little Tahoma

1964 Members of the first American-Mount Everest Expedition practiced on Mount Rainier.

1965 Both Crystal Mountain and White Pass ski areas opened.

1966 The Henry M. Jackson Visitor Center opened at Paradise. The Paradise Ice Caves were closed for the second consecutive year, as entry was considered too hazardous. Approval was given for fish poisoning in Tipsoo Lake. Publicity on the possible eruption of Mount Rainier caused some second thoughts in Puget Sound, following the publication of aVolcanic Hazards Study.

1973 Last tow ropes were operated at Paradise.

1988 1.7 million acres within Olympic, Mount Rainier and North Cascades National Parks were designated as wilderness areas.

Airplanes and the Mountain

Probably the worst recent summit story we've heard was the one about the climbing party who finally made it to the summit, was standing around savoring the moment and catching their breath, and in flew a jet helicopter. Out jumped a dandy in a business suit, who walked around the summit snow mound for a minute, jumped back into the plush corporate helicopter, - and flew off!

In 1951 a young Army Air Force pilot tried the same feat with slightly different results. Lieutenant John Hodgkin flew a ski-equipped 85 horsepower J-3 Piper Cub up from Spanaway and deliberately landed in the saddle between Columbia Crest and Point Success to demonstrate mountain rescue possibilities and to take pictures which he hoped to sell to a national magazine. He only made one mistake. He turned off the key.

When it came time to leave, he made the unsettling discovery the plane wouldn't restart. After a cold night spent in the cockpit, he finally managed to take off in a powerless glide, soon landing the little craft on frozen Mowich Lake. Meanwhile about a half hour after he had flown off, the rescue party who had climbed all night to assist him, reached the empty summit. The stunt cost him a $350 fine and 6-month suspended jail sentence. *(Seattle P.I. & TNT 4/15/51)*.

Early Flights Around the Mountain

The first airplane flights over the park and around The Mountain were made in July of 1920. Three planes circled the mountain and the third then "bravely flew over the summit. "

Almost immediately several people saw the commercial potential in 'around the mountain flights,' although it took several decades until Jimmy Beech successfully made a business of it. In 1927 Pacific Air Transport Company sent a 6-passenger Fokker Monoplane to scope out the possibilities. It was the pilot's first flight to the mountain, and after a quick circle of Paradise and a good scare, he was back in Tacoma 22 minutes later. *(TNT 6/21/27)*. A succession of other aviation services had the same idea, but usually after one or two flights they had a problem finding pilots willing or able to do the job.

Seeing Mount Rainier from the Air

When you find perfection, quit! That's what one early-day air tourist did after seeing the great mountain from the air. Famous 1920's song writer Carrie Jacobs Bond known for writing "The End of a Perfect Day," and "I Love You Truly" had a passion for taking sight-seeing tours by air. However her flight around Mount Rainier was so unspeakably beautiful, and so inspiring, that she made the grand pronouncement (in the newspapers, no less), that she had "found perfection," and that her sight seeing tours by air had ended! She went on to explain that no other flight would be as inspiring as that around Mount Rainier, and consequently she had no desire to fly again. Ever! "This one is perfection." We agree.

The Paradise and Longmire Airports

An article in the *Tacoma News Tribune* in July, 1920 announced daily flight service to Paradise was about to begin, with passengers landing just 300 ft. from the Inn. It sounded like a done deal, but they neglected to say it had never been tried.

The next mention of an airport at the mountain, was 1960 when an airport was not only proposed at Longmire but included in the government National Airport Plan for 1960. The announcement was made jointly by no less than Senators Warren G. Magnuson and Henry M. Jackson. The proposed field was to have a 4,300 ft. runway. This one was not to be for public use, but for fire fighting planes.

And where is this airport? Alas, the best laid plans of even powerful politicians don't always come to fruition.

Early Aerial Photos

Photographer W. G. Stoeser and pilot Lt. Ned Schram fearlessly "faced death" August 23, 1922 to take the first aerial photo of Mount Rainier. It made news in Tacoma and Seattle, and long articles about their 3-hour, 350-mile flight around Mount Tacoma related all the details and dangers. They started their perilous flight from 'Camp Lewis.' *(TNT 8/24/22)*.

Two years later, the next aerial photographer really did face death in trying to get his pictures. From his precarious perch in an open bi-plane, the photographer had to stand up and wrap the seat belt around his leg to hold himself in. As the pilot tried to maneuver the plane into a position where the photographer wasn't just getting a shot of the wings, there was an even bigger problem. The photographer also had to balance the huge heavy camera and try to aim it while his fingers and face were freezing, and the prop wash walloped him with an icy blast. *(TNT 10/21/28)*.

In 1930 the first award was won for an aerial photo of the mountain. A very tiny photo of the mountain! Captain Albert W. Stevens successfully photographed Mount Tacoma from a distance of 227 miles away, aiming his camera by compass. The award was given for Stevens' meritorious contribution to aviation by his long distance photo. *(Ledger 1.27/30)*. (A feat which because of air pollution, could only be duplicated today by NASA.)

Jimmy Beech

Jimmy Beech was Mount Rainier's aviation legend! Operating out of a small dirt "uphill" landing strip near Ashford, Jimmy flew the mountain like no other pilot. He carried everything from fingerling fish on air drops to their new remote mountain lake homes, to thousands of tourists on "round the mountain" flights. He did "scouting" flights, oxygen and medical supply drops, charter flights, checking for forest fires, search and rescue missions, and missions of mercy. When all else failed, Jimmy would be sent up to look for missing hikers or climbers, and with his bird's eye view and ability to get in close, he was pretty good at finding them.

Many of the now-famous Mount Rainier aerial photos were taken with Jimmy at the controls angling the plane in for just the perfect shot. All the photographer had to do was push the button. His secret of success in knowing just how far he could go, and how close he could get, was to watch the birds for updrafts.

Three decades of incomparable skillful mountain flying came to an end when Jimmy died in his plane May 22, 1992, not on Mount Rainier, but against a hillside near Eatonville.

Aircraft Accidents/Incidents on the Mountain

When aviation was young, early pilots probably didn't have a clue about the dangerous updrafts, downdrafts, turbulence, icing and windshears around the mountain. Flying over and around it wasn't as easy as it looked, as some pilots learned the hard way. There's a wry humor among pilots about flying into clouds with rocks in them. Quite a few pilots have actually done that at Mount Rainier too.

1945 An Army A-24 airplane crashed on the Mountain near Fan Lake between the Williwakas and Cowlitz Glaciers.

1946 December 10, 1946, a Marine C-46 crashed into Success Cleaver killing all 32 men aboard. The plane and its dead scattered onto the South Tahoma Glacier 7,000 feet below. The wreckage wasn't discovered until the following July. The Glacier itself, crossed and criss-crossed by deep crevasses, had swallowed most of the remains. *(Seattle Times, 9/20/70)*. In 1982 the glacier yielded another piece of the plane. *(TNT 9/19/82)*.

1951 A ski-equipped Piper Cub landed on the summit. (page 173). While rescue parties went up, the pilot flew off, this time to Mowich Lake.

1959 A geology professor from Western Washington State College, Dr. Calder Bressler, showed symptoms of pulmonary edema at the summit while participating in the "Project Crater" study. Since the group had a limited supply of oxygen with them, a local Civil Air Patrol pilot, Harold Horn, experienced in making airdrops on the mountain, and a friend, Charles R. Carman, took off on a late evening flight in a Cessna 140 to drop the much needed oxygen cylinders on the summit. The drop failed to occur, and the plane never returned to Thun Field.

The following morning Dr. Bressler died, and a week-long storm moved in, making it impossible to search for the downed aircraft. Eventually a wheel of the plane was spotted from the air, just east of Point Success. The plane was upside down, and Horn and Carman had died on impact. Because of the impossibility of removing their frozen remains from the plane, their bodies and the plane were left at the crash site on the summit. Horn was operations officer of the Washington Wing of the Civil Air Patrol. *(TNT 9/9/59).*

1964   The wreckage of a single-engine Mooney was left on the mountain after a crash which killed four, a man named Gordon Berry, his wife and two other people.

1965   Five civilians died in the crash of a four-engine DC-6A military cargo plane which was headed from Boeing Field to Hill Air Force Base in Utah. The plane hit the mountain at the 10,200 foot level "on the peak's west slope" and slid down to 9,600 feet. The crash was attributed to bad weather. (See salvage story below). *(TNT 4/24/65).*

1968   An Air Force T-33 jet trainer enroute from Sacramento to McChord AFB flew into the Mountain at about the 10,500-foot level, scattering debris across the Van Trump Glacier and Wilson glaciers. The plane with two aboard, vanished from radar and radio as it made its landing approach to the air base. Both occupants were killed and the bodies were never recovered. The pilot was an Air Force Colonel.

1976   Helicopters have crashed at the mountain too. One chopper involved in a rescue near the summit unexpectedly encountered a violent downdraft and crashed into the summit snowfield. Fortunately no one was seriously injured. *(Mount Rainier News, August 1976)*

1979   In late January, a Cessna-140 carrying two men on a sightseeing trip from Tacoma crashed on the summit. Sucked down by a downdraft, they hit a few feet shy of the NW lip of the summit crater. When the wheels touched down, the plane flipped and slid backward 400 feet. The men remembered hearing about the steam caves and scrambled back up to the crater and found a small cave where they were forced to spend the night in -35°F weather with no survival gear. They were rescued the next morning after a three-hour wait while rescuers disagreed over whose jurisdiction it was. They both survived the crash without so much as a scratch, however one man suffered the indignity of having second degree burns on his buttocks when he sat on the plane's seat cushion over a steam vent. (This was the second Cessna 140 to crash on the summit.) *(Nat'l Transportation Safety Board report)*.

1985   Navy P-3 Orion Anti-Submarine plane off the U.S.S. Constellation, went into the Success Glacier, killing five.

1989   On a clear day, a Cessna 210 pilot departed Boeing Field enroute to Wenatchee, but flew in a straight course to Mount Rainier. It's unknown why, but he flew directly into Willis Wall. The plane hit so hard it was virtually welded into the Wall and stuck straight out of it for several months. Pilot William Saul had a commercial rating. His body was never recovered. *(The Olympian, 3/20/89)*

1990   In late January, a Piper Super Cub military aircraft piloted by Ronald McDonald crashed on the summit while sightseeing. McDonald and his passenger, Randall E. Bates, were both killed. The following month, while leading a mid-winter ascent, Summit Guide Eric Simonson saw McDonald's plane in the crater. Two years later, on another climb in September of 1993, upon descending into a steam cave, Simonson saw the plane again, suspended in the ceiling of the cave as if it were in a flight museum. It had taken two years to melt through 30 feet of ice. The remains of the plane were never seen again.

1990   Another Cessna 210 ferrying four champion Rodeo cowboys between events in Pendleton, Oregon and Penticton, Canada, crashed at about the 12,600 foot level on the Kautz Glacier. There were five fatalities. Among the wreckage at the scene were cowboy hats, huge silver belt buckles and lariats, trophies of the rodeo circuit.

1991   During the winter, two died in a small Cessna in the East Crater.

Salvage Operation

Following the crash of the DC-6A in April 1965, two entrepreneurs decided to salvage the aircraft for parts. They purchased the rights to the aircraft remains from the insurance company, and got permission from the park service to remove it from the mountain. The salvagers, Lee Nelson and Rip Collins, "blasted parts of the plane loose from the glacier." The venture brought them $10,000 for the landing gears which weighed 1,800 lbs. each. They got another $10,000 for the cargo door, plus another $10,000 each for three engines. They lost the fourth engine in a bergschrund when they blasted it loose.

Legal Aircraft

According to the Federal Aviation Administration, there is no restricted air space over the park. It is not illegal to fly over or around the mountain, it is only illegal to land there! (This is not to say we're advocating the practice of overflying the Park, we're just quoting the law. While it may be legal, it may not be prudent. Anyone contemplating flying over the mountain anyway, should seek the advice of professionals who are familiar with the hazards of any such flight.)

What the law says is *"Except as specifically provided for in this (Wilderness) Act, ...there shall be... no landing of aircraft (and) no other form of mechanical transport..."*

But there are exceptions. Helicopters are brought in legally under certain circumstances and for specific purposes. These include rescue operations and bringing in heavy equipment and materials for such projects as rebuilding the old suspension bridge over Tahoma Creek, and supplying the guide service bunkhouse at Camp Muir with propane and food staples. They also carry out waste, are used in rehabilitation and repair projects, carry outhouses in and out, and occasionally do such things as lifting wrecked airplanes off the mountain.

Aircraft Noise

Most people don't like the annoyance of aircraft disrupting their quiet backcountry experience, and knowing this, unless there's an emergency, the Park Service tries to schedule their own helicopter use after Labor Day, when most of the people are gone.

As for civilian and military aircraft overflying the park, the opinion of such flights depends on who you're asking. The park administrators and wilderness purists would be happiest if absolutely nobody ever flew over the park. A 1992 Forest Service $1.5 million-dollar study found that most visitors to wilderness areas were not bothered when jet fighters and other aircraft flew overhead. The study was ordered by Congress as the result of complaints about aircraft noise in Grand Canyon National Park.

It found there were "few adverse impacts to wilderness users resulting from aircraft flights over Forest Service managed wilderness. The worst case found was a fairly small percentage of wilderness visitors who experienced varying degrees of noise-induced annoyance." Most complaints were generated by lowlevel military jets which fly at tree-top level. This isn't too much of a problem at Mount Rainier though, even though it is in the back yard of both McChord Air Force Base, and Whidbey Island Naval Air Station. The National Park Service is planning on conducting their own separate study. *(Seattle Post Intelligencer 9/10/92).*

Want to Fly Around the Mountain (*Legally!*)?

The following air services offer "round the mountain" flights, and all stress they make every effort to be as responsible and unobtrusive as possible.

From Seattle:

Northwestern Executive Air, Boeing Field (800) 24HRJET

From Renton:

Sound Flight, Renton Airport (206) 255-6500
Puget Sound Aviation, Renton Airport (206) 226-0300

From Tacoma (Tacoma Narrows Airport - Gig Harbor):

Davis Aviation, 1-800-359-2210

From Puyallup (Pierce County Airport):

General Aviation, Inc. Thun Field (206) 840-8570
Spanaflight, Thun Field (206) 848-2020

From Bremerton:

Pegasus Air, Bremerton National Airport (360) 674-2542

Small Airports Around the Mountain

General aviation airfields in communities around the park are:

Asplund Airport (5 miles W of Eatonville)
Swanson Airport? (1 mile E of Eatonville)
Cougar Mountain Airport (10 miles SE of Yelm)
Enumclaw Airport (1 mile W of Enumclaw)
Flying B (4 miles S of Yelm)
Kapowsin Field (1 mile N of Kapowsin)
Moss Field (2 miles N of Graham)
Packwood Airport (1/4 mile WSW of Packwood)
Ranger Creek Airport (30 miles SE of Enumclaw)
Shady Acres Airport (4 miles ESE of Spanaway)
Spanaway Airport (1 mile SE of Spanaway)
Strom Field (1/2 mile ESE of Morton)
Swanson Field (1/2 mile NE of Eatonville)
Tieton State Airport (1.5 miles S of Rimrock)
Thun Field (6 miles S of Puyallup)
Yelm Airpark (2 miles E of Yelm)

For additional information on Round the Mountain flights, look in the Yellow Pages under Airports and Aircraft Charters.

The *VERY* Best View

To get a genuine bird's eye view at no additional cost, try for a view from one of the big birds. When flying out of Seattle on an east-west route, ask for a south side (right hand) window seat. Or if flying out of SeaTac on a south run, ask for a seat on the left side of the plane for a dynamite view of Mount Rainier, and Mount St. Helens beyond.

Some fortunate inbound frequent flyers have lucked out when their pilots were ordered into a holding pattern, and the lucky passengers were flown around and around the mountain.

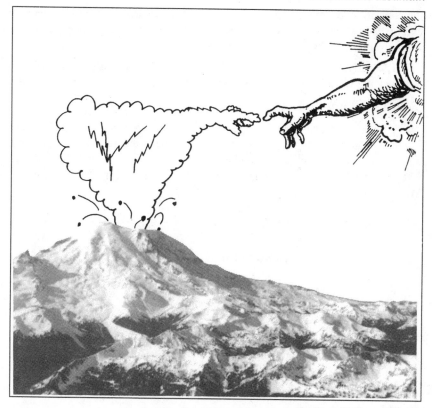

art by Steve McNutt - AVO

God and the Mountain

While Mt. St. Helens had its harmonic tremors, Mt. Rainier had a harmonic convergence. Like a great white shrine, Mount Rainier has been an object of worship and a place of worship.

Many people meet God in the wilderness. Throughout biblical history, mountains have been the meeting place between God and man. Mountains traditionally have also provided a spiritual connection, providing whatever the pilgrim seeks: inspiration, peace, refreshment, serenity, challenge or adventure. People of virtually every faith have found spiritual sustenance at this, and virtually every other mountain. Even non-religious people are struck with the spiritual perspective that comes about in the mountains. Big worldly problems take on smaller more manageable proportions when viewed against the size of a real mountain. Man is so tiny, a mere speck on the slopes, and the mountain is so large.

Mount Rainier has had its share of those who believed they could only meet God on the summit, and then have trudged up to pray, or fast, or meditate on the top. Others believe that isn't necessary. They remember the lesson of Genesis, that God loved to walk and talk with Adam and Eve in the Garden in the cool of the evening. Relaxing Mount Rainier evenings, bathed in alpenglow and over-flowing with the grandeur and beauty of the gardens, are still wonderful times for a similar conversation.

The early Indians did not worship the Mountain, as has been mistakenly reported, but were fearful of the area above snowline.

That Old Time Religion

U.W. history professor Edmund Meany, the proper first president of The Mountaineers, not only wrote flowery poetry while in the backcountry. he wore a jacket and tie while climbing, and always conducted Sunday worship services whenever in the mountains on the Sabbath. Here is one of his works written at Mount Rainier:

Land of the Open Spaces

Edmund S. Meany

O uplifted land of the great open spaces

    O land near the stars and the free higher air,

Where riseth wild echos from glacier torn places,

    From summit to summit - thy God's primal prayer!

As clear silver bells, a sweet music is chiming,

    A music new rivers forever prolong

When heaven and earth are eternally rhyming,

    O nature melodious - God's oldest song!

In gleam of the crag or in gloom of the hollow,

    Yea, even in awe when the storm thunders roll,

Abideth a lure, O, a strange lure to follow,

    For here with your God may you meet your own soul!

The Sermon *of* the Mount

In June of 1910, Rev. Edgar C. Wheeler of Pilgrim Congregational Church of Tacoma took advantage of the publicity surrounding the publication of John H. Williams' book, *The Mountain That Was God* to preach two sermons of the same title. Rev. Wheeler compared the contrasts and similarities of the Mountain's splendor with those of man, and explored why some people fail to climb the mountain, and for the same reason some people fail to obtain heaven.

Briefly, he said: "It was the Rev. F. E. Clark of *Christian Endeavor* who said, 'Nowhere else in all my journeys around the globe have I seen a country where nature is so lavish in her bestowments, where everything is built on a scale so gigantic. It is as if God has grown his biggest samples of everything along the shore of Puget Sound and the surrounding country.' Although Mount Tacoma, or Tahoma, as we are now expected to call it, is not mentioned by Rev. Clark, he must have had it in mind. For there is nothing quite so gigantic in all this country of grand things as the brooding or nourishing mother. Covering an area of over 200 square miles which is nearly twice that covered by the great city of Chicago, with its 2,000,000 people, the noble mountain bears on its ample bosom 12 vast glaciers which with snowfields, cover a surface of 32,500 acres. To walk around the crest would mean a tramp of seven miles.

"Lofty as is its summit and huge its bulk, still scientists tell us that in its battle with the elements it has lost 2,000 feet in height and one-third of its mass. In spite of these serious losses, it stands today imperial in dignity, unsurpassed in the grandeur of its proportions, unequaled in the picturesque panorama, sublime in its appeal to the sensitive imagination, unique among the snow clad mountains of the world in rearing such huge volume from the level of the sea.

"Perhaps at one time in its history, it was a pure cone covered with new snow, a symbol of childhood's innocence. But Mount Tahoma can no longer claim to be youthful. Thrown up above a normal surface of earth thousands of years ago, it has submitted to two processes of destruction.

"One might be called earth's most powerful tool, the glacier. This gigantic plow, drawn by the stolid oxen of gravity, has cut and scarred its fair cheeks and breast until the original smooth contour has gone forever. In other words, Mount Tahoma appeals to the happy and favored denizens of Western Washington because it symbolizes the one really great thing in life -- character.

"They tell us that Mount Tacoma is made up, according to appearances, of snow and ice and agglomerate masses of broken volcanic stone. It really rests on a vast foundation of solid granite. If this is true, and there is no reason to doubt it, the real mountain is not the unstable mass of stones and boulders, nor the transitory snow and ice which are always in the process of change, but is a mighty and permanent invisible substance that has not been reached by the forces that beat upon the surface. Has this any parallel in human life? Can it not really be said that all the trials and cares and defeats and burdens of life fail to hurt the real self?

"There is something else upon the great mountain besides glaciers. Let old John Muir, the famous mountaineer, tell us what it is. In his book *'Our National Parks,'* he says, 'Of all the fire-mountains which, like beacons once blazed along the Pacific Coast, Mount Tahoma is the noblest in form. Its massive white dome rises out of its forests like a world by itself.

"Above the forests there is a zone of the loveliest flowers, 50 miles in circuit and nearly two miles wide, so closely planted and luxuriant that it seems as if nature, glad to make an open space between woods so deep, were economizing the precious ground and trying to see how many of her darlings she can get together in one mountain wreath - daisies, anemones, columbines, larkspurs, etc., among which we wade knee deep and waist high, the bright corollas in myriads touching petal to petal. Altogether this is the richest sub-alpine garden I ever found, a perfect floral elysium.'"

Rev. Wheeler went on to compare the abundance of vari-colored flowers and the growth of the vegetation, with periods in the lives of human beings. He said:

"The baser temptations of the flesh disappear out of one's life as he rises in the scale of godly living. Like the flowers, fortunate the one who has to work and plan and struggle for a living, for in such a life the weeds of sin find the least encouragement. These than, are the lessons that the mountain would have us take to heart: that life cannot remain in the colorless condition of innocent childhood, but must submit itself to the graving tools of experience which alone can produce the character of sons of God. And in this character there is not only the period of toughening the moral fiber and development of strength, but crowning this there issues an efflorescence that not only gladdens the eye of man, but must, we believe, rejoice the heart of God."

Other Religions and the Mountain

Another group which left two indelible marks on the mountain was a small group of "Theosophists" from Tacoma. They bestowed the name "Narada" (meaning "uncontaminated") on the lower Paradise River falls below Paradise. Narada was a spiritual being worshipped by the Brahman people of India. They also left the name "Theosophy Ridge" on the south-central slope of Paradise Park.

Then there are those who use their trip to the mountain as an opportunity to defend their beliefs. At the old bridge across the Nisqually near Cougar Rock, there once was a sign which read "only pedestrians allowed on this bridge." To which one indignant hiker sputtered, "the U.S. government has no right to dictate any man's religion."

Mount Rainier's Glaciers: The Gates of Heaven?

In 1954, a man declared God had appeared to him at the foot of the Carbon Glacier, and that he was subsequently given the revelation that twelve of the glaciers were in fact the gates of heaven and that the rivers flowing from them were the "rivers of life." He wrote a four-page account, entitled "the testimony of Ed'son" which declared that each glacier contained a large gate of solid pearl. His conclusion was that Mount Rainier was in fact, the new holy city of Jerusalem. He attempted to correlate his beliefs with scripture and apparently he even convinced a few people because references to the glaciers as "the gates of heaven" did show up several times in old documents.

Heavenly Harbingers: (Right Planet, Wrong Mountain)

Then there was the time in late 1994 when several hikers came back to Longmire saying they had met an angel on the trail who told them that there was going to be an earthquake-eruption the next day. Hark, the herald angels must have lost their bearings. It was Mount Rabaul in New Guinea on the other side of the world that erupted the next day. ("Gee God, we're sorry we told the wrong hikers. We knew it was one of those big volcanoes that started with an R.")

Legends and Superstitions

For years an Indian who worked with the loggers in the Rainier foothills, told of the time when he was very young, that his father took him behind a waterfall at Mount Rainier. He scratched the wall with his knife, and it was pure silver.

A similar legend concerns Indian Henry. He purportedly had a gold mine at the mountain, and when he needed money he would journey to it and fill his pockets with nuggets. However one of Henry's neighbors who knew him for many years disputed that story, and claimed that Henry was always broke. The gold myth persists to this day, with claims that the Indians still know where the gold and silver is, but they won't tell. Another variation of the Indian gold story is that their source is "Big Creek*," and the gold is still there. The Indians probably wish this one was true. (If it were, they'd all be driving B-mers.)

*Big Creek flows south of, and parallel to the Nisqually River. It flows to the west, and is about 1/2 mile south of the Sunshine Point Campground to well outside the Park.

Monster Sightings

J.Z. Knight, the New Age spirit-channeler from nearby Yelm has forewarned her followers of "murderous lizard-people", (half-man, half-lizard aliens) who supposedly will come out once the mountain erupts. Knight was channeled this information via Ramtha, the 35,000-year old warrior-king from the lost city of Atlantis. Ramtha added that the lecherous lizard people could be bought off with gold.

The sasquatch, another old favorite usually associated with Mount St. Helens, the next mountain south, apparently has ventured north. Periodically, tracks of the hairy man/ape-like creature have supposedly been found at Mount Rainier. One weekly tabloid actually paid good money to somebody for this story, and reported a woman's tale that Bigfoot fathered her child during an encounter at Mount Rainier. Come to think of it, we have seen a few monstrous big-footed kids at Mount Rainier.

Then there's Batsquatch, a large blue Bigfoot-type creature with wings who reported was spotted at the mountain in April, 1994.

"These stories, like the angel reports, involve alien creatures," said William R. Seaburg, a linguistic anthropologist and professor of American Indian studies at the University of Washington. "It seems to me that for some people it's important to create a non-human entity," Seaburg said. "It's boundary setting. It helps define being human." *(Tacoma News Tribune, 10/14/94)*

Actually the first 'monster' sighting was an encounter with "the Old Man of the Crater," reported by Major E. S. Ingraham, after whom the Ingraham Glacier was named. During his second ascent of the mountain, Major Ingraham and his companions explored the steam caves. Later that night, while his companions slept, Ingraham returned to further explore the caves.

"I quickly stepped within a recess in the wall of ice on my left and awaited developments, " he wrote. "I had not long to wait, for almost immediately there came, rolling, now making an attempt to crawl, a figure of strange and grotesque appearance, down the passage. It stopped within a few feet of me, writhing and floundering very much as a drowning man would do, when drawn from the water as he was about to sink for the last time. Its shape was nearer that of a human being than of any other animal. The crown of its head was pointed, with bristled hair pointing in every direction. The eyeballs were pointed too; and while they appeared dull and visionless at times, yet there was an occasional flash of light from the points, which increased in frequency and brilliancy as the owner began to revive. The nails of its fingers and toes were long and pointed and resembled polished steel more than hardened cuticle. I discovered that the palms of its hands and the soles of its feet were hard and calloused. In fact the whole body, while human in shape, except the pointedness of the parts I have mentioned, seemed very different in character from that of the human species. There was nothing about the mysterious being, however, that would make it impossible that its ancestry of long ages ago might have been human beings like ourselves. Yet by living in different surrounding and under entirely different surroundings and under entirely different conditions, many of its characteristics had changed.

"By degrees this strange being began to revive. Gradually an electric glow covered the entire body with light-centers at the ends of those pointed nails, the eyes and the top of the head. It seemed to accomplish its revivification by rubbing its hands vigorously together. As soon as it was able to stand, it began to rub its feet rapidly upon the floor of the cave. This increased the glow of its body and caused the light-centers to shine with increased brilliancy. It seemed to receive some vital fluid from the earth that at once gave new vigor to its whole system. Involuntarily I imitated its actions and immediately found myself undergoing a very peculiar sensation. I seemed to be growing in accord with the strange being who then for the first time noticed my presence. He at once redoubled his former movements. He would rub his hands vigorously together and then quickly extend the points of his fingers in my direction when sparks of light would dart therefrom. Having become deeply interested in this strange exhibition, I went through the same manoeuvre with a similar result although apparently in a much lesser degree. The effect was magical! I was becoming en rapport with the Old Man of the Crater! I could see a brilliant point of light gradually forming on the crown of his head. Feeling my own hair beginning to rise I removed my knit cap and felt my hair bristling upward to a common point. The light from his crown seemed to form an arch above and between us and WE

WERE IN COMMUNICATION. There, in that icy passage connecting the unknown interior of this earth with the exterior, by means of a new medium, or rather an old medium newly applied, two intelligent beings of different races were enabled to communicate, imperfectly at first of course, with each other. For an hour I received impressions from the Old Man of the Crater. It is a strange story I got from him. While the time was comparatively short, yet what he told me, not by voice or look, but by a subtle agency not known or understood by me, would fill a volume of many pages. Finally expressing doubt at what he communicated, he commanded me to follow him. I had anticipated such a demand and was ready to resist it. So when he turned to descend, to the hot interior of the earth as I verily believe, by a superhuman effort I broke the spell and hastened upward and back to my sleeping companions.

"This is no myth. The old man told me of his abode in the interior, of another race to which he belonged and the traditions of that race; of convulsions and changes on the earth long, long ago; of the gradual contraction of a belt of matter around the earth until it touched the surface hemming in many of the inhabitants and drowning the remainder, and of the survival of a single pair. All was shut out and the atmosphere became changed. Gradually this remaining pair was enabled to conform to the new order of things and became the parents of a race which for the want of a better name I will call SUB-RAINIANS. This Old Man of the Crater had wandered far away from the abode of his race in his desire to explore. Far away from my home we had met, each out of his usual sphere." (Today if you told your therapist you had had this experience, they'd chalk you up as suffering from anoxia.)

Monster Sounds

Probably the most accurate "Monster" account we found was an old Natural History Field Observation Report written by a ranger working late one night many years ago. He wrote: "Something snarling and spitting from the top of nearby tree. Didn't stay to find out what it was." Smart Ranger.

Indian Mythology

The Indians did not worship the mountain as God, however they did believe that spirits inhabited the mountain. They were a superstitious people and respected those spirits and their powers. One entity they desired as a guardian spirit, was the Thunderbird, whom they believed lived in a cave on Mount Rainier. Many young Indian braves went to the mountain on spirit quests.

Another significant mythical factor was in the "sun rising out of the mountain" phenomenon, referring to the alignment of the rising sun at the moment it first appeared over the crest of the mountain.

In prehistoric times, this phenomenon was thought to be the sun emerging out of the mountain. It was awaited with great anticipation and was the basis of some of the deepest beliefs of the Salish people. The Tacoma area, including the Puyallup watershed, was considered to be the Holy Land of the Salish. They

"The Magic Moment"   Photo by Katherine Kowalski

believed that the boundaries between this world and the spirit world was weaker here than in other places, and that there was a doorway to the spirit world in the Tacoma area.

They believed it could be opened during their most important ceremonies, but it also opened on its own on the shortest day of the year, if the conditions were right. Those "right conditions" were when the first rays of sunlight emerged from the summit. Then the doorway opened and a viewer could see into the realm of the spirit (or heaven). No one could pass through, however, and the door closed immediately when the sun cleared the summit. *(Doug McDonnell, Tacoma News Tribune).*

UFO's

NASA is a Johnny-come-lately when it comes to Mount Rainier's outer space connections. On June 24, 1947 while flying over Mount Rainier, private pilot Kenneth Arnold, reported seeing nine "shiny pulsating objects" zooming by at an estimated 1,200 miles per hour. This momentous occasion marked America's first "flying saucer" sightings.

At about 3 p.m. Arnold was in a single-engine Cessna searching for the missing Marine C-46 transport plane with 32 men aboard, (see Aviation section) when he noticed the objects flying in and out of formation. He described the objects as each being as big as a DC-4 passenger plane, and "flat like a pie pan." He also described them as flying as if fastened together, - if one dipped, the others did too.

A UFO (Unidentified Flying Object) group lead by Wayne Aho bought a meeting site near Ashford. They believed that the mountain was the site of an ancient civilization and a source of power. Aho formed a non-profit organization in the 60's called the New Age Foundation, and it was this group which built Cedar Park Ranch, five miles past Ashford on Highway 706. The "Spaceport Earth" was complete with a spaceship replica , which was described as sort of an intergalactic decoy to attract aliens. It also had a homing beacon (a chromed pipe pyramid to beam earth's energy to the heavens.)

Being the positive thinkers that they were, the believers also prepared a "SPLAASH site for visiting space ships. (SPLAASH refers to "Spaceship Protective Landing Area for Advancement of Science and Humanities.")

Occasional UFO sightings around Mount Rainier are still claimed today and UFO groups continue to keep the faith and await sightings and meetings.

Church Services

Some folks come to the mountain for recreation, and others for re-creation. The Manufacturer's Handbook tells us in Psalms 121.1 "I will look unto the hills from whence cometh my help," and many a person has indeed had their spirit refreshed in the great green Cathedral of the outdoors. Take time to step aside from the cares of the world and let the enormity of this marvelous piece of God's handiwork dwarf your concerns and give you a renewed perspective on the truly important things of life. Whether you go to an organized service, or have a private moment with your Maker, receive the regeneration freely available to all to come here.

In-Park Church Services:

Inter-denominational Christian Services in the Park campgrounds are sponsored by "A Christian Ministry in the National Parks." Many of the services are conducted by volunteer student ministers who work at jobs with the Park Service during the week. Services are usually held every Sunday from July 1 through Labor Day.

> **Paradise Inn Lobby:** 8:30 a.m. & 7:30 p.m.
> **Cougar Rock Campground:** 9:00 a.m. & 7:00 p.m.
> **Ohanapecosh Campground Amphitheater:** 9:00 a.m. 7:00 p.m.
> **White River Campground Fire Circle:** 9:00 a.m. 7:00 p.m.

Nearby Church Services:

> **Roman Catholic Services:**
> > Eatonville (Our Lady of Good Counsel) 10 a.m.
> > Morton (Sacred Heart) 10:45 a.m.
> > Wilkeson (Our Lady of Lourdes) 9 a.m.
> > Packwood, (held at Presbyterian Church) Saturday 5 p.m.
>
> **Eastern Orthodox Liturgy:** - Wilkeson (Holy Trinity) 10:00 a.m.
> **Lutheran:**
> > Elbe Church, Elbe
> > Grace Lutheran Church, Buckley
> > Hope Lutheran Church, Enumclaw
>
> **Assembly of God:**
> > Mount Rainier Christian Center, 43811-244th SE, Enumclaw

Fun Activities

***Acceptable* Fun Activities in the Park**	***Unacceptable* Activities in the Park**
Bicycling	Bathing in hot springs
Birding/Birdwatching	Bungee jumping
Camping	Gold panning or mining
Canoeing	Golfing
Climbing	Hang Gliding
Fishing	Hunting
Flowergazing	Ice fishing
Glacier Viewing	Jetskiing
Hiking	Motor boating
Horseback riding	Mountain biking
Huckleberry picking	(OK - West Side Road only)
Limited boating	Off-road vehicles
Mushrooming	Picking flowers for drying or preserving
Picnicking	Rockhounding
Running	Rollerblading
Sightseeing	Scuba diving
Snorkeling	Skinny dipping
Snowmobiling (closed roads only)	Trapping
Snowshoeing	Waterskiing
Tubing (Inner-tubing)	Wind Surfing
Volcano study	

Fun

Tourism

If Mount Rainier has an industry, it's tourism. Each year people follow the tug on their heartstrings to come revel in the beauty and soak up some flower-perfumed air. Mount Rainier is one of the state's top three tourist attractions. It shares the honors with the Space Needle and Pike Place Market.

Tourism has never again duplicated the "high" of two and a half million visitors who came in 1977. In 1994 Mount Rainier was visited by "only" 2,206,083 visitors. It was still crowded on weekends, however since about half of those visitors arrived in June, July and August. The peak months were July and August which saw 542,527 visitors and 523,040 visitors, respectively. The annual attendance fluctuates each year depending on the weather. The peak season runs between 138 to 148 days (May through September), with the "off-season" (January to May and September to December) referred to in Mount Rainier trade talk as "the shoulder months."

Where did all these visitors come from? Over half (59%) of all respondents to a recent visitor survey, were from Washington state, with 44% of those residing in the four counties surrounding the park (Pierce, King, Lewis and Yakima). Washington visitors from all other counties constitute another 15%. Remaining visitors were from California (5%), Oregon (3%), foreign (3%) and all other U.S. (30%).

The survey also concluded that most park visitors are well-educated, employed in managerial and professional occupations, and had an average age of 43. Most of those surveyed were traveling with their families, with nearly one-third accompanied by children under age 16.

Most visitors were day users (with most staying less than seven hours in the park). Of overnight users, about half stayed in frontcountry campgrounds, with the remainder evenly divided between backcountry camping and staying at one of the park inns.

Their favorite destination was Paradise, which was visited by about 71% of respondents. The most popular activity was driving to view the scenery, followed by day hiking.

These people came via various modes of transportation. In 1994, for instance, 752,515 vehicles entered the park, including 40,062 recreational vehicles, and 71,290 who came to tent camp.

All these people obediently heeded Washington state's unofficial motto, "Keep Washington Green - Spend Money." It's estimated that the Park adds over $200,000,000 to the state economy each year.

Comparative Attendance Figures 1967 - 1994

Year	Visitors	Vehicles
1958	1,115,815	298,037
1959	1,105,072	291,618
1960	1,538,663	411,125
1961	1,592,829	421,063
1962	1,905,302	508,528
1963	1,544,300	408,653
1964	1,439,922	382,071
1965	1,643,142	439,141
1966	1,722,258	457,704
1967	1,805,863	479,525
1968	1,682,740	447,929
1969	1,795,238	476,113
1970	1,925,131	515,015
1971	1,742,611	483,021
1972	1,682,379	452,936
1973	1,528,186	411,462
1974	1,495,514	404,193
1975	1,521,302	411,163
1976	1,972,334	533,063
1977	2,437,332	658,738
1978	2,094,372	578,413
1979	1,981,454	536,726
1980	2,001,002	540,811
1981	1,964,846	701,732
1982	1,536,014	531,404
1983	1,581,987	548,902
1984	1,669,193	572,356
1985	1,638,837	561,574
1986	1,830,751	633,309
1987	1,825,629	635,473
1988	1,799,978	617,329
1989	2,023,900	700,069
1990	1,936,215	669,739
1991	2,235,591	773,293
1992	2,358,296	815,737
1993	2,192,062	752,515
1994	2,206,083	_____

These figures are predicated on a factor of 2.8 persons per car on weekdays, weekends and holidays from September to May, and 3.0 persons per car for June

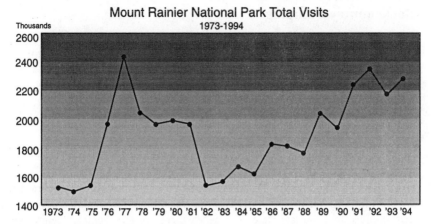

Mount Rainier National Park Total Visits
1973-1994

Economic Impact of Park Tourism

(Based on 1993 figures).

1993 Recreation Visitor Days	1,646,472
Visitor Sales	$193,625,107
Sales Tax Revenue	$15,102,758
Jobs Created	5,808

Sources: NPS Money Generation Model, US Dept of Commerce, Bureau of Economic Analysis, Regional Multipliers, May 1992, Runzheimer International Inc., Quarterly Travel Cost Index, Summer, 1994

Accommodating All

Disabled and handicapped visitors can safely navigate the first half of the Trail of the Shadows at Longmire, which is graded and compacted gravel.

Safety and resource messages are available in English and eight other languages for foreign visitors to the Park. Those languages are German, Spanish, French, Korean, Russian, Vietnamese, Japanese, and Chinese. They are also available in large type for the visually impaired.

Fun

Fun things to do at Mount Rainier are more than could all be done in one trip. Some can be done spontaneously without pre-planning, while others require forethought and preparation. Mount Rainier's smorgasbord of fun activities includes (alphabetically):

Amphitheater Programs

Fact-filled campfire programs ranging from talks, slide shows, movies, or demonstrations, are conducted by naturalists or rangers most weekends of the summer at the amphitheaters at Cougar Rock, Ohanapecosh, White River Campground and Ipsut Creek. Check with the ranger for times and directions.

Backcountry Camping

Don't just strike off without first getting a permit and reservations. There is no casual unauthorized camping allowed in the Park's backcountry. Permits can be gotten at the Hiker Centers up to a day in advance (page 260). In 1994, there were 48,574 camper nights spent in the backcountry at 38 trailside camps which have 144 individual sites, 23 group sites and 4 stock use camps.

Bicycling

Interminably steep grades, winding roads, steep drop-offs, and no shoulders, discourage most cyclists from "doing the mountain." But if this is your sport of choice, obey the number one rule. **Absolutely do not hold up traffic for long periods of time.** Bicycles must obey the same traffic rules as automobiles, and the law states that when there are five vehicles behind you, you *must* pull over and let traffic pass. With only one road encircling the mountain, and hundreds of visitors all using it at the same time, one bicyclist could singlehandedly create the mother of all traffic jams. Also note that helmets are mandatory, and it is also against Park regulations to ride bicycles on any trails.

Bicycles and motorbikes may be operated in the campgrounds on the roadways only. Skateboards are not permitted in the park.

There are only two regular annual organized bicycling events within the Park.

RAMROD: (Ride Around Mount Rainier in One Day) Want to feel your legs drop off? Circumnavigate Mount Rainier in a day. This 156-mile ride has gone on since 1984, and is usually held the last week of July. It is sponsored by the Redmond Cycling Club. Participant cost is $55.00. For more information contact Patrick Merrick, (206) 361-5064.

RAMROD Statistics

Direction: Counter-clockwise

Start/Finish line: King County Fairgrounds, Enumclaw

Amount of elevation gain: 9,300 vertical feet

Number of participants in 1995: 608 riders

First finisher's time: 8-1/2 hours

Usual mileage: 156 miles

1995 mileage: 195 miles because of construction detours

Stalwarts: Louise Miller, 60, has made the ride 12 times

Unusual participants: Tandem bikes and bicycles made for three

Biggest dangers: potholes, cars, the wheel of the person in front of you

Downhill speeds: 60 mph

The second event is an autumn **3-day Mount Rainier Loop Tour** sponsored by the NW Bicycle Touring Society. This event has gone on for over 20 years. For more information, call Pete Maas (206) 255-4192.

There's usually a late summer one-day **West Side Road Ride** too. This one is a Mountain bike ride, leisurely to moderate pace. The ride is sponsored by the Backcountry Bicycle Trails Club. (206) 283-2995.

Occasionally permits are issued for other groups to have one-time rides within the park. Check the bicycling newspapers for those.

Birding

Western Washington ("the Pacific Flyway") lies on major migration routes between Canada and points in California and Mexico, and many flocks of birds can be seen passing over the west side of the Park. Especially watch for the thousands of Canadian geese and pintail ducks which pass through while migrating. A complete list of park birds is on page 397.

Birders might also want to check out The Federation Forest on Highway 410, just north of the Park, a real birder's paradise. They have a pamphlet with a checklist of ninety-four birds visitors might see there.

When coming to the mountain, bring binoculars. Everything looks even better close up.

Boating

Non-motorized boating is allowed on all park lakes except Frozen Lake, Reflection Lakes, Lake Louise, and Tipsoo Lake. Canoeing, row-boating or inflatable boating is a great way to view the wildlife. Mowich Lake is an especially good canoe spot. The deep aqua-blue water is so clear, one can see far into the depths of the lake.

Campground Camping

There are a total of 600 vehicle campground spaces at five locations within the Park. Class A sites are at Ohanapecosh, Cougar Rock and White River. Class B sites are Sunshine Point and Ipsut Creek. Class C group sites are at Cougar Rock and Ipsut Creek.

Reservations

Advance reservations are accepted only for group sites in Class B campgrounds (Cougar Rock and Ipsut Creek). They can be made for camping between June 1 and October 15, and are accepted up to 90 days in advance of the intended visit. All other campsites are allotted on a first-come, first-served basis. To obtain group reservations, write: Group Campsite Reservations, Mount Rainier National Park, Ashford, WA 98304 or call (360) 569-2211.

Length of Stay

A 14-day camping limitation applies to all July and August camping.

Campground Fees:

There are five drive-in frontcountry campgrounds plus one walk-in campground with a total of 600 camp sites.

Ohanapecosh (A): 205 sites, no group sites. $10.00 per night

Cougar Rock (A): 200 sites, 5 group sites. $8.00 per night

White River (A): 117 sites, no group sites. $8.00 per night

Sunshine Point (B): 18 sites, no group sites. $6.00 per night

Ipsut Creek (B): 29 sites, 2 group sites. $6.00 per night

Extra vehicle $4.00 per night

Mowich Lake: No Fee

Group Campsites: $3.00 per night per person.

Fees for use of group facilities at Cougar Rock and Ipsut Creek Campgrounds are also $3 per person per night.

Classes of Sites

Class A sites: Well defined roads, campsites and parking spaces. Piped drinking water, flush-type toilets and refuse cans. Individual sites equipped with parking pad, tent pad, fireplace and table/bench combination. Parking space may not be an integral part of a walk-in site, but is provided.

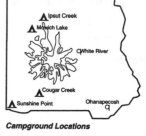

Campground Locations

Class B sites: Well defined roads, campsites and parking spaces. Piped drinking water, pit-type toilets and refuse cans. Individual sites equipped with parking and tent areas, fireplace and table/bench combination.

Class C sites: Group sites in developed campgrounds. Multiple tent site area with central fireplace parking and table/bench combinations by reservations only.

Campsite Capacity

One vehicle per campsite is the usual rule. Parking for additional cars is available in a central campground location. A fee of $2.00 is charged for additional vehicles. A maximum of two tents per site is allowed.

Fuel Sources

Plan ahead and bring your own firewood. Otherwise plan on purchasing wood from the wood concessionaire (at Class A sites only). Gathering wood from the forest is not allowed at any campground, however it *is* permissible to gather wood from riverbeds at Sunshine Point and Ipsut Creek campgrounds. The Longmire General Store usually carries firewood too.

Build fires only in designated places. Don't burn garbage. Do not leave fires unattended and report unattended fires to park officials. Use water to extinguish embers before leaving, and make sure the fire is dead out!.

Some stove fuel is available at the store at Longmire, and at numerous locations outside the Park. (page 419).

Hookups

No utility or hookups of any kind are available at any campgrounds and draining waste water onto the ground is prohibited. RV sink drains may empty into containers outside the vehicle but these must be emptied into service sinks or toilets only. Be considerate and don't use water fountains or spigots for cleaning purposes. Dumping stations are located at Cougar Rock and Ohanapecosh campgrounds.

Interpretive Programs

Park Naturalists present free evening campfire programs and guided walks throughout the summer. For details see activity schedules in *Tahoma*, the Park newspaper given to you when you entered the Park, visitor centers and campground bulletin boards. Self-guiding nature trails and wayside exhibits are available around all campgrounds.

Laundry Facilities

There are no facilities in the Park, however there are coin-operated laundries are in Ashford, Eatonville, Enumclaw, Morton and Packwood. Public showers are in the Jackson Memorial Visitor Center at Paradise, and just outside the park in Ashford, Packwood and Eatonville (page 419).

Pets

Pets are allowed in the park *only* if they are on a leash, in a cage or confined. They are prohibited on all trails, in the buildings or amphitheaters, or in the backcountry, even under restraint. Pets are defined as dogs, cats and other small animals. (Seeing-eye and hearing-ear dogs excepted). It might come as quite a surprise if a cougar were to swoop in and have little Muffy for dinner right before your eyes. If leaving Muffy in the car and it's a warm day, remember leave the window open enough for good ventilation.

There is only one pet relief area in the entire park (at Sunrise) and don't plan on using the flower fields, parking lots or campgrounds or you will be ticketed if caught. Also, if a ranger catches a hiker with a pet on a trail, they will be issued a citation.

Preserve Natural Resources

Do not drive nails in trees, or dig ditches around tents.

Quiet Hours

Quiet hours are maintained between 10 p.m. and 6 a.m.

Security

There have been countless thefts from campsites and camper vehicles. It seems thieves enjoy coming to the Mountain too. To help prevent thefts, lock possessions out of sight in your trunk, and keep wallets, purses and cameras with you. When leaving your campsite, even for a short time, lock your vehicle.

Supplies

Limited camper supplies are available at the National Park Inn at Longmire and at Sunrise. Ice is sold at Longmire and in all nearby towns. Larger selections of camping supplies are available outside the Park at White Pass Sporting Goods in Packwood, the Growly Bear just outside the Nisqually entrance, and the Elbe Mall Mini Mart at Elbe. On the north side full supplies are available in Enumclaw and Buckley, and limited supplies are at Wilkeson and Greenwater.

Leave foodstuffs in your automobile trunk or suspended from bear wires to avoid tempting Yogi and BooBoo.

Motor Homes, 5th Wheelers, Camp Trailers, etc.

There are no trailer utility hookups at any campsites, but trailer, 5th wheel, and motorhome camping is allowed at Sunshine Point, Cougar Rock*, Ohanapecosh* and White River Campground* (*denotes waste disposal).

Vehicles

Vehicles (including bicycles) must stay on the constructed roadways or parking pads. They are not permitted on trails, paved paths or off roadways. Remember, even the small track left by something as simple as a bicycle or tricycle could be the beginning of a new erosion channel.

* * *

Children's Activities

Children will probably enjoy many of the regular programs such as the evening slide shows at Cougar Rock, the campfire programs at the other campgrounds, and the ever-popular "Shadows of the Past" living history program at Longmire. They may be greeted by James, Martha and Elcaine Longmire, Fay Fuller or John Muir along the Trail of the Shadows if they happen to be in the park during the four or five times a year the "old timers" make an appearance. Check with the park newspaper "Tahoma" for dates they are expected to reincarnate.

Programs specifically for children are usually held Wednesday, Friday and Saturday afternoons at 2:00 p.m. at Cougar Rock Campground during the summer. Also check with rangers to see if there are any "Junior Ranger" doings.

Junior Rangers

Junior Rangers is a program designed to teach good conservation habits at an early age. The youngsters get an informative activity booklet which requires answers about one of the four areas of the park, or attendance at one of the formal interpretive programs. Participants in the program receive "Don't Be A Meadow Stomper" button, Ranger cloth patches, decals and certificates.

Junior Ranger programs are conducted at Longmire (Cougar Rock), Paradise, Ohanapecosh, Sunrise and Carbon River.

Fine Dining

Some folks' idea of a good time at the mountain is a hearty meal at one of the many fine restaurants. The dining rooms at Paradise Inn and Longmire offer excellent fare at reasonable prices, and outside the Park, a variety of restaurants have selections ranging from exotic to "down-home" cooking. A complete list on page 421.

Fishing

No fishing license is required to toss a line in Rainier's streams and lakes. Fishing season in lakes and ponds is from April through October. (However most lakes are not ice free until early July, and ice fishing is not permitted.) In rivers and streams the season is usually from late May through November. Since the Park Service stopped stocking the lakes back in the 60's, fishing isn't what it used to be, however that doesn't deter a few diehard Rainier anglers who like the setting as well as the fish. Four species of trout, plus two of charr are native to the park. Specific regulations and closures are listed at ranger stations. Anglers are encouraged to use barbless hooks and to release uninjured fish.

Probably the most popular fishing spots are the Carbon and White rivers, which fish enter to spawn in the clear tributaries (June Creek, Ranger Creek, and Ipsut Creek). Sculpin (bullheads) have been caught in the Carbon River, about a mile or more above Ipsut Campground. The Carbon and Nisqually Rivers, even though silty, also yield Dolly Vardons and cutthroat trout.

Hiking

240 miles of trail network the park. See the Trail section, page 259

Horses/Stock

Nearly 100 miles (or a little over 1/3) of park trails are open to horse use, and four trailside camps may be used by parties with stock. Horse use of trails in the park is infrequent. Mount Rainier trails are steep with long uphill and downhill stretches, frequently with exposure. Horses used in the park should be in good physical condition, and trailwise in mountain travel and fording rivers. Stock is not permitted in the most scenic and fragile subalpine meadows, and most trails open to stock are in wooded areas offering limited views.

To help protect the trails, horse parties are required to follow the following rules: Stock parties are limited to a maximum combination of 12 people and stock on the Pacific Crest Trail, and a maximum of 5 people/5 stock on other park trails. Horses can be used only on those trails and camps signed for their

Horse Trails

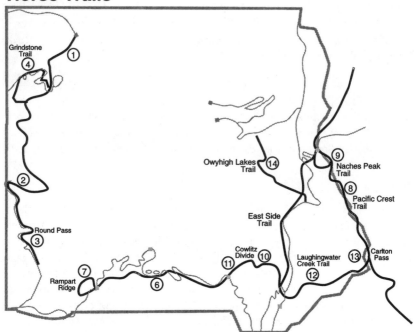

use. They are not permitted in auto campgrounds or picnic areas. Neither saddle nor pack animals are allowed within 100 years of trail shelters, backcountry campsites or above such sites or waterways. *Horse parties must carry their own stock feed.* Grazing is not allowed! Horses should be tethered to hitching rails or away from the root zones of trees. To prevent the spread of exotic plants, stock should be fed compact feed for at least two days prior to entry into the park.

Use of stock on park trails should not be attempted until early-mid August, since trails are muddy or may be snow covered before then. Stock waste may not be dumped or left in parking areas or along roadways.

The term stock includes horses, donkeys, burros, llamas and pack-goats. Bring your own horse, or make arrangements with one of the rent-a-horse outfits outside the park to deliver one to the trailhead for you (page 422).

Areas Open For Stock Use (West)

• Wonderland Trail from Ipsut Creek campground to North Puyallup stock camp (dismount and lead along the road shoulder at Mowich Lake).

• North Puyallup Trail from North Puyallup stock camp to Klapatche Point at the north end of the Westside Road.

• Westside Road (gravel) from Klapatche Point south to Dry Creek (road barricade).

▪ Mowich Lake west on the Mowich Lake Road to the Grindstone Trail, cutting across the road's switchbacks on the trail, and continuing west on the road to the trailhead at Paul Peak (0.7 mi. inside the park on the Mowich Lake Road).

▪ Paul Peak Trail from the Mowich Lake Road to the Wonderland Trail near North Mowich stock camp.

South

▪ Wonderland Trail from Longmire to Box Canyon (along the road shoulder past Reflection Lakes).

▪ Rampart Ridge loop trail from Longmire back to Longmire.

East

▪ Pacific Crest Trail along the east boundary of the park.

▪ Naches Peak Trail from Tipsoo Lake to the Pacific Crest Trail.

▪ East Side Trail from Stevens Canyon Road south to Silver Falls loop trail, and along the Laughingwater Creek Trail to Highway 123.

▪ Wonderland Trail from Box Canyon to the top of Cowlitz Divide.

▪ Cowlitz Divide Trail from the top of Cowlitz Divide to Stevens Canyon Road and Silver Falls loop trail.

▪ Laughingwater Creek Trail from Highway 123 to the Pacific Crest Trail near Carlton Pass.

▪ Owyhigh Lakes Trail from Highway 123 to White River Road.

For Current Trail conditions call (360) 569-2211 ext. 3314.

Llama Trips

Llamas are allowed on any trails open to horses.

Mountaineering

Mountaineering (originally known as "alpinism,") is any activity which takes place in and on mountains, including ice, snow or rock climbing, hiking, rock "scrambles" and ski touring. Each of these activities is covered by separate chapters in this book.

Naturalist Walks and Programs (Paradise)

Interpretive Programs are presented daily from late June to early September.

10:30 a.m. Alta Vista Walk 2 hour walk	1:30 p.m. Flower Walk 1 hour walk
2:30 p.m. Nisqually Vista Walk 1.5 hour walk	
3:00 p.m. Oh! What A Paradise .5 hour audiovisual program	

At 9:00 p.m.there is usually an evening one-hour audiovisual Program. Fridays through Wednesdays from late June through early September, at 7:00 p.m., there's a 1 hour evening stroll.

Each Thursday evening at 7:00 p.m. there's a 1 hour "Music for Parks" walk.

Wednesday, Friday and Sunday from July 1 through early September, at 10:00 a.m., there's a 3-hour Explorer Hike.

This schedule may be preempted by some special more timely topic if events warrant. Check for schedule changes on the activity boards or ask the rangers at the information counters.

In addition to these regularly scheduled activities, the Paradise Interpretive staff presents specially requested on-site programs (such as snowshoe walks, flower and geology walks, map talks, etc.) for schools and groups.

Photography

If a picture is worth 1000 words, you'll have to stop counting at Mount Rainier. Million-word photo opportunities are every place you look.

Whether you wait for alpenglow on the Mountain, catch a just-blooming flower, or capture streaks of sunlight slanting through corridors of the deep forest cathedral, Mount Rainier National Park is a photographer's paradise.

Today's "smart" automatic cameras can take out the work of having to know speeds and settings that used to be essential to good pictures. But photographing mountains, especially big snowy white sentinels like Mount Rainier, will yield better results by following these few simple tips from the old Rainier photomeister himself, Ira Spring.

"One aid to overcoming the mountain-to-valley contrast is shooting at a time when the peak is partly in shadows. Certain times of the day, the sun will leave shadows on the steep icy cliffs, yet be shining brightly on the lower slopes.

"This cross lighting, generally recommended for scenery shots anywhere, is especially important at Mt. Rainier for shooting the peak itself. The resulting shadows give dimension to its massive bulk and show contours of jagged cliffs and deep crevasses otherwise lost in the flat glare of ice and snow.

"Cross light occurs at different times on different sides of the mountain and varies with the seasons of the year, but we're principally concerned with summer. From Sunrise, the mountain's contours show best from 9:00 to 11:00 a.m.; at Paradise, from 6:00 to 9:00 a.m. and from 3:00 to 4:00 p.m.; from the end of the West Side Road (which only hikers can now reach) from 11:00 a.m. to 1:00 p.m.; at the Carbon River-Moraine Park area, the morning sun slants over the sheer Willis Wall in summer, but hardly touches it the rest of the year. Of course, interesting cloud patterns or high overcast upset our theoretical shooting schedule completely.

"From close up, snow and ice create other problems. To give shape to white snow and ice, we always use side or back lighting."

From *Camera Adventuring on Mount Rainier* by Bob and Ira Spring

Reprinted with permission

Ira also is known for not having the mountain dead center in his photos. He makes his shots more interesting by aiming a little off to one side or the other.

Other tips to get good pictures at the mountain are - vary your viewpoint. Don't take all your photos from eye level. If shooting flowers, get down low for single flowers or small clusters of flowers, then shoot from a higher angle to photograph the whole bed.

In scenic shots, don't get too much sky. The interesting matter is the big picture and what's in the foreground.

Want to learn more?

Seattle Mountaineers have frequent "Photo Outings" at the Mountain. They also offer a Nature Photography Course once a year. For more information, contact:

Seattle Mountaineers
300 Third Avenue W.
Seattle, WA 98119
(206) 284-6310

Picnicking

There are eleven different picnic areas with a total of 320 tables within the park plus there are another 211 roadside tables and one picnic shelter scattered around the park. (Total: 531 picnic tables). They are at:

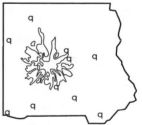

Picnic Areas

• **Box Canyon:** On the Stevens Canyon Road at Box Canyon between Ohanapecosh and Paradise.

• **Carbon River:** Ipsut Campground picnic area

• **Cougar Rock:** Across the road from Cougar Rock Campground. Closes for the winter in mid-October.

• **Falls Creek Picnic area:** 3 tables

• **Ohanapechosh:** Across from the Ohanapecosh Visitor Center in Loop A of the Campground.

• **Paradise:** Located .25 mile below the Jackson Visitor Center. Closes for the winter mid-October or when closed by snow. An indoor picnic area is available in the Jackson Memorial Visitor Center at Paradise on weekends and holidays, as well as a downstairs lounge during weekdays.

• **Paul Peak Picnic area:** 2 tables

203

- **Sunrise:** Below the Interpretive Center in the old campground.
- **Sunshine Point:** .25 mile inside the Nisqually entrance, and 6 miles west of Longmire.
- **Tipsoo Lake:** One of the more scenic picnic settings.
- **White River:** A nice wooded lunch setting.

Power Running

Power runners, those legs-of-steel human running machines have taken to pounding around the Wonderland Trail in three thirty-mile legs on three successive days: (Longmire to Mowich, Mowich to White River, White River to Longmire). This rugged trail normally takes 10-14 days and entails daily elevation gains and losses of 3,500 feet per day. Doing it in three days changes the daily elevation gain/loss to up to 15,190 feet per day, and that's a lot of up and down, by anybody's standard! This event has gone on for the past 13 years.

As mentioned on page 274, one power runner did it even faster. He ran the entire trail in 29 hours and 10 minutes.

For further information, contact the Washington or Oregon Trail Runner's Associations. (503) 646-RUNR

Resorts

If time and money permit, treat yourself to a leisurely weekend or mid-week respite at the mountain either at Paradise or Longmire, or one of the many fine hostelries nearby. A complete list of accommodations in on page 417.

Self Guided Nature Trails

From Longmire there is Trail of the Shadows and the Kautz Creek Mudflow Area. Continuing around the mountain, there's Sourdough Ridge, Nisqually Vista, Ohanapecosh Hot Springs, Stevens Canyon at Box Canyon, Grove of the Patriarchs, the Carbon River Rain Forest, and Emmons Vista at Sunrise. These trails are generally easy, well maintained, and well worth taking.

Sightseeing

This is probably the universal activity at the Mountain. There's something new to see at every turn, and most of the two million annual visitors come simply to see what there is to see.

Occasionally, as northwesterners so surrounded by beauty wherever we look, we grow unappreciative and start to take our beloved mountain for granted. Bailey Willis had some words of wisdom for such a time.

"I have seen the glories of Switzerland, the grandeur of the Andes, and the grace of the beautiful cone of Fuji, but among the most renowned scenery of the world, I know of nothing more majestic or more inspiring than the grandeur of my own old camping ground, Mount Rainier."

Stargazing

Stargazing is particularly good at Mount Rainier (especially in the backcountry) because it's remote, dark, and smog-free. Gazing is best when there's no moon. (The darker the night, the better the stellar performance.) Look for a high, open area and avoid snow cover because it will reflect light. Take a good pair of binoculars (7X recommended), a plastic tarp (for protection from moisture), a good closed-cell foam pad or air mattress, and a sleeping bag. Find a comfy contoured rock, jump in the bag, lie back and watch the heavens go by.

If you don't care to hike after dark, Ricksecker Point is a good place for viewing sunsets, alpenglow and stargazing.

Visitor Center Exhibits

Natural history exhibits are at Longmire, Paradise, Sunrise and Ohanapecosh.

Volksmarching

"Volksmarches" are leisurely walks that are usually 10 kilometers (6.2 miles) in distance and offer a variety of trails and scenery. Each participant chooses his own pace and decides how often he wants to stop and enjoy the scenery.

The last big Volksmarch at the mountain was in 1989 in celebration of Washington's State's Centennial. Under honorary walk director Lou Whittaker, the group offered both 10-kilometer and 20-kilometer walks. The walk was sponsored by the Park Service, and proceeds went to the Foothills Rails to Trails Coalition. For info on future Volksmarches at the Park, call (206) 838-6981.

Winter Fun

Igloos

Another fun group to watch is the igloo builders. Designs range from traditional to creative. For those who want to try their hand, a Winter Camping Seminar is held annually every January by the Everett Parks and Recreation Department. They offer a four-week course, culminating in a campout field trip on Mount Rainier. For more information contact the Everett Parks Department at 802 Mukilteo Boulevard, Everett, WA 98203; (206) 259-0300.

Snow Camping at Paradise

Camping is allowed at Paradise when there is at least four feet of snow on the ground to protect fragile underlying meadows. Permits are available at the Jackson Visitor Center, Longmire Museum and most ranger stations.

Choose your campsite with care. The site must be a minimum of 200' from plowed areas to avoid being buried by snow blowers, and at least 100' from lakes and streams. Be very certain that you park in an authorized overnight area lest your car be eaten by a snowplow. Also be sure morning plowing operations have been completed and the road is open to Longmire before driving downhill.

For your own safety and that of others, be sure to collapse igloos and snow caves when breaking camp so someone does not fall through the roof of your abandoned shelter.

Snowmobiling

Snowmobiles are permitted on designated roads only, when such roads are closed by snow to normal traffic. Four areas within the park are designated for snowmobile use. Out of Longmire, there's the West Side Road, and roadways within the Cougar Rock Campground. The other two are the Stevens Canyon Road (from the Stevens Canyon junction with Highway 123 to Box Canyon) and in the White River Area, from the north park boundary on Highway 410, southward to the junction of the White River-Sunrise Road, and then west on that road to the White River Campground.

Snowmobiles are *prohibited* on Highway 123 north of the Stevens Canyon Road junction, and west of the Box Canyon tunnel. They are also prohibited on the Sunrise Road beyond the White River Campground Road, and south of the Highway 410-White River Road junction.

Snowmobile rules are:

- ❏ Do not attempt to travel cross-country, on trails or on undesignated roads.
- ❏ The snowmobile must be properly registered according to state law.
- ❏ The snowmobile must be equipped with brakes in good working order.
- ❏ The snowmobile must exhibit a white lighted headlight and a red taillight from one-half hour after sunset, to one-half hour before sunrise, or when persons and vehicles are not clearly visible for a distance of 500 feet.

The following acts are prohibited:

- ❏ Operating a snowmobile that makes excessive noise.
- ❏ Racing or operating a snowmobile in excess of 45 mph.
- ❏ Operation of a snowmobile by a person under age 16 unless supervised within line of sight by a responsible person over age 21
- ❏ Operation of a snowmobile by a person under age 16 unless riding on the same machine with a responsible person over age 21.
- ❏ Towing of persons on skis, sleds, or other devices by a snowmobile.

Registration is not required, *but do let Rangers and others know of your plans.* Check with a Ranger for current avalanche forecasts, and *stay alert for possible avalanche danger on all steep areas, and on obvious avalanche chutes.*

Snowshoeing

Snowshoeing has been described as walking on water the hard way. On winter weekends from December through March, snowshoe walks along the Nisqually Vista Trail are led by Park Naturalists. These two-hour walks are offered daily during the Christmas holiday period, and Saturdays and Sundays thereafter, at 10:30 a.m., 12:30 p.m. and 2:30 p.m. About 1,500 people a year take the snowshoe hikes. Sign up at the Paradise Visitor Center. If going on your own, beware of avalanches if you go off the marked trails. Snowshoes can be rented from Rainier Ski Touring, (360) 569-2283 at Paradise.

Snow Sliding

Innertubes, soft platters, sleds and toboggans may be used in designated play areas only. Sliding on snowbanks results in several injuries each year, some serious. Snow can hide rocks, cliffs or streams. Sledders also frequently run into trees and go off high banks into parking lots. In the springtime, snow bridges over streams can collapse under a person's weight. If sliding, sledding or innertubing, be sure there's a safe runout and that you are well out of the area where people may be walking. If the budget permits, the park prepares specific groomed snowplay areas and staffs the area with Snowplay rangers.

Avalanches

Ken Hopping photos

Here's one that dropped about 4,000 vertical feet off Willis Wall

There's very little real estate at Mount Rainier that hasn't been covered by an avalanche at one time or another. The big mountain has all the ingredients: tons of snow, steep slopes, and gravity. Even in summer, evidence of avalanches is all around. Every trail crosses avalanche gulleys, the steep chutes that are scoured by so many avalanches, that it's virtually impossible for baby trees ever to get a foothold, or if they do, they're grotesquely twisted from the tons of snow periodically churning over them.

Higher on the mountain, avalanches are a daily occurrence year round. Then there's Willis Wall, where they rain off like clockwork.

Avalanche Safety

- Cross avalanche prone areas one person at a time.
- Always wear an avalanche transceiver and use fresh batteries.
- Don't leave a victim; stay and search for them. Every minute counts.

If Caught in an Avalanche

- Call out so other members of your party can observe your course in case you are buried.
- Discard your poles, pack and skis.
- "Swim" in the snow in order to stay on the surface, and if possible move to one side of the moving snow.
- If you become buried, cover your face with your hands. This will help keep snow out of your nose and mouth, and create a breathing space.
- Remain calm and conserve oxygen supply while waiting to be rescued.

Some Recreational Fatalities

When most people go to the mountain for a day of fun, the possibility of getting killed there is the farthest thing from their mind, and yet it happens. For some it's as a result of something they did or failed to do, but for others, it's just a matter of being in the wrong place at the wrong time. For instance, on August 7, 1959, the "Rolling Stones" (not *THE* Rolling Stones) a happy-go-lucky group of outdoor-oriented New York Teenagers, came awed by the grandeur of the park, but left scarred by tragedy. The group was on a tour bus, which was stopped awaiting bridge construction on the Nisqually River Bridge. As the bus sat on the road waiting for the signal for go, a massive tree stump came tumbling down the mountainside and crashed into the bus, crushing and killing a young woman chaperone. *(TNT 8/7/59).*

In 1964 a rockslide thundered down on two hikers on the Nisqually Canyon Nature Trail, killing both. *(TNT 7/27/64).*

Another somewhat similar accident happened in 1967 on the Stevens Canyon Road when a rockslide hit a station wagon containing four tourists. The vehicle was hit by three large rocks, one the size of an office desk, which pushed it to the edge of a 100-foot cliff. Another boulder weighing 100 tons landed on the roadway beside the wagon. The vehicle was totaled, but no one was injured.

In 1968, Lt. (jg) Martin J. Quinn, stationed aboard the USS Enterprise out of Bremerton, became the eighth person to die on the mountain in the past year and a half. (All deaths occurred below the 10,000 ft. level). Quinn and a companion were climbing in a rockslide area 500 yards from a trail east of Ipsut Creek Campground. Quinn slipped and fell 300 ft. down a rock chute. *(TNT 8/30/68)*.

A Portland man, Robert Linderman, 23, was killed while snow sliding on an air mattress, when he suddenly plummeted over a cliff and hurled down a waterfall. He fell 35 feet into Edith Creek and went over 50-foot high Myrtle Falls, then slid under a frozen snowbank below the falls. *(TNT 5/28/73)*.

In July, 1977, Julie Fillo, a 20-year old summer park employee, embarked on a 19-mile hike alone. She was doing the Wonderland Trail and intended to go from Summerland over Panhandle Gap to Indian Bar. She never returned and in spite of an intensive search, there wasn't a clue of what had happened to her. Finally in 1984, her remains were found in the Cowlitz Chimneys *(TNT 9/19/84)*.

In 1979, Two and a half miles from Paradise, hiker Gary Baldwin was struck by lightning. It blew a hole through his boot and cotton and wool socks and left him with a first degree burn on his foot. "I saw the glow of blue, and an arc went from my foot to the ground. There was a loud crack and I was thrown to the ground." He was the only one in his party wearing a backpack. *(TNT 8/30/79)*

A Vancouver boy, 6, drowned in the White River when he decided to go wading. His body was found 3/4 mile away on the opposite bank. *(TNT 7/23/81)*.

McChord AFB 1st Lt. Harold J. Steiss, Jr. of Florida and a friend parked at Cougar Rock and set off on a cross-country hike in 1983. They decided to climb Ricksecker Point, but had no ropes or gear. Steiss was killed when he fell 250 ft. off the steep rock, then slid another 500 ft. *(TNT 6/13/83)*.

Fun Activities *OUTSIDE* The Park

Bicycling

Mountain bike enthusiasts look forward to the annual August "Fat Tire" weekend at Crystal Mountain Resort, which features four different competitions for mountain bikers of all levels. The first event is the Poker Run Fun Ride, which is a 6.4 mile (moderate terrain) course where riders pick up a poker card at 5 different checkpoints and the one with the best hand wins the race.

There's also the Dual Slalom, a timed hillside race which features head-to-head racing through flagged gates. There's also a downhill race, observed trials, and an obstacle course with varying ability levels. The second day there's a cross country race, a grueling race with an elevation gain that is geared to people with varying ability and classifications and staggered start times. For information and entry fees, call (360) 663-2265.

Also outside the park on the north side, trails open to bicyclists are Suntop, Skookum Flats, the Dalles Ridge Trail and Ranger Creek Trail.

On the southwest side of the mountain, early each August, there's the 8-mile Snapple Slurp and Burp ("made from the best riders on earth") in the Elbe Hills State Forest ORV area. Sponsored by Northwest Mountain Bike, this is one of a series of races with $30,000 in cash and prizes. Call NW Mountain Bike (Tacoma) 565-9050 for more information.

Caving

The best known cave near Mount Rainier is 400-foot long Boulder Cave 27-miles east of Chinook Pass. Turn right across the Naches River at the Cliffdell Bridge. Take two more right turns on Road 1704 to the picnic area 1.2 miles from the highway. The mouth of the cave is 200 feet wide and 50 feet high. The cave was cut by the creek through collapsed lava-flow basalts. Bring a flashlight and wear good hiking shoes.

Layser Cave southeast of Randle offers a unique archaeological experience. The cave was used by Indians 4,000 years ago, and the floor was left scattered with animal bones and stone tools. The cave is on the lower slopes of Lone Tree Mountain, and is reached by taking Highway 12, to Forest Road 23. (Go 7.3 miles to the junction with road 23.083). Follow the signs to the parking area.

Christmas

"Christmas in August" is the big end-of-year celebration held for all seasonal employees at Paradise each year. But this is a tame version of the annual "Nut House Ball" which was the forerunner of this event. That costumed event, was won one year by the dining room crew who came as the Dionne quintuplets, Mr. and Mrs. Dionne, Dr. Dafoe and the nurse. The buggy they arrived in was a wheelbarrow.

Big Christmas tree lightings are held each year at Eatonville and Morton. Morton's is special, since it features the lighting of the tallest living Christmas tree in the United States.

Cowlitz River Canoe Trip

Begin this 9-mile trip six miles NE of Packwood. Put in at La Wis Wis Campground in the Gifford Pinchot National Forest for this scenic intermediate whitewater Class II run. Prepare for rapids and good views of Mount Rainier. Take-out is at the Skate Creek Bridge in Packwood.

Present day recreational canoers also recommend the Nisqually River lower stretches in the Nisqually Flats and Refuge.

Federation Forest

On the north side of the mountain, 16 miles southeast of Enumclaw, this 619 acre State Park is an ecosystem showcase. It is a low-elevation old-growth forest with some of the largest western red cedar in the state. The Catherine

Montgomery Interpretation Center features exhibits and murals of the seven biotic or life zones found in Washington State. Part of the old Naches Trail, the pioneer trail James Longmire came over on, passes through this park. The park also offers 47 picnic sites, two kitchen shelters, fishing, cross-country skiing, and several nearly level nature trails with easy hiking for those who aren't up to more strenuous trails. This park came by its name because it was purchased and developed by the Washington State Federation of Women's Clubs in 1940. (360) 663-2207.

Hang Gliding

Though hang gliding is not allowed in Mount Rainier National Park, enthusiasts soar off nearby Dog Mountain near Glenoma, a small community a few miles west of Morton. The landing zone is Kosmos Flats, located down the Champion-100 Road. This area is known as the hang gliding capital of Lewis County. Qualified teachers and classes are available. Contact the Morton Chamber of Commerce for details. (360) 496-6068. And yes, even though it's illegal, Mount Rainier has been successfully hang glided. *(Outside Magazine)*.

Horse Back Riding outside the park

Crystal Mountain Corral (360) 663-2589, has group trail rides, overnight barbecues, fishing, hunting and photography trips. Prices start at $25 for a short trail ride, $55-95 for a full day ride, and $135 for an overnight ride with steak fry and cowboy breakfast. You can stay at the Crystal House Motel for $40 more.

EZ Times Outfitters (360) 569-2449, has horse rentals for all levels of rider. They also offer trips by the hour or day, for pleasure or hunting trips in the Elbe Hills State Forest. Reservations are advised but not required. 18703 SE Highway 706 (Mountain Highway) Elbe, WA 98330

Indian Creek Corral (509) 925-2062, eight miles east of White Pass on Highway 12 offers horseback rides from 1 hour to 3 days long. 1-3 hour rides cost $10 an hour (kids must be over 12 or experienced). There's an all-day scenic trip for $50 per person, or a 3-day wilderness trip for $250 with a limit of five per trip. They also have a pickup/dropoff service for hikers for $75 for 75 pounds. Write them at Star Route Box 218, Naches, WA 98937

Nicholson Horse Trail System. This 50-mile trail system is situated on 7,000 acres of State managed land along the southerly edge of the Elbe Hills State Forest. This trail system provides great views of Mount Rainier and the Nisqually Valley. There are three trailhead parks, and the Sahara Creek Camp (near the Mountain Highway) has 18 campsites with water.

No mechanized vehicles (and no bikes) are allowed on the horse trails. It is open *only* to horses and hikers. (On narrow trails, bicycles spook horses.) An excellent map showing all trails (ski trails, horse trails, jeep trails in the Elbe/Tahoma State Forests is available in the catalog at the back of this book.

Ice Fishing

While ice fishing is not allowed in the park, it is allowed in many lakes of the surrounding areas.

Kayaking/Rafting/River-running

River-running by any means is not allowed within the Park. In 1971 one couple kayaking on the Ohanapecosh River barely escaped with their lives when they were almost swept over Silver Falls.

Kayak devotees do recommend the Nisqually River below the dams. Rafting fans like the White River near Greenwater. Guided float trips are also available on the White River, which offers light rapids. Full day and half day excursions begin near Alta Crystal and run March through August. (360) 663-2500.

The new Cowlitz Falls Hydroelectric Project will open up a number of new recreational areas and access to lands and activities which have previously been inaccessible. One new benefit will be a kayak take-out facility for those who use the Cispus River.

Logging Shows

Early every August, the annual Morton Loggers Jubilee draws loggers out of the woods from all over the country to compete for the title of "Bull of the Woods" (the best all-around logger). The show features a wide variety of skill contests, including sawing, chopping, birling, speed climbing, tree topping and operating antique saws. The event also has an old fashioned parade, lawnmower races and bed races (not together) and GOOD food. These folks really know how to have a good time, and it's a good chance to meet some REAL loggers up close and personal. This show is so good, it's rated one of the top 100 events in the National Tourism Information Guide.

A smaller logging show (demonstrations of speed climbing, tree topping, underhanded and standing block chop, choke setting, obstacle pole bucking, single and double bucking, ax throwing and log burling) is held during the King County Fair the 3rd week of July each year at the Enumclaw fairgrounds. This "oldest county fair in the state" also features a PRCA Rodeo, and a bounty of crops grown in the rich volcanic soil from the old electron mud flow.

Another great one in the shadow of the mountain, is the Buckley Logging Show, which takes place in early June each year. You'll see real loggers here and it will be a fun/educational show for the kids and a bit of Americana.

Markets

Weekend Farmer's Markets, Arts and Crafts Markets and Flea Markets are held at several towns on the way to the mountain. Occasionally some old mountain memorabilia turns up when descendents of one of the old timers cleans out the attic or garage.

Mount Rainier Scenic Railway

Another fun way to "do the mountain" is to experience the Golden Age of Steam by riding the rails in an old steam train. The 1912 Heisler steam engine was originally used in logging and mining operations. Two types of trip are offered, a scenic ride, and a dinner train.

The scenic trip: The steam train leaves Elbe for the 14-mile, 1-1/2 hour ride over bridges and through the woods with live music accompanying the gorgeous scenery. From June 15th on, the train runs every day at 11 a.m., 1:15 p.m. and 3:30 p.m. The train leaves from Elbe on Highway 7. Prices are $8.50 for adults, $7.50 seniors, $6.50 teens and $5.50 for kids. Reservations are not required for the scenic train. (360) 569-2588.

The Cascadian Dinner Train: A unique 40-mile, four-hour steam railroad excursion with a fine dining experience in a 1920's dining car. Departs (Summer) Saturday evenings at 5:30 p.m. Fares are $55 per person, and advance reservations are required. Call or write for reservations: Box 921, Elbe, WA 98330. (360) 569-2588.

In 1907, the round trip fare from Tacoma via the Tacoma Eastern Railroad was $6.00. This included the stage ride to Longmire and return as well. The train came as far as Elbe and eventually it went on to Mineral, then Morton.

Music

The (annual) Parnassus Chamber Music Festival featuring Bach, Beethoven and a champagne brunch, against a backdrop of Mount Rainier in full glory, is held three times each summer (May, June and September) in the Day Lodge at White Pass. For tickets or information call (360) 494-5321 or (509) 453-8731.

ORVs

Legal ATV/ORV use is allowed on the **Elbe Hills ORV Trail System**. Elbe Hills is a large tract of state timber land which has a network of multiple-use trails. It can be reached from Highway 706 west of Ashford. ORV is defined as CJ-5 [short wheel-base type] jeeps, mountain bikes, motorcycles and ATVs. The ORV trail system was constructed using monies generated by ORV users (ORV permit fees, and ORV Gas Tax revenues). The trails were designed and built for challenging off-road recreation, with the help and cooperation of volunteers from four-wheel drive and trailbike organizations, the DNR and the IAC. An excellent inexpensive map showing all three trail systems (the Elbe Hills ORV Trail System, the Nicholson Horse Trail System, and the Mount Tahoma Ski Trails) is available at the end of this book.

On the north side of the park, Off Road Vehicle area is **Evans Creek Park** which is located 12 miles past Wilkeson. This ORV area provides 40 miles of trails, a 26-unit primitive campground and spectacular views of Mount Rainier.

The trails and campground are maintained by volunteers from the Pacific Northwest 4-wheel Drive Club.

The free-use campground has tables, fire-rings and vault toilets. There is no potable water or garbage collection.

To reach the Evans Creek ORV Area, follow Highway 162 to Buckey, then Highway 165 toward the Mowich Lake Entrance. Evans Lake is 12 miles past Wilkeson. For more information, contact the White River Ranger District office at (360) 825-6585.

Rules of the Road

The Forest Service (which manages the area) asks that the following regulations be adhered to: All ORVs must have standard ORV tabs, issued by the State Department of Licensing. To operate on Forest Service Roads, an ORV must be street legal, meaning the vehicle must have a license plate and current vehicle tabs. Drivers must be licensed.

The speed limit on forest management roads is 25 mph, and in the camp and picnic sites, is 5 mph. Officials also warn ORV drivers to take precaution when at numbered Forest Service roads used by the general public. Some of the ORV trails end or cross these numbered roads. Also remember logging trucks, heavy equipment and other vehicles use these roads, so be ready to yield right-of-way.

Running

Mount Rainier to the Pacific Relay Run - Begins at Mount Rainier (Longmire Campground) and ends at Northshore High School, Ocean Shores, WA, a distance of 186 miles. The run comes out Skate Creek Road to Highway 706, then to McKenna, Yelm, Tenino and on to the coast. The entire run takes place on paved secondary State routes, and is run under a permit from the Washington State Department of Transportation.

This event, now going into its 8th year, is always held the second Friday of July. This is a major event with 3,000 runners (total) plus several hundred more support workers. Participants came from 22 states and 3 foreign countries, including a team representing the Korean Army. There are 11 people on a team, with each runner going 3-5 mile legs. The run is sponsored by the Oregon Road Runner's Club of Beaverton, Oregon.

The record time for the run is 14-1/2 hours. For more information, contact ORRC at P.O. Box 17086, Seattle 98107 (503) 646-RUNR. There's also a run from Mount Rainier to Tacoma, a "Ranger Run" from the Nisqually Delta to the summit, and an annual "Dam Rod Run" in Mossyrock each July.

Rockhounding

Although no rockhounding is allowed within the National Park boundaries, centuries of volcanic and glacial activity in the Cascades have left many deposits of minerals. Some suggested places outside the park to look are:

Greenwater River, 16 miles east of Enumclaw. Many sites along Forest Roads 7000 and 7200 yield petrified wood, jasper and agate. (Mount Baker-Snoqualmie Forest).

Rodeos

The first weekend of August is the National Rodeo Association Junior Rodeo held in Randle each year. Another rodeo is a PRCA Rodeo held two nights during the King County Fair in Enumclaw each July. Nightly events include bareback riding, calf roping, saddle bronc riding, steer wrestling, team roping, ladies barrel racing and bull riding. Dress warmly. The show runs late and even in July, the nights get *cold*.

Scenic Chairlift Rides

Nearby Crystal Mountain offers a high-speed quad chair-lift ride to a birds-eye view of Mount Rainier from this 7,000'-high next-door mountain top. It's a chance to see from Canada to Oregon, and also an opportunity to stay and watch the sunset on the mountain while enjoying dinner at the state's highest restaurant. For information or reservations, call (360) 663-2300.

Silver Springs Campground

Between the Park and Enumclaw lies the National Forest Service Silver Springs Campground, in a beautiful old-growth forest on the banks of the White River. This park contains a surprise seldom seen in a park of any kind, - a grave. At the west end of the campground, left of campsite #12 is a primitive trail. About 1/4 mile down the trail lies the marked grave of Henry C. Allen, (1848-1896) who was an early homesteader and Civil War veteran who won the Purple Heart. The grave is protected and maintained by the Forest Service.

Smelting

An event eagerly anticipated by fish lovers who don't fish, is the annual Smelt Run in the Cowlitz River every Spring. The tasty little fish are so prolific, catching them requires only a net with which to scoop them up. Throngs take advantage of the easy catch by picking their spot along the Cowlitz Plain off I-5 between Olympia and Vancouver. Smelt are one of three fish in the state which don't require a fishing license. Catching them is free! There is a 20 pound per day limit however.

Smelting gear consists of a 10 to 20-foot fine mesh dip net (no larger than 36 inches across the bag frame) and a bucket. If the smelt are in deeper water, you might want to have a pair of hip waders too.

The technique is to drop the dip net upstream from where you're standing and using both hands, quickly sweep it downstream. (The smelt will be heading upstream). The smelt tend to hug the river bottom, so keep the net low. Smelting is good both day and night. All smelt must be kept regardless of size or condition.

University of Washington
Charles L. Pack Demonstration Forest

Established in 1926, and originally called The Pack Demonstration Forest, 2000 acres of land were donated to the University of Washington by Charles Lathrop Pack. The University's Forestry School met here during spring and summer quarters and studied surveying, erosion control, forestry and conservation. They also did laboratory work in entomology and made field trips to the Wind River Nursery.

On exhibit at the entrance is a section of a large Douglas fir log with 727 rings. Adjacent to the log is a topo model of Pack Forest and an erosion model, contrasting wooded with denuded hills. The highest point of land in the Pack Forest is Hugo Peak, named for Dean Hugo Winkenwerder of the UW College of Forestry. He is recognized as the father of the UW Arboretum in Seattle.

Lathrop Drive is a seven-mile loop encircling the major part of the demonstration area. "The Camp" located on the road up the hill from the entrance, includes a laboratory, a cookhouse, a recreation hall, and a classroom. A sawmill stands about 600 feet from the camp. The facility has now grown to 4260 acres.

White Water Rafting

This is a popular activity on the White River near Greenwater.

Windsurfing

The closest windsurfing site to Mount Rainier is on Riffe Lake near Glenoma, a few miles west of Morton. 11,830-acre Riffe Lake, with 53 miles of shoreline, was created by Mossyrock Dam. Windsurfing teachers and classes are available by contacting the Morton Chamber of Commerce: (360) 496-6086.

Climbing

If there's a summit theme song, it must be "Nearer my God to Thee."

Climbing Chronology

Climbing Mount Rainier Yesterday

1833   Dr. William F. Tolmie, a medical officer and botanist who worked for the Hudson's Bay Company, made the first exploration and ascent in the area of Mount Rainier. It has been concluded he probably climbed Hessong Rock.

1852   R.S. Bailey, S.S. Ford, Jr., John Edgar and Benjamin Franklin Shaw "reached the highest altitude" in two days according to Shaw's account. Shaw was a hero of the Indian wars of 1855, and was considered an honest man. As recently as 1979, the Park Service accepted this as a legitimate summit climb. *(Seattle Times, 7/17/70).*

1854   According to Len Longmire, three men, B. F. Shaw, and Benjamin and Sidney Ford made an attempt on the mountain. (This may be another record of the above party.)

July 15, 1857   July 14: Lt. A. V. Kautz of the U.S. Army, Dr. O. R. Craig, the Fort Steilacoom post doctor, two soldiers named Dogue and Carroll, and their Indian guide Wapowety of the Nisqually tribe, attempted the climb, but had to turn back. Most think they only made it to the saddle east of Point Success.

August 17, 1708   General Hazard Stevens and Philemon Beecher Van Trump made the first successful ascent via the Gibralter Route. In October 1870, S. F. Emmons and A. D. Wilson of the 40th Parallel Corps, USGS reached the crest via the Cowlitz Glacier - Gibralter route.

August 1883   P.B. Van Trump, George B. Bayley and James Longmire made the third successful ascent of the mountain again via the Gibralter Route. It was on the way down that Longmire discovered the mineral springs.

August 20, 1885   The first ascent via the north side was attempted by Rev. Warner Fobes, Richard O. Wells and George James of Snohomish, WA. Coming in via Mowich Lake and Spray Park, they got to about 11,000 ft. before getting turned back. They went further east and made a second attempt via the Winthrop and Emmons Glaciers. It too failed. Their third try was successful. Upon reaching the summit, they found a walking stick protruding from the snow, and "a piece of lead with four names inscribed on it" near one of the vents inside the crater.

1885 or 1886   The first undisputed Indian ascent. A party of 7 or 8 Yakima Indians together with Allison L. Brown climbed via the Cowlitz Divide over the Whitman and Ingraham Glaciers. (This climb and route aren't clearly defined.)

August 14, 1888   The first photo was made on the summit. A party of seven: E.S. Ingraham, John Muir, Photographer A.C. Warner, Charles Piper, P.B. Van Trump, D.W. Bass, and young Joe Stampfler summited via the Gibralter Route. They named their bivouac Camp Muir in honor of the famous naturalist in their midst. A. C. Warner carried a large and heavy plate camera to the summit.

August 10, 1890   The first ascent by a woman, Miss Fay Fuller of Yelm, WA. Also in the party was Len Longmire, Rev. E.C. Smith, Mr. Parrish and Mr. Amsden. The late hour forced them to spend the night in the crater.

July 30, 1891	Three Longmires stood on the summit at the same time: Len (guide), Elcaine and 13-year old Sue Longmire. It was also a notable climb in that it was the second and third ascents by a woman (Sue Longmire and Miss Edith Corbett, a teacher from Yelm), Dr. Stafford, Hans Polson, Edward Allen, (son of Professor O.D. Allen) and others.
1891	P. B. Van Trump and a man named Riley climbed via Tahoma Glacier, after starting at Indian Henrys.
	First ascent by a dog. Dr. Warren Riley's wolfhound.
August 20, 1892	According to Major E. S. Ingraham, 'a total of 38 persons (including three women), have been upon the highest point of Rainier.' Also this year for the first time, two separate parties were on the summit at the same time (both parties having climbed by way of Tahoma Glacier). After spending the night in the crater, both parties united and achieved the first ascent of North Peak, now known as Liberty Cap.
	P. B. Van Trump and George B. Bayley made the first ascent via Success Cleaver and Tahoma Glacier after coming in from Indian Henrys.
July 18, 1894	Three more women made it to the summit: Miss Helen Holmes (age 15), Miss Annie Hall and Miss Bernice Parke. They climbed as part of a party of 14 guided up the Gibralter Route by E. S. Ingraham. (Ingraham's 3rd climb.)
July 23-24, 1896	The first "Cross-over" climb: I.C. Russell, Bailey Willis, Geo. Otis Smith of USGS and two packers named F. H. Ainsworth and W. B. Williams, crossed from one side of the Mountain to the other via the summit. They went up via the Emmons Glacier and descended via the Gibraltar Route.
	The first "speed " record: A. B. Wood of Tacoma set a 12-hour time record from Reeses Camp at Paradise Valley to the summit.
1897	The first large group encampment at the mountain. 200 Portland Mazamas arrived with 4 tons of supplies, two beef steers, and seven milk cows. Fay Fuller made her second ascent with this group. It was during the descent from this climb that Professor Edgar McClure fell to his death. He was descending after dark from Camp Muir. It is believed his lengthy barometer probably caught in a rock and threw him off balance.
May 18, 1905	First ascent from Spray Park via Ptarmigan Ridge by Mr. Lee Picket and unidentified companion.
July 24, 1905	During a joint outing of Sierra Club, the Portland Mazamas, the American Alpine Club and the Appalachian Mountain Club, 112 climbers made the summit, the first large group climb. Fifty three Sierra Club people climbed the mountain via the Gibralter Route. One among the party who reached the summit, was Stephen Mather, who ten years later became the first Director of the National Park Service and guided it through its formative years.
	While the groups camped at Paradise, evening campfire talks were given by General Hazard Stevens (who had made the pioneer ascent 35 years before), J. N. LeConte of the University of California, Henry Landes, State Geologist of Washington, Dr. Marcus Lyon of the Smithsonian and a Swiss guide.
1905	First ascent via the Success Cleaver Route. John R. Glascock and Ernest Dudley then made the descent via the Gibralter Route.

July 30-31, 1909	62 Mountaineers members made ascent via Emmons and Winthrop Glaciers, starting from Glacier Basin.
1910	This year 159 climbers successfully made the summit. F. E. Matthes of USGS began a topographical mapping project.
July 2, 1912	Joseph Stampfler, Phil Barrett and Frank Kandle climbed via Success Cleaver Route and descended via Gibralter Route.
August 20, 1913	A USGS Survey Party under the direction of C.H. Birdseye climbed Mount Rainier for the purpose of completing the first topographical map of the region. It was begun under the direction of F. E. Matthes in 1910. Their determination of 14,408' as the height of the mountain stood for many years.
July 28, 1914	Joseph Stampfler, Dr. K.F. Meyer, W. Ellis, F. Vinton and Alvin Bogardus went up via Success Cleaver, descended via Gibralter.
1914	The Mazamas of Oregon established a new record, that of a single organization taking such a large party to the summit. Seventy-five began the climb. 71 reached the summit. Their route was the Winthrop Glacier.
July 26-28, 1920	Hans and Henry Fuhrer, Harry Myers and Roger Toll, climbed from Van Trump Park via the Fuhrer Finger route and descended via Gibralter.
1921	J.T. Hazard, O.B. Sperlin, Wallace Burr and Stella Shahan retraced the route of Lt. Kautz, and concluded Kautzs ascent had gone to about 12,000'. Current wisdom is that Kautz reached the saddle east of Point Success (14,000').
February 13, 1922	First winter ascent via the Gibralter Route made by Charles Perryman, Jacques Bergues and Jean and Jacques Landy. They made motion pictures at the summit.
1924	Hazard and twelve companions retraced the Kautz route again, completing it this time, and proving that the route was practical.
1925	Balthasar Hauser, a middle-aged Austrian became the first person to spend two consecutive nights in the steam caves. He climbed wearing overalls, and had no gear or warm clothing.
1929	The first climbing fatalities on the popular Gibralter route. Five people on one rope team slid into a crevasse, killing a guide and one climber.
July 4-6, 1934	Hans Fuhrer and Alfred Roovers climbed from Klapatche Park, up via Tahoma Glacier, descent via the Gibralter Route.
Sept. 7-8, 1935	Wolf Bauer and Jack Hossack climbed via Ptarmigan Ridge and returned via Gibralter Route.
Sept 28-Oct 1, 1935	Ome Daiber, Will Borrow, Jr., and Arnold Campbell made the first successful ascent of Liberty Ridge.
July 19-21, 1937	Wendell Trosper and Fred Theime climb via Puyallup Glacier and Sunset Amphitheater (Tahoma Glacier Icecap)..
	The Gibralter Route, pioneered by Stevens and Van Trump in 1870 was the route of choice for most climbers until 1936. During the winter of 1936-37, part of the narrow ledge along the face of Gibralter had fallen away.
1939	Sunset Amphitheater - Sunset Ridge climbed by Hans Grage and Wendell Trosper.

1946	Nisqually-Gibralter Chute -climbed by Paul Gilbreath, Stan DeBruler and (?) Hewitt.
1948	The Nisqually Icefall was first climbed by R. W. Craig and Dee Molenaar.
1948	New ledge route on Gibralter climbed by "K" Molenaar and George Senner.
1956	Ptarmigan Ridge - Liberty Cap Glacier -Fred Beckey, J. Rupley, Herb Staley
1957	Mowich Face (Edmunds Glacier Headwall) first climbed by Fred Beckey, Tom Hornbein, John Rupley, Herb Staley, and Don Claunch.
1957	Dee Molenaar and Pete Schoening do the Willis Glacier Headwall. That same day, Gene Prater and M. Schuster do Curtis Ridge. Six weeks later C.E. Robinson and G. R. Senner conquored Kautz Cleaver.
1958	South Mowich Icefall - Tahoma Sickle climbed by Mark and Monte Haun, Larry Hagerness, Ed Drues, Leroy Ritchie, A. Van Buskirk and F. Walton.
1959	Tahoma Cleaver mastered by Paul Bellamy, Tony Hovey, Don Keller, Herb Steiner and Klindt Vielbig.
1960	Two notable first ascents: Russell Cliff (Upper Curtis Ridge) by Don Jones, Jim Kurtz, Dave Mahre and Gene Prater, and Success Glacier Couloir, climbed by George Senner and Dick Walstrom.
1961	Willis Wall finally climbed (West Rib, to ice cliff, upper Liberty Ridge and summit) by Charles Bell.
1962	Willis Wall climbed again, this time via upper Curtis Ridge, by Ed Cooper and Mike Swayne.
1962	Nisqually Ice Cliff climbed by Barry Bishop and Lute Jerstad.
1963	Four new routes successfully climbed:
	Sunset Ridge via Edmunds Glacier Headwall (by Fred Dunham, Dave Mahre, Gene Prater, Fred Stanley and Jim Wickwire); Willis Wall (East Rib, through the central icecap) by Don Anderson, Fred Dunham, Dave Mahre and Jim Wickwire; Kautz Glacier Headwall by Pat Callis, Dan Davis and D. Gordon, and South Tahoma Headwall by Fred Beckey and Steve Marts
1964	The Park Service opened the mountain to winter summit climbs.
1965	Willis Wall (Central Rib through central icecap) climbed by Dean Caldwell and Paul Dix. Sunset Amphitheater direct to Liberty Cap by Dave Mahre, Don McPherson, Gene Prater, Fred Stanley and Jim Wickwire.
1966	The Central Mowich Face (Route 1) climbed by Dee Molenaar, Dick Pargeter, Gene Prater and Jim Wickwire.
1967	Central Mowich Face (Route 2) climbed by Bill Cockerham, Ed Marquet, Bill Sumner and Del Young.
	This same year, Fred Dunham and Jim Wickwire climbed Nisqually Cleaver.
1968	Route 1 on the North Mowich Headwall was done by Bill Cockerham, Dan Davis, Mead Hargiss and Mike Heath. This same year, Don Jones, Paul Myhre and Roger Oborn made it up Liberty Wall to 12,000 feet
1970	A party of "Centennial climbers", led by Lou Whittaker made the climb to commemorate the Stevens and Van Trump ascent in 1870. It marked Whittaker's 100th climb.

In July, on the other side of the mountain, Jim Wickwire and R. Schaller successfully did the North Mowich Headwall (Route 2).

1971   Liberty Wall by Liberty Cap by done by Gary Isaacs and Dusan Jagersky.

1972   The first ascent of Fuhrer Thumb was done by Charlie Raymond, Jim Wickwire and Tom Stewart

1974   Joe Horiskey becomes the second guide in modern era to reach 100 climbs.

1982   Phil Ershler becomes the first person ever to make 200 successful climbs. Since then six more have reached 200.

1989   Phil Ershler becomes the first person to make 300 successful climbs (since then followed by George Dunn.)

Old Mount Rainier Climbing Camps

Although some of these are no longer used, these are the "camps" which were used by the early climbers.

Avalanche Camp (10,900') on Curtis Ridge along the east side of Willis Wall, between the Carbon and Winthrop Glaciers. Avalanche Camp was named by the Mountaineers during club's first ascent of Mount Rainier in 1909.

Camp Comfort [Camp No Camp] (12,550') on SE slope of Rainier, near the top of Gibralter Rock. It was renamed Camp Comfort in 1888 by Major E.S. Ingraham to contrast it to Camp Misery, below Gibralter, which was also named by Ingraham at the same time.

Camp Curtis (9,000') below Steamboat Prow near the head of Inter Glacier. The name was suggested by Professor Meany for the high camp of The Mountaineers in 1909 in honor of Asahel Curtis, leader of the outing.

Camp Ewing below Gibralter Rock

Camp Hazard (11,300') the rock cliff below the Kautz Ice Fall. The Mountaineers suggested this title in honor of Joseph T. Hazard and Mrs. Hazard, who located and used the camp while leading an exploration of the Kautz route in 1924.

Camp Misery (11,033') on the crest of Cowlitz Cleaver near the lower end of Gibralter Rock. A well-named camp.

Camp Muir [Cloud Camp] (10,062') on SE slope. Named in honor of John Muir in 1888.

Camp of the Stars [Camp Delight] (12,000') On the SE slope near the foot of Gibralter. A night at Camp of the Stars was said to be indescribable, both for the grandeur of the outlook and the bodily discomforts.

Camp Schurman (9,500') at the upper base of Steamboat Prow. Named in honor of revered Clark E. Schurman, Chief Climbing Guide 1939 -1942.

Camp Starbo [Starbo Camp] (5,800') the mining camp at Glacier Basin.

Eagle Nest Camp on Cowlitz Cleaver.

Early-Day Guides

Leonard Longmire set himself up as the first "professional" (paid) guide and charged a fee of $1.00 per person for the trip to the top from Camp Muir. Business wasn't exactly booming, and by 1898 he left the Mountain to search for gold in the Klondike. That didn't last long, and he soon was back.

left - Phil Barrett; center - Joe Stampfler; right - Frank Kandle. Taken August 2, 1912 at Indian Henrys before an ascent via Success Cleaver

John Reese employed guides at his "Camp of the Clouds" above Paradise as early as 1903. One of them was Joseph Stampfler, a very popular young guide, who from the age of 14, had lived with the Longmires. As a small boy, he had accompanied the Muir party of 1888. "Little Joe" also operated his guide service out of the tent-camp at Indian Henrys Hunting Ground from the late 1800's until 1914. His younger brother Jules also guided at various times between 1914 and 1918. On August 14, 1909, two climbers perished in a storm. In 1911, as a result of those deaths, Park Superintendent E. S. Hall instituted an "Official Guide System" for Mount Rainier, copied after the Swiss system. Each climbing party was limited to eight persons. Four persons were authorized to act as guides, one of whom was not permitted to guide to the summit, nor across any glacier."

1912. Seven people were authorized as summit guides.

1914. At least four guides were authorized, three to be paid $25 per trip.

The Guide Service - Yesterday

If one doesn't count Len Longmire and a handful of self-appointed guides, the first "real" professional guide service was installed at Mount Rainier by the Rainier National Park Company in 1916, with a contract they were to hold for the next 26 years. First hired were Asahel Curtis, Major Ingraham and Crissie Cameron, who comprised a chief-guide committee of three. Curtis held the post only one year, and eventually went on to become the most famous outdoor photographer of his day. Curtis was followed as chief guide by O. B. Sperlin in 1918 and Joseph T. Hazard in 1919.

In 1919 the Rainier National Park Company brought in Swiss brothers Hans and Heinie Fuhrer, who worked as summit guides between until 1925.

Names of the early guides read like a history of the mountain. There was Peyton Farrer, Frank Jacobs, Will Duggan, H.B. Cunningham, Ben Thompson, Frank (Swede) Willard, Wendell Trosper, Gene Jack, Clark Schurman, Ed Kennedy, Bill Dunaway, Chuck Welsh, Roby Albouy, Ollie Chiseaux, Jim Whittaker, Dr. Paul Gerstmann, Dick Krisman, Dick McGowan (had the guide service from 1956-1965), Jack Melill and, since 1968, Lou Whittaker.

Mountain Guides at Mount Rainier

1890s through 1969

List compiled by Dee Molenaar

Bold facing signifies this man was in the 10th Mountain Division, ♦ signifies he was also a ranger

P.B. Van Trump,	1890s	Frank "Swede" Willard,	1928-35
Len Longmire,	1890s-1910(?)	(chief guide 1935)	
Joe Stampfler,	1890's-1912	Forrest Greathouse,	1929 (assist.,
Henry M. Sarvent,	1890s?	(killed in crevasse fall in 1929)	
Henry Carter,	1892-"many years"	Bob Strobel,	1929 (assist.)
Jules Stampfler,	1900-18	Harry Webster,	1929 (assist.)
Dan Riley,	1905-10	Worth McClure, Jr.,	1929, 1940
F.H. Tuell,	1914	Henry Swanson,	1928, 1930-31
H.A. Loss,	1914	Doug Ward,	1928, 1930-31 (assist.)
Harry Greer,	1914, 1918-19	William J. "Bill" Butler,	1930-31
David Crockett,	1915-16	(with NPS, 1932-31)	
John Reese,	1916	Al Bellaine,	1930
Asahel Curtis,	1917	Leroy Grandy, Jr.,	1930
(1st chief guide under RNPCO		Ken Selby,	1930
-Rainier National Park Co.)		Bill Odom,	1930
Otis B. Sperlin,	1918	Willard Widman,	1931
Fairman Lee,	1918	Ben Thompson,	1931-33(?)
Jake Shidell,	1919	Darroch Crooks,	1931-34
Joseph T. Hazard,	1919-20 (chief guide 1919)	J. Wendell Trosper,	1933-36
Errol Rawson,	1919-20	(chief guide 1936)	
Alma Wagen,	1919-22	Frederick Thieme,	1933-37
Wesley Langlow,	1919-26	Carlton Weigel,	1933-34
Hans Fuhrer,	1920-24	Ariel Edmiston,	1933-36
Heinie Fuhrer,	1920-25	Wolfgang Lert,	1934
Peyton Farrer,	1920 (chief guide)	Gene Jack,	1934-38
Thomas Hermans,	1920-20	(chief guide 1937-38)	
Wilford Playter,	1921-22	Oscar Anderson,	1934-35
Emma Vaughn,	1922-23	Wally Gettings,	1935
William T. Duggan,	1923-24	Les Yansen,	1935-42 (assist.)
Nulsen Widman,	1923-30 (assist.)	Ken Syversen,	1936
Waldo Chamberlin,	1924-29 (assist.)	John Carey,	1936
Harry B. ("HB") Cunningham,		Neal Jacobus,	1936-38
chief guide,	1925-32	George Broz,	1937-38
Leon Brigham,	1925-29	Mel Pederson,	1937-38
Ed Arthur,	1925	Don Stewart,	1937-38
Joe Griggs,	1925, (assist.)	Bob Svare,	1938
Seymour Todd,	1925 (assist.)	Harold O'Connor,	1938
Clyde Adams,	1926-28 (assist.)	Clark E. Schurman,	1939-42 (chief guide)
Ken Olson,	1927-29 (assist.)	Bruce Smith,	1939
Stuart Twiss,	1926	James L. Wortham,	1939-40
John Swan,	1926 (cashier)	Robert W. Hoxsey,	1939-40
Ernest Durranmatt,	1926	♦**Robert W. Jamison,**	1939
Lewellyn Jordan,	1927 (assist.)	Lyman Boyer,	1939
Sam Flemming, Jr.,	1927 (assist.)	➢ Dee Molenaar,	1940-41, 1947
Marcom Wallace,	1927	(and some weekends through 1962)	
Jim Zelandos,	1927 (assist.)	**Ken Spangenberg,**	1940
Rurie Todd,	1928 (assist.)	Robert W. Weber,	1941-42
Bob Strain,	1928 (assist.)	➢ Maynard M. Miller,	1941
John W. Day,	1928-30 (assist.)	**Dennis Huntley,**	1942
Jerrold Bellaine,	1928-31 (cashier)	Marion Marts,	1942

♦**Ed Kennedy,**	1946 (chief guide)	George Heuston,	1966-68
➤♦**William R. "Bil" Dunaway,**	1946-47	Tony Anderson,	1967
1951 (chief guide)		Tom Hammer,	1967
♦**Gordie Butterfield,**	1946	Don McPherson,	1967
Jim Nussbaum,	1946 (assist.)	➤ Fred Stanley,	1967 (?)
Robert W. Parker,	1947	Jim Ullin,	1967-68
Charles E. Welsh,	1947, 1949	John Rutter, Jr.,	1967-69
Roby Albouy,	1949-50	Jay Springer,	1967-68
Ollie Chesaux,	1950	Bill Cox,	1968-69
➤ Robert W. Craig,	1949	Dave Stelling,	1968
➤ James W. Whittaker,	1951-52, 1954	Tom Falley,	1968
➤ Louis Whittaker,	1951-52, 1954-55,	Bill Lehman,	1968
(chief guide 1968 to present)		Daryl Bennett,	1968 (assist.)
Dr. Paul Gerstmann,	1953 (chief guide)	Nancy Brown,	1968 (assist.)
Dick Krisman,	1953	Kathy Christianson,	1968 (assist.)
Gordon Tebb,	1955	➤Joe Horiskey,	1968-present)
➤ Richard E. McGowan,	1956-65 (chief guide)	➤ Adolf Weissensteiner,	1969
Gary Rose,	1956-59	➤ Phursumba Sherpa,	1969-present
Gilbert Blinn,	1958-59	Leonard Faulks,	1969
➤ Luther G. Jerstad,	1960-62	Gary Olsen,	1969
Adolf Bitterlich,	1960	Ed McAlpine,	1969
Herb Staley,	1961-64, 1966	Dave Kazeck,	1969
Roy Schwitters,	1963-65	Larry Cotton,	1969
➤ Gary Ullin,	1964-66	Ron Fear,	1969
Jay Ullin,	1965-66, 1968	➤ Del Young,	1969
Robert Schaeffer,	1965-68	Pat Barr,	1969
Bruce Davis,	1966	(guides from 1969 to present will be in future
Karl Span,	1966	editions.)

➤ denotes climbed in Himalayas

Dee noted that many of RMI's guides have climbed in the Himalayas, Andes, Africa, Alaska, Mexico, the Antarctic and New Zealand, and several have reached the tops of Everest, K2, and Kangchenjunga. Ed Viesturs has done Everest 2-3 times without oxygen, and K2 without oxygen

The Guide Service - Today

The present guide service, Rainier Mountain-eering, Inc., (RMI) is co-owned by Lou Whittaker, attorney Jerry Lynch, Joseph Horiskey and Lou's son, Peter Whittaker. Lou has been guiding on the mountain since 1951 and has guided thousands of people to the summit. RMI is the oldest continuously operating guide service and climbing school in the U.S., and currently employs up to 60 guides, five of whom are women. Of those 60, eleven have climbed Mount Everest (Larry Nielson, Phil Ershler, Ed Viesters, Robert Link, Mark Tucker, Eric Simonson, George Dunn, Dave Hahn, Brent Okita, Kurt Wedberg and Andy Politz). Two of the Everest veterans, Ed Viesturs and Larry Nielson, are the only Americans ever to climb

Lou Whittaker

Everest without using oxygen. Another of RMI's occasional guides is Nawang Gombu, the Sherpa who accompanied Lou's twin, Jim Whittaker, the first American to climb Everest. Nawang started guiding at Rainier in 1971, then returned in 1973, 1976, 1978, and several times since. In 1970, Joe Kennedy III, Bobby and Ethel Kennedy's son worked for a season as an apprentice guide. *(Sports Illustrated 7/6/70)*

Climbs run from May through September. Once the decision is made to make the climb, get your application in early. Slots fill up fast and there's a long waiting list. 1995 prices were $403.50 for the three-day Summit Climb Package via Camp Muir (one-day school and two-day climb) or $489.58 for the four-day Emmons Glacier summit climb.

For further information, contact Rainier Mountaineering, Inc.:

Winter Address (October-April)
Rainier Mountaineering, Inc.
35 Dock Street, Suite #209
Tacoma, WA 98402

(206) 627-6242

Summer Address (May-September)
Rainier Mountaineering, Inc.
Guide House
Paradise, WA 98398

(360) 569-2227

Lady Guides

The first female guides were limited to taking visitors for walks to Paradise glacier, and occasional assistance on summit climbs. The first such guide was Alma Wagen, a Tacoma teacher who worked at the park in 1918. Alma also had the distinction of being the federal government's first female guide anywhere in the U.S. In 1923, another woman, Emma Vaughan, was hired as a guide.

Marty Hoey, a much loved and respected Rainier guide from 1973 to 1981, was killed on Mount Everest in 1982.

Current female guides are Heather MacDonald, Catie Casson, Leslie Mittendorf, Jen Wedberg, Emily Johnston, Ann Keller and Heidi Eichner.

Climbing Routes

Climbers need names for features of each climbing face and landmarks along the various routes. On December 9, 1977, the Washington Board of Geographic Names approved a series of proposals developed by Dee Molenaar and others which documented names for most of the locations on the south-side routes. There are 56 climbing routes up the mountain, with varying degrees of difficulty and technicality. Even with so many choices, eighty percent of all climbers use just the "standard" Disappointment Cleaver (Ingraham) route, and the Emmons route. Other well known routes are Gibraltar (ledge), Fuhrer Finger, Kautz Glacier, Success Cleaver, Tahoma Glacier and Liberty Ridge. Liberty Ridge has claimed a disproportionate number of lives, Success Cleaver has the distinction of being the longest route, and Fuhrer Finger is the shortest. One climber who holds a major route record is Dan Davis who has climbed 22 different routes since 1959.

Camps Muir and Schurman

225

Camp Muir

In 1916 a hut at Camp Muir was completed at a cost of $555.00. The building's dimensions were 8' x 20' with walls 3 feet thick. Not only did the small rock building look like a fortress, it was a fortress against the elements which continually buffet the upper reaches of the mountain. In 1921 a bigger shelter was built, and the smaller shelter became the domain of the guide service (now

RMI cook shack). The larger one was designated for public use. Another building for the climbing service has since been added, as has a small ranger shelter. The old stone privies have been replaced with one pit toilet which has to be shoveled out by hand, and two solar toilets. The old ones were precariously perched overhanging the glacier, and the freezing updrafts used to give users a wake-up jolt like none other.

Reservations are not accepted for indoor hut space at the high camps and Camp Muir's 25-person hut fills up fast, so be prepared to camp outdoors.

Some have described Camp Muir as half way to Heaven, while a few others claim it's half way to Hell. It probably depends on what condition the climber is in. In any event, it's definitely half way to the summit.

Camp Schurman

By the mid-50's, it became evident a mid-point shelter was needed on the east side. Today, if building one, a Huey helicopter would make short work of

hauling the materials and supplies up the mountain, but in the late 1950's it went up the old-fashioned way: a human's back!

Under the leadership of Mountain Rescue veterans Max Eckenburg, John Simac, Ome Daiber, Bill Butler, and other Mountain Rescue friends, volunteers from Explorer Scouts, summit guides, ex-Park personnel, Mountaineers, and a varied assortment of climbers and hikers, tons of heavy corrugated steel and cement went up the mountain. The main qualification was a strong back and a willing heart. Materials were donated or paid for out of funds raised by a memorial-fund committee. "The Big Carry" started in 1958 and went on for six years before the much-needed cabin was completed. The cabin was named for beloved Clark E. "Pappy" Schurman, who, after years of serving as a Boy Scout executive, served as chief guide at the park from 1939 through 1942. He was a sensitive man who treasured the beauty of the mountain, and made countless contributions to his loves of mountaineering, Scouting, and safety on the slopes. He presented these final words about the mountain he loved at the close of his nightly lantern-slide programs in the Paradise Guide House.

> Last campfires never die. And you and I
> On separate ways to Life's December,
> Will always dream by this last fire
> and have this mountain to remember.

At 9,500 feet at the base of Steamboat Prow, Camp Schurman is six miles from the White River Campground. It has bunk space for 18, but would shelter 55 in a pinch. That's rather a moot point now, because in the mid-70's the shelter was taken over by the Park Service for their own exclusive use. Climbers must camp outside. The quonset-hut shaped cabin is kept permanently stocked with rescue equipment, emergency food and gear, and a radio.

High Camp Capacities

Camp Muir	110 person max limit
Muir Snowfields	36 person max limit
Ingraham Flats	36 person max limit
Camp Schurman	35 person max limit

Why Climb Mount Rainier?

There's a lot of truth in the old adage "because it's there," first said by Britisher George Leigh-Mallory, who disappeared on Mount Everest in 1924.

And, the words of P. B. Van Trump could also still be said today:

"I obtained my first grand view of the mountain in August 1867, from one of the prairies southeast of Olympia. That first true vision of the mountain, revealing so much of its glorious beauty and grandeur, its mighty and sublime form filling up nearly all of the field of direct vision, swelling up from the plain and out of the green forest till its lofty triple summit towered immeasurably above the picturesque foothills, the westering sun flooding with golden light and softening tints its lofty summit, rugged sides and far-sweeping flanks -- all this impressed me so indescribably, enthused me so thoroughly, that I then and there vowed almost with fervency, that I would someday stand upon its glorious summit, if that feat were possible to human effort and endurance."

Different things motivate different people to climb Mount Rainier. For some it's the drive to succeed at this ultimate test of stamina and endurance. For others it's the adventure of crossing glaciers and peering into the blue depths of seemingly bottomless crevasses. For still others it's the victory over fear of failure. Whatever the motivation, there's little as sweet as savoring the knowledge that you stood on top! For every person who "conquers the mountain," hundreds more conquer something within themselves!

Climbing Mount Rainier Today

When someone tells you they've climbed Mount Rainier, be impressed! Mount Rainier is considered the longest endurance climb in the conterminous states. It involves a vertical elevation gain of more than 9,000 feet over a distance of eight or more miles. It requires determination, stamina, strong legs, stronger lungs, and a good cardio-vascular system. It will probably be the most physically demanding experience of most people's lives. Many people have died in the attempt. Kenneth Cooper, author of *"Aerobics"*, and world authority on breathing and conditioning, calls his climb of Rainier "the hardest thing I've ever done, - at least as hard as the marathon." It should not be undertaken by the under-equipped and unprepared. Surprisingly, women have a higher success rate than men in making the summit.

While private climbs are allowed if qualification requirements of the Park Service are met, most people make the climb with the aid of RMI, the professional guide service. Climbers under 18 need written permission from a parent or guardian. Solo climbing is strongly discouraged. All private climbers must register at a ranger station before and after their climb.

Depending on the route taken, there are two parts to a guided climb. Part one for hopefuls is the successful completion of a one-day school which teaches the fundamentals of travel on glacial ice and snow, ice-axe self and team arrest, team travel with ropes and walking using crampons. About 10 percent of potential climbers wash out at this point.

The actual climb begins at Paradise (5,400 ft.), with a strenuous 4-5 hour climb to Camp Muir. (10,000 ft.) Most climbers go to Camp Muir the first day, from Puget Sound (sea level) to 10,000' in a span of just a few hours. As Lou Whittaker has pointed out, this is more elevation gain than a climber will experience on Mt. Everest in a single day. The final ascent begins shortly after midnight, after a brief night's *attempt* at sleep. The objective is for the party to make it to the summit (about a 5-to-7 hour climb from Camp Muir) and be back down off the glaciers before the heat of the day.

Jet-stream winds, cloudcaps and snow storms aren't the only problems climbers battle. Sometimes it's the air (or lack of it) in their lungs that does them in. At 14,000 feet, the air pressure is half that at sea level. Lethargy is a common problem. From the top, the party descends the entire 9,000 feet back to Paradise in just a few hours.

The long Emmons Glacier Route is different only in that it is an even more physically demanding route, and takes 2-1/2 days instead of two. This climb begins at the White River Campground for the strenuous pack up Inter Glacier and is made via Glacier Basin, Steamboat Prow and follows the Great Corridor up the Emmons Glacier. The final assault from Camp Schurman takes 8-10 hours.

Lou Whittaker summed up the sentiments of most who have made it to the top. "I meet them later, many years later. Some tell me that this fact - the conquering of Mount Rainier - changed their whole lives." It truly is the accomplishment of a life time. If you can climb Rainier, you can do anything!

Glaciers are Wilderness Areas Too: Permit Required

Anyone climbing to Camp Muir, Camp Schurman or any route, or planning to travel on a glacier, must obtain a climbing card. Those going to Camp Schurman also need a wilderness permit. Climbers must also register in *after* a climb too. For additional information, write: Backcountry Desk, Mount Rainier National Park, Tahoma Woods, Star Route, Ashford, WA 98304, or call (360) 569-2211, extension 3317 or 3303.

The Climber's Reward

The Summit

Seen from Seattle and Enumclaw, Mount Rainier looks like a huge rounded mound of ice cream. From Tacoma and the Mountain Highway, it has been described as a giant jagged tree stump. The reason is that there are three "points" on the summit: Point Success (14,150 ft.) formerly named Peak Success by Stevens and Van Trump, Liberty Cap (14,133 ft.) formerly known as North Peak and Peak Takhoma, and Columbia Crest formerly known as Columbia's Crest

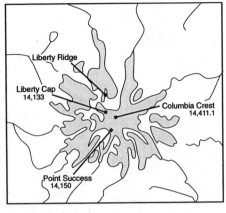

(14,411.1). Columbia Crest, (called by Stevens and Van Trump "Crater Peak" or "The Dome"), the true summit, is on the western rim of the East Crater which is 2,000' in diameter. For many years it was thought to be the highest point in America. The East Crater is actually the younger crater, and it "cuts" or truncates the West Crater. The high point of the mountain is where they intersect.

The rim is usually bare of snow as a result of high winds and volcanic heat on the summit. The wind frequently blows at velocities between 35 and 100 miles an hour. The depression is filled with snow, and rimmed with a series of caves and caverns formed by steam jets and volcanic heat "fumeroles."

The View From The Top

To the northwest, the distant Olympic Mountains blocks the view of the Pacific Ocean, however Puget Sound is spread out beyond the lowlands like a shimmering blue-green carpet with even the ferryboats visible. To the north, east and south, the Cascade Range is punctuated by other volcanoes, Mount Baker, Glacier Peak, and Mounts St. Helens (50 miles distant), Adams (48 miles), Hood (103 miles) and Jefferson. Other significant sentinels are Mount Shuksan, Chimney Rock and Mount Stuart. The summit offers 360-degree views for those with 360-degree eyes.

Climbers report that at night, city lights clearly define all the Puget Sound cities, and they can also see the lights of Yakima and Ellensburg. In daylight on a clear day, the tall Columbia Center building in Seattle can be seen.

The Steam Caves

The notorious summit steam caves have provided welcome emergency shelter since they were first discovered by P.B. Van Trump and Hazard Stevens in 1870. But spending a night in them is not without the unique problem of freezing and roasting at the same time. If you get too close to the fumeroles, you

Old Summit Cave System

△ Columbia Crest

Lowest accessible point

Surveyed Passage	————
Unsurveyed Passage	- - - - - -
Guide Trail on Surface	— — —
Main Entrances	◯

also get wet! Even that ordeal beats the alternative of freezing all over! Early climbers called the steam caves "Pluto's fires," and according to Indian legend they were "giant puffing otters." P. B. Van Trump and Hazard Stevens, during their 1870 climb, were the first to spend a miserable night in a steam cave at Columbia Crest.

There were other observations of the summit steam caves by Dr. Russell in 1898, and Dr. Flett in 1912. C. H. Birdseye, a USGS Surveyor working on an elevation study to determine the height of the mountain in 1913 wrote: "If anyone thinks that American glaciers are play glaciers, or that the weather which may be encountered at the summit of Mount Rainier in August is uniformly balmy and spring-like, let him climb Mount Rainier during one of its summer blizzards. The steam caves in the crater are not the most pleasant of places imaginable to spend the night in, but had they not been there, not one of us would be alive today to tell the tale .

"Here we sought shelter in one of the steam caves, where during the long night we were thoroughly steamed and half frozen in turn. Strenuous measures were employed by the men to keep from falling asleep and freezing to death. As it was, their fingers and ears were badly frozen."

In 1954, while scaling Mount Rainier Jim and Lou Whittaker were the first to seriously explore the Columbia Crater ice caves. Their experience piqued the interest of many cavers in the Seattle area, particularly the Cascade Grotto and the National Speleological Society (NSS). A team of climbers and cavers from the two groups, led by Dick Mitchell and Dr. William R. Halliday began the ambitious project of mapping the summit caves in 1968.

Between 1970 and 1975, a study of North America's highest, (and the world's largest) known cave system in a volcanic crater was conducted at Mount Rainier. In 1970 Dr. Eugene P. Kiver of Eastern Washington State College, Dr. William K. Steele, Bill Lokey and others mapped over 7000 feet of ice passages in the steam caves. In some areas the tunnels were over 30 feet high and 100 feet wide. Elsewhere the passages were just big enough for a man to crawl through. The deepest passage was over 350 feet below the surface ice. Dr. Mark Meier and Dr. Mumma, both of USGS did studies, and another study with Dr. Maynard M. Miller, Michigan State University, as the chief scientist and principal investigator, was sponsored by the Foundation for Glacier and Environmental Research (FGER) and was funded by the National Geographic Society. *(Explorers Journal, 9/73)*.

In 1970, a large "amphitheater" or "room" measuring 120 feet by 120 feet with a ceiling about 70 feet high was again seen.

A few hardy lichens and mosses grow in the steam vents of the summit crater, sustained by the warm moist steam. There are also spiders and insects which inhabit the warm, moist exposed volcanic rock of the summit. There are at least 30 entrances to the summit steam caves. *(TNT 7/17/81)*.

In 1996, Mr. William Klimack will lead the Mount Rainier Steam Cave Project. The study will map the caves, as well as doing a potential hazards study of Mount Rainier steam Caves.

"Crater Lake" (the lake in the crater)

Beneath the ice plug of the west summit crater lies a small lake about 150 feet below the surface. A small passage leads down from the perimeter passage to the lake grotto, which is nestled on the floor of the deepest chamber in the west crater. The lake, about 25 feet x 130 feet, by about 19 feet deep, is terminated by a vertical ice wall. The temperature of the rock on the floor of the grotto exceeded 70°C in places, but the water temperature was only 0.5°C.

The lake wasn't discovered until the 1971 exploration of the summit steam caves, but existence of a pool was first suspected in 1954 by Jim and Lou Whittaker who, when descending through the labyrinth of tunnels under the ice cap (in the east crater), rolled rocks down the slope, and heard them go quite a ways before concluding in a splash.

Five men have actually taken a little dunk in the nation's highest lake. Four Tacoma fire-fighters, Lee Nelson, Damon Herd, Bob Newberg and Ralph Guelfi did polar-bear type dips in the 32° water wearing cut-offs, and Bill Lokey, then in charge of the "Project Crater" enterprise of the Foundation for Glacial and Environmental Research, and now Director of Pierce County Department of Emergency Management, made the world's highest wet-suit dunk.

According to the World Almanac, Hawaii's Lake Waiau, at 13,020 feet is the highest conventional lake in the nation. Lake Titicaca on the Peruvian-

Bolivian border, at 12,506 feet, is the highest lake in the world on which steamboats ply, but this secret little summit lake, at 14,260 feet, in the crater of Mount Rainier, is the highest lake in the world!

Who Climbs Mount Rainier?
How Many Climb It?

If climbing to the summit makes you king or queen of the mountain, Mount Rainier has roughly 4,500 royalty on top per year. In 1994, for instance, 9,220 climbers made the attempt, and 4,411 actually succeeded. Of those, RMI took 2,500 people up, and that was their biggest year. (In 1964 only 300 summited).

There is a Park Service summit register at the top at Register Rock. It is housed in a Mazama summit register box. When the registers are full, they are put into the Park Service archives.

The Big White Classroom

For four decades, Mount Rainier has been the training ground for nearly all major American climbing expeditions. In September 1962, the American Mount Everest Expedition held their training maneuvers there. Ex-Rainier climbing guide, Jim Whittaker, used his Rainier-learned skills to become the first American to stand atop Mount Everest. He was followed to the top of Everest by four other climbers who had either been Rainier guides or had climbed on Rainier. (Lute Jerstad, Barry Bishop, Willi Unsoeld and Tom Hornbein)

Interestingly, during the ten days of training the Everest team spent on Mount Rainier, the weather was so bad, the group never made it to the summit. They went on to conquer Mount Everest, but Rainier didn't submit to them.

Expeditions to Alaskan, Andean, Yukon and Himalayan peaks have also used Mount Rainier as a proving ground, honing team techniques, climbing skills and testing equipment. They all came to the same conclusion: Mount Rainier can dish up conditions equal to the worst to be found anywhere in the world.

The Champs

All of the following climbers are legend! Each of them (except the few deceased old timers) could surely write books of their own about the mountain and their adventures on it. Within the ranks of these climbers, there's a friendly camaraderie and jousting over status. Joe Horiskey was the first climber in the modern era to get 100 climbs. Then Phil Ershler passed him up and has been in the lead ever since. Those footsteps closing in on Phil belong to George Dunn, who will probably pass Phil's record by the time this book makes it into print. Tracy Roberts is breathing down Eric Simonson's neck, while Jason Edwards breathes down Tracy's, and so it goes...

George Dunn holds the record for the most climbs in one year. He succeeded in 30 out of 40 attempts (from May through September) in 1976.

Conspicuously absent from the lists, is an exact figure for Lou Whittaker - who over his 40 years of teaching and climbing on the mountain, has lost count of his exact figure. Lou, his brother Jim, and son Peter, are without question America's first family of climbing.

The Iron Men: (left to right:) George Dunn, Eric Simonson, Phil Ershler

The Century Club	**The 150+ Club**	**The 200+ Club**
(100 Climbs)		
Dan Boyd	Lou Whittaker	Phil Ershler 352+
Curtis Fawley	Peter Whittaker	George Dunn 349+
Dave Hahn	Larry Nielson	Eric Simonson 250+
Marty Hoey (female)	Ed Viesturs	Tracy Roberts 250+
Gary Isaacs	Hans Fuhrer*	Jason Edwards 220+
Craig John	Heinie Fuhrer*	Craig Van Hoy 210+
Drew Kacmarcik		Joe Horiskey 210+
Paul Maier		
Brent Okita		
Andy Politz		
Ned Randolf		
Jules Stampfler		
Gary Talcott		
Dan Tobin		
Greg Wilson		

*Hans and Heinie Fuhrer each made over 150 ascents according to the American Alpine Journal, Vol. 2, #3, 1935 p. 320. Jules Stampfler had 128 trips up as of 1916. (22 seasons of climbing.)

The "civilian" Energizer Bunny Award should go to Mike Banner of Federal Way who just keeps going and going and going. He has climbed Mount Rainier for thirty-one consecutive years, climbing it first in 1965.

The Alumni Club

Harry (H.B.) Cunningham, chief guide at the mountain from 1925 through 1932, made his first climb with none other than Major E. S. Ingraham. Cunningham went on to climb the mountain 67 times in all.

In 1972, Cunningham held a reunion of sorts to celebrate the publication of Dee Molenaar's *"The Challenge of Rainier"* and to get many old Mount Rainier friends together to reminisce about their times on the mountain. At least one member of the incredible assembled bunch, was present at, or took part in, every major climb or rescue during the last two-thirds of this century.

Bill Butler, the shy, soft-spoken "living legend" was there. Butler left a legacy of rescues and almost superhuman physical feats, like the time he carried a kitchen range on his back, filled with grub, from Narada Falls to Paradise.

Also at the get-together were former Mount Rainier chief guides Wendy Trosper, Gene Jack and Jim Whittaker, as were former guides Wes Langlow, Molenaar, Leon Brigham and Dick Klinge. Noted climbers present were Jack Hossack, Paul Gilbreath, Harvey Manning, Willi Unsoeld, Pete Schoening, and Arne Campbell. Mount Rescue Council founders Wolf Bauer and Ome Daiber were there, along with John Townsley, superintendent of Mount Rainier National Park. Most of the mid-20th-century men of Mount Rainier were all assembled in one room.

It was like a *Who's Who* of Mount Rainier greats.

Climbing Statistics and Records

Speed Records

The first mention of speed in climbs appeared in the *Tacoma Daily News* in 1909. "Longmire Springs, July 24 - (Special.) Since the fast ascent of the mountain made by the party headed by C. E. Morford of Seattle last Saturday in seven and one-half hours, considerable controversy has arisen as to what is the record climb. Prof. Olof Bull of Tacoma, who is a Mazama and had made several trips to the summit, believes the one made in 1896 by A. B. Wood in six hours and 35 minutes is the fastest yet made. But old residents of the springs are of the opinion that even this time has been beaten. Guide Stampfler says that the trip from the springs to the summit and return, a distance of 25 miles, has been made in 12 hours, and he is confident that the ascent from Reese's has been accomplished in less than six hours. "Cain" (Elcaine) Longmire, who has been here since the first ascent, and Joe Stampfler, brother of the guide, are preparing a list of all the ascents made so far, and when this is completed, the matter will be settled definitely." (Ed. Note: We haven't yet found Elcaine and Joe's list yet, but Dee Molenaar's list is on page 223.)

The next printed mention of a speed record was in *"Scooting Skyward"* published in 1912. The fastest "scoot to the top" author Woodrow Bridges knew of was one up and back from Reese's Camp (Paradise) which was done in 11 hours.

Without fanfare, in 1933, young Delmar Fadden made a solo summit climb up the Emmons Glacier, leaving Sunrise at midnight, took a picture of himself on the summit at 10 a.m., spent 2 hours before starting down, and arrived back at the Sunrise parking lot at 6 p.m., thus accomplishing this very long route in

18-hours flat. The next mention of speed was in 1936 when Ranger Bill Butler made a round trip to the summit via Fuhrer Finger in 11 hours and 20 minutes.

In July 1959, twins Jim and Lou Whittaker and Oregon outdoorsman John Day made a round-trip time of 7 hours and 20 minutes, climbing from Paradise to the crater rim via the Gibralter Route. Two weeks later, two guides, Dick McGowan and Gil Blinn shaved that down to 6 hours and 41 minutes, but they didn't sign the register. They climbed via the Cadaver Gap-Ingraham Glacier route.

In 1977, a group of climbers from California who were going throughout the west making one day summit climbs of virtually every major peak, raced up the mountain and back before heading off to their next conquest.

Recent rapid round trip efforts started again in the early 1980's. In 1981 Rainier climbing guide Craig Van Hoy made the round trip from Paradise to the top via the Disappointment Cleaver route in 5 hours and 20 minutes, but remembered to take time to sign the summit register. What did he write? "Praise the Lord!" He received a silver bowl from *Sports Illustrated* for being mentioned in the magazine's "Faces in the Crowd." *(TNT 9/13/81).*

Two years later, Van Hoy did it again, this time with fellow guide, John Smolich. Wearing a full load of gear, the two made it to Columbia Crest in 3 hours, 50 minutes. Van Hoy blew into Paradise in 5 hours, 20 minutes, followed five minutes later by Smolich. Both had taken time to sign the register.

In July 1985, Ken Evans of White Pass, and a companion, Matt Christensen of Yakima, traveling light (with only ski poles and wearing running shoes instead of boots), made the round trip in 5 hours and 9 minutes. They didn't bother to sign the register.

Van Hoy, Smolich, and another guide, Jason Edwards, have since set round-trip speed records on several climbing routes: Success Cleaver (13 hours), Sunset Ridge (14 hours), Nisqually Icefall (16 hours), Central Mowich Face (19 hours), Liberty Ridge (21 hours), and Ptarmigan Ridge (22 hours). All are car-to-car times.

Camp Muir Speed Times

Today's power runners have pared the normal 6-hour climb to Camp Muir to little more than a jog around the block. It is now routinely done in an hour and a half. Until recently, the fastest trip on record, was the dynamic duo of Park Ranger Bundy Phillips and U.S. Biathalon competitor Josh Thompson. Thompson steamed into Muir (barely breathing hard), in 1 hour 4 minutes, with Phillips right behind him a minute later. In 1993, Paradise Ranger Scott Wanek, set a new time of 54 minutes flat, and did it inadvertently. He didn't even set out to break the record!

The Muir Legends

Many gasping-for-breath Muir-bound hikers have marveled to see two diminutive senior troopers steam by them. They've probably just seen 70 year-old Bronka and (husband) Aki Sundstrom, 78, who consider hiking up to Camp Muir for lunch, their favorite "date." And they date a lot. In 1993, they hiked to Muir 50 times. In 1994, they went up 38 times. The first time up each season, it takes them four hours, but by the end of the summer, they're doing it

Aki and Bronka Sundstrom

in 3-3-1/2 hours. It's not like they get out of shape in winter. Then they don their cross-country skis and go down to Box Canyon for lunch. Tiny Bronka weighs just 95 pounds, but she and Aki must have the hearts and muscles of 16-year olds.

Why do they do it? These are two people who truly do count their blessings. Tiny (Polish) Bronka survived a Concentration Camp as a young woman, and a few years back, (Swedish) Aki lost an eye to cancer. They took stock of their lives, and made a commitment to spend the rest of their years enjoying each other and doing the things they loved best: - mountaineering. In 1967 they built a "weekend" house in Nisqually Park, just a few feet outside the park entrance so they could be closer to their beloved mountain.

One month before St. Helens blew in 1980, they moved to their Nisqually hideaway full time, and began exploring every inch of the lower reaches of the mountain. They've never been to the summit, but their names are in the register. The RMI guides and climbing rangers all know of their Herculean efforts, and said with all the miles the pair has logged on the slopes, they've done the equivalent of summiting many times over, and thus they were credited with "honorary" summits.

Bronka has a word for other retirees. "Cherish today! Spend your golden years actively, and appreciate the day for whatever it is. We even appreciate the rain. Without it, we wouldn't have any of the other things we love, the snow, the trees, the flowers. We have it so good here. We don't relate to many others our age who while away years on cards and TV. We'd much prefer to be out with the younger people, enjoying the mountain."

Bronka and Aki, in turn, have run into other Muir hikers whom they admire. At the top of their list, was an older lady they met one day who was setting a respectable pace going up the mountain, and then told them she had just had a hip replacement!

Camp Schurman Speed Times

1994 saw Paradise Ranger Scott Wanek set another speed record. He and seasonal ranger Stefan Lofgren, climbing on a single rope, went from Camp Schurman to the summit in 2 hours and 30 minutes, beating the old record by 20 minutes. It isn't official, but they probably also set the speed record coming down. The descent took one hour, which put them back in camp and in the sack sawing logs by 4 a.m. as if nothing had happened!

Other Mount Rainier Legends

Youngest Climbers

By 1891, the very first climber under age 21 to climb the mountain was 13-year old Sue Longmire.

The next young climber of record to make the summit was 13-year old Jesse McCrea, the same young man who carried the first mail into the Park. He liked to hike barefoot, and it is reported that twice he hiked without shoes up Muir Glacier to a point above present Camp Muir. When McCray was 13, he accompanied Hazard Stevens on the latter's last climb of the mountain. *(Seattle Times 5/3/59)*

In 1939 an 80-pound boy of 11, Bob Melzer, chalked up a record with his climb. Not only did he make it up Mount Rainier, it was the 60th peak over 14,000-feet he had climbed. He and his father had already bagged 50 high peaks in Colorado and nine in California since the boy was 7 years old.!

Former Washington state Governor Dixy Lee Ray climbed the mountain in July of 1927, when she was just twelve.

The youngest climber to ever make it to the summit was a little half-pint of a girl, 58-pound, 7-year old Laura Ann Johnson of Tacoma.

The famed Olympic ski champion Mahre twins (Steve and Phil) first climbed Rainier when they were thirteen.

In 1969 a ranger's children set a family record. Nine year old Rice Anderson made the climb, one day after his 12-year old sister Laura made it, and one year after 13-year old sister Connie summited. *(TNT 8/5/69)*.

It was done again by Aaron Kirkpatrick, a nine year old Idaho boy in 1981.

Oldest Climbers

In 1958 retired Manson, WA orchardist Burr Singleton climbed Mount Rainier and completed a goal he had set only two years earlier. At age 73 he decided to take up mountaineering and climb every major peak in the state. He began with Mount Shuksan, then picked off Glacier Peak, Mount St. Helens, Mount Adams, Mount Baker and saved the best for last, doing Rainier at age 75-1/2. He explained that operating an orchard left no time for mountaineering, but now that he was a widower and retired, he had time. *(Spokesman Review 10/19/58)*.

For years the oldest climber on record was Julius Boehm, the Issaquah, WA candy maker, who climbed it in 1968 when he was 70, then did it again in 1978 at age 80. An opera lover, he stopped enroute on his climb to sing a few bars of "Der Rosenkavalier" by Richard Strauss. Boehm's record stood for 14 years until it was broken in 1992, by Jack Borgenicht of Long Valley, N.J., age 81.

Famous Customers

The first "noteworthy" customers of the Rainier National Park Company climbing service were the John D. Rockefeller, Jr. party. Their guide was the first woman guide of record, Alma Wagen. Not to be outdone, a party of daring DuPonts also made the climb as did a bevy of famous Firestones.

In 1964, Tenzing Norgay, the Sherpa guide who was one of the first two men in the world to scale the highest peak in the world, Mount Everest, also climbed Mount Rainier. He climbed Mount Everest in 1953 with Sir Edmund Hillary, but he climbed Mount Rainier ten years later with Jim Whittaker, Lute Jerstad and Dr. Tom Hornbein, three of Washington state's Everest veterans. *(TNT 7/22/64).*

The world of sports has contributed a few climbers. Ex-football coach Don James of the University of Washington Huskies and his coaching staff (the James Gang) climbed it, as did Jim Zorn and Steve Largent of the Seahawks. Steve Raible, former Seahawk and KIRO sportscaster did too. Bill Russell, while coach of the Sonics made it to 11,000 feet before he got weathered out. His biggest problem prior to the climb was finding a pair of climbing boots big enough for his size 18 feet.

Political Climbers

Dan Evans climbed the big mountain in 1965 with guides George Senner and Dee Molenaar, while he was governor of Washington State. Governor Booth Gardner climbed it with Jim Whittaker, and Governor Dixie Lee Ray climbed it as a child. Senator Slade Gorton not only climbed it, he also bicycled around the mountain. Colorado's former Governor Richard Lamb and his wife climbed it with Phil Ershler guiding, and the governor of Tennessee climbed with RMI guide Drew Kacmarcik.

In 1966, U.S. Secretary of Defense Robert S. McNamara, his wife Margaret, and daughter Kathleen climbed it with Lou Whittaker. In 1969, at age 15, Robert S. Kennedy's son David climbed the mountain. Then in 1970, Ethel Kennedy came out to visit the mountain while son Joe Kennedy III was working as an apprentice guide. She didn't make the climb, but she did zip up to Camp Muir in a respectable time.

In 1992, John Kennedy, Jr. attempted the climb, but was turned back by ice. This was the famous "Ice Summer" when it rained, then froze hard and the whole mountain turned to ice. Nobody made it up for three weeks.

Unfinished Business

There are some things in life which just need closure, and if not done, pass on to later generations to complete. Climbing Mount Rainier seems to be one of those unfinished achievements.

The first such case of record concerns the not-quite-successful 1857 climb of Lieutenant August V. Kautz. Although he went on to have a brilliant military career, his failure to make the summit of the mountain ate away on at least one family member. In 1957, exactly 100 years later, his granddaughter Jean put the Kautz name on the summit, when she finally completed the Kautz Route with a party of Mountaineers.

In 1994, another grandchild repeated his grandfather's feat, going to the summit exactly 100 years after his grandfather had. Only in this case, granddad had made it to the summit, he just never got credit for it.

According to the recently-disclosed old diary and photos, in 1894, Walter Bosworth was commissioned by the federal government to survey Mount Rainier. He and two other men took the train to Wilkeson and followed the Carbon River up to the Carbon Glacier. The three, Bosworth, Arthur French and Guy Evans, were the first to circumnavigate the mountain at timberline, and the first to reach the summit via Emmons Glacier. They also claimed to be the ones to name Fryingpan Creek. The diary related that when the party threw their packs across a creek, a frying pan fell out and was washed away.

At the summit, the diary noted, they found the tattered flag left by the Ingraham-Muir party of 1888. They also found a smaller flag and note left by one of the first women to reach the summit. The note was probably left by Susan Longmire, who at age 13 was the first young woman to climb it.

While not exactly unfinished business, in 1990, a group of 33 women from various parts of the country did a 100-year commemorative climb in honor of Fay Fuller's historic first-woman-on-the-summit climb in 1890. The women climbed under the auspices of the Northwest Chapter of (Minneapolis-based) Woodswomen, and Women Climbers of the Northwest.

A second group of ladies from the Ashford-Elbe area also did a "Centennial Climb" in honor of Fay Fuller's historic feat.

Mount Rainier: An Equal Opportunity Mountain

Climbing or hiking Mount Rainier, as pointed out previously, is probably the most physically demanding undertaking most people will ever attempt. The challenge is there, for all who will or can, to accept. Many able-bodied people have done just that, and failed. The flesh was willing, but the spirit weak, or vice versa. Then there those few, who by all logic, are not expected even to try. But occasionally, try they do -- and succeed!

One of the first handicapped persons to rise to the challenge, was Jack Graves, a one-legged amputee, who in July, 1978, skied alone from the summit down the Ingraham Glacier. Graves was the owner of a prosthetics company, and used an artificial leg he had designed especially for skiing and climbing. It worked exceedingly well, even helping to stop him when he slipped.

In 1981, a group of eleven handicapped people ("Project Pelion") made a summit attempt with the assistance of fifteen helpers. Among the climbers were seven blind members, two deaf, one mute, one epileptic and a Viet-Nam Vet with one leg. The climb was led by Jim Whittaker, and the helpers included Jim's wife, two doctors, a cinematographer and reporter. Nine of the eleven handicapped climbers succeeded in making it to the summit. The following week they were invited to the White House where they presented then President Reagan with an American flag they had carried to the summit. The expedition was named Project Pelion, after a mythological Greek mountain called the giants' stepping stone to heaven.

The next one-legged climber was Don Bennett, who made it all the way on July 17, 1982, on his second attempt. (He was turned back by a storm just below the crater rim during a 1981 attempt.) Bennett made it on his "hop to the top" with the help of special crutches fitted with large ski baskets and a spike tip.

The next honors went to amputee Sarah Doherty on August 3, 1984 when she too made it aided by special ski-pole crutches. A year later, she became the first amputee to make it to the summit of 20,300-foot Mount McKinley in Alaska. *(Molenaar)*

Perhaps the most daring hiker we've heard about, was a fellow Mount Rainier expert Bob Arnold met on the trail several years ago. Bob watched the man cross Van Trump Creek via a log crossing on his hands and knees. It was only after Bob met him further on, and suggested to him that he might do better on the trail if he stood upright and didn't lean into the hill. It was only then the man told Bob he was blind.

The Most Courageous Climbers

There's one gutsy group of 14 women for whom climbing Mount Rainier is the second biggest challenge of their lives! These dauntless women have already beaten an even more dangerous challenge: breast cancer! The 1994 Breast Cancer Survivor's Mount Rainier Expedition - an assault on breast cancer, was conceived by Laura Evans, an Idaho mountaineer who was once given only a 15 percent chance of living. The women scaled Rainier to heighten awareness of the disease, raise funds for research and pay tribute to women whose lives have been taken by breast cancer. Roberta Fama, one of the climbers, noted, "we're not trying to say that survivors should climb mountains, but they should reclaim their lives."

Another climber who attempted an almost super-human climbing feat, was quadriplegic Don Hayden of Ashford. Using a system of ropes and pulleys attached to a handle to pull himself up, Hayden and nine companions attempted the climb in first in 1987. A severe storm came in and even though Hayden wore waterproof gear, the driving rain and icy snow turned the party back. In 1993 Hayden was back and this time they got as far as Camp Muir. This tough young man will doubtless be back.

From the Depths to the Heights

A climb took place in July 1991 that has had life-changing ripple effects ever since, and will continue to have them for years to come. Jim Hinkhouse, a man with a love of the mountains, and particularly of Mount Rainier, saw the relationship and similarities between climbing a giant peak and achieving any difficult goal, by doing it in steps, -- one at a time. Jim had learned that lesson both through mountaineering and personally. He was a recovering alcoholic.

Jim founded "One Step at A Time" (OSAT), an outdoor activity club which is for members of 12-step recovery program, and in 1991, took 36 members on that momentous climb of Mount Rainier. Most people start their climb at Paradise, but for many of this group, their climb had begun in Hell. In their wildest dreams, they had never imagined themselves standing on the top of Mount Rainier.

But through Jim's own new lease on life, he dedicated himself to helping others maintain sobriety and immerse themselves in the great adventure of life. He saw no limits to what anyone could accomplish, and through his patience and inspiration, hundreds of people now climb mountains, hike and run. The incredible joy experienced by those 1991 climbers continues to multiply and rub off on others with the big climb still ahead of them.

Jim was tragically killed on a climb of Mount McKinley in Alaska the week of May 23, 1995. But OSAT continues to thrive as a result of the dedication and commitment that so many now hold. For them, the sight of Mount Rainier is a symbol of what can be achieved, by doing it one step at a time, and of the kind man who taught them that invaluable lesson.

Call the OSAT HOTLINE (206) 236-9674 for the time and location of weekly meetings or for membership information, or write to OSAT, P.O. Box 6461, Lynnwood, WA 98036.

A Big Climb for Big Bucks and a Good Cause

Since 1988, Lou Whittaker has led annual climbs for the American Lung Association's "Kids with Asthma" program, and charged corporate personnel $5,000 each for the privilege of participating. The first few climbs raised $50,000 to $60,000 for the cause, but the dip in the economy cut the number of participants for a couple years. The climb is now being opened to corporate personnel for all over the U.S. instead of just Washington. Interested executives with the necessary "entry fee" are invited to contact Lou in care of R.M.I.

International Peace Climb

1989 saw another first. Climbers from China, the Soviet Union and the United States climbed together for the first time. Some of the finest climbers from each country got together for a get-acquainted practice run up Mount Rainier. Their ultimate goal was the Earth Day 20 International Peace Climb, a symbolic expedition to the top of Mount Everest in 1990. Soviet climber Alexander Tokarev broke the ice by showing up for the climb wearing a pair of Groucho Marx glasses with a fake mustache. They were then borrowed by Liu Da Yi, leader of the Chinese team who wanted some souvenir pictures wearing them. *(TNT 6/25/89).*

Other Summit Celebrants

Northwesterners are a zany bunch, and their creativity knows no bounds when it comes to celebrating The BIG Achievement of making it to the summit.

Among other things at which the summit has been the site, are a number of weddings, a couple divorces, happy birthdays, engagement announcements, banquets, barbecues, board meetings, music recitals and other pronouncements of various kinds. It has had fireworks set off to celebrate the 4th of July and bringing in the New Year. One man in 1896, Mr. Olof Bull, gave a violin recital on the summit. It even had a book signing. Aubrey Haines had an autograph party on the summit to kick off his new book, *"Mountain Fever."*

Countless bottles of champagne, Rainier and other beers, booze and assorted other beverages, watermelons, birthday cakes and other accouterments of celebration have been hauled up the big hill. Also lugged up were flags, skis, rocks and mementos from other states and countries, assorted musical instruments, dolls, teddy-bears, good luck charms, bibles, crucifixes, carrier pigeons, telescopes, and a few munching mice inadvertently carried up in packs. One father and son who were caught on the top in a whiteout for eight days, swore one thing they would never climb without again, was a deck of playing cards.

Yes, there have been ashes scattered on or over the summit (as well as other places around the mountain.) Most want to be scattered on the sides visible from Seattle and Tacoma so friends and relatives can look and see "if so-and-so's out today."

Last but not least, with the advent of cellular phones, "you'll never guess where I'm calling you from..." has become a more commonplace greeting. (And if you're calling Puget Sound from the summit, it's a local call.)

Coldest Tootsies and er...

Climbers come in all shapes, sizes and hues, and one blue one that showed his stuff was a chapped chap who climbed in the buff in the 1950's.

The second strangest was a barefoot climber in 1971. The climber had to start off with boots, to get past the rangers. How did these guys endure the cold and climb barefoot? Your guess is as good as ours.

A License for Bragging

Several years back when Washington State decided it was time to redesign their license plates, they held a contest. The winner: a stylized rendition of a light blue Mount Rainier on a white background with red lettering. For $45, motorists can order custom license plates with up to seven letters on them, and of course, the names "Rainier," "Tahoma," and "My Mntn" were among the first to go.

A driver noticed that the car ahead of him had an X marked on the top of the Mount Rainier on his Washington license plate. At a stoplight he hopped out for a closer look. "I stood there!" it read.

Mountain Rescue

Following World War II, not only did most Northwest boys come home to "God's Country," so did many of the GI's and Swabbies who trained here or were stationed here. With the war won, and the years of rationing and deprivation behind them, people indulged themselves in some well-earned recreation. At the top of that list was taking to the hills for climbing, hiking and skiing.

When the inevitable happened, and people had accidents, it soon became evident there was a need for skilled people to go find the unfortunates, administer first aid, and haul them out of the mountains. Thus it was, that a number of expert climbers from the Seattle Mountaineers (Wolf Bauer, Ome Daiber and Dr. Otto Trott, being the nucleus) made themselves available to be on call at all hours of the day and night to slog off into the mountains in search of the accident. By 1948 they formally organized as The Seattle Mountain Rescue Council. Today there are similar groups all over the country, all a part of the Mountain Rescue Association which had it's humble beginnings in part on Mount Rainier.

Rescue and recovery efforts on the mountain are usually responded to first by guides from Rainier Mountaineering, Inc. and Park Service personnel since they are already at hand and can start to the scene of an accident immediately. Once word comes in of an accident, rescue forces are coordinated by the Park's chief ranger, who dispatches what aid is available, then puts out the call for additional help. Tacoma Mountain Rescue is the first "outside" group which responds to rescues at Mount Rainier, with additional backup help provided by Seattle and Olympic Mountain Rescue, Pierce County Sheriff's office, Explorer Search and Rescue, Civil Air Patrol then if need be and MAST helicopters from Fort Lewis. (Occasionally other units are used.)

These Good Samaritans usually work under the worst of all conditions, and have to retrieve their mangled charges from impossible predicaments and places, often at their own peril. By their very nature, mountaineering accidents are not nice neat clean little mishaps requiring an aspirin and a Band-aid. The brave rescuers usually have to walk miles, in the dark, in raging storms to retrieve people and bodies from cliffs, crevasses, raining rockfalls, rivers, under waterfalls, and any other dangerous situation people can get themselves into.

The annual number of search and rescue incidents ranges between 25 and 42 per year. The total number of carry-out incidents has increased 33% since 1992. Early in 1995, the Park Service inaugurated a $15 per climber fee (or $25 for an annual pass), which will be used to defray *the park's portion* of rescue costs. If a helicopter is required, the public still pays. An Army Chinook helicopter runs about $400 per hour, and that comes out of the Army's training budget. *(TNT July 7, 1989)*. (The rescuers from Search and Rescue, the various Sheriff's departments, other military and any other groups who participate, still pay their own expenses. The fees collected by the Park will not be shared with them.)

In just the first two months, the new $15 fee raised $25,000, and the park administration estimates it will bring them $150,000 per year. The fee applies to all climbers going above 10,000 feet.

Climbing Deaths

It wasn't until **1897** that the first fatal climbing accident occurred. It followed an effort to get the first barometric reading of the elevation of the mountain. After a long day, University of Oregon Professor Edgar McClure was returning to Paradise by moonlight, carrying his fragile yard-long glass barometer. He veered off course while descending the Muir snowfield, and ended up on what is now known as McClure Rock, where he fell and died.

1909. The next fatalities were in August, when T.V. Callaghan of West Seattle and Joseph W. Stephens of Trenton, N.J., perished above Gibralter in a blizzard. Their alpenstocks were found, their bodies were not. *(The Ledger 8/14/09).*

1911. A young man employed at the Indian Henrys tent camp, Legh Osborn Garrett, wearing a light shirt, trousers, and tennis shoes, disappeared while on a solo ascent on Success Cleaver. A 30-hour search turned up nothing but a few footprints made by his tennis shoes.

1915. C.W. Ferguson, Seattle, was crushed under falling ice in an ice cave beneath the Paradise glacier.

1916. J. A. Frisch, a member of a seven-man climbing party fell into a crevasse above Gibralter during the descent. He was rescued and brought down to Camp Muir where his primary problem appeared to be that he was "dazed." Doctors at Paradise examined him and declared him not seriously injured except for being dazed. He stayed at Paradise Inn, where two days later, he suddenly died.

1917. Dorothy Haskell, Tacoma, fell 75 feet to her death on Paradise Glacier.

1924. A Stanford University student, Sidney W. Cole, was hit by a falling rock in the chute by Gibralter Rock. He died the following day.

1929. The first major tragedy struck. In what came to be known as "the Greathouse accident," a climbing party of six was plucked off an icy slope one at a time after a sick member fell. Following a long slide which culminated with all falling into a deep crevasse, guide Forrest Greathouse and a client, Edwin Wetzel, were killed. The others, though badly injured, made it off the mountain. Efforts to retrieve the bodies took six days, and earned the first citation for heroism ever given by the Department of the Interior to Ranger Charlie Browne, who had climbed alone, at great personal peril, in an effort to locate and assist survivors.

1931. July 4th weekend. A group of climbers, many of whom were ill-prepared, spent the night at Camp Muir. A storm the following morning, discouraged all but several small parties. Two brothers, Kenneth and Robert Zinn, tagged along unroped, behind a party of nine Mazamas. Nearly at the summit, one brother (Robert) fell. He slid a distance of about 3,400 feet. Three days of searching crevasses finally located his body.

1936. The first winter climbing disaster happened in January, when 22-year old Delmar Fadden made an unauthorized solo winter climb via the Emmons Glacier. Film found in his camera showed he had made it to the top, but apparently he fell on the descent, was knocked unconscious and froze to death. The entire effort of locating his body and getting it off the mountain took many rescuers two weeks.

1943. Donald Kershmyer, 28, of Everett, got sick at the 12,000 foot level of the mountain, and was brought down to Camp Curtis (9,500') where he lapsed into unconsciousness. He was carried down to Glacier Basin, but died on the way to the hospital, probably of pulmonary edema. *(TNT 7/24/43)*.

1957. A snow bridge near the summit collapsed, with climbers disappearing amid huge falling blocks of ice and snow. One young Pennsylvania man, Bill Haupert, (having suffered a broken back) was dug out, but died several hours later, while still on the mountain. *(TNT 10/2/57)*.

1959. Geology Professor D. Calder Bressler of Western Washington State College died on the mountain of pulmonary edema. Two of his rescuers, the pilots who attempted to drop oxygen for him, also perished when their light plane crashed near the summit near dark.

1967. Elmer Post, 40, and his nephew David Post, 19, of Tacoma, both died when a snow bridge on the Muir Snowfield collapsed. They died of exposure when a blizzard came in and prevented their rescue. *(TNT 9/11/67)*.

1968. Two more climbers died after a fall into a crevasse on the Paradise Glacier at about the 9,000 ft. level. They died of exposure. *(TNT 2/19/68)*. Seattle Climber Pat Chamay, a member of the Boeing Alpine Club, died on Liberty Ridge of pulmonary edema. *(TNT 6/25/68)*.

Milton G. Armstrong, 54, a retired Navy officer from California, left a note on his pack at Camp Muir saying "Do not disturb. Back at 3 p.m.". His body was found two years later near the Beehive area. Armstrong was an admirer of John Muir, and told friends he just wanted to hike around Camp Muir as a part of his study of the man. He apparently slipped and fell on loose rock. *(TNT 9/18/68 & 9/27/70)*.

1969. saw the first fatalities on a Mountaineers climb. Two climbers, Mark Kupperberg and David Stevens were killed when they fell on rock-hard glare ice, and their rope partner couldn't arrest them. They slid 2000 feet down the Winthrop Glacier before falling into a 125-ft. deep crevasse. Theirs marked the third and fourth deaths of the year. A man named George "Tim" Dockery was killed in a rockslide on upper Curtis Ridge in June. Others were injured by the same rockfall, and the resulting rescue was one of the most difficult ever attempted on the mountain. Also a lone skier had died in an avalanche. *(TNT 7/15/69 & 5/17/89)*.

1971. Michael A. Ferry, 24, of Seattle, became the mountain's 18th summit climbing fatality, when he fell 65 ft. into a crevasse. *(TNT 8/2/71)*.

1974. A fresh snow avalanche, started by David Taylor, carried him over rocks below. His body was never found.

1975. Mark Jackson, 17, was killed by rockfall while ascending the Mowich face. Jackson, a summer employee at the park, was the son of an administrative assistant to then Representative Floyd Hicks.

1977. A bad year for climbers. First, Jack Wilkins, a popular Tacoma News Tribune reporter, was killed in a fall which took him off a cliff on Success Cleaver. Next Dean Klapper, unroped and not wearing crampons, slipped and fell 1000 feet before going in a crevasse. Then a woman, Mary Gnehm was killed when her rope team slid 1,500 feet down upper Ingraham Glacier.

1978. An Alaska man, Todd Davis, was killed by an avalanche while climbing Fuhrer Finger. The avalanche swept his party 2,000 ft. down the mountain. *(TNT 6/2/78).* Two days later, and around the mountain, another slab avalanche struck. Two parties were climbing east of Camp Muir. The slide swept one party of four, led by Lou Whittaker, 600-700 ft. onto the Cowlitz Glacier. The other party, led by Lou's son Peter, managed to arrest their descent after a 20-30 ft. slide. Young Whittaker suffered a broken ankle. *(TNT 6/1/78).*

Two climbing instructors died on the peak. Shirli Voigt, 30, of Denver, and Guillermo Mendoza, 28, of Saltillo, Coahuila, Mexico, died of hypothermia. They told rangers they intended to camp on the summit, but their tent was found in their car, and a sleeping bag was left at Camp Muir. Voigt was director of a mountaineering school for the Colorado Mountaineering Club, and Mendoza was an instructor for a Mexican mountaineering school. *(TNT 9/15/78).*

1979. (March) Willi Unsoeld and Janie Diepenbrock, a student from Evergreen State College, were killed in an avalanche at Cadaver Gap when they (and twenty students) got caught in a storm and decided to take a shortcut back to Camp Muir. (May) Seattle attorney Stimson Bullitt, 59, and son Ben, 22, were rescued by helicopter from separate bivouacs after being caught in a fierce snowstorm. (June) John Donlou, 34, a California physician, was rescued after he was hit by a 300 lb. chunk of ice about 1,000 ft. from the summit. His arm was later amputated. His helicopter rescuers snatched him off the mountain at 9:39 p.m., with just ten minutes to spare before it was too dark to fly. *(TNT 6/26/79).* Climber Dale Click fell in a crevasse and died of hypothermia just as rescuers arrived. *(PI 9/4/79).*

1981. (May) Doug Fowler 21, and Bruce Mooney 20, both of Tacoma, fell 3,000 ft. to their deaths on the steep face of Liberty Ridge. A Chinook helicopter equipped with a device called a Jungle Penetrator winched their bodies off, as the giant rotor blades whipped just inches from the mountain. *(TNT 5/29/81).*

(July) Peter Brookes, 26, Huntington Beach, CA, also died in a fall from Liberty Ridge after unroping from his climbing partner at Thumb Rock. He was never seen alive again. (July) Seattle climbers Brian Sullivan, 23, and Dan Stage, 26, were fortunate to escape the same fate. They were rescued by helicopter from Liberty Cap. *(TNT 7/19/81).*

1981. 18-year old Peter Brooks died in a fall from Liberty Ridge.

1983. A party of three climbing to Camp Muir in fog, fell over a cornice above Anvil Rock, and into a deep crevasse below. The body of climber Doug Vercoe was never found.

A rescuer died. Christopher Hal Bligh, a 25-year old Lake Stevens, WA, plunged to his death while rescuing a woman from a crevasse. He died when he moved to avoid the woman who had just been hauled out, and fell approximately 100 ft. into the same crevasse. He had unroped while working on the rescue. *(TNT 5/31/83).*

Two Fort Lewis soldiers who failed to register, and climbed with inadequate equipment (no ice axes or crampons), were killed in an 800 ft. fall from Disappointment Cleaver. Spec. 4 Patrick V. Hill 26, of California, and Pvt. E-2 Douglas J. Velder 19, of Colorado took off on an impromptu recreational climb. Their fall was witnessed, but rescuers were unable to save either man. They died of severe head and chest injuries and multiple broken bones. *(TNT 10/6/83).*

Climbing Deaths

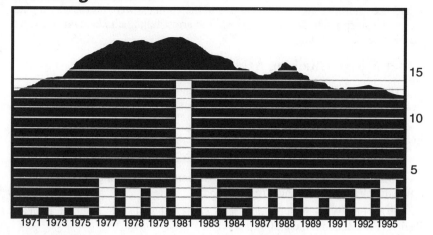

1971 1973 1975 1977 1978 1979 1981 1983 1984 1987 1988 1989 1991 1992 1995

1985. Fuat D. Dikmen, 28 of Madison, WI disappeared while climbing alone on Liberty Ridge. His body was discovered the following May at the 11,800 ft. level on the Carbon Glacier. *(TNT 5/17/89)*

1987. John Weis, a doctor, and Don Weltberger, a nurse, both 31, died in a tent at the 13,000 ft. level where they had taken refuge in a storm. *(TNT June 21, 1987).* A few days later, Tacoma Fireman Kurt Fengler died when a snow bridge he was crossing collapsed. *(TNT 6/28/87).*

1988. Three climbers, Craig Adkison, a 37-year old Boeing electrician and two Californians, David Kellokoski of Paradise, CA and Greg Remmick of Citrus Heights, died on Liberty Ridge near Thumb Rock. They had hoped to climb Mount McKinley after bagging Mount Rainier. A helicopter was able to snag their climbing rope and pluck the bodies off the mountain. *(TNT 5/21/88).*

1989. Richard Mooney became another Liberty Ridge casualty when he died of altitude sickness and hypothermia at the 13,700 ft. level, and Peter Derdowski 26, of Stateline Nevada, plunged 3,000 ft. to his death off Liberty Ridge, onto the Carbon Glacier. *(TNT 5/17/89).*

1992. A Colorado man, Mike Price, died of a broken neck when a snow bridge collapsed under him 1,200 feet above Camp Schurman. *(TNT 6/23/92).*

All told, between that first fatality in 1897 and 1995, 67 people have perished in climbs of Mount Rainier. In 1992 there were three killed, two on Fuhrer's Finger and one on the Cowlitz Glacier.

First Ranger Rescuer Fatalities

August 13, 1995, marked the first deaths of climbing rangers, when two rangers fell to their deaths while trying to rescue an injured climber. They were trying to reach a climber with a broken ankle on Emmons Glacier, and fell at about 1,300 feet on nearby Winthrop Glacier on the north side of the mountain. The rescuers, Sean Ryan 23, of New York, and Philip Otis 23, from Minnesota, were experienced seasonal rangers. Exactly one week later, two more climbers were killed in a fall from a spot just 100 feet from where the rangers had fallen.

The area of the infamous falls was not only steep, but had identical conditions. It had been hot, the snow had melted, and the climbers were on rock-hard glare ice on the steep pitch. Ice axes work well to arrest falling climbers on snow, but act like ice skates on ice.

Other MRNP Climbing Accidents

1912. Charlotte Hunt, Seattle school teacher, fell to her death from Pinnacle Peak. *(TNT 7/25/33).*

1921. In August, Jack Meredith, a young climber from Portland was killed in a fall from Little Tahoma.

1924. A guide, Paul Moser, plunged to his death from Unicorn Peak.

1932. Prof. Richard J. Pearce of the University of Washington, was killed in a Paradise Valley avalanche. *(TNT 2/22/32).*

1970. Eric Weigel, an off-duty RMI guide fell while solo climbing Pinnacle Peak. He fell at about the 6,500 ft. level. *(TNT 7/31/70).*

1989. A 26 year old Michigan man was killed in a climbing accident on Unicorn Peak. Andre Genereux suffered fatal head and chest injuries when he pulled a large rock loose, which then fell on him. *(TNT 7/7/89).*

1993. There was another fatality on Pinnacle Peak.

America's Worst Climbing Accident

1981 was the year of the largest climbing catastrophe on the mountain and the worst accident in American climbing history. An icefall with blocks of ice the size of cars came hurling down the mountain at speeds of 130 mph and swept 11 climbers to their deaths through burial in a deep crevasse. The climbers, roped together, had nowhere to go and it was all over in 30 seconds.

The climb was under the auspices of RMI, which had successfully led thousands of climbers over the same route. Twenty-nine climbers were going up the Ingraham Glacier, the most popular and traditionally trouble-free route to the summit. The climb was proceeding under what seemed like ideal conditions. The weather was cooperating: there was little wind, temperatures were in the upper 20's and the sky was clear when the tragedy struck. RMI guide Tom O'Brien was among those killed. The bodies of the lost climbers were never recovered. The only remains ever found were a headlamp, eyeglasses, a camera, a backpack, and a piece of rope. Eighteen survived the mishap.

A year after the tragedy there was a service at the mountain for friends and relatives of the victims. Several families have returned for their own private services over the years.

The Suddenness of Mountain Death

Willi Unsoeld's death on Mount Rainier shocked the climbing world. It created a newfound respect for the familiar peak most took for granted.

"If the mountain can kill a guy like Willi Unsoeld, it can kill anybody," they said.

Over the years, the casualty list climbed, some years faster than others. The above 1981 accident is the third worst tragedy in world climbing history. The worst was when a Russian avalanche killed 42. Second worst was in the 1930's when 16 members of a German climbing party were killed in the Himalayas.

In Washington state, the previous most deadly accident occurred on Mt. Baker on July 23, 1939 when six people were killed in an avalanche. In 1975, another avalanche killed five members of a University of Puget Sound climbing party at Mount St. Helens. It swept down on them as they prepared to go to bed. *(TNT 6/22/81).*

Do The Glaciers Ever Give Up Their Dead?

After reading all the above grisly statistics, one soon realizes that many mountain climbers and hikers (plus aircraft accident victims) not only died on the mountain, but are still up there. Do the glaciers ever give up their victims?

The most famous case of one that did, was the famous Grindewald Glacier in Switzerland. Two climbers disappeared on it in 1870, and their bodies were found nearly 90 years later at Grindewald's terminus.

Knowing when and where to look requires knowing the elevation of the last known location of the victim and the speed at which the glacier moves. (The South Tahoma Glacier moves about 500 ft. per year, for instance.) Added to this is the calculation of changes in the speed of the glacier, and whether it is advancing or receding.

For years many people kept an eye on the terminus of the South Tahoma Glacier in hopes it would yield the victims of the Marine Transport crash of 1946, but the only thing it ever gave up were some pieces of the aircraft in 1982.

Ken Hopping photo

Here's a view of Little Tahoma that few but climbers ever see.

Skiing

Early Skiers

The first recorded skier at the mountain was a young lady named Miss Olive Rand, who came with a group of Tacoma Mountaineers in 1912. Miss Rand brought with her two long slabs of wood with turned-up ends and fastened to her feet with hoops. She explained that the contraptions were skis, and proceeded to demonstrate their use. To those who had been making the pilgrimage to Paradise on big heavy snowshoes, the prospect of being on boards gained instant popularity. It proved to be easier and a lot more fun. The sport became so popular that soon there were rope tows at Paradise, and more at Cayuse Pass. The rolling meadows made superb ski runs, and the well-named Paradise was found to be as appropriate for skiers as for flower lovers. For the more adventuresome, a climb to Camp Muir gave the down-hillers a vertical drop of nearly five thousand feet in four miles on the return trip. As if there wasn't enough land to ski on, some joker would always amuse the weekend crowds by skiing off the roof of Paradise Inn.

In 1920 the Northwest Ski Club held a ski jump competition at the mountain. The winner won with a standing jump of 95 feet. An audience of over a thousand watched. In 1923, Nels Nelson, world amateur ski champion made a record jump of 240 feet at Alta Vista.

Everybody wanted to get in on the act of winter fun at the mountain. Seattle had an annual Spring Snow Sports Carnival at Paradise, complete with the crowning of "Queen of the Carnival." Then Tacoma had the "Tacoma Day Winter Carnival" at Longmire, with ski and snowshoe races, tobogganing and other snow sports. Around the 4th of July each year, a large annual ski ball was held at Paradise Inn.

In 1936 the Olympic Ski trials were held at Mount Rainier, and the National Downhill and Slalom Championships were held at Paradise..

Silver Skis

The big annual event in the mid-1930's was the internationally famous Silver Skis Race, sponsored by the Seattle P.I. At 4.5-miles from Camp Muir to Paradise Valley, it was the longest downhill race in the country.

Old time climber Wolf Bauer remembered being in the second race in 1934. "We all started at one time. There were sixty-nine of us in one line, and we all funnelled down two miles to the first gate; there were only three gates on the entire course." The 5,000 foot drop was run in 7-1/2 minutes, and only forty-four of the sixty-nine racers finished. That particular race was the first and only one where all racers were started at one time.

In 1940, a skiing tragedy occurred. Skier Sigurd Hall was killed instantly when he crashed into fog-shrouded rocks. The accident, along with our entry into Second World War resulted in the end of the races.

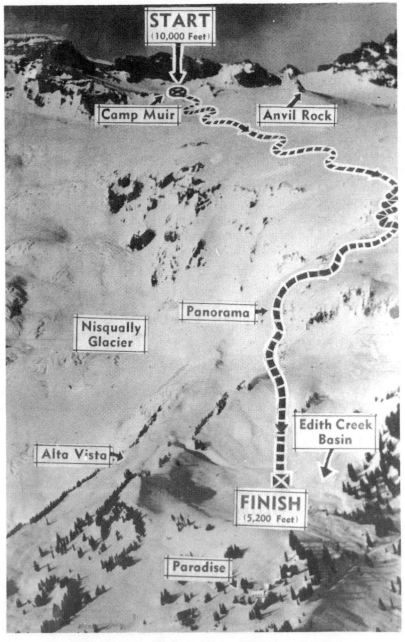

START
(10,000 Feet)

Camp Muir

Anvil Rock

Panorama

Nisqually
Glacier

Edith Creek
Basin

Alta Vista

FINISH
(5,200 Feet)

Paradise

Seattle Post Intelligencer Collection, Museum of History and Industry

Mount Rainier Ski Ascents/Descents

The first ski *ascent* of the mountain was made July 1, 1939 by Sigurd Hall (who was killed the following year during the Silver Skis race.) The first ski *descent* wasn't made until 9 years later, on July 18, 1948, when four Mountaineers, - Dave Roberts, Charles E. Welsh, Kermit Bengtson and Cliff Schmidtker, used ropes and an ice axe in place of a second ski pole, to make it safely through the heavily crevassed passages near the top .

A second ski descent was made in 1955 by Marcel Schuster and Robert McCall of the Yakima Ski Club. They descended via the Emmons Glacier. *(Molenaar)* The Whittaker brothers also did a ski descent this same year.

The first ski descent via the Ingraham Glacier was accomplished June 18, 1961 by John Ahern, Bill Briggs, Roger Brown, Gordie Butterfield, Joe Marillac, Roger Paris, and Jim and Lou Whittaker. *(Molenaar)*

Another noteworthy record is that of that of Frank Danes, professor emeritus of physics at University of Puget Sound. He used to ski the Nisqually Glacier from Glacier View to the bridge two times a day. He also used to hike the mountain to get seismology readings with his students. He still runs marathons at 70+ years of age!

First Ski Encirclement

The first Nordic ski trip around the mountain was accomplished in June of 1983 by Air Force triathlete and astrophysicist Dana Rush, and librarians N. L. Kirkland and Karen Goettling. Nicknaming their encirclement, "the Skywalk," they looped most of the mountain on skis at about the 10,000 foot level. At this elevation, the distance is 25-miles around. Inspired by Dee Molenaar and Harold "Hal" Foss's earlier 4-day encirclement at this level on foot, the trio decided to try it on skis. They had already bicycled and hiked around the mountain in addition to climbing it by several routes. *(News Tribune 6/5/83)*.

Three years later, May 24-30, 1986 the feat was repeated by Kirkland, Rush, Terry Pritchards and Dr. Roy Walters *(Molenaar)*.

The latter group traveled clockwise, taking seven days to make their way across the glaciers and through the icefalls. All went well until Kirkland took an unexpected detour into a deep crevasse on the South Mowich Glacier, nearly suffocating in the process.

Skiing Fatalities

Prior to Sig Hall's Silver Skis fatality, in 1936 skier Jack Northrop was killed below Narada Falls by an avalanche, and suffocated under 7 feet of snow. When finally found he was rushed to the Narada Falls Ranger Cabin, but it was too late. *(TNT 3/27/36)*.

Telemark skier Pamela Benton Lee, a popular Evergreen State college student nicknamed "Mountain Woman" was killed when she was caught in an avalanche off Plummer Peak. *(TNT March 8, 1988)*.

Skiing at the Park Today

Cross Country Skiing - In the Park

For those who love the tranquility and physical challenge of ungroomed trails and no ski lifts, there are several marked cross-country courses in the Paradise area. They run to Narada Falls, Edith Creek Basin, Barn Flats, Deadhorse Creek, Mazama Ridge, Nisqually Vista Loop and the trail over the Inspiration Point saddle to Reflection Lakes. Pick up a map from the Visitor Center, and heed the park's safety instructions. Choose a destination which is appropriate for your abilities and existing avalanche conditions, and be sure to sign the trail register at the Ranger Station or Visitor Center or at the Narada Falls Comfort Station. Remember cross-country skiing and snowshoeing are wilderness activities.

In 1993, for the first time in 20 years, there was again a ski patrol at the mountain. Members of the Washington Ski Touring Club volunteered to perform ski patrol duty at remote locations throughout the Paradise area. They were a welcome sight on the slopes. The group decided to take over Nordic Ski Patrol duties when one of their members, Jim Kampe got lost in a whiteout, and was never seen again.

There's also a cadre of cross-country aficionados who hike in from the (northern) Highway 410 road closure and ski around Cayuse Pass and Sunrise. Beware of avalanche danger if going off the beaten track! Be aware too there are no Park personnel or ski patrols to bail you out if you get in trouble on the north or east side.

Cross country and telemark ski lessons and ski rental equipment are available within the park from Mount Rainier Guest Services. Inquire at the (Longmire) National Park Inn Gift Shop.

Difficulty Levels

The park service uses the following criteria to determine your ranking:

> **Novice:** This is your first trip or season. You ski slow and straight ahead.

> **Intermediate:** You can climb uphill and turn downhill. You are aware of hazards such as avalanches and hypothermia.

> **Advanced:** You have instructed others. You can ski well downhill. You are skilled in staying safe and alive.

Telemark Skiing

Telemarking is an old time sport that's regaining popularity. It's a free-heel cross-country ski technique which was developed in Telemark, Norway.

Recently RMI guide Ned Pandolf telemark skied the Kautz Route (including the chute) and the Wilson Headwall. Liberty Ridge was also telemarked by Jimmy Katz in 1989.

More recently, Jim Drannan, a civilian nuclear instructor at the Puget Sound Naval Shipyard set another telemark record, in large part, at the mountain. Drannan's achievement (which changes monthly), is seeing how many months he can (telemark) ski on Washington State snow. When all other snow is long gone, old faithful Mount Rainier still has all the good skiing one could possibly want. As of December 1995, Drannan's record stood at 74 consecutive months. Hardy soul that he is, even after a serious spill on Frying Pan Glacier which left him with a broken wrist, a mangled shoulder, a brain contusion, and a couple nasty cranial gashes, he dragged his bones six miles down the trail to his car, and stopped at the hospital in Enumclaw long enough to get put back together. The next month, complete with cast, he was back maintaining his record.

Avalanche Hotline

To check conditions before leaving home, call the Forest Service's Northwest Avalanche Information Hotline (206) 526-6677.

Skiing Outside the Park

Cross Country Skiing - Outside the Park

Mount Tahoma Scenic Ski Trails: The 100 miles of the Mt. Tahoma Trail System with hut-to-hut skiing begins not far from the Park's Nisqually entrance. X-country skiers can make a weekend of it and ski to their heart's content on snow-covered logging roads in the beautiful hills of the west side, just outside the Park boundary. Snow covered clearcuts and natural openings offer great telemark skiing opportunities. These trails are open to all types of skiers and snowshoers only. (No motorized equipment.) The trails to the huts and yurt are kept groomed, volunteers and weather permitting.

Mount Tahoma Trails Association operates under a cooperative agreement between the Department of Natural Resources, the US Forest Service, Champion International and Mount Rainier National Park. This is a happy marriage of government agencies and private owners.

Mount Tahoma Trail System Difficulty Statistics:

- 25% easiest. (Easiest = gentle terrain, basic x-country skills required.)

- 53% more difficult. (Steep terrain; requires endurance and the ability to stop and turn at will.)

- 5% most difficult. (Very steep terrain, requires full control of skis at all times.)

- 17% backcountry/expert. (Off trail or unmarked trails; Requires same skills as Most Difficult, plus knowledge of route finding, avalanche assessment, weather, winter camping and survival.)

Elevation ranges of trails are between 2,200 and 7,500 + feet.

Mount Tahoma Ski Trails Sno-Parks are:

Copper Creek - 10.8 miles East from Elbe via Highway 706. Turn north on USFS Road 59, continue 3 miles north on Road 59 to parking area; groomed; 20 spaces. (This lot also joins a Cross-country ski/snowmobile Parking Lot.)

DNR Road 1 - 6.5 miles East from Elbe via Highway 706, then South on 553rd St., 6 miles South on Road 1 to parking area; 20 spaces.

DNR Road 2 - 6.5 miles East from Elbe via Highway 706, then South on 553rd St., 7.4 miles South on Roads 1 and 2 to parking area; 20 spaces.

DNR Road 23 - 6.5 miles East from Elbe via Highway 705, then South on 553red Street, 6.6 miles on Roads 1, 2 and 23 to parking area; 20 spaces.

DNR Road 92 - 6 miles East from Elbe via Highway 706, then North .5 miles on 278th Street East, continue 5 miles North on Roads 8,9, and 92 to Parking area; groomed; 20 spaces.

Sno-Park Permits

State Sno-Park Permits for the Central and South Districts cost $7/vehicle for a one-day pass, $10 per vehicle for a three-day pass and $20 per vehicle for a winter pass. Permits are available at the Ashford Valley Grocery, Elbe Mini Mall and over 125 retail locations. The permits must be displayed in the lower left corner of the windshield. Proceeds are used exclusively for non-motorized

Sno-Park facilities. The money is used to provide snow removal, sanitary facilities, trail grooming, signing, mapping, parking lot construction, and maintaining the Sno-Park Program.

Champion Tree Farm Access Permits:

Champion offers North District access, good for the trail season from Jan. 1 through June 30. The fees are: one day - $8.00 adults/$6.50 seniors; three day - $20 adult/$16 senior; and full season $100 adult/$80 senior. 10-day permits are also available ($55adult/$40 senior). There is no fee for children under 18 when accompanied by an adult. Seniors are 65 and older. For information, write Champion International, 31716 Camp 1 Road, Orting, WA 98360, Attn. Bob Graul, or call their recreational information number (1-800-782-1493) for retail locations. Permits are NOT available at the gate. Also call for gate access times and holiday closures. Permits do not have to be used on consecutive days.

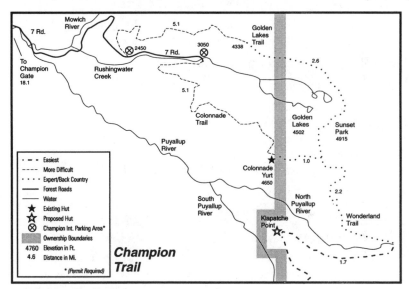

Hut Vital Statistics

- **High Hut:** 8 berths, South District - 4,760'
- **Snow Bowl Hut:** 8 berths, South District - 4,300'
- **Copper Creek Hut:** 12 berths, Central District - 4,200'
- **Colonnade Yurt:** 6 berths, North District - 4,650'

MTTA Huts

Three overnight huts and a yurt offer welcome backcountry shelter for skiers, but make reservations early, as they fill up early. (The whole season's weekends are usually booked by December). All you need is food, a sleeping bag and survival gear. (Also bring your Ten Essentials, a garbage bag and camera.) There is no charge to stay in the huts, but a refundable deposit is required. Weekdays are usually no problem, so ski midweek if at all possible. (Reservations: (360) 569-2451). Consider volunteering to help out too.

Other Cross Country Skiing Opportunities

Crystal Mountain Ski Resort: Yes, Crystal is best known for its downhill runs, but it's also a favorite haunt of cross country skiers who like the convenience and safety of having Ski Patrol nearby. The cross country area is the big Silver Basin just off chair 4. (No groomed trails though). Ski Patrol will monitor your whereabouts if you ask them to (check in and out). They'll also sell you a good topo map of the area for 50 cents. For info, call (206) 825-6585.

White River Ski Trails Sno-Parks are:

Silver Creek - 32.4 miles East of Enumclaw via Highway 410, then .2 miles east on Crystal Mountain Road; 25 spaces.

Sun-Top - 24.8 miles East of Enumclaw via Highway 410, then 1.4 miles South on USFS Road 73; groomed; 20 spaces.

Recommended Backcountry Equipment:

In addition to the ten essentials, backcountry skiers are also advised to carry:

- Avalanche transciever
- Unbreakable shovel
- Avalanche probes
- Repair kit
- Winter survival skills and equipment
- Weather radio

Downhill Skiing

Crystal Mountain

Crystal Mountain, site of the 1972 World Cup Championship, is Washington's premier ski resort. It offers outstanding winter Nordic and alpine skiing, Crystal also offers hiking, fishing, swimming tennis, horseback riding and chairlift sightseeing the rest of the year.

White Pass

White Pass Ski Area, about 55 miles west of Yakima on Highway 12, offers a 2-1/2 mile run, a 1,500 foot vertical drop and 650 acres of skiing, served by a high speed quad, 4 double chairs, a poma lift, and rope tow. Amenities include a ski school, child care, cafeteria, bar and privately owned condos. Don't knock the relatively short drop. Phil Mahre, the 1st American to win a World Alpine Cup championship learned to ski here, as did his Olympic medalist brother, Steve. His dad, Dave Mahre, a Mount Rainier climbing veteran with several first ascents to his credit, has been manager of the White Pass Ski Area for going-on 30 years. For more information, phone (509) 453-8731 or (509) 672-3100.

Trails

Wilderness Management System

Prior to 1973, there were few regulations governing back country use, and destructive practices such as multiple campfire rings, trees stripped of branches cut for firewood and bedding, and polluted water supplies caused the establishment of a Backcountry Management Plan. Backcountry usage was severely restricted through a limited permit process, capacities were established on the number of people allowed in any one area, shelters were removed, and for the first time, what practices could and could not be done in camp and on the trail were clearly spelled out.

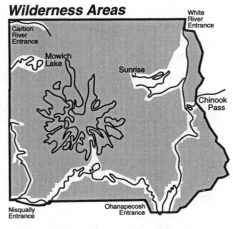

Wilderness Areas

On November 16, 1988, 228,400 acres (nearly 97 percent) of the park's 235,612 total acres became a part of the Washington State National Parks Wilderness Act which designated Mount Rainier backcountry as wilderness. Excluded areas are Camps Muir and Schurman, portions of the water supply, road systems and roadside developments.

Wilderness and Backcountry Use (1994)

Backcountry Camps: 19,681 users
Cross-Country Zones: 2,626 users
Alpine Zones: 7,386 users
Total Wilderness Visitor Use Nights: - 29,693

Camp Muir: 6,062 users
Camp Schurman: 1,716 users
Sunrise Camp: 1,655 users
Paradise: (winter) 3,099 users
Total Backcountry Visitor Use Nights: - 9,433

Total Visitor Use Nights: - 39,126

Conservation

The qualities we find in the wilderness, the bracing clean air, the "pure" rushing waters, the outrageously breathtaking scenery, are all beyond price. Being the only human being ever to view the perfection of a virgin flower bursting in bloom through the snow, anxious to add its beauty to the great panorama, is a gift from God. The conservation of these priceless resources can be summed up in five simple words: *enjoy it, don't destroy it!*

As individuals, we may not be able to save the Brazilian Rain Forest, but we can save our own little Carbon River Rain Forest. Conserving these things is not something to be done by the next person, or some environmental organization, or the government. It's up to each of us who uses and enjoys the wilderness.

Conservation is simply each person doing his own small bit to protect the natural resources with which he comes in contact. Like taking the flowers home as photographs, and leaving the "originals" for others to enjoy. Or simple things like carrying out even the smallest piece of litter, even if it's not "yours," and not shortcutting across switchbacks causing new erosion gullies to start.

It's simple, but that's what it's all about. Use it, but don't abuse it.

Rules of the Trail Written and Unwritten

Permits for backcountry travel are required year round.

If going into the backcountry, don't go alone unless you are very experienced. Hike with a partner or group, and keep the party together. Hiking alone is risky. *Leave a trail and trip schedule with a responsible person.* Don't just take off without telling anyone where you're going. Each year several searches must be launched for people who are missing. A search for an overdue hiker whose destination was known is far easier for than one for whom there isn't a clue as to where they could be.

Know your own limitations. Don't hike in any further than you can hike out. Take short rest stops often to enjoy the scenery and study the terrain. Look back often and remember the way home. Mentally mark every fork or trail junction. Be prepared for sudden and extreme weather changes. **Always carry the Ten Essentials**. The one time you don't take them, will be the time you'll need them.

If backpacking, carry a lightweight stove and fuel. Extinguish cigarettes and put campfires out. Start *no* campfires in the backcountry.

Early Naturalist John Muir stated that a great deal of enjoyment in outdoor recreation is derived from an ability to "read the trailside." Look down often, not only to keep from breaking your neck, but to savor the small wonders at your feet.

Leave plants, rocks and animals where you find them. All natural features, (including rocks, plants, trees, leaves, and animals) are protected by law, and must be left in place and unharmed.

Be a courteous hiker. Step aside for the descending hiker. Give a pack horse the right of way by stepping to the side of the trail, and standing quietly while it passes. Be careful on the descent. That's when most mishaps happen, and at Mount Rainier, "down" can be a *l-o-n-n-n-g* way down!

Stay on the trails or constructed pathways while enjoying the luxuriant fragile flowers. Trampling them not only kills the flowers stepped on, but future crops too. They can't propagate if they can't live long enough to mature and go to seed. If that isn't enough incentive to stay on the trails, then do it because it's the law. Off trail hikers can be fined.

Again, *ALWAYS* carry the ten essentials.

Trails

There are 240.238 miles of Park trails (not all maintained). There are enough different trails and types of trails, that there's something for everyone. There are short easy trails to pretty places, and long hard trails to pretty places. There's the 92.2 mile Wonderland Trail, which encircles the mountain. There are trails to fire lookouts, trails to glaciers, trails to rivers, trails to viewpoints, trails to flower fields, and trails to other trails.

If you want solitude, there's still all the privacy you want. Jim Whittaker said, "I can hike from Paradise and in ten minutes not see a soul. That can be on a busy weekend." (Jim Whittaker, *Cascade Voices*)

Hiker Centers

For information regarding current trail conditions, backcountry camping and permits, call (360) 569-2211, Ext. 275. Backcountry hiker permits may be gotten at any Hiker Information Center (which are located at Longmire, Paradise, Ohanapecosh, White River, and Carbon River).

Hiker Center Locations

Hiker Permits

1973 marked the end of an era. As of that year, anyone going into the backcountry for an overnight trip MUST have a backcountry permit. The number of permits is limited to control the number of people impacting the remote areas of the Park. Permits are required year-around, and are issued on a first-come, first-served basis.

In the whole of the backcountry, there are only thirty six trailside camps, with 131 individual campsites, and 20 group sites each with a maximum party limit of 12 people. (Most have far fewer). A few hikers may be given cross-country permits, requiring them to camp out of sight and sound of the trail. These permits are given only to those with proven back country experience. About 80-115 violation notices are issued each year for resource violations with camping in non-designated campsites making up the largest percentage followed by destruction of natural features, illegal fires and wildlife violations.

TRAILSIDE CAMPS

Individual camps have a capacity of 5 people or one immediate family. Group sites are limited to a capacity of twelve people. All sites are on a first- come, first-served basis on the first day of your climb.It's hard to get sites on Friday or Saturday, so come early or plan to start your trip mid-week if possible.

H = Horse sites available.

Camp	Individual Sites	Group Sites	Elevation Feet
Berkeley Park	4	-	5600
Camp Curtis	5	-	8200
Camp Muir	110*	-	10000
Camp Schurman	35*	-	9510
Carbon River	4	-	3100
Cataract Valley	7	1	4700
Deer Creek (H)	3	-	3125
Devil's Dream	7	1	5000
Dick Creek	2	-	4320
Dick's Lake	1	-	5680
Eagle's Roost	7	-	4700
Fire Creek	3	1	4600
Forest Lake	1	-	5600
Glacier Basin	5	1	5960
Golden Lakes	5	1	5000
Granite Creek	2	-	5732
Indian Bar	3	1	5100
Klapatche Park	4	-	5400
Lake Eleanor	3	1	5000
Lake George	5	1	4320
Lower Crystal Lake	2	-	5510
Maple Creek	4	1	2800
Mowich River (H)	8	1	2600
Mystic Camp	7	2	5620
Nickel Creek	3	1	3350
N. Puyallup River (H)	3	1	3600
Ollalie Creek	2	1	3800
Paradise River	3	1	3950
Pyramid Creek	2	-	3760
Shriner Creek	3	-	5800
Snow Lake	2	-	4600
S. Puyallup River	4	1	4000
Summerland	5	1	5900
Sunrise	8	2	6300
Tamanos Creek	4	1	5200
Three Lakes (H)	2	1	4650
Upper Crystal Lake	2	-	5800
Upper Palisades Lake	2	-	5840
Yellowstone Cliffs	2	-	5100

Backcountry Shelters

Thirteen log and stone shelters, dating from between the 1920's and 40's used to be spaced periodically around the Wonderland Trail. Most were three-sided affairs, although a few had the fourth side partially enclosed. Most of the shelters has a large "Lincoln-Log" look, but two had rock walls, and one had board walls. A 1924 map showed seven shelters around the mountain. Today most of the originals are gone and only four later-model shelters remain. The remaining Wonderland Trail shelters are at South Mowich (built in 1924), Summerland (C.C.C.-1934), Indian Bar (C.C.C.-1940) and Nickel Creek (C.C.C.-1933). A non-Wonderland shelter is at Lake George.

Ed Walsh photo

Although because of Mount Rainier's hostile weather conditions, shelter cabins* were considered vital to backcountry travelers, the 1973 Backcountry Management Plan marked a change of philosophy on the part of the Park Service, which substituted protection of the environment as the top priority, in place of man's creature comforts and safety. (*Early reports likened the need for back country shelters to monasteries in the Himalayas or on the Crusade routes of Europe).

Shelters were removed to take pressure off the meadows and to put camps in Forest Zones instead. The Mystic Lake Shelter was removed in 1973. The lovely old log shelters at Van Trump Park and Klapatche Park now exist only in photo albums and memories.

Hiker Preparedness

Ten Essentials

If going into the back country, even on a short hike, at least carry a knapsack or fanny pack with the following lifesaving essentials: fire starter (matches or lighter), candle, extra food, extra clothing, first aid kit, compass, map, flashlight, knife, and light tarp, tent or survival blanket. Properly used, these will give you warmth, shelter and energy to survive. The addition of these few simple items to your pack will provide everything you need to survive until found.

Equipment Rental

Summer mountaineering gear can be rented from RMI at Paradise, and Cross-country ski gear can be rented at Longmire in winter. The closest gear rental places outside the park are in Seattle and Issaquah.

Hiking Difficulty

Probably the biggest surprise among out-of-staters who come to hike at Mount Rainier, is the degree of difficulty arising from the amount of elevation gain and loss. Every place you look, it seems, is an incline.

There's a handy little rule of thumb for estimating the true difficulty of a hike. For each thousand feet of elevation gain, add a mile to the total distance of the trip. For each mile of elevation loss, add half a mile. Thus a six mile trip that includes 2000 feet of ascent and 2000 feet of descent, would be the equivalent of nine miles of level hiking.

Backcountry "Permanent" Bridges

There's no guarantee anything is permanent at Mount Rainier, let alone a bridge. But the steel suspension bridges over Tahoma Creek and the Carbon River come about as close to permanent as a man-made structure pitted against the forces of nature can be. There are dozens more bridges over the various river and stream crossings, however many disappear with every heavy rainfall.

Crossing Rivers

Several "rules of thumb" apply to crossing Mount Rainier's rivers. The waters are higher in summer than in winter, and higher in the afternoon when it's warm, than in the morning when it's cold. They change hourly depending on how much water is melting off the glacier up above. If you need to cross, look for a bridge or if fording is necessary, wait until the cool of the evening or early morning. Because of the rock flour suspended in the water, it's often impossible to tell how deep the water is. Listen to the boulders and cobbles pounding together underwater, and think of what one of those boulders could do if it slammed into your legs.

If you must ford, cross at a diagonal angle to the flow. Use a sturdy stick as a depth probe and for three-point suspension against the swift water. Plant the stick downstream so each step is supported, and unfasten pack waist straps so you won't be dragged underwater by a waterlogged pack if you fall in. You may lose your pack, but at least you (hopefully) won't lose your life.

Drinking Water in the Backcountry

If going into the backcountry or away from the visitor centers, plan on treating all drinking water.

Few people try drinking the brown or grey "rock water" from one of the glacial rivers, but willingly drink the cool clear water from a lake or stream.

It may look inviting, but where has it been and what's in it?

The first thing to think about is Giardia Lamblia, (Giardiasis), more commonly known as "beaver fever" or if acquired at Mount Rainier, it's called "Tahoma's Revenge." Beavers aren't the only culprits responsible for this nasty little micro-organism. It's found in the fecal material of people and both wild and domestic animals, and remember the 1,500 elk, 500 deer, 150 bear, 450 mountain goats and assorted smaller Mount Rainier critters don't wear diapers. If an animal or human with it defecates too near a lake or stream, the organisms find their way into the water and can spread over a wide area miles from the source. (This isn't just true of Mount Rainier. Most city water supplies come from backcountry sources, and all water is subject to animal input.)

Symptoms of the resulting major gastro-intestinal disorder include chronic diarrhea, severe abdominal cramps, vomiting, bloating, fatigue, and needless to say, loss of appetite. It requires medical treatment to get rid of it.

Also unseen in the streams is mouse scat, probably a dead animal or two upstream, and some of the tons of airborne pollution captured by the mountain. (Why do you think the pretty white glaciers get so dark by the end of summer?)

Purifying Mount Rainier Water

Only water from faucets around the Park is considered safe to drink. If going into the backcountry, treat water by boiling, filtering or chemical treatment. Water must be maintained at a rolling boil for twenty minutes to kill all possible micro-organisms. Chemical tablets such as Halazone work, and are easy to use, but some leave a chemical taste. There are a number of good filters on the market these days, all of which will give good tasting water.

First Aid

Emergency help and first aid are available at any ranger station. All full time rangers are trained in First Aid and CPR.

Typical First Aid emergencies at Mount Rainier are: sprains, strains, dislocations, cuts, abrasions, contusions, fractures, twisted ankles, head and neck injuries, respiratory problems, circulatory problems, and burns. Other emergencies are abdominal distress, back injuries, fainting and passing out, seizures, and several of a miscellaneous nature.

Snow and Sun - A Warning

People usually equate sunburns with beaches, but burns acquired on snow are equally nasty or worse! At high altitudes, even on a cold overcast day, it's possible to get a 3rd degree burn. Sunburn is caused by exposure to ultraviolet B rays, the type of radiation that actually burns the skin and poses a long-term cancer risk. Most sun screens block against UV-B rays.

A number of factors increase the amount of sun exposure, including summertime exposure, time exposed to the sun between 10 a.m. and 3 p.m., increased altitudes (5% increase per each 1,000 feet of elevation), snow reflection (reflection of 85% of ultraviolet rays) and water reflection. Of these factors, altitude may be one of the most significant, especially if one combines altitude and snow exposure. The degree of harmful effects is also related to the amount of previous tanning of the skin, as well as the skin type of the individual.

Sun screens are rated in regard to sun protection factor (SPF). The sun protection factor is a number which should be multiplied by the number of minutes of unprotected exposure in which the average person will get a burn (20 to 50 minutes is the normal range). A sun protection factor of 10 may thus allow approximately 200 to 400 minutes in the sun before burning occurs.

The bottom line is, if going on snow, even for a short time, put on sunscreen or sunblock, with at least a (UVA/UVE) SPF of 30, on highly sensitive areas such as the nose. Apply it 30 minutes before going out, and reapply every two hours or after water immersion. Protect your scalp from excessive sun with a hat or bandana, or by applying sun screen to the part in your hair and any bald areas. Remember too the places where you'll get reflection glare burns: the backs of your knees, the underside of your chin, under your nose and your lips. It is important to use a separate product on the lips, such as a lip balm with a minimum SPF of 15.

Exposure

More people die of exposure in the outdoors than any other cause. At Mount Rainier, people have been known to survive calamitous mishaps or falls, then die of hypothermia. It is a simple condition where the body's inner core temperature drops below 78° due to getting cold or wet, and continues to drop until death results. The "cure" is to restore warmth to the body and do it quickly. Exposure will soon overtake even a minor injury.

As one's temperature starts to drop, the brain and heart cease functioning normally. Thinking and judgment is impaired and general comprehension is dulled. Muscular coordination is affected. Visible symptoms are uncontrollable shaking, drowsiness, confusion, weakness, diminished mental capacity, irritability and problems breathing. Cover the victim's head. 50% of body heat loss is through the head, followed by the hands and feet.

Once hypothermia is recognized, stop at once and get the victim into dry clothing and into a sleeping bag, If necessary, have someone warm strip down and get in the bag with the victim. If conscious, administer warm liquids.

Don't think this only happens to climbers. Hypothermia can happen at any elevation. Three back to back incidents in 1977 proved that. The first was a 17-year old boy who took off without telling anyone, and went snowshoeing along the Nisqually River near Longmire. When he was found six hours later, he had taken off his snowshoes, and was struggling in waist-deep snow. He was well into hypothermia.

A month later, two young men attempted to ski from Paradise to Longmire. When a search finally got underway, they were found soaked to the skin, crouching in a hole in the snow near the Paradise River five miles from Longmire. Both were in advanced stages of hypothermia and would not have survived the night. Two days later, a teenage girl clad in a cotton sweatshirt, jeans and tennis shoes, wandered away from her companions at Paradise. She was accidentally found near Panorama Point by four snowshoers returning from an outing. She lapsed into unconsciousness before rewarming treatment could be started, but miraculously survived.

Remember, cotton kills. *In winter at the mountain, wear wool and/or thermal garments.*

Human Waste in Backcountry Areas

The years when one ducked behind a tree to answer "nature's call" are gone. Human waste in alpine areas, where decomposition is slow, poses a tremendous problem. The corridor to the summit is not the pristine sight one envisions, especially around the traditional pit stop locations. The icy temperatures and ultra-violet radiation severely limit decomposition.

For the past several years, the park has worked with scientists at Oregon State University to identify human waste problems in backcountry areas. They also gathered together a committee of technical experts (hydrologist, soil chemist, geologist, plant ecologist, algologist, and stream ecologist) to provide a peer review of backcountry human waste issues and management. The result is that a number of pit toilets have been relocated away from lakes or streams, (Wilderness standards require a minimum distance of 200 ft. from surface waters.) Different types of toilet (solar, chemical, composting, etc) have been tested and used with varying degrees of success.

The seven to nine tons of human waste which accumulate at the high climbing camps must be helicoptered out at the end of summer. Various other means (from human 'mules' to llamas) have been tried to remove it. The men could begrudgingly be talked into hauling it out. The llamas just put on the brakes and declined the opportunity to perform this service to mankind, thank you.

Ideally, one would carry out one's own waste. The next best solution, for hikers, at least, is to find a secluded spot at least 300 feet from any water source, dig a "cathole" at least 7" deep (within the biological decomposition layer) then cover the hole with soil and duff.

Firearms

Firearms are not allowed in the backcountry. All guns must be unloaded, broken down, and packed away out of sight. Hunting is prohibited.

Accidents

The beauty of the mountain frequently disguises the danger, and lulls people into a false sense of security about the place. The danger comes in many forms: avalanches, rockfall, drowning, falling off cliffs or into crevasses, freezing, dying of exposure, and a myriad of other ways. The beautiful glaciers hold a grisly secret. They are the icy tombs of many people, some from climbing accidents and some from aircraft accidents. It may be many years before they finally yield whatever remains that make it to the melting edge.

Another major cause of many backcountry accidents is poor judgment. People strike off into the wilderness completely unprepared for the weather, terrain and conditions. In a showdown between man and nature, nature often wins. There's no 911 service in the back country, and rescues are very expensive undertakings. The day has finally come when the Park Service has instituted a $15 user fee to cover the cost of rescues, a sort of "Pay to Play" fee.

Rescues

When helicopters are needed for rescues at the mountain, they usually come in from MAST (Military Assistance to Safety & Traffic) at Fort Lewis. Don't plan on calling for one if you just get tired of hiking. They're used only for "life-threatened" accident victims. The flight is free, the hospital is not. And the flight may not be free much longer.

According to overall (national) Park Service statistics, "by percentage, hikers, boaters and swimmers are the biggest users of the Park Service's rescue fund. Climbers come in fourth nationally, but first at Mount Rainier. NPS representatives emphasized that the intent is not to charge individuals for the cost of their rescue, but to spread the cost among all users.

The bottom line is be prepared to rescue yourself. Do not count on a great whirling machine to drop out of the sky and save you.

Rescuers

The unsung, and usually unheralded heros in mountaineering, are not the guys getting their pictures taken on the summit, but the rescue volunteers and rangers who have to risk their own necks to go in under the icefalls, the crevasses, and other dangerous places where the bodies land, to bring out the living and dead who didn't make it.

Rock Safety

Rocks and trails can be icy, even in summer. Wet logs and mosses can be as slippery as ice too.

Wear adequate footwear on trails. Thongs are not adequate. A jagged rock can cause a nasty gash on an unprotected foot. A twisted or broken ankle miles from the trailhead is guaranteed to be a major problem.

Climbing routes and hiking trails are frequently more difficult than they appear on maps. Before attempting the unknown, prepare yourself with proper training and equipment. Rock climbing and scrambling continue to be among the leading causes of injury and death at the mountain.

Rocks are the cause of other types of accidents too. People are so busy looking at the scenery, they trip over them. Rocks also fall from cliffs and hillsides, and several deaths have come from falling rock. Don't throw them, or allow children to throw them. They could hit someone, or start a rockslide. If you do kick rocks loose, even when hiking, yell *"ROCK!"*

Historic Trails

The very first trails in the park were aboriginal trails. The trails to Yakima Park, and the Cowlitz Divide Trail were used by the Indians for centuries.

In the northwest corner of what is now the park, the first trail was the Grindstone Trail (1881-83) originally called the Bailey Willis Trail. It went up from Wilkeson, crossed the Carbon River, then went up Voight's Creek drainage to the place called Grindstone Camp. The Forest Palace was where the North and South Mowich Rivers joined outside the Park. There the trail forked. One branch went toward Ashford and National, the second branch went to Mowich Lake and Spray Park, and a third to the South Mowich Glacier. Remnants of this trail can be found in only a couple small places now.

The Grindstone Trail was primarily designed to aid in the survey of mineral resources of the region, principally coal. In 1896 Willis was placed in charge of a USGS survey party which made the extensive geological investigation.

The trail from Ashford to Paradise was referred to as "the Yellow Jacket Trail" and the section between Longmire and Paradise was called "the Pony Trail."

Old Camps

Palace Camp, also known as Barktown, was a large cabin and several smaller buildings near the North Fork of the Puyallup River. It was built by Bailey Willis as the headquarters for the construction of the Bailey Willis/ Grindstone) Trail. It got the nickname of Barktown because the cabins were made of large slabs of bark by the trail laborers. The trail came into being in the 1890's after the Tahoma Mining District was organized.

Camp of the Clouds. (5,947') In August, 1886, a party of Olympians were camping at Paradise on the east side of Alta Vista waiting out a summer storm, and when it finally cleared, the mountain "came out" inspiring the group to call their campsite, "Camp of the Clouds." The name caught the fancy of all who heard it, and a man named Major Skinner developed a commercial tent camp of the same name on the east shoulder of Alta Vista. He abandoned the venture a few years later when gold was discovered in the Yukon. The following year it was purchased by John Reese of Ashford who then ran it for the next twenty-some years. This is not to be confused with Cloud Camp, the original name for Camp Muir.

Reese's Camp. (5,800') In 1897 John Reese set up a second camp ("High View") on Theosophy Ridge, just below Alta Vista. After taking over Camp of the Clouds, he consolidated the two camps, and moved the single camp (which he called 'Reese's Camp') to Theosophy Ridge. Until 1916 when Paradise Inn opened, Reese's Camp was the only public accommodations at Paradise. This popular camp had 25 housing tents, a dining room tent, and another which was a big social or "sitting room." It was distinguished by a large stove and lines of drying socks. This was the camp used by the climbers and the guide service. This camp operated until 1915.

Hall's Camp. [Wigwam Camp] (5,300') a tent and log cabin camp operated by George B. Hall in Indian Henrys Hunting Ground. A 1912 Government bulletin said Hall charged $.75 for a bed, $.75 for dinner or a weekly rate of $15.00. Packing freight from Longmire to Indian Henrys was $.02 per pound.

The First Round-the-Mountain Hike

1911 Professor J. B. Flett of Tacoma traveled completely around the Mountain. He gave many talks about his adventure, and illustrated them with "lantern slides." Audiences were spellbound as they saw for the first time, the hidden wonders of the backcountry of Mount Rainier. He succeeded in whetting their appetites to go see it for themselves.

1915 Mountaineer Outing Camps

Scouting expeditions around the mountain were made in 1911, 1912 and 1913 to check out the feasibility of a large party of Seattle Mountaineers encircling the mountain as their annual "outing." Even though the trail around the mountain was not complete, the scout's recommendations were affirmative, and in 1915, over 100 men and women embarked on "the trip of a lifetime." They came with hobnailed boots and fancy hats, plump dunnage bags and high spirits. They spent three weeks traveling clockwise, and took time out to climb the mountain, and finish hewing out the final section of trail over Panhandle Gap as they went. Their route was frequently the shortest distance between two points, whereas the heavily laden pack train with their food, tents, clothing and gear took the lower trail route and frequently was late in catching up with them.

This historic club outing established several "firsts". It was the first 'group' encirclement of the mountain which had previously only been done by a handful of reconnaissance scouts, men doing geological exploration, and trail builders. It included the first mass assault on climbing the mountain. The name "The Wonderland Trail" was first used after their trip around the mountain. The "camps" were the first organized encampments in the backcountry. They took the first pack train around the mountain. Their glowing reports of the trip put the Wonderland Trail and the glorious Mount Rainier backcountry on the map!

Camp One (5,400') Paradise Valley
Camp Two (7,000') Van Trump Park "near a roaring creek"
Camp Three (5,400') Indian Henrys Hunting Ground at Mirror Lake
Camp Four (3,800') St Andrews Park (two nights)
Camp Five (5,300') Elbow Lake in Sunset Park
Camp Six (4,929') Mowich Lake (then called Crater Lake)
Camp Seven (5,800') upper Spray Park below Hessong Rock
Camp Eight (5,700') Mystic Lake (two nights)
Camp Nine (5,900') Glacier Basin (base camp while climbing)
Camp Ten (5,900') Camp Curtis (Summerland) (two nights)
Camp Eleven (5,100') "Ohanapecosh Park" (Indian Bar) (two nights)
Camp Twelve (3,300') Nickel Creek "in the deep forest"
Camp Thirteen (6,100') Mazama Ridge near Sluisken Falls
Camp Fourteen (2,150') Tahoma Creek "in the Robin Hood forest" beyond Longmire

The record notes: "Each camp can be found today by a triangular aluminum plate fastened to the trunk of a tree. The last read, "The Mountaineers' Camp, No. 14, August 22, 1915."

Trails Within The Park
Out of Longmire

Eagle Peak: from Longmire to the summit of Eagle Peak via the Nisqually River suspension bridge. 3.5 miles

Rampart Ridge-Van Trump: from Longmire to Van Trump Park via Rampart Ridge. 5 miles, 1,900' elevation gain. Very steep terrain.

Carter Falls Walk: Enjoy the lowland forest along the Paradise River. 2.2 miles along Wonderland Trail to Falls.

Indian Henrys: from Kautz Creek bridge to Indian Henrys via the divide between Tahoma and Kautz creeks. 7 miles.

Tahoma Creek Access Trail: West Side Road to Wonderland Trail. 2.1 miles.
South Fork Trail: West Side Road to Wonderland Trail paralleling the South Puyallup River. 1.5 miles

St Andrews Creek Trail: West Side Road to Klapatche Park. 2.5 miles

Skate Creek: from Longmire to Packwood Trail. 1.5 miles

Van Trump Creek: from Christine Falls to Van Trump Park via Van Trump Creek and Comet Falls. 2 miles.

Pinnacle Peak: from Reflection Lakes to Pinnacle Peak. 1 mile.

Panorama Point: 3 hours, 2.5 miles, 1,050' elevation gain.

Snow Lake Trail: 3 hours, 2.5 miles, 700' elevation gain.

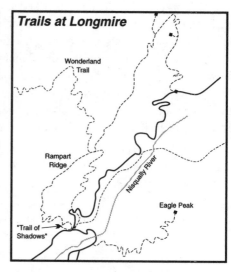

Trails at Longmire

Longmire to Paradise: travel via Paradise River and Narada Falls. 6 miles.

Out of Ipsut Creek

Northern Loop Trail: Ipsut Creek to Frozen Lake out of Sunrise. 19 miles

Out of Ohanapecosh

Silver Falls Walk: Walk through the lovely lowland forest along the Ohanapecosh River. 3 miles round trip.

Trails out of the Sunrise Area

Emmons Vista: A short easy trail with good views of the mountain and the Emmons Glacier. 0.5 mile - 30 minutes.

Sourdough Ridge Nature Trail: A self-guiding loop with great views and lots of wildflowers. 1.5 miles - 45 minutes.

Fryingpan: from the White River Road paralleling Frying Pan Creek to Summerland. 5 mile

Pet Exercise Loop: The ONLY trail on which pets are allowed. 1.5 miles

Skyscraper Peak: off the Wonderland Trail. 6 miles round trip.

Sunrise Rim Trail: An easy 3 mile loop which takes about an hour and a half.

Sunrise Camp: A walk-in backcountry camp near Shadow Lake. Permit required. 3 miles round trip.

Sunrise-Frozen Lake-Shadow Lake: Wonderful views & flower display. 5 miles round trip.

Silver Forest: White River Valley views. 2 miles.

Sourdough Ridge-Dege Peak: See Cowlitz Chimneys and Mt. Adams. 4 miles.

Mt. Fremont: Visit the lookout tower and see Grand Park. 4 hours, 1,200' gain.

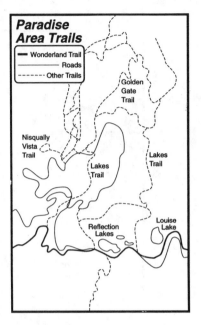

Burroughs Mountain: Knockout glacier views. First Burroughs: 5 miles - 3 hours. Second Burroughs: 7 miles - 5 hours. 1,000 foot elevation gain.

Berkeley Park: Great wildflower displays. 5 miles round trip. - 3 hours.

Grand Park: An incredibly beautiful flat park. 13 miles round trip.

Sunrise-White River Campground: Switchbacks all the way down and back up. 6 miles round trip. 2,000' elevation gain/loss.

Emmons Moraine Trail: Visit the moraine near the terminus of the Emmons Glacier. 3 miles.

Glacier Basin: See the remnants of the old mining camp. Trail begins at White River Campground. 6.5 miles round trip.

Palisades Lakes: Trail begins at Sunrise Point. 7 miles round trip - 4 hours.

Trails out of Paradise

Alta Vista Loop Trail: out of Paradise. 1.5 miles. Pass through the flower fields to a knoll overlooking Paradise.

Nisqually Vista Walk. An excellent view of the Nisqually Glacier. 1.5 miles.

The Wonderland Trail

If you think the mountain is pretty from the tourist areas, you should see it up close! The 92.2 mile Wonderland Trail hugs the mountain, crossing each new river just born from under a glacier, up the ridge beside it to the park at the top, then down the other side. It repeats this process thirteen times around the mountain to accumulate a total elevation gain of 22,786 feet in doing the whole trail. That's enough climbing to actually go to the summit 2-1/2 times!

Hundreds of people may be admiring the flower fields of Paradise, but in the backcountry you can have acres of your own private flower meadows. From the highest point of 6,750' (Panhandle Gap) to the lowest at 2,300' (Ipsut Creek), each turn of the trail brings a new wonder and discovery. The history, Indian lore, geology, mining sites, and natural sciences all come alive under your feet.

Wonderland Trail

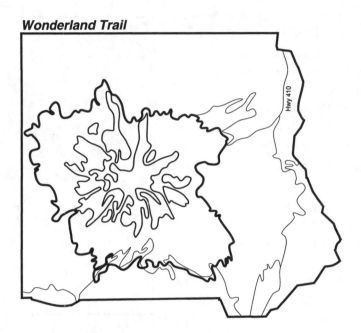

Whether done piecemeal or all at once, doing the Wonderland Trail is a once in a lifetime experience. Locals can plan short segment trips based on 5-day forecasts so hiking can be timed to coincide with good weather. Direction (going clockwise or counter-clockwise) can dictate a minimum amount of climbing or descending (whichever your legs like best.) The author of this book has also written a detailed guide entitled *"Discovering the Wonders of the Wonderland Trail encircling Mount Rainier".* This book is highly recommended to all who might be interested in doing the trail some day.

The book is designed to help do the trail with a maximum of ease and safety, as well as pointing out the features and wonders along the trail as the hiker passes each. (In other words, it isn't just "pretty", the reader will know what the pretty is, and how it got there.) Book ordering information is in the catalog at the back of this book.

The first use of the term "Wonderland Trail" appears to have been in 1920 by Superintendent Roger Toll.

The Wonderland Speed Record

By most people's standards, the demanding Wonderland Trail requires 10-14 days to do comfortably. But in 1984, Ken Evans, who had previous set a climbing speed record, did the incredible feat of doing the entire Wonderland

Trail in just 29 hours and 10 minutes. He even took time out to fall in the Mowich River in the middle of the night while crossing it in the dark.

Trail Infrastructure

For those who like minutia, Mount Rainier's front and backcountry trails contain:

- 577 bridges
- 693 culverts
- 7085 feet of drainage
- 4411 ft. of boardwalk
- 495 trail signs

Trails Adjacent To The Park

Mount Tahoma Trail System

The Mount Tahoma Scenic Trails Association (MTTA) and the Department of Natural Resources are promoting year-round use of this new 103.5 mile trail network on the west side of Mount Rainier. Skiers, mountain bikers and hikers can make use of the three huts and a yurt along the trail. High Hut, Snow Bowl and Copper Creek are accessible from the Ashford side, and require Sno-Park permits for parking.

The "base camp" for the Mount Tahoma Trail System just outside the Park, is at Lou Whittaker's Bunkhouse in Ashford. The office is staffed only on ski-season weekends from 9 am to 4 pm. Then volunteers fill information requests, make hut reservations and handle membership applications. Up-to-date trail conditions are always available by phone. Their number (360) 569-2451 is answered only during weekend operating hours. A recording gives conditions at other times. Their mailing address is P.O. Box 206, Ashford, WA 98304. The Bunkhouse is located at 36205 Highway 706 in Ashford. Call for a flyer giving particulars on MTTA's excellent trails and overnight huts on the spectacular west side of Mount Rainier.

Champion Tree Farm Trails

The Colonnade Yurt, just outside Mount Rainier National Park (just west of Sunset Park on the Mount Tahoma Trail system is reached through Champion Tree Farm, and requires a separate visitor entry permit. To ski on Champion land you must join MTTA. Call 800-782-1493 for the current cost of the permit, gate hours and closures.

Visitor permits may be purchased at the following retail outlets:

- Kapowsin Grocery; 39833 Orting/Kapowsin Highway, Graham, 98338
- Orting Hardware; 212 Washington Ave., Orting, 98360
- Handi Stop Grocery; 30323 Meridian E., Graham, 98338
- Ohop Valley Grocery; 33916 Mountain Highway, Eatonville 98328
- Al's Sporting Goods; West Highway 410; Buckley 98321

Pacific Crest Trail

The Pacific Crest Trail used to be called the High Crest Trail, and legend has it that it was built by the Indians centuries ago. It was considered neutral ground, and the standing (Indian) rule was that you had to pass an enemy in peace when on the trail.

Today the Pacific Crest National Scenic Trail stretches from Manning Park in Northern British Columbia to the US/Mexican border in California. 450 miles of it pass through Washington state. Of that, four miles touches Mount Rainier park boundary. The section east of the park runs between White Pass (Highway 12) and Chinook Pass (Highway 410), a leg of about 26 miles.

The entire 2,500 mile Pacific Crest Trail was established as one of three national scenic trails by congressional action on October 2, 1968. The other trails so designated are the Appalachian Trail, and the Continental Divide Trail.

Weyerhaeuser Trails

Weyerhaeuser has begun charging a fee for motorized vehicles using its White River Tree farms. Any vehicle entering the farms is required to have a permit in the windshield. Permits cost $50 per year and are available at area sporting goods stores, or call 1-800-433-3911. Access on foot will continue at no cost.

Get permits for the White River Tree Farm (Grass Mountain Gate) at:

- Black Diamond: Diamond Sports Shop; (206) 886-2027
- Buckley: Al's Sporting Goods; (360) 829-0174
- Enumclaw: Tuttle's Gun Shop; (360) 825-6100
- Enumclaw: Rainier Sportsman (206) 825-6121
- Issaquah: Buffalo Bills (206) Sporting Goods 392-0228

The fee is used to combat vandalism, garbage dumping, theft, safety hazards to employees and environmental degradation. The farm is open daily from one hour before sunrise to one hour after sunset. Security contractors patrol parking areas to check for permits.

Trail System Development

1884   First trail constructed to Longmire Springs by the Longmires.

1895   The first trail to Paradise valley was constructed by the Longmires.

1904   Three Rangers were hired to patrol the back country.

1906   Cowlitz Indians were still making occasional hunting expeditions into the Cowlitz Divide, Indian Bar, Ohanapecosh and Summerland.

1915   Mountaineers finished the Wonderland trail section over Panhandle Gap

1914   A telephone line was strung to distant ranger stations at a cost of $60 per mile. The telephone line paralleled existing trails.

1915   The Cowlitz Divide Trail is the old Indian Trail. It is marked by a series of 4-chop marks high in the trees.

1916   Cedar shake cabins were built along the East Side Trail for use as telephone stations. The telephone wire circuit was completed from Narada Falls to the White River, via Stevens Canyon and the East Side Trail.

1917   The Wonderland Trail was considered to be a 7-day trip. Hikers were told to expect to average 20-miles per day. In actuality, the trail today is 92.2 miles, and was probably close to that then. Mountaineers made the trip in 3 weeks time. Additional trail shelters were proposed 10-15 miles apart.

1921   Conventional wisdom now dictated that doing the Wonderland Trail by horseback required 12 days. Seventy signs were put on trails. A proposal was made that hotels should be built at intervals around the trail so hikers wouldn't have to carry food.

1923   The only actual shelters are miner's cabins at Berkeley Park, one near Mystic and one at Nickel Creek.

1924   The Northern Loop Trail was constructed primarily by prospectors, then improved by Rangers. The Huckleberry Creek Trail was much used by prospectors and hunters, and unfortunately in recent years, by poachers.

1927   The round trip from Sunrise to Mystic Lake and back was considered a day hike. The only trips considered overnighters were Sunrise to Indian Bar and Lake James.

1929   A Patrol Cabin was built at Lake James.

1930   The Mt. Fremont and Tolmie Peak Lookouts were built. 1,000 boundary signs were ordered.

1931   A study showed that for 3 months, an average of 12 people per day used the Frying Pan Trail to Summerland.

1932   The Frying Pan to Cowlitz Divide section of the Wonderland Trail was voted the most popular trail section. This would probably still be true today.

The Windy Knoll Fire Lookout was built this same year.

1933   Nine more shelters were built by the C.C.C. at "strategic points" around the Mountain, including those at Summerland, Berkeley Park and Windy Gap.

1937   Fire at Summerland burned 140 sq. acres.

1938   The roof of the Indian Bar Shelter cabin caved in from snow.

1940   A new stone shelter (the present one) replaced the log cabin at Indian Bar.

1941   Technology came to the Mountain. Radios were used by Lookouts as backups for the unreliable telephones.

1973   Permit system   went into effect for overnight backcountry travelers.

Roads

Pemco, Webster and Stevens Collection, Museum of History and Industry

Early Roads

The early roads were little more than dirt trails, seas of mud that went around and between the big trees. Soon slab wood or poles were laid side by side over the impassable sections, and these were called puncheon or corduroy roads. The many hills in the area and the never-ending mud made travel hard on horses as well as humans. Riders frequently had to get off the poor beasts or out of their wagons and walk up the hills to spare the horses.

In 1903 Congress appropriated $10,000 for a survey to determined the most practicable route for a wagon road into the park. The Secretary of War directed the U.S. Army Corps of Engineers to carry out the survey and ensuing road construction. The Corps assigned a remarkable civilian engineer, Eugene Ricksecker, as the overseer of the work crews. Oscar A. Piper carried out the survey. With Longmire as the zero point, Piper surveyed both east toward Paradise, and west to the Nisqually Entrance. In the understatement of the decade, he concluded the latter road followed the old pack trail, and was very rough and never dry.

In 1904 Congress appropriated $30,000 to begin construction, and Ricksecker was raring to get building. The first thing he did was revise the location of the road as it passed through Longmire. He said of his revision, " It avoids the big bend on the flat near the Springs, passes close by the springs and present hotel, affords a fine view of the Springs from the clearing at the new bend, is some 400 feet shorter, and is considered preferable to the old route, it crosses a portion of the Longmire Claim."

Museum of History and Industry photo

Washington State Historical Society photo

Captain H.M. Chittenden, the famed road builder of Yellowstone National Park, was horrified when he visited Mount Rainier. He wrote that the existing road below Longmire, "was, without exception, the worst I have ever traveled over. It required four and one-half hours with a single-seated light rig and a good team to cover a distance of ten miles." He urged that the Nisqually-Longmire section of road be given the highest priority. Standards for the road were that the roadbed was to be 18 feet wide with 3 feet on each side for ditches, and a total width clearing of 30 feet. The first 10-1/2 mile section was projected to cost $65,000 to complete, with the Longmire to Camp of the Clouds segment to cost about $250,000.

In 1907, automobiles were allowed to enter the park and drive as far as Longmire Springs. During the year, 60 automobiles entered the park, as compared to 950 vehicles of other types (horses and wagons).

The original road from Longmire to Paradise crossed the Nisqually River at approximately the same location where the bridge is now. Eugene Ricksecker, the young genius and idealistic United States assistant engineer who designed the road, had as his goal to build roads to "God's grand places" in the Park, while preserving the surroundings.

Some hoped the road could be open in time for the Alaska-Yukon Pacific Exposition which was to be held in Seattle in 1909, but in reality it didn't open to the general public until 1915. Optimists convinced of Ricksecker's road-building ability, actually proposed extending the road to Camp Muir! An Interior Department inspector visiting the park in 1911 investigated the possibility of a road to Indian Henrys Hunting Ground.

The as-the crow-flies distance from Longmire to Paradise is twelve miles, but the final (current) road covers a distance of twenty miles, with no grade exceeding four per cent. The elevation gained is 3,800 feet. Early motorists marveled that with the elimination of the one-way road control system, the time from Puget Sound cities to Paradise Valley was reduced by fully one hour.

On the north side, before there was a road to the Park from the outside, a portion of road was constructed inside the Park alongside the Carbon River. It was done by miners who wanted to show improvement on their claims.

Getting to the Park - Yesteryear

In 1904, it was like an answer to prayer when the Tacoma and Eastern Railroad finally completed a line to Ashford, just six miles short of the park boundary. Originally the line was to be a logging railroad, but immediately the pressure was on to begin carrying passengers from Tacoma and Seattle. From Ashford, "four-horse tally-ho's" took the adventurers the remainder of the way to Longmire. There was also a stage coach depot behind and slightly west of the present Copper Creek restaurant. There were wagon tracks around the building and old stage coach receipts were in a glass case for many years, according to Judy Wootan, long-time owner of Copper Creek.

You had to come all the way to Elbe to cross the River to get to Morton and Mineral. After they built Alder Dam, all that changed.

Outside the park, across the Mountain Highway from Alpine Gallery was a little cabin that was the first restaurant for people hiking in to the park. During the early days, the entrance fee to the park was $5.00 per auto, a hefty sum for the time. The fee dropped as low as $1.00 and has now climbed back to $5.00.

C. Frank Brockman, early Park Naturalist, said the sign prior to Longmire read "Slow-Village" His comment: "Indeed it was a slow village in 1928."

On the north side, the first road (1924) was the Carbon River road which went all the way up to the glacier. The Mowich Lake Road was designed and surveyed by M. Ricksecker. The road was dedicated in 1933. There was an entrance station, a large rustic log structure, and a monument to Dr. Tolme dedicated in 1933, 100 years after he came to the area.

Railroads and the Mountain

Miners were among the first white people to explore every nook and cranny of the Mount Rainier area. Discovery of coal in the 1860's near Wilkeson, brought hundreds of prospectors into the Carbon River Valley. Bailey Willis explored the Valley primarily to map coal deposits. The added discovery of glaciers was exciting, because they were thought to exist only in Europe. By 1876 The Northern Pacific Railroad laid the track to Wilkeson to ship coal to Seattle. It turned out coal became the second most important product behind timber. Coal mining operations began in 1879. The railroad billed Wilkeson as "but 23 miles from the summit."

Wilkeson was named for Sam Wilkeson, Secretary of the Board of the Northern Pacific Railroad. To reward the railroads for opening up the west, the government gave them land, in fact every other section of land along the right of way. This was done through the 1872 Post and Road Act, which was done as an effort to get people to go west after the Civil War. (To this day, the railroad still owns a great deal of land around the Park.) Northern Pacific Railroad is now Burlington Northern. Their sub-enterprises are Glacier Real Estate, and Plum Creek Timber Company.

The advent of the railroads brought about another large industry in the Northwest - tie mills. The ever advancing railroads required an enormous quantity of railroad ties. Gandy dancers or Gandy hoppers were men who maintained the railroad tracks.

In 1886, the fare from Tacoma to Wilkeson, a distance of 30 miles, was $2.40. There was another line from Kapowsin, called the "Electron Speeder" which went to "the upper end of the long flume" (wherever that was). From the end of that line, one would hike to the old Conrad cabin, then follow the Puyallup River to the junction of the Mowich on the north side.

The Mountain as Railroad Tourist Destination

On the south side of the mountain, the Tacoma and Eastern line from Tacoma to Ashford, made short and pleasant work of the trip to the mountain. In 1910, the Chicago, Milwaukee and Puget Sound Railroad went all out to create a national advertising program to exploit (their word) the beauty of the mountain. A party of several railroad officials spent several days at the mountain exploring points of interest, drinking in the scenic wonders and dining on venison.

Particular note was made of their trip back to Ashford to catch the Tacoma Eastern back to town. William Estes, the mountain ranger who was in charge of the upper stretches of the reserve, drove the party down in a coach to which was hitched "a cayuse, and a spirited nag." The group was impressed with the driving skills of the ranger who could turn the rig within four feet anywhere on the mountain, and who managed to get them to Ashford in time to catch the train.

It didn't take long for their promotional efforts to pay off, and soon the wonders of Mount Rainier were known from coast to coast, and visitors began coming to the mountain from all over the country.

A.A.A. - The Earliest Road Proponents

Even before the roads were fit for automobiles, both the Tacoma and Seattle Automobile Clubs were enthusiastic cheerleaders in promoting "machine" travel to the mountain, and calling for improving the roads. Much of the credit for the continual upgrading of the roads belongs to these organizations, because without the pressure they kept on all concerned, the much needed improvements would have been much longer in coming.

The clubs made good use of the existing roads, and organized large auto excursions to the park. They tirelessly taxied any and every politician who could help them in their crusade for better roads, so they could see for themselves the need for funds. Among their passengers in 1910 was Secretary of the Interior R. A. Ballinger who pledged his full support after the trip.

In addition to the 'political pressure' for more road funds, the Tacoma club also commissioned moving pictures of Tacoma automobiles on the picturesque road to the mountain. The films were sent all over the country, and shown in 'moving picture houses' to be seen by enthralled audiences, who marveled at both the beautiful scenery and convenience of getting about in the wild west.

The automobile clubs also were the ones who in 1908 measured the roads to the park and made road signs and mileage signs. They proclaimed it was fifty-six and one-tenth miles from the Tacoma Union Station to the Nisqually gateway. They also devised a visual system of putting a white post every mile, a red one every five miles, and a blue one every 10 miles.

Lady Drivers

In 1917, when women won the right to vote, they also wanted the right to drive. The first lady who tried to exercise this right at the mountain was Mrs. Edward D. Palmer, wife of a Seattle Attorney, who was refused permission to drive to Paradise because "the drive was too dangerous for a female driver." The Park powers-that-be based their decision on the fact that a woman had almost driven her car off a cliff on an earlier occasion. The Park administrators wrote that "women looking over steep areas suffer dizziness." "And" they added, "if we let one woman drive, we must let them all." The superintendent added that he had driven the road himself, and the rule must remain in effect.

Needless to say, that was not the end of the story. Public pressure, particularly from the feminine quarter, was intense. The avalanche of letters nearly equaled the sixteen feet of snow which fell at Longmire that winter. By

March, the administration buckled, and after announcing that the roads were now improved, women were allowed to drive to Paradise.

1911 MRNP Regulations

Saddle horses, teams or pack trains have the right of way. Autos and motorcycles will take positions on the outer edge of the roadway, regardless of the direction in which they are going, taking care that sufficient room is left on the inside for horses to pass. Horses have the right of way, and automobiles and motorcycles will be backed or otherwise handled to enable horses to pass with safety. Speed will be limited to 6 miles per hour when approaching teams. In no event shall it exceed 15 MPH. Signal with horn at every bend. No hitchhiking in the Park.

From Tacoma to The Mountain

The old Mountain Highway begins at the foot of Pacific Avenue in Tacoma, and ends in Paradise on Mount Rainier. On the way, it passes through Parkland, skirts the Fort Lewis Military Reservation, then continues on through Spanaway, Elk Plain, LaGrande, Elbe, Ashford and Longmire. On the Tacoma end, it begins as State Route Seven, and at Elbe it becomes State Route 705.

'Round the Mountain' Road

Once those living within sight of the Mountain discovered it was even more beautiful close-up, there was no stopping the hoards of visitors who wanted to come revel in the Mountain's pleasures first hand. Just as with today's Washingtonians, it was *their* Mountain, and they couldn't get enough of her! Each glorious glimpse just made the viewer want to see more and more. Soon plans were afoot for "The Wonder Road", a highway to completely encircle the Mountain.

In 1907 Major Hiram Chittenden was the first person to conceive of an actual road around the lower slopes of the mountain. He recommended first building a horse trail which could later be enlarged into a wagon road. The endeavor was to be a 102 mile road, intended to encircle the Mountain within park boundaries. When completed, it was projected to cost $11 million. Since roads of sorts already existed or were proposed for all sides of the Mountain except on the west, that side received top priority.

In 1913, surveys for the road were begun and by 1920, the plans for the road were completed. In 1924 Congress, via the National Park Highway Law, authorized funding to build the road northward from the Nisqually Road to as far as the South Puyallup River plus fifteen miles of road southward from the Carbon River road to the North Mowich River. By 1935 the road was punched northward from the Longmire Road just inside the Nisqually entrance, to as far north as the North Puyallup River. Two handsome stone-faced arch bridges were built, one on the South Puyallup River, the other on St. Andrews Creek.

Even though the old timers were an ingenious bunch when it came to road building, they finally had to conclude it was not feasible to build a road up Ipsut Creek to Ipsut Pass. It was just too steep. The only alternative was to build a road from the west park boundary to Mowich Lake.

Also in 1935, they ran into even more insurmountable problems: lack of funds, an upcoming war, and politics. The incredibly difficult terrain was suddenly the least of their problems. Then some people began to question the whole plan and by then the war brought construction of the road to a halt, never to be restarted.

In fact, so completely was work shut down, that the road to Mowich Lake never opened to the public until 1955.

The Roads Within the Park Today

The primary road within the park loops only the south and east sides. There are a total of 147.288 miles of road, plus the 12.076 miles of the West Side Road which for the time being is closed. Of this figure, 116 miles are paved, the rest are dirt or gravel. Along these roads are 31 bridges, 683 drainage structures and 67 box culverts.

The Westside Road Today

Since 1993, only the first three miles of the road are open to vehicle traffic. A 1988 mudflow wiped out three-quarters of a mile of road, and a 1989 flood and several smaller subsequent flows re-damaged it. Temporary repairs have not resolved the problem, and plans now rest with Superintendent Briggle's promise to reopen the road only after it is resolved that the annual mudflows are over.

The road beyond the Dry Creek problem area is still used by the Park Service vehicles, but is open only to foot and bicycle travel by the public. Hopefully until it is reopened to the public for vehicular traffic, a shuttle service will transport hikers to the various West Side Road access trails.

Those wanting to drive in and see the spectacular beauty of the west side will have to do so on Forest Service and Champion property logging roads. You can't get very close to the Park boundary, but you can get some great views. Champion does charge a fee, and you will be sharing the road with logging trucks, so drive accordingly.

Highway Bridges in The Park

1909   The Nisqually Glacier Bridge - Elevation 4,000 ft. America's first bridge by a glacier. In the late 50's, the massive concrete Nisqually Bridge, a lower version of the present bridge, fell victim to a flood, and was swept in chunks ten miles down-river.

1924   Nisqually River Suspension Bridge #1

1926   Paradise River 2nd Crossing Bridge

1926   Paradise River 4th Crossing Bridge

1926   Edith Creek Bridge

1927   White River Bridge

1928   Christine Falls Bridge

1928   Narada Falls Bridge

1929   Deadwood Creek Bridge (Replaced 1993/94)

1929   Dry Creek Bridge

1929   White River Bridge

1930   Klickitat Creek Bridge

1931   Fryingpan Creek Bridge

1931   St. Andrews Creek Bridge

1931   South Puyallup River Bridge

1934   North Puyallup River Bridge

1935   Laughingwater Creek Bridge (Replaced 1993/94)

1935   Sunbeam Creek Culvert

1936   Chinook Pass Entrance Overpass

1937   Stevens Canyon Tunnel

1939   Deer Creek Bridge

1939   East Side Tunnel

1941   Stevens Creek Bridge

1952   Muddy Fork Bridge at Box Canyon

1952   Nickel Creek Bridge

1952   Nisqually River Suspension Bridge #2

1957   Nisqually Glacier Bridge This replacement bridge is higher and stronger and hopefully will withstand any future floods.

1994   Laughingwater Creek and Deadwood Creek Bridges replaced

(Mount Rainier Park flyer: Mount Rainier Roads and Bridges, 1992)

Mather Memorial Parkway

This historic 53-mile long highway began as an Indian trail, then became a mining road. By 1918, the State of Washington began construction of a state highway up the White River, getting as far as the Dalles, 29 miles beyond Enumclaw. Originally it was alternately called McClellan Pass Highway or the 'Naches Pass Highway', although the road ran several miles south of both McClellan and Naches Passes. The construction contract was let in 1929 and the road finally opened in 1931-32.

The first director of the National Park Service, Stephen Tyng Mather, was personally familiar with Mount Rainier and was one of the champions in working to have it established as a National Park. He had climbed the mountain with the Sierra Club expedition of 1905.

In 1928, Mather visited Mount Rainier and toured the new state highway (now Highway 410) which was to connect eastern and western Washington. He was particularly concerned that the natural beauty of the area be preserved and he emphasized that saving both the timber and scenery was essential.

In January 1929, Mather left Washington, D.C. to travel again to the northwest to campaign for saving the timber along the road. While in Chicago, he suffered a severe stroke, and a year later he died. The section of road he so dearly loved and wanted to preserve was named in his honor as the Mather Memorial Parkway. A plaque commemorating him was on Highway 410 at the entrance to the Park. It has now been moved to Longmire beside the Hiker Information Center.

The Parkway runs from the west boundary of the Mt. Baker-Snoqualmie National Forest, through Mount Rainier National Park, to the east boundary of Wenatchee National Forest. It follows the White River, passing below Yakima Park, then on through Cayuse Pass and Chinook Pass to Yakima while passing through old growth evergreen forests and alpine lakes. The road, including the portion passing through the park, is maintained by the Washington Department of Transportation.

1994 saw a major change in the road as construction began to widen it and bring it up to current standards. The project was not without controversy, as a number of old growth trees had to be cut.

The East Side Road

Throughout the 1930's work proceeded on connecting the state highway at Cayuse Pass to Ohanapecosh Hot Springs. In 1933 the road from Packwood to Ohanapecosh opened. The road was finally opened to traffic in 1940, enabling motorists to drive the length of the east side of the park, go up to White River Campground or Yakima Park, or drive eastward over Chinook Pass to Yakima.

Stevens Canyon Highway

By 1931 the road to Yakima Park was pretty well finished, and development of Yakima Park was well under way. The first official fee-paying visitors to the area were Mr. and Mrs. G.O. Johnson of Seattle who drove up July 17, 1931.

But Superintendent Tomlinson was already weary of the roundabout 135-mile long trip from Longmire to Yakima Park. He felt that the distance, physically and psychologically, amounted to having two separate national parks. He envisioned a more direct route via the south and east sides of the park.

Strong disagreements broke out on exactly what route the new road should take. The park planners favored a route past Reflection Lakes, down Stevens Canyon and up the east side.

Asahel Curtis, chairman of the Rainier National Park Advisory Board, favored a higher, more scenic route. Curtis wanted the road to be high on Stevens Ridge, then past the snout of the Cowlitz Glacier, and up on the Cowlitz Divide.

The dispute was finally resolved in 1932 with the decision to route the road down Stevens Canyon to Muddy Fork, then south around Backbone Ridge and the Cowlitz Divide, then northeasterly to join the new East Side road near Silver Falls.

Even with the route established, some people wondered if the Stevens Canyon Highway would ever be built. Construction came to a halt with the advent of World War II. The C.C.C. boys and construction crews all went off to war. During the war, brush and trees grew up on the roadbed, and by the time the war was over, all road construction had to be started over.

Begun again in 1951, Stevens Canyon Highway was finally completed in 1957.

Carbon River-Mowich Lake Roads

In 1921 Congress appropriated $50,000 for a road up the Carbon River. Simultaneously, the U.S. Forest Service began building three miles of road on its land to connect the park and state roads. By late 1923 the road extended to within a mile of the snout of the Carbon Glacier. With much disappointment it was discovered that the proposed extension over Ipsut Pass to Mowich Lake was impossible.

The Highways to the Park

Getting to the Park - Today

Longmire is 63 miles southeast of Tacoma, 86 miles southeast of Seattle, and 94 miles west of Yakima. Driving time from Seattle is about 2 hours one

Road mileages between points within Mount Rainier National Park and nearby cities

	ENUMCLAW	TACOMA	SEATTLE	PORTLAND	YAKIMA
NISQUALLY ENTRANCE	57	55	80	149	100
LONGMIRE	63	61	86	155	94
INSPIRATION POINT	69	71	95	165	84
PARADISE	71	74	98	168	87
BOX CANYON	61	79	98	166	76
STEVENS CANYON ENTRANCE	51	77	88	156	66
OHANAPECOSH	52	78	89	155	64
CAYUSE PASS	40	66	77	167	65
CHINOOK PASS	43	70	80	170	61
WHITE RIVER ENTRANCE	38	64	75	172	69
SUNRISE	52	78	89	186	83

way, without stopping. From Seattle there are two ways to get there. The first is either through Auburn or Maple Valley to Enumclaw. From there it's 40 miles through a forested route to the White River Entrance on SR 410. This entrance is closed in winter. The other route is via Puyallup or Tacoma, and takes you to the Nisqually Entrance. From Tacoma there are also two ways: either as above, through Puyallup and Eatonville, or Via South Tacoma Way.

Bus transportation is a convenient and energy-smart way for many folks to come to the mountain and leave the driving to someone else. Gray Line of Seattle runs sightseeing tours daily from May through October (weather permitting) from Seattle. The bus departs from the Seattle Sheraton at 8:00 a.m., and stops at Sea-Tac Airport (the Gray Lines booth outside United Baggage Claim) at 8:15 a.m. Prices at this writing, are $32.00 for a sightseer one day round trip, or $22.00 one way/$44.00 per person round trip *(payable in advance)* rate for backpackers.

It's a 10-hour round trip and goes to both Longmire and Paradise. On the return trip, the bus leaves Longmire about 2:15 p.m. Because of the popularity of the trip, 30-day advance reservations are recommended (but call anyway in case there's been a cancellation). Early or late season trips are canceled if there aren't enough people.

Gray Line of Seattle also offers a daily "Mount Rainier Overnighter" with a night at Paradise Inn. This package includes round-trip transportation and lodging, but not meals.

Call 1-800-426-7532 for reservations or more information. (They'll send a brochure.) Gray Line of Seattle, 720 South Forest, Seattle, WA 98134

Information

Up to date information on the park roads, trails, weather and facilities is available 24 hours a day by calling (360) 569-2211. If driving, near the

Nisqually Entrance you can turn your AM radio to 1610KHz. The TDD information number is (360) 569-2177. In an emergency, just call 911.

Road Reports

To check road conditions on the way to the mountain call (206) 649-4366.

Speed Limits Within the Park

Obey posted speed limits. Limits vary within the park, but most are 35 MPH. One exception is the Ipsut Road, which is 25 MPH. Another is Highway 410, which is 50 MPH to near Cayuse Pass, then 35 MPH.

Gateway Cities

The title of "Gateway City to the Park" is claimed by Seattle, Tacoma, Olympia, Yakima, Enumclaw, Elbe, Eatonville, Puyallup, Graham, Wilkeson, Greenwater, Naches, Packwood, Morton, Randle, Ashford, Buckley, Mary's Corner, Auburn and Yelm.

Early and Late Driving

Should you come to the park around dawn, or leave at dusk, watch for deer and elk on the road! These are their feeding times. Deer have been known to jump directly in front of cars, and hitting an elk can definitely ruin your day, not to mention what it does to his. At night the headlights attract them, and they often appear squarely in the path of cars. Especially watch for elk when they've moved down to the lower elevations from late autumn until spring, between the park and Eatonville.

Highway Markers

There is only one official Washington State Historical Highway marker commemorating Mount Rainier. It is located five miles south of Puyallup on State Route 162.

It reads:

Mount Rainier

This monarch of the Cascade Range has been called the Great Pyramid of the United States. No other mountain on the continent exceeds Rainier in bulk of rock masses, number of glaciers (26 active) and extent of base. Nearly all of Mt. Rainier National Park's 337 square miles belong to the mighty mountain. Geologists believe the original peak lost 2,000

Jimmy Beech Photo

291

feet in a volcanic blast creating a crater three miles square. Three cinder cones grew together surrounding the crater rim: Columbia Crest, the central snowy dome, Point Success to the south and Liberty Cap to the north. The British explorer, Captain George Vancouver, discovered the mountain in 1792 and named it for a fellow naval officer, Peter Regnier, now spelled Rainier.

Fuel - Last Gas

Since the little gas station at Longmire closed, there is no longer any fuel sold inside the park. The closest gas station to Longmire is twelve miles away in Ashford. On the north side, the last gas is in Greenwater. On the south, Packwood has several service stations. For those going to Mowich Lake or Ipsut Creek, the last gas is in Wilkeson. If coming up from Yakima, the last chance to gas up is Naches. Remember to fill up before going into the Park. Specific gas station locations are in the directory at the back of this book.

Mechanics are available in Eatonville, Enumclaw, Packwood and Morton.

Winter Access to Park

During winter, all major roads to the park, except one, are closed. The only access is via the Nisqually entrance, with the road to Longmire open as weather permits, and to Paradise only during daytime hours. It is usually gated at 6:30 p.m. and re-opened sometime the next morning after 8:00 a.m. depending upon weather and road conditions.

Winter Road Closures

With about fifty feet of snow falling on the mountain each year, it isn't uncommon for the road to Paradise to be a canyon between walls of snow twenty feet high. If parking overnight at Paradise in winter, park in the lower lot toward the center island. The snowplows blow snow to the outside edge of the lot.

On the north side, Highway 410 is gated at the north boundary arch, just south of the Crystal Mountain Ski Area junction. Cayuse and Chinook Passes are closed. On the south side, Highway 123 is gated just north of the Stevens Canyon Entrance. On the northwest, Highway 165 is normally closed at the Paul Peak Trailhead. Depending on the snow, the Carbon River Road may possibly be open.

Snowmobiles are permitted on designated roadways only, such as when those roadways are closed by snow to normal traffic. They not allowed on trails, cross-country or on undesignated roads. It is legal to snowmobile into the park on a snowmobile via Highway 410 when the highway is snowed in.

Winter Road Travel

When winter driving in the mountains, be prepared for anything. Watch for posted signs along the road indicating traction device (snow tires, studded tires or chains) requirements. Although you may not need chains to drive up to Paradise, you may need them to drive down! If you do need to chain up, do not stop in the roadway. Use a pullout where you will be safe. Carry a windshield scraper, shovel, the "ten essentials" (Page 263) and sleeping bags in the car. Watch out for skiers, sleds, innertubers, falling rocks and icicles, snowplows and animals. Obey the speed limits, exercise extra caution on the mountain's winding roads and wear your seat belt.

Parking

If you choose to go to Paradise on the hottest day of summer, you may conclude it's called the National Park Service because of the gridlock in the parking lot. The debate about what to do about the parking at Paradise has gone on for at least 25 years, and will probably go on at least that many more with nobody happy with whatever the solution. Just about all suggested plans bring forth the gnashing of teeth from the opposing side. The thought of paving over more flower fields drives normally pacifist environmentalists to militancy, and the "mandatory bussing" dream of the park administrators does likewise to the masses.

The Park Service wants to get people out of their cars and onto mass transportation. Under their proposal, visitors would park somewhere outside the park and be bussed to Paradise. A 1990 National Park Service survey claimed that 47 percent favored a Mount Rainier transit system, while 41 percent did not. Furthermore, 72 percent said they would not take a bus from the Nisqually entrance to Paradise if it were offered.

Overnight Parking

There are two overnight parking areas at Longmire: near the National Park Inn, and behind the Longmire Museum. Parking elsewhere could impede the snowplows. Don't set your emergency brake - it could freeze!

Fees

At $15 Mount Rainier's Annual Pass is a bargain, allowing unlimited entries to the Park throughout the calendar year.

A one time vehicle entry fee is $5.00, which is good for the day of issue only. In and out privileges are allowed if the receipt is shown.

Per person entry fees of $3.00 are charged to those persons entering the park on foot, bicycle, motorcycle, horse or commercial bus.

The *best* deal is the Annual Golden Eagle Passport, available at a cost of just $25. This pass allows entry into all National Parks in the U.S. and covers the driver and all occupants in the car.

The Golden Age Passport is for U.S residents 62 years old and older. The Golden Access Passport is for those who are blind or permanently disabled. Both Golden Age Passports and Golden Access Passports are free lifetime entrance passes. In addition, they also carry a 50% reduction in camping fees.

Park Road Rules

Obey posted speed limits or lower speed if conditions warrant. Drive defensively. Use lower gears for climbing or descending ridges if necessary. Watch for drivers who are preoccupied with scenery, also for deer, elk and other animals to dart from the woods. Look out for pedestrians, cyclists and falling rock. Don't take your eyes off the winding road. Pull off the road at the next observation point if you want to take in the view or if people want to pass. *Washington state law requires you to pull over and allow traffic to pass if five vehicles are being held up behind you.*

Park Watch

Mount Rainier has a program called Park Watch with the objective of encouraging visitors to take an active role in protecting and preserving the Park. Be alert for crime, vandalism, poaching, resource violations, uncontrolled fire and safety hazards. If any are observed, report to any park employee or find the nearest phone and call MRNP Communication Center collect (206) 569-2271.

If you observe criminal activity, do not take action yourself. Note the location, description of the people involved, make, model and license number of vehicles involved, and report as above.

Avoid becoming a victim. Don't leave valuables unattended in car at parking area, trailhead or campsite. Mark your gear with indelible ink using driver's license number and state abbreviation. Record serial numbers of camera gear, radios, etc. Check at ranger stations and visitor centers for marking kits and Operation ID stickers.

Car Security Suggestions

1. Lock all valuables in trunk. Put things out of sight.

2. Lock all doors and windows.

3. Keep wallets, purses and cameras with you.

4. Report all suspicious activity to a ranger

Public Rest Rooms on the way to the Park

Enumclaw:

- The Enumclaw Public Library, 1700 First Street
- McFarland Park Chinook Avenue between Porter St. and Chinook Winds
- Enumclaw Activity Center, SE of Highway 410 on 248th Ave SE

Greenwater (Highway 410)

- Federation Forest
- The Dalles Campground, Highway 410, 26 miles east of Enumclaw
- Silver Springs Campground, Highway 410, 32 miles east of Enumclaw

Elbe

- Alder Lake Sunny Beach Point, Mountain Highway (Highway 706)

Morton

- Mains Mountain Center, Morton

Building the Roads

1883   Bailey Willis built a horse trail from Wilkeson to Mowich Lake.

1884   James Longmire constructed the first rough trail to his mineral springs.

1890-91   Aided by five Indians, the Longmire family constructed the original crude road to Longmire Springs. It was a toll road, suitable only for travel in good weather.

1895   A "Toll Trail" ran between Longmire and Paradise. It ran up alongside the Nisqually Glacier, not toward Ricksecker Point as today's road does. It ran to a lateral moraine, then came back towards Paradise Inn and old Nisqually Vista.

1903-10   The Corps of Engineers, under Eugene Ricksecker, began work on the engineering the Longmire-Paradise Road.

1904   The Tacoma Eastern Railway reached Ashford, bringing even more visitors.

     The Army Engineers Corps proposed a wagon road as the most practical route into the park from the east. The 17-mile road was to come in via the American River along the crest of the Cascades over Shriner Peak into the Ohanapecosh Valley, up Olallie Creek and over Cascade Divide up into Cowlitz Park. The estimated cost was $101,490. This road was never built.

1906   Construction of engineer Eugene Ricksecker's road to the mountain from western Washington was begun, following much the same route we use today. Congressman Francis Cushman of Tacoma succeeded in getting the sum of $240,000 appropriated for the construction of Ricksecker's road.

1908   Automobiles could drive as far as Longmire.

1909   Automobiles could drive as far as the Nisqually Glacier Bridge. The road was hailed as the first road in America to reach a glacier.

1911   The first automobile rolled into Paradise, driven by Mr. Lynn Miller. Mr. E.S. Hall, Park Superintendent, and Edward Allen were passengers. The road wasn't completely passable, and the car had to be dragged part of the way by a team of mules. The public was still not allowed to drive to this point until 1915.

1912   Government Bulletin reported, "During the winter, the government road was kept open for sleighs as far as Longmire Springs."

1913   Surveys were begun for "the Wonder Road", a contemplated 'round the mountain highway.'

1914   Mount Rainier Mining Company built the road up the main fork of the White River to Glacier Basin, a distance of 12 miles.

1915   The public was finally allowed to drive to Paradise, although between the Nisqually River and Ricksecker point traffic was one way.

1916   A survey was done for "the Wonder Road" segment going to Mystic Lake, Grand Park and Frozen Lake, to connect with the Starbo Road in Glacier Basin. The estimated cost was to be $15,000 a mile.

1918   Women were given the right to drive on park roads.

1920   The ultimate plan for the 'round the mountain' highway was completed.

1921   A rough road was opened into the Carbon River section of the park. The snow removal method at Paradise was by TNT and hand shoveling!

1924   A suspension bridge was built over the Nisqually River to provide auto access to the Longmire Campground on the far side of the river. A rough private road to Ohanapecosh Hot Springs was punched through. The west side section of the "Wonder Road" was begun, with this segment to run from a point one mile north of the Nisqually entrance to the South Puyallup River. The Carbon River Road was built to near the Carbon Glacier. The road to Paradise was finally opened to unrestricted two-way traffic.

1925   The road to Ohanapecosh was completed.

Meanwhile routine maintenance on the existing roads was driving Supt. O.A. Tomlinson crazy. "No sooner is one rough place repaired than others, worse, are worn. By the time a second or third dangerously rutted section is repaired, the first work must be done over. The worst feature of it all is the gradual deterioration of the old road despite all the work done and expenditures made, giving the impression to visitors that we either do not know how to maintain roads or else we are not cognizant of the needs."

This same year the National Park Service turned over care of the park roads to the Bureau of Public Roads. Supt. Tomlinson breathed a sigh of relief!

1926   Construction began on the southern section of the West Side Road.

1927   The proposed Naches Pass Highway (Mather Memorial Highway) was projected to be completed in 1928.

1929   The Highway to Paradise was widened and improved. The Yakima Park Highway was begun. It opened in 1931.

1931   The road to Sunrise was formally opened in June to unrestricted traffic. The cross-state highway connecting Eastern and Western Washington, the Enumclaw-Chinook Pass-Yakima Park Highway known as the Mather Memorial Highway was completed. The route was between American River, over Chinook Pass and out White River. Scenic pullouts, vista points, and natural rock retaining walls which harmonized with the landscape, were a new idea, inspired probably by the breathtaking views of the mountain from the new highway.

The Frying Pan bridge was completed in another step toward 'round the Mountain' travel. With the White River Road completed, Sunrise development began.

1932   Mather Memorial Highway (also referred to as the Naches Pass* Highway) officially opened, affording the motoring public 60 miles of protected scenic highway, and making the Park directly accessible from the eastern part of Washington. (*Actually the highway is twenty miles south of the historic Naches Pass.)

1933   Construction on the Stevens Canyon Highway began and the Laughingwater Bridge was under construction. An overpass was to be built at Tipsoo Lake. A crude road to Mowich Lake opened, and a highway to Ohanapecosh opened from Packwood.

1934   The road to Ohanapecosh Hot Springs was vastly improved. Work continued on the East Side Road and tunnel. The West Side "Highway" opened as far north as the North Puyallup River.

1935   The road from the Park Boundary to Mowich Lake was graded at a cost of $200,000. Originally intended to link up with the West Side Highway, it never went any further. It also never opened until 1955!

The West Side "Highway" segment of the Wonder Road was completed from the Nisqually Highway to as far north as the South Puyallup River. The next segment, which was to run up the west side of the Park to Mowich Lake, was never built.

1938-39 BIG problems! The state opened Cayuse Pass. 34,000 visitors came to the Park and there were no bathroom facilities. The eastside Deadwood Bridge was completed.

1940   The East Side Road from Ohanapecosh to the junction of the Chinook Pass Road at Cayuse Pass opened, completed at a cost of $1.4 million. This was the first 'through road' in the park.

1941   The Stevens Canyon Road was expected to open in 1944.

1942   The masonry arch was completed over Stevens Creek. The road bridge over Box Canyon was in progress, as was tunnel work in Box Canyon. Two viaducts were built for the Nickel Creek Bridge.

1945   As the war sapped manpower and materials, non-essential efforts such as the park road projects, ground to a halt. The Stevens Canyon Road was completed from the East Side Highway to the Muddy Fork Road, and could be driven from the upper end to within 1/2 mile of Stevens Creek. The Canyon roadwork finally came to a complete standstill because of the War effort.

1948   White Pass Highway construction was underway.

1950   Material and labor shortages still held up resumption of work on the Stevens Canyon Highway. Nickel Creek and Muddy Fork Bridges were still not completed.

1951   The White Pass Highway opened, increasing travel looping through the East side of the Park.

1954   The Mowich Lake Road opened to public auto travel for the first time since it was built. The East Side Road was used for commercial vehicles for one month while Snoqualmie Pass was closed due to slides.

1957   Stevens Canyon Highway finally opened September 4, 1957, twenty four years after it was begun, linking the east and west sides of the mountain.

1960   There was extensive flood damage throughout the Park, including much on the Stevens Canyon Road.

1995   Wilkeson Bridge resurfaced.

]
Weather

> First it rained and then it blew;
> then it friz and then it snew;
> then it fogged and then it thew;
> and very shortly after then;
> it blew and snew and thew again.
> **from an old Woodsman's song**

Carpe Diem (Seize the Day)

Deciding When To Go To Mount Rainier

If there's one word to describe Mount Rainier's weather, it's "fickle." Major storms can descend in minutes, and clear just as rapidly. It's those unexpected changes that make predicting the weather difficult.

Nearly every Northwesterner has had the experience of driving all the way to Mount Rainier only to find themselves in near zero visibility. Not only can they not see the Mountain, they can barely see the side of the road. They look yonder from Seattle or Tacoma or points east and see the Mountain out in all her glory and decide to go for the day. What they don't realize is, that though the *TOP* of the Mountain is out, the bottom can be socked in tight. Clouds or fog frequently can hang like pea soup between three thousand and six thousand feet. Just the reverse can also be true. Though there may be a raging storm on the summit, it can be a glorious day on the lower reaches.

Eric Simonson, summit guide with over 250 climbs to his credit, had this to say about when to come visit. "After guiding for over 20 years, I have learned the most on my worst climbs. If you only come to Mount Rainier during the summer, whether to climb, hike or be a tourist, you only see one side of the Park, and that is often the crowded side. To really know this special place, you need to come during the "off" season. The going is more difficult, the chance of success less, whether that means standing on the summit, or getting that perfect photograph as the clouds clear at sunset or after a snowstorm. If it was easy, everyone would be there doing it. The fact that they are not makes it worth the while."

The bottom line is, *Mount Rainier creates its own weather, and one should be prepared for anything, even in summer!* The mountain reaches into the upper atmosphere and intercepts the flow of moist maritime air coming in from the Pacific Ocean. This accounts for the great amount of rain and snowfall.

299

SEASONS AT THE MOUNTAIN

A Rule of Thumb for all Seasons

You're going to the Mountain for the day, and wonder how warm it will be at Sunrise. There's an easy way to get a fairly accurate idea of the temperature anywhere on the Mountain. It's this: What is the temperature and elevation above sea level where you are? If you're in Seattle, or Tacoma or Olympia, you're pretty close to sea level. Let's say it's a cool day, 50°. At Sunrise (6,403') it's around 34°. How can you tell? Temperature drops 3° for every 1,000 ft. in elevation gain.

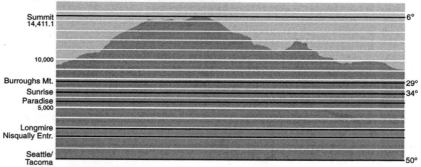

Comparative Temperatures

Summit 14,411.1 — 6°
10,000
Burroughs Mt. — 29°
Sunrise — 34°
Paradise 5,000
Longmire
Nisqually Entr.
Seattle/Tacoma — 50°

Temperature

Longmire's average daytime summer temperatures are in the mid-70°'s, with nighttime temperatures in the high 40°'s. Warmer or cooler temperatures can occur at any of these locations. These are average maximum and minimum temperatures at Paradise and Ohanapecosh.

	Paradise (5400')	Ohanapecosh (1950')
April	44°/27°	51°/32°
May	50°/32°	63°/38°
June	56°/37°	71°/45°
July	64°/44°	80°/48°
August	63°/43°	78°/49°
September	57°/39°	71°/44°
October	40°/33°	52°/38°

Up-To-The-Minute Weather

Those contemplating going to Mount Rainier might want to check the National Weather Service Report (206) 526-6087. Those with weather radios can tune to 162.55 frequency or 162.475 out of Olympia for the Mount Rainier Recreational 48-hour forecast.

Precipitation

1991 Figures:

Longmire	77.40"
Ohanapecosh	74.77"
Paradise	126.62"

Paradise, at about 5,400 feet, is generally greater than 10 inches per month from October through March, and decreases only and inch or two during July.

Water

Sounds of water are everywhere in the park, generated by rain, melting ice and snow, waterfalls, lapping lakes, tumbling rivers, bubbling brooks and gurgling springs. No wonder! With an average of 80 to 125+ inches of moisture annually, as recorded at Longmire and Paradise, all this water has to go somewhere. Not surprisingly, it all runs downhill, then downstream eventually to the Pacific Ocean, then up into the atmosphere where it starts the process all over again..

The Lenticular Cloud

Lenticular clouds are Mount Rainier's weather indicators. They signal the fact there are high winds at the summit, and a storm is usually on the way.

One of the members of the 1963 Mt. Everest expedition noted that one cloud cap had a storm in it as severe as anything he had experienced at 25,000 feet on Everest. The cause is the air masses moving in from the southwest.

Frank Sincock photo

No wonder the lenticular clouds are mistaken for flying saucers

When the warmer air hits the mountain, it cools and forms clouds, snow or super-cooled rain. The cloud forms on the windward side, and dissipates on the lee side.

Climbers on the summit have actually suffered burns inside a cloud cap, caused by sitting on sulfur impregnated pumice, which combined with water to form a weak acid solution. There is always a high wind within the cloud-cap. The most innocent looking caps can have raging blizzards going on inside them. (One pilot reported 150 mph winds). Many an experienced party has regretted going into one.

The Wind Chill Factor

In addition to being forewarned to anticipate lower temperatures at higher altitudes, there's another element which could ruin your day, or at least make for a very uncomfortable hike: wind chill.

Let's continue our trip above. You know it's going to be 34°F at Sunrise, so you take a jacket. But you intend to hike out to the end of Burroughs Mountain (7830' elev.) for a better look at the mountain. Your destination is 1,400' higher than Sunrise, so there's another 5°F temperature loss. Now your problems start.

Burroughs Mountain will give you a full head-on view of 5.5 mile long Emmons Glacier. It will also give you the full brunt of the icy winds sweeping down off the glacier.

Wind chill factor

Wind MPH	Thermometer temperature in F°							
	35	30	25	20	15	10	5	0
	Wind chill temperature							
5	33	27	21	16	12	7	0	-5
10	22	16	10	3	-3	-9	-15	-22
15	16	9	2	-5	-11	-18	-25	-31
20	12	4	-3	-10	-17	-24	-31	-39
25	8	1	-7	-15	-22	-29	-36	-44
30	6	-2	-10	-18	-25	-33	-41	-49
35	4	-4	-12	-20	-27	-35	-43	-52
40	3	-5	-13	-21	-29	-37	-45	-53
45	2	-6	-14	-22	-30	-38	-46	-54

Winds of more than 45 mph add little to the chilling.

What this means to the park visitor, is that winds blowing at only 20 mph can transform a brisk 30-degree day into a frigid bone-chilling 4 degrees. It's especially important to cover everything. Wear hats, gloves, coats, layers of clothing, and extra socks. Above all, try to keep dry, and bundle the kids up too. Storm fronts move in fast on the mountain, and can overtake backcountry hikers very quickly.

Another important factor to add in is air flow. Hot air rises, cold air sinks, thus it's warmer on the hillside than in the gully. Even on hot days, the cold air flowing off a glacier can chill one quickly.

The true temperature of cold plus wind chill can easily be calculated from the above chart.

Spring

Life Springs Eternal

It may be spring in the Puget Sound lowlands, but the flower meadows at Mount Rainier are still sleeping under their thick soft blanket of snow. Spring at the mountain isn't April and May, as it is elsewhere. Spring here comes and goes in about a two week period which usually hits around July.

April and May means maybe it snows a little less. Then the weather just keeps getting better as the months go on, culminating in the very best months being September and October. It isn't uncommon for July and August to experience rainstorms, and even an occasional snowstorm. By the end of October, the winter snows begin to close down the trails, and while Puget Sound experiences a winter of drizzle and rain, it's coming down as snow at the Mountain, only to repeat the process starting again the next May.

Spring months invariably mean the snow plows will be busy clearing the snow and slides from the Stevens Canyon Road, the Sunrise Road, and other remote sections of the Mountain.

Summer

When the Crowds All Come

Even in summer, the cold air currents descending from nearby glaciers make visitors glad they brought sweaters or jackets. Summertime temperatures at Longmire (2,761') average in the upper 40's to mid-70's, and at Paradise (5,400') in the lower 40's to mid-60's. Days which turn out to be "hot" by Mount Rainier standards, can start off with a crust of ice on pots of water left out in the campgrounds. What we think of as summer is actually an accelerated spring-summer-fall condensed into about a four-month period. The plants and animals must hurry through their birth-growth-reproduction cycle before the long winter settles in on them again.

But when summer finally hits, what a glorious time it is! Nature's white quilt is thrown back, and the fresh multicolored cover takes its place. The little

Mount Rainier critter community springs to life and the soothing sounds of nature are everywhere. The fragrance of the flowers and the trees is intoxicating, and even the fresh dirt smells good. Even the most ordinary hot dog or hamburger tastes like a gourmet feast when eaten with a million dollar campground wrapped around it.

Autumn

When the Tourists Go Home

The nip in the air brings many things: fewer visitors, the subalpine meadows and avalanche chutes blaze with scarlet foliage and riotous vine maple, migrating birds pass overhead, and fresh white snow appears on the upper reaches of the mountain. It signals that the wildlife is making final preparations for winter. By mid-October the small animals are busy hoarding the last of the nuts and seeds, and the large animals that winter over in the park are packing on the layers of fat needed to survive the long winter.

Bull elk bugle in the backcountry. It's a wonderful time to drive the loop around the Mountain with a short diversion to Chinook Pass to drink in one last long panoramic view of the mountain. Sunrise traditionally closes down around Labor Day, and some years the road to Sunrise beyond the White River Campground cutoff does too. Come midweek and you may have a picnic area or campground to yourself.

Indian Summer is a glorious time to hike. Good trails for fall color out of Paradise are: Alta Vista, Nisqually Vista, Myrtle Falls and Mazama Ridge. Other colorful hikes are: Pinnacle Peak, Bench lake, Reflection Lakes, Shriner Peak, Tipsoo Lake, Summerland, Frozen Lake, Fremont Lookout and Emmons Vista-Shadow Lake. Trails should be in prime condition, the bugs are gone, and the crowds are too. If backpacking, wilderness permits are still required. Be prepared for inclement weather. Be especially alert to fire danger at this time of year too. Keep in mind too that in just hours, crisp Indian Summer can quickly turn into snowy early winter.

Remember too, all plants are protected and cannot be collected. No collecting of colored leaves is permitted.

Winter

Winter turns Mount Rainier into a virtual fairyland. The giant trees become living Christmas cards. Snow sparkles like ermine.

"So brilliant is the peak on these clear days of winter following the snows that the eye can hardly look upon it, and when the sun sinks low in the west and touches the crests with old rose and gold, the scene passes beyond the ability of words to describe it," wrote Floyd Schmoe.

Now as then, when heavy snows blanket the trails, wilderness travelers should be prepared for routefinding and survival techniques. Even now, wilderness permits are still required if going into the backcountry. Be aware of avalanche danger. Leave your itinerary and schedule with a responsible person.

Some of the real heros among permanent employees are those maintenance crew stalwarts who spend their winters digging tons of snow from the visitor facilities and park roads, and scrambling to get everything accessible for the next onslaught of visitors.

Mount Rainier is a traditional training ground for various mountaineering and outdoor types, and one of the traditional fun spectator sports is watching groups trudge off to practice such things as learning to cross a glacier, hauling somebody out of a crevasse and doing ice axe self arrests. Such groups have usually had several classroom sessions to get the textbook learning down pat before actually practicing the real thing on the mountain.

Mountain Rescue organizations, scout troops, military units, and ski patrol units also practice maneuvers and exercises of all types on the deep snow.

Longmire, at 2761', stays much warmer than the higher elevations, thus snow conditions vary. During mild winters, trails may be completely snow free, or they may have several feet of snow during colder ones. Novice skiers and snowshoers often favor skiing among the trees on these lower trails.

Mountain Weather

Climate

Perhaps the one feature which makes Mt. Rainier unique, is that the climatic zones range from a deep humid rain forest, to conditions similar to the arctic circle, just a few miles apart. Thus going up in elevation is equal to going north in latitude.

At 14,411 feet, Mount Rainier actually generates its own peculiar weather system. The Pacific Ocean's marine air currents keep the mountain covered with a thick blanket of snow most of the time. Snowfall has been reported during every month of the year, including the summer months.

Annual precipitation at Mount Rainier ranges from 60 inches at the lowest elevations to over 100 inches in the subalpine regions. The Big Bump intercepts

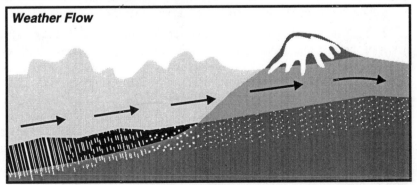

Weather Flow

all the storms coming in from the southwest, and it is all this rain which is responsible for the luxuriant vegetation.

The coldest temperatures recorded in the Park were in 1925 when the thermometer registered 18° below zero at Paradise and 6° below zero at Longmire.

Chief Naturalist Bill Dengler came out with probably the best weather analysis of all time. He suggests that perhaps the name should be Mount Rain-ier and Longmire split to become "Long-mire." Then there were the words of wisdom from a University of Washington professor who learnedly noted, "If you can't see the Mountain, it's raining. If you can see it, it's going to rain."

"In 1983 the total precipitation (rain and melted snow) recorded at Longmire was 86.96 inches, and at Paradise 130.11 inches. There are 231 cubic inches in one gallon, so we calculate that 54.2 gallons of water fell for each square foot of ground at Longmire during 1983, and at Paradise, each square foot of ground received 81.1 gallons. No wonder the level of Alder Lake can rise and fall so dramatically in such a short period of time."

Dressing for Mountain Weather

As previously noted, the number one killer at Mount Rainier is hypothermia, the state where the human body loses heat faster than it can produce and retain heat. If the body's inner core temperature drops below 78°, the heart and brain cease to function. It begins when a person gets cold and/or wet, usually "soaked to the skin." One loses 26 times as much heat in cold water as when dry. Add to that the wind chill factor, and bingo! It doesn't even have to be below freezing for one to become hypothermic. Hypothermia is the silent companion which stalks everyone in the outdoors, quietly waiting to strike the unprepared. Its' victims at the mountain have included climbers, hikers, and Sunday tourists. Don't become another one of them. **BE PREPARED!**

Afternoons may be warm, but mornings and evenings can be bitter cold, so bring extra clothes, and dress in the layer system: if cold, put on a layer, and if overheated, take one off. Use hooded, zippered clothes. People are always getting caught unprepared on trails by changes of weather that come in rapidly and without warning. Many have paid for that unpreparedness with their lives.

Even the always prepared Boy Scouts got caught once back in the 60's in a fiasco of the first magnitude. The boys were holding a big campout at Grand Park, and not heeding their own advice, many hiked in wearing shorts and thongs and took just a minimum of lightweight cotton clothing. Many didn't even take tents, thinking they'd just sleep under the stars. They no sooner got to the Park, and a major blizzard hit. It took a massive rescue effort to get the boys all out, because the rescuers had to take in even such basics as long pants, jackets and shoes and socks. Everyone was brought out safely, but the event produced a couple hundred young evangelists preaching the "Be Prepared" gospel.

Let it Snow

> "Mount Rainier has ten months of good skiing, and two months of not so good."
> -old Mount Rainier cliche

The subject of snow is no small matter at Mount Rainier. It is of great concern to rangers, road crews, tourists, animals, skiers, Mountain Rescue members and all the electric companies (and power consumers) downstream who rely on that snowpack for the water to run their generators. The same snow serves many people and many purposes. And oh, how it snows!

Mount Rainier is the mother of all snow-making machines. The massive monolith reaches nearly three-miles skyward to intercept the moist maritime air flowing eastward from the Pacific Ocean. The resulting confrontation between the mountain and the moisture-laden air creates pea-soup fogs and whiteouts, rains ranging from torrential downpours to gentle grey mists, record world-class snowfalls, plus that old Rainier trademark, the lenticular cloud.

Because the top of the mountain is above the snow-producing storm clouds, the snowfall at the summit is not as great as it is at lower elevations. The greatest snowfall is usually between 4000 to 9000 feet. Above 10,000 feet, the colder air holds less moisture.

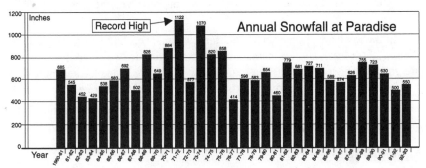

One such record snowfall was the winter of 1971-72 when a total of 1,122 inches (93.5 feet) was recorded at the Paradise Ranger Station. The same place also holds the world record for the greatest depth of snow in a single month, - 25 feet, 5 inches in April 1972. Winter snows routinely reach the gabled third floor windows of Paradise Inn and have to be removed to prevent damage to the roof.

Even in milder years, it isn't uncommon to visit Paradise on the 4th of July, and find not flower fields, but tunnels cut through the snowbanks to access the Inn.

The weight of that volume of snow is no small matter either. The roofs on the Paradise building must support an incredible amount of weight, considering that a cubic foot of very compacted snow weighs 35 pounds, and it isn't uncommon to have 25-feet of snow on a roof. (Formula: 1 foot of loose snow @ 5.2 lbs = 1" to 2" of rain. 1 cubic foot of water = 62.5 lbs.)

Lowlands Rain to Mountain Snows

In the lowlands, from Puget Sound to the Mountain, it rains below 1,500 feet. That same precipitation is snow between 1,500 and 2,200 feet. From 3,500 and 7,000 feet come the heavy snows. Above 11,000 feet, the cold dry air contains little moisture, although there may be violent storms on the summit.

The truth is, Mount Rainier only has two seasons, Winter, and a 2-4 month long condensed spring through fall. It isn't uncommon to have winter snows still on the ground through August, and have winter move in again in late September or October. It's during this brief window the eager flowers pop through the melting snow to live their short lives before passing from Paradise to flower heaven. Some years it seems the winter "intermission" goes directly from blooming flowers to Autumn color, by-passing summer.

The long winter at Sunrise goes unheralded except for an occasional visit from cross country skiers who come in on boards. Even though Sunrise is a thousand feet higher than Paradise, the snowfall is substantially less. Because it is on the lee side of the mountain, it is protected from the Pacific storms which sweep in to the southwest side. It's in the wind, rain and snow shadow of the mountain. When there are 20-25' of snow in Paradise, there are 10-15' in Sunrise.

In the lowlands, Longmire (2,762 feet), Ohanapecosh (1,914 feet) and Ipsut Creek (2,300 feet), snow accumulation seldom exceeds two to six feet. Winter life goes on as usual in Christmas-card pretty Longmire, since it takes more than a little snow to faze the hardy year-round ranger and scientist crew.

Winter doesn't mean back country travel is over. Each year an increasing number of hardy adventurers take off on skis and showshoes.

Snowfall (1993)

Longmire	45" (the lowest in 13 years)
Ohanapecosh	71"
Paradise	550" (100 inches below average)

The first big snowfall of the season came on September 6, 1992, and the last snow fell on June 23, 1993. Paradise was not snow free until July 5. (Eight weeks snow free.)

Volumes of Snow

In the summer of 1984 Hydrologist Carolyn Driedger and a team of USGS scientists did a study of the actual total volume of snow and ice on Mount Rainier. Their conclusions: **there is one cubic mile of snow and ice covering an area of 35.5 square miles that is more than 700 feet deep in places.**

According to 1985 USGS figures there are 37.8 billion cubic feet of ice and snow from a 250.2 million square foot glacier area which feeds the Puyallup River drainage system.

Snow and ice totals for glaciers feeding the other drainage systems are:

Carbon River   - 28.7 billion cu. ft. in volume/130.2 million sq. ft. in area

White River   - 47.2 billion cu. ft. in volume/286.7 million sq. ft. in area

Cowlitz River   - 20.2 billion cu. ft. in volume/145.4 million sq. ft. in area

Nisqually River - 22.3 billion cu. ft. in volume/178.4 million sq. ft. in area

Driedger estimated the volume of ice in the crater from 12,000' (the origin of the old depression of the two craters) to the summit is 8.7 billion cubic feet.

Thickest Glacial Ice

According to the scientists, the thickest ice was in the following places:

Carbon Glacier	705 feet thick	6,200 foot leve
Emmons Glacier	594 feet thick	6,000 foot level
Tahoma Glacier	471 feet thick	7,000 foot level
Nisqually Glacier	436 feet thick	6,000 foot leve
Winthrop Glacier	322 feet thick	9,500 foot level

Paradise Record Snowfall

Maximum annual snowfall: 1,122" (7/1/71 -6/30/72)

(There was over 1,000" two years in a row, since 1970-71 had over 1,000" In 1971-72 the volume of water was so great that water flowed into the old Puyallup River bed.)

Maximum snowpack: 357" (3/55)
Minimum annual snowfall: 313" 7/1/40 - 6/30/41)

Temperatures

Longmire, 1993: The highest temperature recorded for the year was 91 degrees on August 5. January 6 was the year's low with at 7 degrees.

Cold weather on the upper reaches can rival that of Mount Everest, with winds frequently gusting 60-100 miles an hour, and temperatures hitting minus 50°F.

And From the Outside Looking In...

Three times every day, Mount Rainier has its picture taken by a camera on Queen Anne Hill in Seattle. The picture tells a story even if the mountain isn't out. The reverse also happens, a camera at the Fremont Lookout takes Seattle's picture.

If you have the sensation Mount Rainier isn't visible as often or as clearly as it used to be, you're right. In 1993, for instance, Mount Rainier was visible from Sea-Tac Airport only 21 days between April and October (the prime viewing months!)

Where are you, pretty Lady?

Scientists confirm that Mount Rainier is slowly disappearing from view, and the culprit is air pollution. Specifically, it's fine particulate pollution, consisting of tiny particles less than 10 micros in size, the byproducts of burning gasoline, diesel fuel, wood and coal burning and other sulfate-producing activities. One primary characteristic of fine particulates is that they absorb and scatter light and reduce visibility, and thus steal our beautiful views.

Twenty-five years ago, Wallace R. Donaldson, who was then meteorologist in charge of the U.S. Weather Bureau at Sea-Tac, published a paper which covered his long-range visibility observations of the mountain from April to October 1949-1953 and 1963-1967. Donaldson concluded that long-range visibility was decreasing at a much faster pace than previously believed, and projected an even faster degradation by the 1980's. Then in 1990 Frank Van Haren, a visibility specialist with the Department of Ecology, became intrigued by Donaldson's paper and continued the study through 1993. He found, however, that instead of declining after 1967, long-distance visibility actually increased. He attributed the improvement to the Department of Ecology's aggressive efforts in the 1970's and early 80's to reduce air pollution. Then came 1986 and the beginning of another decline in visibility. The number of days Mount Rainier was visible dropped from a high of 60.4 in 1986 to 36.4 in 1993. That time frame corresponds with a vast increase in Puget Sound's population, and an even greater increase in the number of vehicle miles driven.

Also monitoring air quality around Puget Sound is the Puget Sound Air Pollution Control Agency, an agency that's been around since the 1970's. In January of 1994 they began a 5-year, $100,000 study to not only do the photo monitoring, but to install equipment to measure the kind of pollution the camera is seeing. The conclusion: Not only are we in danger of losing our beautiful views of Mount Rainier, the same pollution could be costing our lives. Epidemiological studies, now 20 years old, in 24 cities and communities across the U.S. have found that fine particulate pollution is damaging health and killing people. Fine particulates have been linked to the deaths of 60,000 people annually.

Meteorologist Donaldson's prophesies were accurate, just a little premature. His conclusion: "The atmosphere will not absorb an unlimited amount of air pollutants. The beauty of the mountains is of little consequence if the mountains cannot be seen.," *(Mike Archbold, Valley Daily News 3/15/94)*

Make My Day

The sweetest words to any red-blooded Rainieraholic: **"The Mountain's out!"**

Technology

Hello Longmire

A telephone line from Ashford to Longmire was installed by the Milwaukee Railroad Company in 1911.

The advent of the telephone was revolutionary for its day, and when the 'around the mountain' telephone system went in, it was looked upon as the answer to prayer. For those marooned at a distant ranger station or fire lookout with no means of knowing what was going on anywhere else in the Park, the telephone brought welcome human contact. But installing and maintaining the system was a monumental undertaking, which over the years required hundreds of men and thousands of man hours. Every winter the lines came down, and every summer they would be have to be repaired and put back up again. The frail lines were no match for the heavy Mount Rainier snows. The old crank telephones look quaint to us now, but when they worked, they worked, and were regarded as a life line to those who used them.

One interesting footnote in the records, was a notation by a fire lookout who was alarmed to see fire shooting from his telephone during an electrical storm.

The outmoded system was finally abandoned after World War II when radios came into use. Look up (w-a-a-a-y up) as you hike through the woods. You may be rewarded with the discovery of one of the old ceramic insulators. There are lots of them around, in addition to miles of phone line still up in the trees.

Today's Technology on the Mountain

We've come a long way from the old 'round the mountain' telephone lines. Though to the casual observer, the Park looks as wild and rustic as it has probably always looked, devices of technology are nestled here and there, silently working.

Even the air is monitored at Mount Rainier. Air quality is measured, so is visibility. There's an automated visibility camera at Paradise and another at Mount Fremont, with the data collected sent to Boulder, Colorado for analysis. Acid precipitation is also monitored. There's also a Paradise nephelometer, (which measures pollution) operated by the Washington Department of Ecology. In all, the air is monitored for six different types of pollutants: sulfates, nitrates, ozone, organic carbon, heavy metals, and particulates.

There's an ozone monitor at the Carbon River and a weather transmitter at Camp Muir. There's also a weather station and repeater on Glacier Island.

Eight times a week, from 680 miles in space, a satellite takes the mountain's temperature and relays it to the Goddard Space Flight Center near Washington, D.C. Signals are sent from electrical temperature sensors which were placed in several steam vents in the summit crater.

A variety of pressure sensors, sonic rangefinders, cameras, data loggers, and radios transmitters keep an eye on the South Tahoma Glacier. Time lapse cameras also methodically snap away at various locations around the mountain. Be aware there are also cameras taking pictures of all this stuff, so if anyone tinkers with it, the guilty party will be easy to identify.

Other Infrastructure

There are six electric generating systems, with 93 transformers, five miles of above-ground power lines and 21 miles of underground lines. There are 89 vehicles and pieces of specialized equipment, 76 fuel storage tanks, 1 seismograph and 385 radio, telephone and computer components.

The First Radio Broadcast

The first radio broadcast from the summit was also a three-way world-record breaker. The year was 1933, and two radio devotees, William Gunston and Donald Klumb, carried 32 pounds of radio gear to the summit to conduct the first five-meter broadcast from the mountain top. Besides conducting the five-meter mountain broadcast, they also established a distance record for the same wave length, and the highest altitude broadcast ever attempted except by airplane. Their conversation was heard in Paradise, but much to the amazement of all, it was also heard in Seattle. They conducted a couple of simple experiments, and claimed the radio waves traveled downward instead of outward, as they do under ordinary conditions, and also they found that by putting the 47-inch antenna about six inches off the ice, that the speaker volume was tripled. The event was so newsworthy, it was discussed at the International Radio Convention in Chicago a few days later. *(TNT 7-25-33)*.

Radios Round the Mountain

Most people don't realize that on the 79-million acres under National Park Service control in the U.S., there are nine different electronic surveillance methods in use quietly keeping track of what's going on when park visitors think nobody's watching. These technologies include hidden sensors, scanners, satellites, miniature transmitters, vehicle trackers, and night vision devices. *(Popular Communications/The Monitoring Magazine, Feb. 1987)*

How many of these are in use at Mount Rainier, we'll never know. However those who like to monitor radio, might try listening in to the following Mount Rainier frequencies: 151.895, 155.160, 163.075, 164.475, 164.9875, 166.875, 167.125, 167.15, 169.725, 171.775, 172.45, 172.625 and 406.25. Tom Kneitzel, author of the above article, also suggests that when you go to the mountain, put your handheld scanner into the search/scan mode and see if you can discover any non-NPS frequencies in use at the park.

For park information (near the Nisqually entrance), tune your AM radio to 1610KHz for up to date news on park roads, trails facilities and weather. This station broadcasts 24 hours a day, and messages change as needed.

Computers and the Park

Just as it must have been a quantum leap in communications when all facilities in the park were finally connected by telephone, they're now connected by computer. This enables backcountry hikers to get permits at any place around the park with a computer terminal, and it enables the park service to know exactly who is in the outback and where, and all pertinent information about them: length of intended stay, destination, etc. There are 94 computers in use around the park, with most at Longmire and headquarters at Tahoma Woods. Among other things, forest age stands, forest habitat types, boundaries, roads and trails, geology, meadows, slopes, elevations, rare plant locations, glaciers and Paradise impacts are all tracked via computer.

For those who want to keep tabs on park doings from home via their computer, there are now a number of ways to do it: the on-line services (CompuServe, America Online and Progidy) as well as the Internet, give Park aficionados an Information Highway onramp to news on the parks (but no access to the Mount Rainier computer or any data in it).

The vast Internet is a growing source of information on National Parks, trails, hiking and politics. Both the National Park Service and the National Parks Conservation Association (NPCA) have 'home' pages on the Web. (The National Park Service's URL (the address used with Internet Web's Mosaic/netscape software) is: **http://www.nps.gov/.**

NPS's home page offers information on all national park sites including historical and archaeological sites. You can 'surf' through NPS press releases, publications, heritage site data, etc. The site was new in 1995 and is still growing and expanding (budget considerations notwithstanding...). The NPCA site offers information on NPCA and its activities as well as a list of other Internet sites of interest to hikers and park aficionados. NPCA's URL is **http://www2.ari.net/home/npca/**).

There you can go to pages of :

American Hiking Society **(http://www.teleport.com/~walking/ahs.htm)**

Backcountry home page **(http://io.datasys.swri.edu/Overview.html)** with lots of information on the Rockies and Eastern locales.

American Volkssport Association page with lists of walks in every region of the U.S.

(Washington walks at **http://www.teleport.com/~walking/wayre.htm**)

Other Related Internet home pages:

Pacific Northwest Hiking - **http://www.kcls.lib.wa.us/gpadden/hike.html** (growing collection of trail reports with maps).

Wildflowers - **http://rampages.onramp.net/~garylipe** (good reference data)

The Great Outdoors (associated with CompuServe site, includes a good summary of Mt. Rainier NP information in the National Parks section). **www.gorp.com/default.html**

On CompuServe, NPCA maintains a library and message board in area #5 on the GREAT OUTDOORS Forum. **Enter GO:NPCA** to reach the forum. Email to NPCA should be addressed to **Internet:webmaster@npca.org**, or CompuServe, **7774,2456** or to dkhanna, **73441,1406**.

America Online (AOL) has a **Travels** section with the *Backpacker* magazine in the **Interests and references** area. Besides materials on its monthly magazine and TV show - 'Trailside,' Backpacker offers information on trails and hiking in the **Trailhead** register. (Keyword - **backpacker**). There are great opportunities to find the latest on trails across the nation as well as finding a hiking companion for doing the Wonderland Trail.

America Online subscribers can also type keyword "Network Earth" and select the message boards. E-mail NPCA at "dkhanna" or "**NATPARKS**".

Progidy has a limited section on National Parks (Use **Jump - National Parks**). Some parks are not covered (Mount Rainier should be covered shortly.)

Current trails and parks information on-line is a 'dynamic' process. Information may become available on local bulletin boards, on the Internet or other on-line services at any time. One should check the listings in local computer magazines, like ComputerUser, or keep up with the Internet home pages listed above for the latest data.

Any computer user with access to the Internet can also send and receive E-mail via CompuServe and America Online. For CompuServe, type "**Internet:73441,1406@cis.com**" and for America Online, use the command: "**Internet:dkhanna@aol.com**".

Serious Volcanology on the Information Super Highway

For those with access to a modum and Internet, a major revelation will come with the discovery of the National Center for Supercomputing Application's program called **"Mosaic"**. Mosaic is an information browser that runs on the **"World Wide Web"**. "The Web" offers an endless source of information in the form of text and images for virtually every topic imaginable.

There are several sources of information (called "Home Pages") available that are dedicated to volcanology. Following is a short summary of what is out there along with the addresses (formally called the "URL" for Universal Resource Location) that one uses in Mosaic to get to a specific home page.

Some of the Pages that relate to Mount Rainier and Mount St. Helens are:

The NASA EOS Volcanology Team (URL = **http://www.geo.mtu.edu/eos/**)

EOS will be a set of 23 satellites that will start to fly in 1998, and will collect long-term data sets about the Earth and its climate. This home page includes a general introduction to the EOS mission, a list of the Volcanology Team members and collaborators, a discussion of the volcanic phenomena that are being studied using remote sensing, several slide sets that present illustrations of the volcanoes that are studied by the Team. A lot of other information related to up-coming NASA missions can also be accessed via this server.

Volcano World (URL = **http://volcano.und.nodak.edu/**)

A second project under the NASA Cooperative Agreement Notice is Volcano World: which is run by the University of North Dakota. The intent of Volcano World is to bring the excitement of volcanology to the general public, particularly those who visit **Mt. St. Helens** .This interaction with the community is demonstrated by one of the sections of this home page that enables Internet users to send questions to volcanologists and get an electronic reply.

There are some very useful pieces of information for the layman interested in volcanoes at this Home Page such as how to become a volcanologist, news on current and recent eruptions, images of volcanoes, a tour of volcanoes, volcano lessons, a volcano slide show, and other sources of information about volcanoes.

University of Washington Volcano Systems Center

(URL = http://www.vsc.washington.edu/) Numerous research activities of the Volcano Systems Center are described (along with a list of the faculty conducting this research). These activities include research on Mt. Rainier; volcano monitoring; magmatic processes and petrology; mid-ocean ridge processes; geophysics and tectonics of volcanic systems; volcanic stratigraphy; chronology and geomorphology; volcano-atmosphere interactions; and biology of volcanic environments.

Cascades Volcano Observatory (URL= **http://vulcan.wr.usgs.gov/home.html**)

This server contains an excellent description of the continuing volcano studies at the Cascades Volcano Observatory, including a discussion of volcanic emissions and global climate change and the Volcano Disaster Assistance Program. In addition, there are some fine photographs of many of the **Cascades Volcanoes**, including 50 images (with captions) of **Mt. St. Helens** that show the 1980 eruption from its earliest days, the distribution of the May 18th, 1980 deposits, the growth of the dome in 1981 to 1990, and some interesting "before and after" pictures.

Space Shuttle photos (URL = **http://images.jsc.nasa.gov/html/earth.htm**)

These images are some of the photographs from the most recent Space Shuttle flights. While the content of the home page is not strictly dedicated to volcanology, the astronauts often see a volcano erupting so there are many volcano pictures here. The photographs have been digitized (the original images were taken on photographic film) and are listed by Shuttle mission. The images are sorted by latitude, longitude and time during the mission.

Space Shuttle Radar (SIR-C/X-SAR) images

(URL = **http://www.jpl.nasa.gov/sircxsar.html**)

This is part of the Public Information Home Page at the Jet Propulsion Laboratory, Pasadena, California, and shows some of the radar images that were collected during the April and October (1994) flights of the SIR-C/X-SAR system including one of Mt. Rainier (following).

The Mountain on E-Mail

Puget Sound Internet users have their own set of acronyms to describe various local phenomenon. Right up there with CBC ("catered by Costco"), and BTBB ("bad traffic, both bridges") is TMOT: "The Mountain's out today!"

If you want to contact us, fax us at (206) 277-8780, or you can e-mail us at "**rainier@tcm.nbs.net**"

Outer Space

NASA photo

One of the objectives of the 64th space-shuttle "Mission to Planet Earth" study in 1994 was to take photographs and radar images of Mount Rainier. The purpose was two-fold: to compare them to a similar but more active volcano in Siberia, in the hope they will learn more about potential mudflows that could threaten local communities in the event of an eruption here.

They also wanted to compare the Mount Rainier images with ones taken during a similar shuttle mission earlier in the year. Because the Endeavor flew at a path with a 57 degree inclination to the equator, it produced 3-D images of the mountain while orbiting over it at 138 miles high.

Copies of the above photo may be ordered from Pounds Photographic Labs, P.O. Box 35003, Dallas TX 75235. The cost is $6.00 for an 8 x 10 or $9.00 for an 11 x 14, or $18.95 for a 16 x 20, plus $4.50 shipping and handling. Ask for photo #STS064-51-027. There's also a beautiful shot of Mount St. Helens taken on the same mission. Its number is STS064-51-025. There's also a joint shot of Mounts Adams, St. Helens and Rainier (#STS047-73-058). You can see these on the internet under:

volcano.und.nodak.edu./vwdocs/volc_images/img_Adams.html

Global Positioning Systems

The park service acquired their own system in 1992, a GPS Pathfinder Professional and entered into an agreement with the EPA to use their GPS base station to achieve greater mapping accuracy. They will use their system to inventory and monitor social trails and other impacts, monitor elk plots, record spotted owl observations, map infrastructure and cultural resources, and other assorted projects.

Downstream

Mount Rainier is the headwaters to five major river systems: the Carbon, the Puyallup, the White, the Nisqually, and the Cowlitz., All originate within the park's boundaries and constitute the "life-blood" of downstream communities. All have large hydro-electric generating plants located on them, dependent on the glaciers and waters originating within the Park.

Power to the People

With the advent of electricity, it didn't take long for the good people of Puget Sound to realize that the mountain could give them more than beauty, it could give them POWER! More water descended from the heights of Mount Rainier to the sea, than from any other single area in the lower United States. Early hydraulic engineers estimated that the minimum flow of the mountain's rivers was more than 1200 c.f.s. (cubic feet per second), with an average flow of at least twice that figure.

Tacoma was the first to take advantage of all that wasted power. In 1904, the construction of the Electron plant of the Puget Sound Power Company began. The water was diverted from the Puyallup River about ten miles from the end of the glacier, at 1,750 elevation. It was then carried ten miles in an open flume to a reservoir where four steel penstocks, each four feet in diameter, drop it to the power house, 900 feet below. The original plant generated 28,000 horse power, at a pressure of 60,000 volts, which supplied power to Tacoma, twenty-five miles distant.

On the larger White River, near Buckley, the Pacific Coast Power Company diverted the water via dam and an eight-mile canal to Lake Tapps, elevation 540 feet. From there it went to the generating plant at Dieringer where 100,000 horse power was ultimately produced.

In 1912, a plant was built on the Nisqually which was dammed at the canyon (elevation 970 feet). The water was then carried through a 10,000 foot tunnel and over a bridge to a reservoir at La Grande. From there penstocks carried it down the side of the canyon to a 40,000 horse-power generating plant built on a narrow shelf above the river.

When Electricity came to the Park

Electricity came to the foothills in 1931, but the Park Service was generating their own electricity for two decades before that. The very first power plant was near Christine Falls. Then in 1920, about two miles above Longmire on the banks of the Nisqually River, a new power plant was built (by the Rainier National Park Company) which supplied electricity to both Longmire and Paradise. The faithful team who kept the facilities in power was Bert J. "Dynamo" Brouillet and his wife, who for eleven years, never had a day off together. One of them was always on duty within earshot of the whirling dynamos and turbines, day and night, summer and winter. The reason it was always within earshot, was because the power plant was in the basement of their house. Aside from keeping things humming, they had to clear the dam of rocks and river debris, and chop ice from the dam. As of 1931, Mr. Brouillet was the second oldest Park Service employee from the standpoint of service. He was a 15-year employee at that point.

Older hikers may remember the surprise of first coming upon a beautiful little handmade windmill, then a small cottage with a manicured yard, nestled in the forest above Longmire. Some of the old large wooden-stave water pipes bound with wire adjoining the Wonderland Trail are still there. The small generating plant put out 13,600 volts on the park's power lines.

As a later power plant operator noted, this is a good job. Where else could you work beside a trail called Wonderland, and a river called Paradise?

Populations Surrounding the Mountain

Mount Rainier towers over a population of more than 2.5 million people in the Seattle-Tacoma area. The mountain's drainage system via the Columbia River potentially affects another 500,000 residents of southwestern Washington and northwest Oregon. Pierce County had a population increase of 21% in the last decade, while Lewis County had 6%, and Yakima County 9%.

Dams

Alder Dam: Completed in 1945, Alder Dam is 285 feet high, and has a storage capacity of 244,000 acre ft. This dam straddles Pierce, Thurston and Lewis counties, and covers a drainage area of 286 square miles. The average annual generation is 228,000,000 kWH.

Butterworth Dam: fed by waters from Eden Creek in Pierce County. Built in 1949, the dam is 51 feet high, and is owned by the Washington State Department of Wildlife.

Cowlitz Falls Dam: Lewis County PUD, a new 140-foot high, 700-foot wide dam opened August, 1994. The distinction of this dam is that it took 3 years to build, but 16 years to get through the licensing and permit process. This dam can generate up to 70 Megawatts of power, which is enough to provide 1/3 of Lewis County's total power needs.

Derringer: (Sumner) fed by the White River, this dam was built in 1911, and is 18 feet high. It's reservoir is Lake Tapps.

Electron: (Kapowsin) This was the very first dam to harness power from Mount Rainier waters. Though only 7 feet high, this small diversion dam still generates electricity for Puget Sound Power and Light.

Edith Creek Basin Dam (This is the Paradise water supply).

Frozen Lake Dam (This is the Sunrise water supply).

LaGrande Dam: The first dam was built in 1912, the second in 1945 by Tacoma Public Utilities. 192 Feet high. The drainage area is 292 square miles.

The average annual power generation is 345,000,000 kWH, which is transmitted via two 115 kV lines 25 miles to the Cowlitz Substation..

Lindstrom Dam on Lake Kapowsin (privately owned residential dam).

Mayfield Dam: Built by the City of Tacoma on the Cowlitz in 1963. The drainage area is 1,400 sq. miles. The average annual power generation is 804,000,000 kWH. The energy flows to BPA lines over 230kV lines.

Mossyrock Dam: This 1968 Dam on the Cowlitz River serves a drainage area of 1,042 sq. miles. and generates an annual output of 1,100,000,000 kWH. The energy flows to Bonneville Power Administration lines over 230kV lines.

Mud Mountain Dam: 7 miles SE of Enumclaw off Highway 410, is one of the highest earth and rock flood-control dams. The park features a nature trail, wading pool, playground, picnic areas and overlooks. This dam was built by the U.S. Corps of Army engineers to reduce flooding in the Lower White and Puyallup valleys. There is no power generation from this dam. The dam is open daily from 9 a.m. until dusk. Free admission.

Stud Company Log Pond Dam: Private dam

In addition, Bumping Lake, Clear Creek and Tieton (Rimrock) were built by the U.S. Bureau of Reclamation as storage dams.

Reservoirs Fed by Mount Rainier Waters

Alder Reservoir (lower) is fed by the Nisqually River. Length of the reservoir is 7 miles. Miles of shoreline: 28. Reservoir area at max elevation: 3,065 acres. Reservoir content: 214,500 acre feet. Reservoir elevation (full) 1,207 feet above sea level.

Butterworth Reservoir off Eden Creek in Pierce County. Built in 1949, the reservoir is 70 square acres.

Davisson Lake: Tours begin at the "Hydrovista" near Mayfield. Viewpoint. Museum. Picnic grounds. Two Parks, Mayfield Lake State Park and Lewis County Park, are both on Mayfield Lake. Swimming, boating and trout fishing. Davisson Lake behind Mossyrock Dam also offers recreational facilities.

Eden Creek Reservoir also off Eden Creek in Pierce County is only 10 acres, and is owned by the Washington Dept. of Wildlife.

Electron Reservoir - Puyallup River, has been owned by Puget Sound Power and Light since 1937.

La Grande Reservoir - Nisqually River. On the border of Thurston and Pierce Counties, this reservoir is behind the La Grande Dam operated by Tacoma City Light. First built in 1912 and enlarged in 1945, it provides water for Alder Dam. The reservoir is downstream but north of Alder Lake reservoir on the Nisqually River. The name is derived from the community of La Grande in Pierce County. Reservoir length: 1.5 miles. Miles of shoreline: 3.5. Reservoir area at max elevation: 450 acres. Reservoir content: 2,700 acre feet.

Lake Tapps - White River (Derringer Power Plant) 2,570 acres.

Luhr Creek Reservoir - Nisqually Flats

McMillan Reservoir - Puyallup River, owned by Tacoma City Light and completed in 1912. Size 9 acres, height 30 feet.

Mud Mountain Reservoir (Lake Isaac I. Stevens) White River

Fish Hatcheries

On the Cowlitz: The world's largest salmon and trout hatcheries are at the tiny towns of Ethel and Salkum, are. Both are just beyond two Tacoma City Light dams, Mayfield and Mossyrock. Both are open for inspection.

At the Salkum Hatchery, you can see a high-tech nursery in action when up to twenty-five hundred fish per hour move upriver. Using push button controls, salmon and trout are sorted and routed into various holding ponds. Eggs are first hatched in trays, then moved outdoors into rearing ponds. Eventually the fingerlings are released into the Cowlitz. From there they will head down to the Columbia River, and then out to sea. So strong is their homing instinct, when they return in three or four years, they'd try to get back into the pans they were spawned in if they could. It used to be only the best specimens were used for propagation, now, to maintain genetic diversity, all are used.

Mossyrock: To help the salmon runs, twenty million dollars of rearing facilities augment the blocked upstream spawning beds.

The propagation process for trout is similar. When the annual quota of 480,000 pounds of fish is reached, fish not required for pond rearing are moved in aerated tanker trucks to Davisson Lake behind Mossyrock Dam. There they are released to spawn naturally. A large pipe by-passes the dam so they don't get ground up in the giant turbines.

Nisqually: One interesting note. Some tagged fish from Russia were found going up the Nisqually. Considering the phenomenally accurate homing instincts fish have, this was highly unusual.

Nisqually River Interpretive Center Foundation

With the goal of the establishing a Nisqually River Interpretive Center which would interpret the rich natural and cultural resources of the Nisqually River Basin, a number of federal, state and local government representatives, corporate sponsors and civic leaders banded together to bring the project into reality.

In 1993, they established the Foundation, developed a model for the facility, hired an architect, and searched for a site between Roy and McKenna as the location of the Center. Efforts are now underway to raise funds, acquire land, and continue planning for the proposed facility and program.

William Dengler, the Chief Park Interpreter represents the park as secretary of the Foundation. Donations for the facility may be sent to him at the park.

Rainier water by the bottle

The *purest* sparkling mountain water these days comes out of a bottle.

Entrepreneur Jon Corriveau is first and foremost a lover of Mount Rainier. He has stood on the summit 28 times. One evening a few years ago, as he perched on a ridge watching the sun disappear in the west, he thought to himself, "if a guy could just bottle this..." The idea caught his imagination, and he spent a year wrangling over permits with half a dozen government agencies. In November 1992, after receiving the final blessing of the Department of Ecology, Corriveau backed up a 6,000 gallon truck to the Carbon River just outside the park boundary, and the rest, as they say, is history.

It's then trucked to Everett where an elaborate multi-step graduated filtering system removes the silt, glacial till and organic matter, and voile! Corriveau now offers his snow-flavored nectar of the Carbon as "Tahoma Pure Glacier Water" to a devoted following. Tahoma is the only true bottled *glacier water* in the continental U.S. Other bottled waters use the words "pure" and "mountain", but Jon's says, "Source: Carbon Glacier"

In case you've ever been curious about the chemical makeup of Mount Rainier's water, the analysis run on Tahoma Pure Glacier Water is: Bicarbonates: 8.0, Calcium: 2.4, Magnesium: 0.5, Chlorides: 0.0, Sulfates: 0.0, Nitrates: 0.1, ph: 6.8, Total Dissolved: 30 ppm, Sodium: (per 236 ml): 0.4.

Knowing the mountain as he does, Corriveau realizes his business could go down the drain if Mom Nature has mood swing. "If the Mountain blows, we'll be out of business tomorrow," he says. "We've even thought of marketing it that way: Tahoma Glacier Water: Get it while you can!"

Corriveau, however, was not the first to come up with the idea of bottling the mountain's cool refreshing nectar. In 1904, the Mount Tacoma Water Supply Company held two (mining) claims near Mowich Lake. But it was not gold, silver or copper that the company had their mind on, it was the water! *(Archives, Mount Rainier NP)*.

Some Berry Big Statistics

Copper Creek Restaurant's Jennie Zuelich has baked in excess of 118,214 of her famous Wild Blackberry pies between 1954 and 1994. The figure is actually much higher, (probably closer to 164,000 pies) since there were 15 years when no records were kept.

Volcanology

The Other Side of the Mountain

As we lovingly admire the shimmering gossamer beauty in our big backyard, we tend to forget that Mount Rainier is a volcano, - a dormant, but definitely not dead volcano. Lying silently beneath the white mantle is more energy and power than all the world's nuclear weapons, . . . with fragile flowers adorning the bomb casing. It's somehow like the hippies of the 60's who stuck flowers in the National Guardsmen's rifles. They were still rifles. Mount Rainier is still a volcano.

Rainier's little sister, Mount Saint Helens, gave us a preview of The Big Show. Mount Rainier will be The Main Event. The big question is not if, but when, this life-changing occurrence will take place. As Janet Tanaka, editor and publisher of *Volcano Quarterly* wryly puts it, Mount Rainier is not dead, she's only pausing between eruptions!

The "Ring of Fire"

Like giant beads on a thread, most volcanoes occur in belts or chains. Mount Rainier is a major component of "the Ring of Fire," an arc of volcanoes rimming the Pacific Ocean from North America to Asia. The segment of which it is a part extends from Northern California's Lassen Peak for over 600 miles to the south, (and includes a dozen volcanic peaks), to British Columbia's Mount Garibaldi in the north & are called the Cascade Volcanoes.

The Ring of Fire volcanoes which rim the Pacific Ocean all belong to the subduction-volcano class. Subduction-related volcanoes all occur about 125 miles inland from the oceanic trench, a phenomenon which is probably related to a zone of extensive vertical fractures caused by the buckling of the overlying plate.

The island arcs of New Zealand, the southwest Pacific, Indonesia, the Philippines, Japan, Kuriles, Kamchatka, and the Aleutians comprise the western side of the Ring of Fire. The western spine of North and South America, - the Cascade Range, the highlands of Mexico and Central America, and the Andes Range, complete the eastern side of the Ring.

Other (American) "Ring of Fire" Volcanic Eruptions

Compared to all the reports of volcanic activity a hundred years ago, this century has been quiet. In 1843, pioneer reports said both Mounts Baker and St. Helens were erupting at the same time. (Actually according to Oregon newspapers, St Helens erupted November 22, 1842.) In 1858, they said the clouds over Mount Baker reflected red from the crater. In 1859, The Portland *Weekly Oregonian* reported spectacular volcanic activity and "intermittent columns of fire" emanating from the crater on Mount Hood for two days. The only Cascade eruptions this century were Mounts Lassen in 1914, and Mount St. Helens in 1980.

A forest supervisor reported to the Redding (CA) paper, "Mt. Lassen awoke without a twitch. It is erupting from a new crater on the north slope, close to the summit. The new crater had deep fissures radiating in all directions."

Two weeks shy of a year later, Lassen did it again. Viewers saw a red line appear at the crater rim, then with tremendous explosions, lava spilled through the notch and down the slope for 1,000 feet. The resulting mudflow came down the mountain and then up and over a divide. Boulders weighing twenty tons were swept several miles.

The trees resembled those after St. Helens blew, with all tops pointing away, bark sandblasted away, and grit driven an inch into the wood.

Mount Mazama, in southern Oregon, had a history of thousands of years of violent eruptions with the resulting ash and pumice covering 350,000 square miles, (including a distinctive layer at Mount Rainier). Finally, about 6,700 years ago, it blew out an estimated 42 cubic miles of pyroclastic material, expanded from 16 cubic miles of liquid magma. This undermined the summit, causing it to collapse, and creating one of the world's largest calderas, which is 6 miles wide and nearly 2,000 feet deep. That caldera is Crater Lake.

Evidence of Other Volcanic Eruptions on Mount Rainier

A trip on the trails of Mount Rainier means you may also be walking on a little bit of Mount St. Helens and Mount Mazama as well as some from an older, higher Mount Rainier.

Mount St. Helens left two deposits of pumice on the park, about 3,300 and 450 years ago. There's also a layer of volcanic ash which documents the great eruption of Mount Mazama about 6,900 years ago. It's worth noting that there is so much Mazama ash spread around the Pacific NW and into Canada that it is a very distinctive age marker for timing other geological and archeological events.

The following chart shows a "color key" to the various pumice layers on the mountain. Mount Rainier threw out a small amount of pumice sometime between 1820 and 1854, although the most conspicuous pumice from Mount Rainier is about 2,000 years old. It is found primarily on the east side of the park, and ranges in size from pea to walnut size.

COLOR	SOURCE	AGE IN YEARS	DEPTH	WHERE FOUND
Light gray	St. Helens	15	Sand-1"	All over
Olive-Gray	Rainier	100-150	1"	NE>E
White	St. Helens	450	Sand	All over
Brown	Rainier	2,150-2,500	1/4-8"	N-NE-E
Yellow	St. Helens	3,250-4,000	Sand	All over
Brown	Rainier	5,800-6,600	1/4-6"	E->SE
Brown	Rainier	58,00-6,600	1/4-2"	SE
Yellowish	Mt. Mazama	About 6,600	1-3"	All over
Red-Brown	Rainier	8,750-11,000	1/4-1"	NNE>SSE

Pumice Data courtesy Dr. R. Mullineaux, USGS

When Mount St. Helens Erupted

It had the symmetrical beauty of Mount Fuji, a perfect picture of peace and serenity. But in mid-March of 1980, that 123 years of peace was interrupted by earthquakes. From the time the quakes began, they increased in magnitude and frequency, and by March 25, were occurring at the rate of 40 per hour.

March 27, a gas and steam eruption blasted a crater in the summit, and Mount Saint Helens was officially back from the dead. Each day showed new activity as molten rock moved beneath the mountain. In early May an ominous bulge on the north face began forming, and continued to swell until the May 18 eruption.

Since Mount Saint Helens is the first of the Cascade volcanoes to erupt under present day scrutiny and technology, it gave scientists a first hand look at what might be expected among other northwest volcanoes. St. Helens didn't just spring to life and erupt one day. There were many signs: earthquakes, increases in temperature, the ground swelling, etc., that gave warning something was happening.

The eruption itself began with a magnitude 5.1 earthquake which shook the volcano, and triggered a collapse of the bulging north flank. The enormous volume of rock, snow and ice swept down the mountain's north flank at speeds exceeding 200 mph. Part of the avalanche poured into Spirit Lake, temporarily forcing much of the water onto the surrounding hill sides before pouring back

Mount Rainier as seen from the "new" Mt. St. Helens   Charles Anderson photo

into the basin, and rapidly raising the lake's surface level by 200 feet. A second part of the avalanche went up and over the top of a 1,200 foot ridge. A third section of the debris flow raced down the North Fork Toutle River, filling the river valley to a depth in places from over 100 to over 500 feet - where it poured over the ridge into a tributary valley.

With the sudden loss of the north flank of the volcano, pent-up hydrothermal pressure inside the mountain exploded with an atom-bomb strength lateral blast of pulverized rock, hot gasses and organic material. The blast traveled at speeds up to 250 mph and with a temperature over 600° F. Everything, - vegetation, wildlife, (and a few people) up to 6 miles north of the volcano was exterminated. The heat of the eruption melted vast volumes of ice and snow. Lahars (mudflows) surged down the slopes, picking up and carrying along everything in their path - trees, rocks, bridges, houses, even logging camps. One mudflow eventually poured into the Columbia River, 75 miles away, causing the river's channel depth to decrease from 40 to 15 feet for a distance of 2 miles.

Lightning bolts shot through the clouds thousands of feet high. Soon the ash extended to an altitude of 70,000 feet.

Back at the mountain, pyroclastic flows covered an area of over 6 square miles to a depth of up to 125 feet. The blast affected an area of over 215 square miles. When it was finally over, Mount St. Helens had lost 1,313 feet and was reduced to just 8,364 feet high.

Mount Rainier's Reaction to the St. Helens Eruption

Mount Rainier handled the big event graciously, as if watching a little sister have a temper tantrum. She observed, but did not take part. She recorded St. Helens' earthquakes, but gave no sympathetic rumbles of her own. She just got dusted with the ash.

Closed by Special Event...

"Eruption of St. Helens shut down the park for a few days because of ash difficulty and water turbidity." -*1980 issue, Rainier National Park Daily Bulletin*

An inch of ash rained at Longmire, and the park was closed indefinitely. About 100 permanent Mount Rainier personnel stayed put, but all tourists hurriedly left the mountain. It was feared the park's water supply would be contaminated by the ash.

And what did Mount Rainier do while sister St. Helens erupted? Nothing!

The Saintly Sister

Mount St. Helens, Mount Rainier's hot tempered southerly sibling, has lots of things, but an apostrophe is not one of them. James J. Kilpatrick of *The Writer's Art*, Charleston, SC points out the volcano is named after a man named St. Helens, and is not the possession of some holy person named Helen. In cartography, even in the case of singular proper nouns, the apostrophe has disappeared. Thus it's Grants Pass, Indian Henrys Hunting Ground, etc. *(Volcano Quarterly)*

Viewing Mount St. Helens from Mount Rainier

There are spectacular views of Mount St. Helens from Mount Rainier, however all require hikes of between 1.5 to 7 miles to see them. The problem is that you have to climb high enough to see over the Tatoosh Range.

The best viewing spots are:

- **From Paradise.** Alta Vista Trail. 1.5 miles, elevation gain 540' or Skyline Trail to Glacier Vista and Panorama Point. 5 miles, elevation gain 1,400'
- **From Pinnacle Peak.** 2.5 miles, elevation gain 1,140'
- **From Eagle Peak.** 7 miles, elevation gain 2,955'
- **From Van Trump Park.** 5.5 miles, elevation gain 1,900'
- **From Tolmie Peak.** 5.8 miles, elevation gain 1,010'

Another easy way to see the dangers associated with both Mount St. Helens and Mount Rainier is to view the volcanic-hazards exhibit in the Henry M. Jackson Visitor Center. Equally interesting are the "Earthquakes" and "Glaciers" exhibits in the main exhibit room at the same center. These displays were all prepared for the Park by the U.S. Geological Survey.

The Building of Mount Rainier

The Cascade Range was formed by crustal upwarping during Pliocene time between 5 and 2 million years ago, but Mount Rainier and the other Cascade volcanoes, were formed during the Pleistocene "Ice Ages," since then, and are young by geologic standards. A volcano psychologist would diagnose volcanoes as having manic- depressive mood swings. While lava and pumice work to build a mountain up, glaciers and erosion work day and night to tear it down.

Geologic Time Scale	Years Ago	Geologic Events in Park
Holocene	Present to 3,000	Little Ice Age: Rebirth and re-advance of glaciers. Building of new summit cone.
	5,000	Summit of Rainier destroyed by avalanches that formed huge mudflows.
	10,000	
Pleistocene	25,000	Last major glaciation.
		Birth and growth of Rainier volcano and repeated glaciation.
	2-3 million	
Pliocene		Uplift and erosion of Cascade Range.
	12 million	
Miocene		Intrusion of Ganodiorite. Folding of older rocks. Deposition of Fifes Peak (andesite and basalt flows) and Stevens Ridge (hot pumice flows) Formations.
	26 million	
Oligocene		Deposits of Ohanapecosh Formation (sandstone and breccia).
	37-38 million	
Eocene		Deposition of Puget Group (sandstone, shale and coal).
	53-54 million	

Prepared by Dwight R. Crandell and Donal R. Mullineaux, U.S. Geologic Survey, Denver Colorado. 6/64, Revised 4/66 and 4/71

The Formation of Mount Rainier

50 million years ago, during the Eocene Epoch, Mount Rainier and the Cascade Range did not exist. The broad lowlands were occupied by lakes, rivers and ocean embayments. There were volcanic eruptions both on land and under water, which spread debris across huge areas which formed layers of volcanic breccia of the Ohanapecosh Formation. Eruptions during the Oligocene and Miocene periods formed thick layers of volcanic ash and lava flows on the land. These rocks form the Stevens Ridge and Fifes Peak Formations.

After these rocks formed, they crumpled into folds, broken with faults, and uplifted into northwest-trending mountains. At about the same time, a mass of molten rock moved up into the lower part of the older rocks. As the molten rock cooled and solidified, it formed grandiorite, a pretty light-gray rock, similar to granite. After these northwest-trending mountains were worn down to low hills, the north-trending Cascade Range began to rise across them. Thus before Mount Rainier was born, the Cascades were already a rugged range whose crest was about 6,000 high.

Then between half a million and a million years ago, molten rock began to flow as much as 15 miles from the central vent of what was the beginnings of Mount Rainier. Later eruptions of ash and pumice alternating with andesitic lava flows gradually built up the high main cone. In roughly the same time frame, Mounts Baker, Adams and Hood and Glacier Peak were also forming.

No sooner had the eruptions diminished, than the new volcano began to deteriorate by explosion, erosion and collapse. It is believed that at it's highest, Mount Rainier was about 16,000' in elevation. *(Dwight R. Crandell and D. Mullineaux, USGS)*.

Evidence of Other Volcanic Eruptions of Mount Rainier

Mount Rainier had several minor eruptions in the 19th century, the last being in 1883 according to Charles Wood, editor of *Volcanoes of North America.* Although Indian and pioneer accounts note fourteen minor eruptions last century. (Although most were probably just cloud caps.)

Though most people think of Mount Adams and Mount St. Helens as being Mount Rainier's closest sibling volcanoes, according to Mr. Wood, the even-closer Goat Rocks are the remains of an old stratovolcano, and there are the remains of lava flows just south of White Pass.

Other Mount Rainier eruptions last century were reported to have taken place in 1843, 1854, 1858, 1870 and 1892. Indian legends tell of a great cataclysmic outburst in times past. The most recent pumice from Mount Rainier (found mostly on the northeast and east sides of the park), was thrown out sometime between 1820 and 1854. It is olive-gray in color and is a layer about 1" thick.

The Palisades

At several places within the Park, magma broke through to the surface, initiating a series of explosive volcanic eruptions. Only small remnants of the resulting pyroclastic rocks have survived erosion, but one of these remnants forms the Palisades, a great cliff in the northeastern part of the park. The Palisades are a mass of welded tuff at least 800 feet thick and contain the tallest columnar rock in the world. *(Fiske, Hopson and Waters)*

Andesite Columns

Before the Mount Rainier volcano began to take form, probably early in the Pleistocene era, the first Mount Rainier eruptions were voluminous lava flows of pyroxene andesite. These flows spilled westward down the canyons of the ancestral Mowich and Puyallup Rivers, astride which the volcano grew. There are many good examples of the hexagonal andesite columns around the park.

Remnants of Former Mount Rainier

Remains of the dike systems radiating from the summit known to be remnants of the originally higher mountain help form some of the sharp ridges and spires on Rainier's flanks such as Little Tahoma, the Puyallup Cleaver (including Tokaloo Rock and Tokaloo Spire), the ridge separating Winthrop Glacier and Inter Glacier, and Gibraltar Rock. The former height of Mount Rainier was projected to be 2,000 feet higher.

Unlike recently measured 14,411.1" summit which has felt the footsteps of only a mere few thousand climbers, millions of Puget Sound residents have stood on material that may have originated at the summit of the former higher Mount Rainier. Everyone who has ever set foot in the Auburn-Kent valley has done just that, since that's where the old summit went, as part of the Osceola Mudflow about 5,800 years ago - an eruption at the summit triggered release of chemically and hydrothermally weakened rocks of the old crater area..

Studying the Hazards

For the answers to the concerns about Madam Rainier's internal rumblings and goings on, we look to those doctors of Volcanic gastroenterology and proctology, geologists from the U.S. Geological Survey and various universities. Since their first meeting with Ms. Rainier, they have taken her seismic pulse, and poked and probed her steam vents, fumaroles, fissures and crevasses. They know she's more than just a pretty face!

The Park Service itself lists Mount Rainier as "the most hazardous volcano in the Cascades in terms of its potential for magma-water interaction and sector collapse."

In 1971, some geophysicists from Scripps Institute of Oceanography at La Jolla and the Nuclear Science Laboratory at Los Alamos, NM, topped that. They told attendees at an American Geophysical Union meeting that "Mount Rainier is the most dangerous *of the most dangerous* objects on earth!". They added that it has the potential explosive power of a hundred nuclear bombs like the one at Hiroshima.

If that isn't enough to give one pause for thought, USGS hydrologist Kevin Scott describes Mount Rainier as a pile of volcanic debris nearly three miles high, and so heavy that "the crust underneath is quivering like a bowl of Jell-O." *(Valley Daily News 5/10/95).*

The Greatest Hazard is Just Plain Mud

Geologists worry that much of the volcanic rock in Mount Rainier's foundation could be converted to clay-like minerals by the chemical effects of acid gas seeping from underground.

"You might not even need an eruption or seismic event (to trigger a mudslide)," said Don Swanson, head of the USGS office at the University of Washington. "Perhaps this slow, continual changing of rock to clay is enough."

Jokulhlaups: Ancient "Big Ones"

During post-glacial time (the last 10,000 years), Mount Rainier has produced many large debris flows and avalanches which have periodically inundated parts of the now densely populated Puget Sound lowlands. The largest flows at Mount Rainier originated in huge volcanic landslides known as sector collapses which result in high-velocity debris flows that can be either wet or dry. The presence of water is not essential to their movement. *(Schuster and Crandell, 1984).* Debris avalanches at Mount Rainier probably have contained abundant water, as

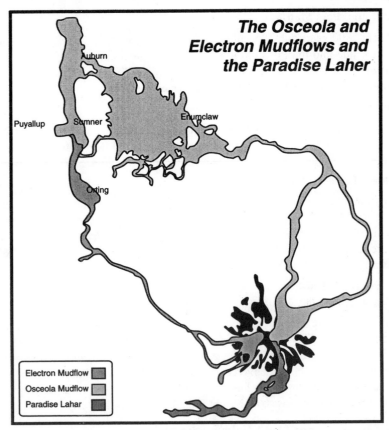

The Osceola and Electron Mudflows and the Paradise Laher

Auburn
Puyallup
Sumner
Enumclaw
Orting

Electron Mudflow
Osceola Mudflow
Paradise Lahar

suggested by their rapid transition to mud flows, common on the flanks of the volcano shortly after initiation. *(Scott and Vallance, 1995).*

The Osceola Mudflow

About 5600 to 5800 years ago one of the largest volcanic events in the mountain's "recent" history took place, when Mount Rainier experienced what has come to be known as the Osceola Mudflow. Violent steam explosions collapsed the summit, and scientists estimate that 2.7 billion cubic yards (about half a cubic mile) of debris the consistency of wet concrete avalanched down the mountain and flowed down the White River valley and across the Puget Sound lowland. It has been estimated that the mass towered 500 feet high when it passed the present site of the White River Campground. The flow spread out over more than 100 square miles, and covered the sites of present-day Enumclaw and Buckley with up to 70 feet of thick mud. The sites of Auburn, Kent, Sumner and Puyallup were also inundated. The height of the mountain dropped from about 16,000 feet to roughly its present height. The sector collapse that produced the Osceola Mudflow penetrated the hydrothermally altered core of the volcano more deeply than most such events. *(Scott and Vallance - 1995).*

The Round Pass Mudflow

About 2800 years ago 200 million cubic yards of volcanic debris came down the west side into the Puyallup River drainage. The volume of the Round Pass Mudflow was enough to temporarily fill the upper Tahoma Creek and South Puyallup valleys with at least 1000 feet of material *(Moir)*.

The National Mudflow

This Nisqually River drainage flow (named after the town of National), 1,200 and 700 radiocarbon years ago, was a hyperconcentrated flow until well beyond the boundary of the Puget Sound Lowland. *(Scott and Vallance - 1995)*.

Tahoma Creek Mudflow

Eight hundred years ago, Tahoma Creek experienced a monumental mudflow which wiped out an 800-year old forest below the glaciers. It began as a debris avalanche which transformed to a lahar. This lahar, of tremendous velocity, was the precursor of the many mudflows the Tahoma has experienced since 1967, most originating at South Tahoma Glacier.

The Electron Mudflow

This flow takes its name from the small settlement near the Electron power plant, near where the Puyallup River leaves Mount Rainier and enters the Puyallup Valley. The Electron occurred about 1350-1400 A.D. and buried the present site of the town of Orting, as well as the entire Puyallup Valley, 100 years before Columbus discovered America. The Electron Mudflow inundated at least 14 square miles of the Puget Sound lowland. And there was no eruption. It may have been set loose by a Mount Rainier earthquake.

The Orting Saga: Old Sticks in the Mud

Geologists have a strange practice. Whenever they see a hole in the ground, they look in it. Pat Pringle, a geologist with the Washington State Department of Natural Resources, happened to be driving through Orting in 1993, when he saw excavations for sewer lines at a new housing development. Piles of stumps and tree trunks, some up to seven feet in diameter, were being unearthed. Much to Pringle's delight, he discovered the perfectly preserved remains of an old-growth forest wiped out by the Electron Mudflow 600 years ago.

In the area of Orting, the mudflow covered the valley floor to a depth of 15 feet. The top several feet of muck finally dried out, but locked in moisture which preserved the wood below. The uprooted trees rotted to about three feet below the surface, but beneath three feet, they were as good as new. Pringle whipped out his handy chain-saw, and cut a collection of tree ring samples from the excavated logs, which he will use to study. The tree cross-sections will read like a diary, telling what the climate in this area was for several hundred years before the stumps were buried. They will also help pinpoint when the Electron Mudflow occurred. Already Pringle has been able to determine that it occurred in the spring, probably April or May.

There's more than idle curiosity to Pringle's interest in the Electron Mudflow. Says he, " There's more to fear from the giant slumbering in our backyard than a full-scale eruption. Rock at the base of the mountain is being severely hydrothermally altered by the acidic steam and hot fluids inside the mountain. At some point," says Pringle, " the wall of rock is going to collapse. We're talking about an enormous, elongated wave of mud. The one that swept through the present-day site of Electron 600 years ago, left a bathtub ring of sorts 100 feet above the valley floor.

It will probably be an hour or two after the collapse at Mount Rainier before the mudflow reaches Orting and Puyallup. That's not a lot of time to evacuate those who live and work in the lowlands."

As evidence of how swiftly the Electron flow moved, he points out that many of the trees he observed in the trench had been ripped out by the roots, and that some of those that hadn't been swept from its path had been eroded by as much as 19 inches in the muddy current. "It was as if someone had cut into them." The largest of the rocks unearthed at the site was a 15-foot chunk that originated at Sunset amphitheater on Rainier's upper west flank. *(Puyallup Herald - 10/15/93)*

Jokulhlaups: *Recent* Big ones

In the park's history, there have been over a dozen witnessed glacial outbursts/mudflows (Jokuhlaups: pronounced "yo-kul-h-loips") more commonly known as mudflows or lahars. A mudflow is a viscous mass like wet cement, which is a mix of liquidized mountain chunks of glacial ice, rocks, dirt, water, trees, vegetation, bridges, buildings, and anything else in its path. Over the years, the glaciers have taken turns trying to outdo each other in power displays.

Kautz Creek. The largest lahar since the establishment of the park occurred about 11 p.m. the night of October 2, 1947. The Kautz Creek mudflow moved an estimated 50-million cubic yards of liquid mountain 5-1/2 miles into the Kautz valley, wiping out or killing everything in its path. It took the builders of the Hoover Dam three years to move 8-million cubic yards of rock and earth. Kautz Creek did six times that amount in fifteen hours and filled in 1/3 of Alder Reservoir's capacity.

South Tahoma. In 1967, The Tahoma Glacier delivered a surprise mudflow, which, it turned out, was to be the first of many. In a matter of minutes, the river reached a high-water mark of 15 feet in the vicinity of the Wonderland Trail before burying the Tahoma Creek Campground downstream. Since 1967, at least 20 such flows have swept down this deceptively quiet little creek, including at least one each year from 1986 through 1990. The erosion of these passing flows has deepened the gorge under the Wonderland Trail bridge from 30 feet to 80 feet just since 1986.

During one 1988 slide, 39 cars and their occupants were stranded when the South Tahoma glacier dumped boulders, mud and car-sized blocks of ice across the West Side road.

Nisqually River. People don't usually think of the Nisqually when they think of mudflows, but the fact is, it's been one of the more active mudflow producers. Jokulhlaups damaged or destroyed bridges over the Nisqually River in 1926, 1932, 1934 and 1955. The present bridge withstood floods in 1968, 1970, 1972, and 1985.

At the Glacier Bridge, look at the levees constructed by debris flows in the 1930's and 50's and at the weathered concrete and twisted rebar standing as memorials to the 1930's bridge that used to stand about 100 yards upstream.

photo courtesy of Larry Penberthy

This 1960's Infra-red image revealed the heat from the mountain.

Hot Spots

Mount Rainier is a dichotomy of side-by-side fire and ice. It is raw power decorated with snowy white icing and garnished with garlands of flowers and evergreens. At the summit there are 175° steam vents beside -23° ice. Around the mountain, geothermally heated water, better known as "hot springs", bubble at far-flung Ohanapecosh and Longmire, 36 miles distant. They're also in Moraine Park, and there are 'mud pots' on the way to the old Paradise Ice Caves. The thermal springs are indicators of the far-ranging subsurface thermal activity. On the flanks, climbers are occasionally startled to hear loud reports and see columns of vapor emit from crevices in the rocks. In 1961 a steam vent opened near Gibraltar Rock, and a column of pressurized vapor shot 200 feet in the air raining debris on the nearby Cowlitz Glacier.

Hot springs are formed by ground water seeping down until it finally reaches either shallow intrusions of magma beneath the earth's surface, or rock heated by contact with the magma. Other hot springs in the area are just outside the park in Packwood, where there's a 70°F trickle on bedrock, in an area often submerged by the Cowlitz River. These springs are reached by private road in the Gifford Pinchot National Forest. Also in the Gifford Pinchot are 70° springs on Deception Creek (no pool or path), and 70°F springs on Orr Creek (no pool, bad bushwhack to get to them.)

In 1969 on the Emmons Glacier, subsurface heat warmed and melted glacial ice into a network of potholes and crevasses, in places opening gaps in the ice wide enough to reveal the bare bedrock beneath the glacier.

The Thermal Groups

The thermal features of the park fall into six separate groups:

- The summit thermal area
- The upper-flank thermal areas
- Winthrop Springs*
- Paradise Springs*
- Longmire Mineral Springs
- Ohanapecosh Hot Springs

* The Winthrop and Paradise Springs on the lower flanks are thought to all be part of a single geothermal system within the edifice of Mount Rainier volcano. The Longmire and Ohanapecosh systems are separate systems of limited extent.

Mount Rainier Natural Resources Inventory

Earthquake faults at the Mountain

Geologists have concluded that the Pacific Northwest experiences a massive earthquake every 300 to 500 years. An earthquake under a volcano serves as a reminder that the real estate on top is not dead, simply dormant. An average of 30 - 40 earthquakes occur under Mount Rainier per year, which makes it the third most seismically active volcano in the Cascade Range after (1) Mount St. Helens, and (2) Mount Lassen, to the south. Over the past 20 years, Rainier has been jolted by more than 800 earthquakes, including six large enough to be felt.

"Seismic monitoring is a quantitative way of saying something about the vigor of a mountain," says Dr. Steve Malone, UW seismologist. "I don't know if it's a valid predictor of volcanic activity, but as a seismologist, that's what I go by. If nothing goes bump in the night, nothing is going to happen. But if the earthquakes come in furious succession, ('swarms,') and continue for three days while growing in intensity, an eruption is likely. Swarms preceded the eruption of Mount St. Helens, but they are missing at Mount Rainier."

Malone believes most of the seismic activity is related to regional tectonics - the Juan de Fuca oceanic plate butting up against and subducting beneath the North American Plate. He hopes new work on Rainier will enable seismologists to hone techniques for distinguishing between tectonic and volcanic events.

For example, the west side of the mountain is more seismically active than the east side. The area, called the Western Rainier Seismic Zone, is 7 or 8 miles west of the mountain, and is about a 30-mile long zone of earthquake activity. The zone runs in a North-South direction, and the quakes are reasonably deep, between 6 to 10 miles. There is no evidence of faulting on the surface. Thus when we hear there was another west side quake somewhere between

Enumclaw and National, they're all a part of the Western Rainier Seismic Zone (WRSZ). Scientists don't think it's one long continuous fault, however, but a series of small faults. If it was continuous, it could generate a quake of 6.0 or so.

Seismic hazard studies have revealed the formerly unrecognized danger from subduction quakes and the newly studied Seattle Fault zone. Mt. Rainier is susceptible to large debris avalanches when violently shaken. More study of non-eruption events (e.g. the Electron Mudflow) needs to be undertaken.

Earthquake Detection Equipment In Use

Six seismographs are located around the mountain: below Fremont Lookout, Camp Schurman, Emerald Ridge, Longmire, Paradise, and Butler Hut at Camp Muir. Two more are nearby, just outside the park west of Mowich Lake and by White Pass. If you come across one in the backcountry, please leave it alone!

Scientists who have monitored Mount Rainier's seismic recordings for many years have learned some very interesting facts. The glacial outburst floods (mudflows) which occur periodically around the mountain produce a seismic record that is clearly distinctive to that type of event. A second type of record has been identified as being typical of the movement of glacial ice. Visitors can see these distinctive recordings for themselves in a new interpretive exhibit at the Henry M. Jackson Visitor Center.

Since the 1960's the Longmire seismograph has been a part of a worldwide network which supplies seismic data to the scientific community worldwide. The seismograph is monitored daily at the park, and constantly at the University of Washington and the USGS. The 1994 massive earthquake that hit Kobe, Japan, was detected at Longmire before it was picked up anywhere else in the U.S.

Inside the Longmire building are three different instruments: the old faithful seismometer, a standard network seismometer and a newer advanced instru-

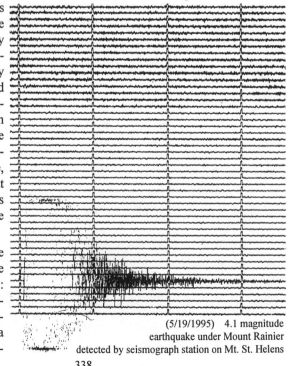

(5/19/1995) 4.1 magnitude earthquake under Mount Rainier detected by seismograph station on Mt. St. Helens

ment. If the earth quivers, the jagged line on the paper, tells much about the time, duration and nature of the quake.

With Mount Rainier's new designation as a Decade Volcano, the seismic records generated at the mountain will receive additional study.

Distant Seismic Detection

On August 16, 1989, at the University of Washington Geophysics lab, Rick Benson, a research scientist, happened to be looking at signals being sent by seismic instruments on and around Mount Rainier. Something was definitely happening. What it was, Benson concluded, was a massive rockslide from Curtis Ridge on the north side of the mountain. He calculated the location and phoned Longmire for confirmation. His finding was news to them, and since the mountain was socked in tight, it wasn't until the next day when the skies cleared that rangers spotted Benson's slide. Tons of rock which had come down on the Winthrop Glacier, --within 1,600 feet of where he had said it was. This was the first time a rockslide had been detected and located remotely.

The Indian Henrys Fault

Benson now has so much experience in analyzing Mount Rainier's every cough and quiver, he can even distinguish between signals caused by ice quakes and rockslides. Let's hope he's at work if the big one hits in our lifetime.

USGS Tectonic Studies

During the 1993 season, researchers used a new 'magneto- telluric' method to produce an image of the subsurface beneath Mount Rainier and the surrounding region. They did this using electrical geophysical and seismic methods to sound and image to depths of 25 miles or more. The east-west profile of deep electrical soundings, was made utilizing a new backpack instrumentation system powered by solar panels.

The surveys will continue in the park along another east-west line north of the mountain. The researchers will then compute revised earthquake seismic tomograms (3-D images) of the region to complement the electrical images. Eventually a display of the new tectonic models will be made for use by park naturalists. *(USGS -Stanley and Benz).*

Slides: Another Way to Rearrange the Real Estate

In May of 1937 climber Ome Daiber reported a bad slide since summer 1936 had sheared off the south face of Gibraltar Rock, a popular summit climbing route. The slide left a sheer face several hundred feet high, impossible to pass. The climbing route was replaced with a new route thru Cadaver Gap, then up Ingraham Glacier onto the Emmons Glacier and on to the summit. The new route is longer and somewhat tedious.

Eight different major slides are evident around the mountain (Page 146).

Mount Rainier Seismology 1981-1995
(Mag. > 0.0)

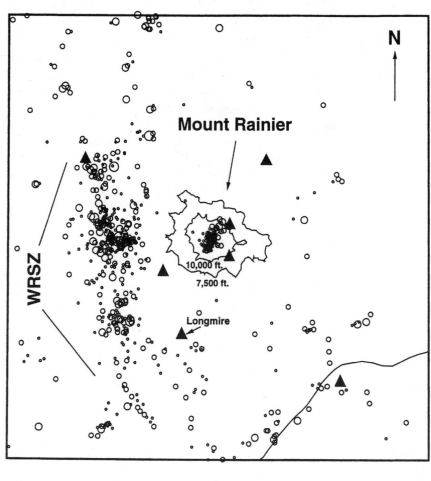

Mount Rainier

WRSZ

10,000 ft.

7,500 ft.

Longmire

N

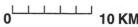

0 ⌞⌟⌟⌟⌟⌟ 10 KM

Earthquakes around Mount Rainier

Magnitude	
·	- 0.0
○	- 1.0
○	- 2.0
○	- 3.0
○	- 4.0

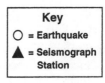

Key

○ = Earthquake

▲ = Seismograph Station

Map by Seth Moran, University of Washington Geophysics Lab

340

Decade Volcano Project

Much of what is known about Mount Rainier's volcanic propensities is based on 40-year old research. According to Steve Malone, University of Washington research professor of geophysics who specializes in volcanic seismology, Mount "Rainier is one of the most dangerous volcanoes around, --a big, 14,000-foot chunk of mountain surrounded by 2.5 million people."

He and other scientists familiar with the mountain say that Tacomans, Seattleites and others who live under the volcano would be wise to harbor a healthy respect for it.

It was this risk, which caused the International Association of Volcanology and Chemistry of the Earth's Interior, or IAVCEI, to deem Mount Rainier as one of nine volcanoes worldwide which warranted extended study. In 1992, top U.S. volcano researchers declared Mount Rainier as their top priority "decade volcano," and drafted a science plan that would guide their studies over the next decade. They also put their funding efforts into the project.

Decade Volcano Project Display

A new exhibit at the Henry M. Jackson Visitor Center at Paradise explains the Decade Volcano Project. Included is an explanation of the geology of the Sunset Amphitheater, summarizing the 1993 field work done as part of the study, and an explanation of the Paradise Lahar that was initiated by a landslide which swept over the Nisqually Glacier and across the Paradise area. The display will be updated as the ten-year project progresses.

The Big One: Will Rainier really Go?

The first question after "will it ever erupt again?" is "what will it do" Will Tacoma turn into a 20th Century Pompeii? What is the primary danger? Lava? Ash? Pumice? Floods? Being inundated by a massive mudflow?

The most recent geological review of the Electron Mudflow *(Scott and Pringle, in press)* estimates that a flow of similar size and composition would reach Orting in 1 to 2 hours, with a flowing depth of about 30 feet, and leave the town buried about 15 feet deep. Even though the Electron Mudflow apparently occurred without an accompanying eruption, it is used by scientists and emergency-preparedness planners as the design event to be expected from a major eruption of Mount Rainier. *(Tanaka).*

Ash-flow-producing eruptions are another significant volcanic hazard previous unrecognized at Mount Rainier.

▪ The greatest risks are from mudflows. Studies of past flows yield the most meaningful estimates of what could be expected in size of flows, as well as frequency, dynamics and extent. Such mudflows might well be caused by a steam eruption, which would melt some of the vast snow and ice reserves, causing a disastrous mudflow, rather than a violent explosion similar to Mount St. Helens in 1980.

■ One scientist *(Frank - 1985)*, believes that a northeastward sector collapse is especially likely at Mount Rainier because the summit cone formed in a depression oriented in that direction, is like a "greased bowl." The White River drainage would be affected by such a collapse. The same report suggests the precipitous headwaters of the Carbon River might also be affected by that renewed failure. It also noted that the Cowlitz River has a much lower probability of a sector-collapse lahar.

■ A major earthquake could precipitate a major problem. Triggering by earthquakes or steam eruptions could destabilize the volcano's continuously active hydrothermal system, and cause a large and dangerous flow to occur. *(Scott and Vallance, 1995)*. Canada's largest historic landslide is believed to have occurred in response to an earthquake of magnitude 3.2. *(Evans - 1989)*.

■ The least likely scenario is a debris flow of lake-breakout origin. The small lakes on or near Mount Rainier are mostly cirque lakes with stable sills. Only a few are old, moraine-dammed lakes that have previously broken out. Lake water displaced by a landslide is a possible, although unlikely source of local flooding or debris flows. *(Scott and Vallance, 1995)*.

Is Anything Being Done?

The thing that worries the scientific community most is the number of people living and working in the hazard area. They also worry about development moving closer to the mountain, and what may happen if and when the mountain moves closer to the people!

Pierce County, the most likely recipient of anything Mount Rainier may deliver, has prudently taken an aggressive stance in hazard-awareness education and emergency preparedness. Much like the messenger who had to be the bearer of bad news, they took a firm stand when the Orting School District wanted to build a school in what would be the path of a repeat of the Electron Mudflow. Not only was the school not built, hazard planners now meet with teachers from Orting to brainstorm ideas for classroom materials for use in educating grades K-9 about volcanic dangers.

Local emergency planners also have evacuation and services plans in place should mudflows inundate areas along the Puyallup, White and Nisqually rivers.

Will The Dams and Reservoirs Hold Back a Mudflow?

The Nisqually, Cowlitz and White River systems contain reservoirs which could, depending upon flow size, either lighten or aggravate the effects of a mudflow. A flow may be contained by a reservoir, or the impact of the wave may cause dam failure. Such factors as reservoir size, dam type and whether it's full or empty would all be factors. The Mud Mountain Dam on the White River is exclusively a flood-control structure of earth and rockfill construction which is normally empty, and thus would greatly reduce, or at least slow (but probably not eliminate) downstream risk.

Other downstream dams, Mossyrock Dam (Riffe Lake on the Cowlitz River), and Alder Dam on the Nisqually River, would serve a similar function. However their reservoir levels vary from season to season, so the degree of risk mitigation would depend on their water level at the time of a mudflow. *(Scott and Vallance - 1995).*

How fast would a Mudflow travel?

Few will forget the speed with which the Toutle River carried the volumes of debris flow material from Mount St. Helens to the Puget Sound lowlands. The Osceola flow is estimated to have been 45 MPH. Distances from Mount Rainier to the lowlands or to the nearest downstream reservoir, range from 24 to 48 miles. Travel times range from 2 to 3.6 hours. *(Scott and Vallance - 1995).*

What would it be like when Mount Rainier erupts?

What will Puget Sounders face? Ash? Lava? Pyroclastic flows? How far will things flow? How fast will it come? Since anything about how, what, when and where a Mount Rainier "event" will occur is pure speculation, we hereby present a little science fiction of four hypothetical scenarios. Not science fiction as in flying saucers, but fiction based on what science knows about what mountains like Mount Rainier can do when they "come to life."

Four Scenarios

These scenarios are the work of Mrs. Janet Cullen Tanaka, a pioneer in volcanic hazards management studies, who published the first urban and regional planning study of Mount Rainier hazards, using the Puyallup Valley as an example. These were written in 1972 (a mere instant in the life span of a volcano), but note how accurately Mount St. Helens followed pieces of Ms. Tanaka's script. The real event may resemble any one of them, a combination of several, or none of the following. All names are ficticious.

Scenario #1: Steam explosion and mudflow

The hypothetical Wire Service report reads as follows:

(Seattle) October 8: Late season tourists and Park Rangers at Mt. Rainier National Park were shaken up this morning by a major steam explosion and avalanche on the mountain. The explosion, the largest ever witnessed on a Cascade volcano since the coming of the white man, occurred shortly after 9:00 a.m. The only warning, park personnel reported, was a series of "half a dozen" sharp earthshocks during the fifteen minutes immediately preceding the blast.

"They put us on our guard," Chief Ranger Andy Adams told reporters. "We had a feeling something was going to happen--and man, it sure did!"

Geologists from the University of Washington and the state's Department of Natural Resources say that the massive explosion was caused by a pocket of steam coming into sudden contact with the cold ground water and frozen rock beneath the head of the South Tahoma Glacier on the southwest side of the old volcano. The blast apparently broke the surface just above the 10,000 foot level, involving the entire head of the glacier and portions of the ridge known as "Success Cleaver".

Ice, rock, and steam shot over a thousand feet into the air with a sound one observer described as being: "like all the thunderclaps I ever heard rolled into one." The earthquake accompanying the blast proper knocked dishes off the shelves at the ranger station.

While astonished tourists watched and wondered if the volcano were erupting, a huge fall of rock and blocks of ice broke from the blast area and caromed off the glacial slopes into Tahoma Creek Canyon. A party of climbers on Pyramid Peak, above the Canyon, said they could see "tremendous" amounts of water coming out of the glacier near a big column of steam.

The wall of water, rock, mud, and debris which geologists call a "lahar" poured through the canyon and over the Tahoma Creek road only minutes after the initial explosion.

"If there was anyone in there," said ranger Bob Bridger, "they sure never had time to get out!"

Early reports say the bulk of the massive mudflow came to a halt at the junction of Tahoma Creek and the Nisqually River, where it is currently creating a partial dam. High water is reported on the Nisqually as far down as Alder Dam, over thirty miles downstream from the blast site. Officials from Tacoma City Light and the Army Corps of Engineers said that there is no apparent danger downstream from the dam, but warned that flooding may occur in lowland areas on the upper Nisqually due to the breaking-up of the dammed mass of mud and debris. The Dept. of Emergency Services has ordered threatened areas evacuated.

Scientists from the U.S. Geological Survey who have been studying Mt. Rainier for the past 20 years say that the dormant volcano has not shown any signs of impending eruption. Carl Chandler, head seismologist on the Rainier project, told reporters that there had been no significant seismic buildup of the kind normally expected before a regular ash or lava eruption.

Dr. David Daniels, number one Rainier watcher for the USGS, pointed out that the mountain has been the site of several moderate steam explosions and mudflows in the last 50 years.

"This one," he said, "was just bigger and louder. But there is no doubt that there is a hot area under South Tahoma Glacier. We've had a lot of rockfall activity there in the past few years."

It is not yet known whether there are any casualties.

(The above scenario is a fictional account)

Scenario #2 A Scientific Paper (entitled):

The Recent Eruption of Mt. Rainier Volcano, Washington, U.S.A.

Minor hydromagmatic and ash eruption beneath summit crater lake with lahars and ashfall

by: David A. Daniels, Everett Edwards, and Frances Fox

Mt. Rainier, a dormant andesitic volcano, erupted briefly during the month of June, following approximately 150 years of quiescence. The activity was presaged by six days of intense microearthquake activity beneath the summitarea. Beginning 10 days before the eruption, thermistors located in the walls of the summit crater showed an apparent rise in temperature. This was confirmed at minus 8 days by IFR. At minus 3 days considerable breakup appeared in the ice filling the east summit crater. By minus 24 hours a large crater lake had formed.

On the evening of June 24 several earthshocks occurred. These were felt over a radius of 50 miles from the volcano. Observations just before dawn on June 25 revealed the lake to be bubbling in places, with a large column of steam and sulphurous gases rising from fissures in the crater wall surrounding the lake.

The eruption proper began at 10:20 am on June 25 with a steam explosion which breached the crater walls, releasing the crater lake onto the southeast quadrant of the mountain. Barographs recorded 47 separate explosions in a 2-1/2 hour period.

The emptying of the crater lake caused major ice breakup and lahar formation from the Emmons, Ingraham, Cowlitz, and Nisqually Glaciers. Lahars averaged heights of 25-100 feet in passage down the river valleys draining the affected glaciers. Measurement of total volume of both lahars and ashfall are still in progress at this writing. The shortest mudflow extended approximately 5 km. from the terminus of the Nisqually Glacier. The longest originated from the Emmons Glacier and was contained in the reservoir behind Mud Mountain Dam, approximately 75 km. downstream.

Ash eruption began 2 hours and 5 minutes after the first steam explosions. Over the period from June 25-29 a moderate volume of ash was expelled, the major portion on the first and third days. Deposits from the first day are composed primarily of fragments of older rock from the summit and conduit walls, ranging in size from a coarse sand to blocks 4 meters in diameter. (Larger blocks were loosed by the subsequent avalanching, but to date these mentioned are the largest apparently due to explosive activity at the crater area.) Subsequent deposits range from a coarse brown sand to greyish colored pumice measuring from a medium sand to 20 cm. chunks. Heaviest deposits occur on the northeast flanks of the volcano and in the immediate vicinity of the crater. A depth of 20 cm. was measured at the Silver Creek Ranger Station approx. 22-1/2 km. from the summit crater. Ash deposits extend to 150 km., with a fall of less than 1 cm. at Wenatchee, approximately 130 km. northeast of the volcano.

The last ash explosions were recorded near 11 pm on June 29. By the afternoon of July 3 the seismic activity had fallen to near seasonal normal. At this writing (Aug 1) all eruptive activity seems to have ceased. It is assumed that the June eruption was similar to Rainier's previous minor eruptions.

Structures and roads on the affected sides of the mountain were heavily damaged or destroyed by the lahars. Seismic and thermal warnings were heeded, and the low-lying valley areas on all sides of the volcano were evacuated by civil and military authorities prior to the beginning of the eruption. There was one fatality. A television news reporter crossed state patrol barriers and was swept away with his vehicle by a lahar.

(The above scenario is a fictional account)

Scenario # 3: Major Eruption

(Letters from a young seismologist)

Seattle, July 1

Dear Greg,

No vacation for me! Dr. Harry laid his cold, clammy hand on my shoulder this morning. Seems Rainier is doing funny things earthquakewise again. So sun yourself this weekend and think of me slaving over a hot seismograph.

Love,

Irene

July 6

Dear Greg,

You should have come <u>here</u> for the weekend! We had some real excitement on the 4th. There was an intensity V earthquake under Paradise. It shook the heck out of the lodge for about 20 seconds and dropped an avalanche off the upper end of Nisqually Glacier. Dr. Johnson from NW history was climbing on Nisqually Cleaver, and he said it felt as though the mountain was trying to shake him off the way a dog shakes off water. One of their party had his ankle cracked by a falling rock.

Total event count is up over 100 for this week and only about 10% of that is normal tectonic stuff. You suppose Rainier is trying to tell us something??!!

Yours,

Rene

July 10

Greg--

A quick one. Event count went over 30 <u>yesterday</u>. The USGS people from Menlo Park and Denver are descending on us tomorrow. Dr. Harry is threatening to sleep in the lab.

July 12

... Count doubled yesterday. The Emergency Preparedness boys, the USGS, and our staff had a big meeting this a.m. The consensus seems to be that ye olde mountaine is going to ERUPTE--maybe. Love from the Very Junior Asst.

July 15

Greg--

Drop everything and come to Seattle! Rainier's got a terrible case of the shakes and she's starting to run a temp. There were two Intensity VI shocks today. One dropped a rockfall onto the highway between Longmire and the Nisqually Bridge.

The infrared pictures from day before yesterday show a definite new hot area on the SW side below Point Success. The runoff from Nisqually and S. Tahoma and Kautz is way over last week's. All ground temps are increasing, according to the USGS gang. Dr. Harry screameth and lo I must runneth. See you for the "rock festival."

Rene

July 20

Dear Greg,

I think it's pretty rotten of your boss not to let you come to watch the eruption! You would major in microbiology!

They pulled the plug on Alder Dam yesterday. They figure it will take a couple of days to empty out enough water to contain a mudflow in the reservoir. The southwest glaciers are putting out a lot of mud and water. All the streams on that side are approaching flood stage--in July yet.

We're having 3 or 4 strong earthquakes per day and the monitors look like they have hiccups.

An evacuation order was put out today for the valleys on the SW. Park is closed until further notice.

And the tourists! They're swarming in by the hundreds. Not to mention the scientists. I've never seen so much geo-physical brass all assembled in one place. A couple of Japanese professors set up an "eruption pool" yesterday. Everybody kicks in a dollar and the one who guesses the closest time to the beginning of the eruption wins the pot.

You've got to get away from those bloomin' protozoa!

July 23

Dear Greg,

I saw it, but I don't believe it! The balloon went up at 6:45 this morning. What a blast! TV couldn't do it justice!

Thanks to Dr. Harry, I had a ringside seat. I was one of the "front-line" corps at the UW-USGS observation station set up about 8 miles due south of Rainier. He virtually yanked me into the lab and introduced me to the team as: "My junior assistant, Ms. Ives, who is doing her doctoral dissertation on this eruption." (Which is the first I'd heard of it!)

Nobody got much sleep between the excitement and the earthquakes. By dawn's early light things were really shaking. Pieces were coming off some of the glaciers right and left. Our Russian observer was a little apprehensive about being so close.

Anyway at about 6:25 there were some steam explosions at the 13,000 foot level at the right of Point Success. A whole line of steam-spouting fissures opened almost all the way across to Cowlitz Cleaver. There was steam and rock and blocks of ice blowing up like crazy! (I suppose a volcanologist could describe it better, but I'm just a V.J.A.S. who's never seen a volcanic eruption except on TV.)

We could see big fountains of water and debris splashing across the top of the glaciers.

At about 6:42 there was one really tremendous shock-- it sure played heck with our recording equipment. We no sooner stopped shaking ourselves when the whole fissure opened up with a tremendous banging, whooshing sound. It started at the lower end and seemed to spread toward Point Success. In just a few seconds it blew Point Success and all the glacier around it clean off the mountain! One minute there was this huge outcrop of rock and the next--blam--this big cloud. Honest. Then there was this kind of doughnut shaped cloud that started rolling out from the bottom of the main cloud. One of the guys from the GS said it was a "base surge".

Then there was just a fountain of pieces of rock--great chunks of it mixed with a cloud of steam. A minute or two later the ash started coming. Wow! Just like the pictures you always see of Vesuvius. Big grey clouds of ash just boiled out of that hole where point Success was.

Fortunately the wind was blowing due east. As it was we got peppered with little pieces of pumice up to an inch across. It wasn't as hot as I thought it would be, but it was plenty warm. The noise was so loud we had to yell at each other. Dr. Kamirov kept saying things about Bezymianny and urging us to retreat to a safer distance. I for one agreed with him!

Later in the day we did move to about 12 miles out, much to Dr. K's relief (and mine). I must tell you about the mudflows. They were really spectacular! All this water and ice and rock was just pouring off the glaciers where the fissures had opened. The Kautz Glacier was taking the worst beating. (That was the one you took all the pictures of last March.) The Nisqually was having a pretty bad time of it too. The little glaciers down below were getting peppered with hot pumice, and the So. Tahoma was just covered with chunks of rock that must have been as big as houses.

We weren't where we could see much of the canyons, but Daniel from the USGS said that the muddy mess was running up over a hundred feet deep in places. He and some guys from glaciology were up in a forest service helicopter. The bridge at the foot of Nisqually Glacier went out. They said you couldn't even see where the creekbed of the Kautz was: it's all filled with mud. Longmire meadow is all covered with mud and rocks and a lot of debris has come down at Paradise, too.

All the roads in the valleys on the SW side of the park have been washed out or swallowed up in mud. The Nisqually River is over flood stage down as far as Alder. The last I heard, Alder Dam is still holding.

Right now it's almost dark and we can see the glow in the sky above the new crater. So far no lava, just pumice and ash. It's sure hard to believe this is Rainier.

Love, Rene

P.S. Oh yes, I split the eruption pool with Pat from the Geology office and a Dr. Ramirez from NOAA.

July 25

Dear Greg

Glad to hear you got your color TV in time to watch the show. But, nothing, NOTHING, compares to being here and seeing, hearing, feeling, and (yecchh) smelling it in person. Dr. Harry is right--I'm going to do my dissertation on some of the seismic aspects of the eruption.

The eruption continues with no let up in sight. Still all ash and pumice. A white line of cinder cones (pumice cones?) has built up at the fracture where the initial breakthrough occurred. Kautz Glacier is done for, and so are the smaller ones. Nisqually is still breaking up, but old So. Tahoma is bearing up bravely under a pile that looks like half the mountain's guts. The only way you can really tell there's still ice is by the flood of water gushing out.

Alder Dam is holding but discharging water as fast as it comes in. The winds continue to blow due east, and the Yakima farmers are pretty upset about the ash.

And you simply wouldn't believe the tourists!! The state police and military have had to erect barriers to keep them back. They are coming right into the park on the north and west sides. The highways are lined with cars. People are setting up their tents and parking campers all over. The farmers and suburbanites have got smart. They're renting their land and yards and charging whatever the traffic will bear.

So far no one has been killed, but I don 't know why. A lot of good land has sure gone under.

August 15

Dear Greg,

Well, Rainier seems to have set her mind on being a semipermanent attraction. There are three new craters below the first, and yesterday the lowest, at the 8000 foot level where the Kautz Glacier used to be, started putting out some thick lava flows. Dr. Lowell says it is dacite. Dr. McCormack says it's a dacitic andesite. (I'm glad I'm a seismologist.) Anyway, it doesn't really flow. It oozes along at about 8 or 9 feet a day. (That's what McCormack tells me, anyway, and I'm too chicken to go up with them and measure it myself.)

The first casualties happened yesterday. A planeload of Army Engineers got caught in an updraft from the eruption cloud last night and crashed into the mountain. There weren't any survivors.

Alder reservoir is becoming the world's biggest mudbath. Tacoma City Light said it would be cheaper to abandon the dam than to try to dig out the reservoir. It's solid. The water goes over the dam in places, but it's still holding.

The winds have let down and the fruit crops may not have suffered too badly. The ag boys are telling the farmers that the ash will be good fertilizer in a few years, (ED: another accurate prediction.) but it doesn't make them any happier right now.

By the way, would you be just as willing to marry a volcano-seismologist as a plain garden variety earthquake chaser? I think the pumice has got in my blood!

Love, R.

Sept. 1

Dear Greg,

Well, it seems to be all over but the digging out. Rainier is still steaming, but her heartbeat says she is napping again. There have been no new lava extrusions for five days and the pumice turned off on the 25th. Alder dam still stands, and people are returning to their property---if they can find it. The tourists are going home, but I suppose there will be new batches along after Labor Day.

Maybe Rainier has had her fling. Probably she's just taking a breather for a few weeks or months. Anyway, Dr. Harry says I'm number one in charge of the old girl's cardiology from now on, so I should be the first to know.

What that means, dear heart, is that I've been made Senior Assistant Seismologist. So any thoughts of my coming to join you at M.I.T. are O.U.T. But if you're still so inclined, there is a position just opened for a good research micro-biologist at the University of Washington Hospital......

Love,

Irene

(The above scenario is a fictional account)

Scenario #4: A Book Review about Catastrophe

If, indeed, the great eruption of Santorin was the cause of the plagues and phenomena of the Red Sea described in the book of Exodus, we can deduce that the whole affair may have spanned no more than a few weeks. If Santorin brought about the fall of Crete, archaeological records reveal that the major part of the catastrophe took no longer than that.

The climax of the great eruption and collapse of Krakatoa took less than a week. Katmai's demise came about in only two and one-half days. Indian legends indicate that the fall of Mazama took place in a matter of days.

There is no reason to assume that Rainier would take any longer to undergo an all-out caldera-forming eruption. A summarized review of the event might sound something like these excerpts from the popular book: *The Great Eruption of Mt. Rainier*, by Dr. Norman Nobeaver and Ms. Oshi Ozumi, published by the University of Washington Press in 1986.

"Looking back on the Rainier event, scientists are now in agreement that the great eruption was the outcome of a number of happenings which began at least as early as 1969. In that year a number of events took place which alerted scientists that all was not well--or perhaps was all too well--with the mountain." p.12

"...in all fairness to the ladies and gentlemen of the scientific community, it should be pointed out that the years of 1971-79 were the 'calm before the storm'. In the autumn preceding the cataclysm it became apparent that Rainier was about to take up where she had left off.

"Seismic activity began to intensify in October, at the time when it would normally have been quieting down. With the exception of a brief drop in the event count during December, both felt tremors and micro-earthquakes underwent a staggering rise from 15 per week in September to 950 in the week immediately before the eruption. Application of the Tokarev-Nicholaev seismic strain release formulae clearly showed that an eruption of a very large magnitude was due to occur within a short time." p.15

"The second indicators of potential trouble were the biaxial tiltmeters placed on the mountain in the 1970's. Shortly after the first of the year they began indicating definite changes of level on the east side of the mountain." p. 20

"It is of value to note that the really significant changes in ground temperature did not appear until 10 days before the start of the eruption. Rainier, like all dormant volcanoes, already contained enough inner heat to cause periodic steam explosions and glacier outburst floods. Large scale thermal anomalies began to appear on infrared photographs only in the four weeks previous to the start of the eruption proper.

"Glacier runoff, which would have been apparent during the summer, was no doubt cut down considerably by the normal sub-freezing temperatures of the High Cascade winter." p. 30

"It was the eyes of human observers, rather than instrumentation, which first detected the large scale melting taking place in the ice caves of the east summit crater. A climbing party reported in late March that the large cavern in the crater was filling with meltwater.

"By the middle of April there was a well-established crater lake in the east summit crater. Its temperature was barely above freezing and large chunks of ice were observed floating on the surface....Several fumaroles at the edge of the lake were discharging steam and sulphurous fumes with an audible hissing. Clouds of steam could be seen rising from the summit on clear days.

"Strong earthquakes began to be felt in the park area." pp. 39-40

"Preparations for a full-scale eruption were begun on May 1st and 2nd. Alder and Mud Mountain reservoirs were ordered emptied. A high rate of glacial runoff and several small-scale mudflows were already being experienced.

"Valley floors on the east and northeast side of the mountain were ordered evacuated, as was the upper Nisqually Valley. Cross-mountain highways through the park were closed to all but emergency traffic. Tourists and scientists alike began to converge on the state. It now began to look as though the grand old mountain would *have* to erupt to keep Washington from 'losing face'." p. 49

"Sharp earthquakes were felt for over a one hundred mile radius beginning on May 5th." p. 50

"The Seattle-Tacoma area was literally brimming over with earth scientists of every description--as excited as a bunch of children waiting for the circus to begin." p. 53

" 'If this were happening in pioneer days the only warnings would have been some clouds of steam--which could be mistaken for ordinary clouds, rising rivers--which might have been attributed to normal spring runoff, and some earthquakes---which might have been attributed to the perversity of nature. No wonder people talk about volcanoes erupting without warning!' Dr. Juan Ramirz, NOAA, on KIRO-TV, May 5th." p. 55

"The eruption began at slightly half-past eight on the evening of May 8...the anniversary of the fateful explosion of Mt. Pelee. No series of earthshocks led up to the opening curtain. At 8:30 the steam cloud rose placidly above the mountain. At 8:31:53 a tremendous steam explosion blew a hole in Emmons Glacier at the 12,000 foot level. The fracture must have extended completely across the width of the ice face. Explosion followed explosion, finally undermining the east crater area of the summit, spilling the contents of the crater lake onto the rising molten material and gases.

"A stupendous hydroexplosion lifted the east side of the mountain from the summit cone down to the 11,000 foot level. The base surge was well-defined and photographed from several angles." p.64

"At precisely 9:00 pm a deep orange glow in the sky over the eastern side of the ravaged cone signaled the arrival of the magma." p.65

"By dawn on the 9th the eruption was going full tilt. Huge cauliflower clouds of ash and pumice rose tens of thousands of feet above the mountain. Lightning bolts flashed in the clouds and the booming of the thunder mingled with the roar of the volcano. Rainier had truly lived up to all expectations. Let the Hawaiians have their stew-pots: here was a *real* volcano!" p. 67

"The Geological Survey's predictions of huge mudflows were fulfilled. Lahars to rival the great mudflows of the past filled the valleys of the White and Ohanapecosh. Lesser flows, though still sufficient to cause widespread damage came down the Paradise, Cowlitz, and Nisqually valleys." p. 72

"The lahars, particularly the catastrophic White River flow, fell into a rough pattern as follows: (1) increased glacial runoff due to melting of the ice prior to the eruption proper, (2) large, debris-laden flows resulting from the explosive ousting of the crater lakes and the explosions beneath the Emmons Glacier, (3) lesser flooding during the first part of the eruption, (4 increased floods as glowing avalanches swept the flanks of the volcano on the southeast side, (5) a decrease leading to a gradual cessation of flooding on the east side, and finally (6) catastrophic flows of ash and debris accompanying the collapse of the summit. Heavy rains during the Autumn months contributed to later mud and wet ash flows from the side of the still-steaming hulk." pp 73-74

"Although loss of life was certainly on a minor scale during the 'opening gun' of the Rainier event, the White River Mudflow more than made up for it.

"The seeds of the tragedy were laid in the inability of geologists and public officials to convince residents of the lower valleys that they were really in danger. Thus, when the east wall of the summit collapsed at 3:50 on the morning of May 11th, there was no longer sufficient time to awaken the ill-fated residents of Enumclaw, Buckley, and East Auburn in time for orderly evacuation.

"Fortunately many of the residents of the lowest-lying area had been forced from their homes by the earlier flooding. Unfortunately, a number of them had simply taken up temporary residence within a few miles of their flooded homes and still in the lowlands." p. 76

" 'It was, I guess, about 7:30 on May 10th that we were grabbing a sandwich, when the other guys from the Survey and Dr. Suji came in. They were looking pretty grim. They'd run some rough figures through the computer, based on the amounts of material put out and the change in the chemical composition of the ash. What they came up with was that it looked like the magma chamber was being emptied, and it looked like we might be going to have an honest-to-God caldera forming eruption...

" 'And when it finally did come, we thought it was pretty dirty of Rainier to do it in the middle of the night. Well, hell, we didn't get any decent photographs at all!'" Quoting Dr. Terry Taylor, Center for Volcanology, Eugene, Oregon. p. 77.

"The collapse of the summit sent vast amounts of material avalanching down slopes already mantled with fresh ash and saturated from the torrential rains which broke out from time to time during the eruption...Measurements made in early July led to the conclusion that as much as half the eastern side of the summit may have fallen outward, while the remainder plunged into the eviscerated mountain." p. 81

" ' At any rate, we sent out emergency warnings telling the people to get out of those lower valleys. I don 't care how many times we told them about the old Osceola Mudflow, they just wouldn't believe that they were in danger of being buried in mud in the United States of America in the last quarter of the twentieth century!'" Dr. Terry Taylor. p. 82

"The final estimated death toll from the White River disaster stands at 25,000, with over 2000 others still missing and unaccounted for. Like most of the tragedies associated with volcanic eruptions it was one that never needed to have happened.

"The eruption itself was successfully predicted several days in advance. Even the fact that it was to lead to the collapse of the east side of the summit and the formation of a caldera was predicted several hours in advance by scientists. Every potential danger was known. As much as 8 hours in advance of the catastrophe, warning was given of the potential for a major mudflow too large to be contained by any dam or reservoir. It was a warning that went unheeded by nearly 30,000 people." p. 85

"Although the loss of life in the lower White and Green River Valleys was staggering and the accompanying property damage in the tens of millions; the greatest economic blow dealt to Washington by Mt. Rainier was the temporary loss of the major portion of its fruit-raising industry.

"During the 3 days of the eruption strong west-south-west winds deposited 10-12 inches of ash on the orchards of the Yakima and Wenatchee valleys. Acid rains accompanying the fall literally stripped the foliage from the trees.

"The fact that the ash would, in time, create a richer soil was scant compensation to people whose livelihood was (at least temporarily) wiped out, and for which no insurance policy would give compensation." p. 90

Summary

The great eruption of Mt. Rainier lasted for approximately 75 hours. It was presaged by several years of sporadic pre-eruptive preparations. Before the eruption proper there were 7 months of heightened seismic activity (with 3 days of felt shocks), 4 months of deformation measurable with tilt-meters, and 6 weeks of detectable thermal activity.

"The eruption began at approximately 8:32 pm on May 8 with a massive steam explosion at the 12,000 foot level beneath Emmons Glacier. It built to a climax on May 10 with the continuous expulsion of the contents of the magma chamber, both from the new crater and from fissures on the east side of the mountain. In the late evening hours of May 10, there was a lull in activity, followed by more explosions and the collapse of the eastern portion of the summit at 3:50 am on May 11. Weak explosions continued from collapse until just before midnight.

"At the beginning of the eruption Mt. Rainier raised a magnificent snow-capped peak to 14,410 feet. It was clothed with glaciers and surrounded by forests, rippling streams, and abundant wildlife. It was ringed with highways and facilities for human recreation.

"At its end, Rainier is a battered hulk. On the western side, a chaotic pile of rubble reaches to 12,300 feet. On the east side there is a vast bowl, whose easternmost rim stands at barely 9700 feet. The remains of her western glaciers are buried in ash and debris. On the northeast side there is a desert of ash and pumice reaching 15 miles from the base of the mountain. The former canyons are filled with steaming ash flows.

"The White River Valley below Mud Mountain is filled to depths of 25-150 feet with mud and debris. The towns of Buckley and Enumclaw are unrecognizable beneath 25-30 feet of lahar cover. The lower section of the city of Auburn sustained flows up to 10 feet in depth, with lobes of mud up to five feet thick extending into the city limits of Kent.

"Other mudflows extended 15 miles down the Ohanapecosh, 12 miles down the Cowlitz, and filled the Alder reservoir in the Nisqually Valley. Depths up to 10 feet have been measured in the Nisqually Valley just above the Reservoir.

"Rainier spread a layer of ash to 12" at Wenatchee, 7" at Coulee Dam, 3" at the Canadian border, and 1" at Helena, Montana Up to 2" blanketed areas of Idaho, and as much as 1-1/2" fell on Northeast Oregon. Some fine ash drifted into sections of Quebec.

"The known death toll, principally from the White River Mudflow, stands at 25,310, with another 2500 unaccounted for in the lower White River area. Twenty-eight persons died in the crash of an Army jet which flew into the ash cloud. One scientist from the Geological Survey died of a heart attack.

"On the positive side of the ledger, profits from tourists visiting the site of the catastrophe topped two million dollars in the first year. There is no doubt that visitors will continue to tour the area for many years.

"The science of volcanology made tremendous strides in the understanding of the Cascade volcanoes and the mechanisms of caldera-forming eruptions. A permanent laboratory has been erected by the USGS and UNESCO for the continued study of the volcano." p.103.

(The above scenario is a fictional account.)

Guidelines to Components of Events

Event Type	Earthquakes	Steam Explosions	Snow/Ice/Rock Avalanches	Mudflow & Flood	Pyroclastic Flows	Tephra Fall	Lava Flows	Probability of Occurrence
Minor * Non-Magmatic	Possibly none except as trigger	Possibly none except as trigger	Small, near source	Small to foot of mountain & valley heads	None, but steam blast could cause "cold" pyro. surges	Small amounts of old rock materials	None	I
Moderate * Non-Magmatic	Possibly none except as trigger	If present, small to moderate sized	Moderate-size to foot of mountain & valley heads	Moderate-size involving upper valleys downstream sedimentation	None, but steam blast could cause "cold" surges	Moderate amounts of old rock material < 2 inches	None	II
Major * Non-Magmatic	Possibly none except as trigger	If present, probably large-scale	Large volume, involving upper portions of valleys	Large volumes, involving large areas or whole valleys	None, but steam blast could carry "cold" surges	Large amounts of old rock material at least 20 miles	None	V
Minor Magmatic	Some	Initial vent clearing. Other small scale	Small, near source	Small, to mod. to foot of mountain & upper valleys	None, or small near vent	Old and new material <2" within park limits	None or very small, in vicinity of vent	III
Moderate Magmatic	Many	Initial vent clearing, small to moderate	Moderate to large size, involving upper valleys	Moderate to large size, involving upper and middle valleys	None, or small near vent	Old and new material <2" within park limits	None or very small, in vicinity of vent	IV
Major Magmatic	Many, including several strong	Initial vent clearing, small to very large scale	Large volume, involving upper valleys	Large volume, involving entire valleys- comparable to hazard map MI 836	Large, involving slopes and upper valleys	Old and new material as far as Eastern Washington, 6" of pumice < 12 miles	Small to moderate volume, from central or flank vents	VI
Catastrophic	Many, probably some very strong	Many of all magnitudes	Extensive, large volume collapse of edifice	Large volume, involving whole drainage systems. Collapse of edifice	Voluminous, from central and satellite vents, empty magma chamber, extending 20-40 miles down all valleys.	Immense volumes of old and new material, <20" to 60 miles. Ash cloud carries around the earth.	Moderate to large volume, from vents on or near volcano	VII

*The large flows which go all the way to Puget Sound are associated at least as much with non-magmatic activity as with magmatic activity. Behavior and Hazards of Debris Flows at Munt Rainier, WA USGS Professional Paper 1547, U.S. Government Printing Office, Washington, D.C., 1995, Authors: K.M. Scott, J. W. Vallance and P.T. Pringle

And if she *Does* go...

here's where you don't want to be!

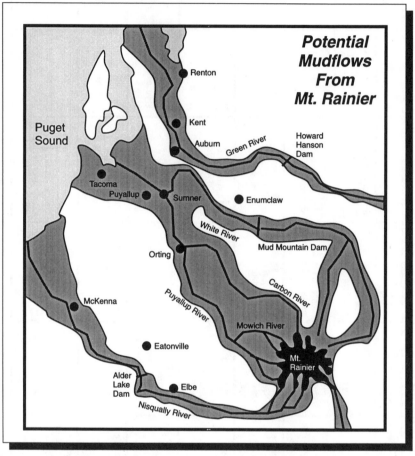

Potential Mudflows From Mt. Rainier

Some general safety rules for those living in the shadow of a volcano (or the possible path of a mudflow) are:

1. Always keep your car gassed up, and always park with your car facing out (so you don't have to waste time backing out if you only get a couple minutes warning that a mudflow is coming).

3. Keep an emergency blanket, a supply air filter masks, a spare air filter for your car, and gallon or two of water either in the garage ready to grab on the way out, or in your car.

4. Know every possible way to get to the highest hills around. Learn back ways to get to high places. Freeways will be jammed and freeways are in valleys, and that's where the mudflows will go.

5. When you're anywhere around the mountain, always have a working car radio or portable radio turned on.

6. If you hear a mudflow is coming, don't waste time packing, get the family out immediately and head for high ground.

Natural Resources

Mount Rainier Natural Resources Inventory

Plants
- Native Plant Species: 787
- Exotic Plant Species: 107

Birds
- Native Bird Species: 126

Animals/Amphibians
- Native Mammal Species: 54
- Native Reptiles and Amphibians: 17

Forests
- Lower elevation forests: 132,630 acres
- Old Growth forests: 91,140
- Subalpine (forests and meadows: 53,870 acres
- Alpine (not permanently covered with snow): 25,373 acres

Glaciers and Snowfields: 23,237 acres

Watersheds
- Watersheds: 9
- Glacial systems: 7
- Clear water systems 2

Lakes: 382

Rivers and Streams: 656 miles
- Separate tributaries: 470

Scientific Studies

The names of many of the early explorers of the area remain in the names of flora and fauna they observed and discovered. Early examples are Clark's Crow, Lewis's Monkey Flower (Mimulus Lewisii) and Lewis' Woodpecker, all named after Lewis and Clark who studied and collected samples during their famous 1804-06 journey to the Pacific. The Douglas fir is named after David Douglas who explored and botanized up and down the west coast. about 1825.

Dr. William Fraser Tolmie was not only the first white man to enter what is now the park, he came for the primary purpose of studying the local plants, and gathering herbs for medicinal use.

The first rock study was done in 1883, when Prof. Von Zittel, a renowned German paleontologist, collected rocks which were examined in Germany by K. Oebbeke of Munich. He worked with Bailey Willis during his geological investigation of 1881-83.

The first studies of the animal life of the mountain were made in July and August, 1897, by a Biological Survey party led by Dr. C. Hart Merriam, accompanied by Vernon Bailey and Walter K. Fisher. They collected 183 specimens of mammals and 25 birds. After study, this collection became a part of the 'United States National Museum,' now the Smithsonian Institution.

In 1896, I.C. Russell did the first study of the glaciers.

In 1905 the Sierra Club spent several weeks in the park, during which Professor N. LeConte of the University of California, a member of the party, made the first investigation of the rate of flow of the Nisqually Glacier. The results were published in the Sierra Club Bulletin of January 1907.

In 1919 the Biological Survey spent an entire summer in the Park collecting bird and animal specimens. When they left, the park had 363 fewer mammals and 172 fewer birds.

Once the mountain came under government control, more formal studies were made of the various aspects of the geology and natural sciences of the mountain. In recent years, numerous research programs have been carried out. The local universities (University of Washington, Washington State University, Western Washington University, University of Puget Sound, Oregon State University, etc.) take full advantage of the living laboratory in their back yards.

The park produces an annual scientific studies summary for those who may have need of one.

Science in the Park Today

In 1992 the National Park Service and the National Research Council issued a joint report on "Science and the National Parks." The report reviews the status of former and current research projects.

At just about any given time, numerous studies of various things are going on in the park. In 1994, for instance, thirty scientists conducted field studies.

Special Collections

The first herbarium in the Longmire museum came from the vast collection of botanical specimens of Dr. Oscar D. Allen, a Yale botany professor who came to the mountain for his health in 1895, and ended up settling in the Upper Nisqually Valley, just outside the park. Professor Allen made numerous excursions to the south and west sides of the mountain for the purpose of studying and collecting plants.

The next herbarium was housed at the Administration Building in Longmire and contained 200 specimens and 150 separate pieces collected and mounted. Although the colors have faded, most of the plants are in excellent shape, and are now considered valued collector's items. Labels on the original specimens bear such historic names as Bailey, Brockman, Danner, Landes, Lindsay and Scheffer.

In 1978 under the watchful eye of Resources Management Specialist Stan Schlegel, a new collection consisting of 200 specimens and 150 separate pieces were collected. Several rare plants were encountered, and all three endemics (plants found only at Mount Rainier) were found. These specimens are available for occasional displays, interpretive programs, and as aids for visiting botanists and researchers.

Also, five hundred 3x 4 glass slides from the 30's were given to the park by Harry Lemon, an early naturalist.

The first exhibits in the old museum were handpicked bouquets of flowers displayed in mayonnaise jars. One visitor remarked that the most remarkable thing about all the wildflower displays was the tremendous amount of mayonnaise that had to have been consumed to make them possible.

Scientific Findings

1833 Dr. William Fraser Tolmie made "botanizing expeditions" in Mount Rainier backcountry. In his diary, he stated that he collected "a vasculum of plants at the snow."

1841 Lieutenant Johnson crossed the Cascades via Naches Pass, and collected many specimens and made various scientific observations.

1870 Samuel Franklin Emmons and A.D Wilson of the 40th Parallel Corps, U.S. Geological Survey, did geological field work on the east side of the mountain. They made the first collection of Mount Rainier rocks. The rocks were later studied by Hague and Iddings of U.S.G.S. who concluded that "Mount Rainier is formed almost wholly of hypersthene andesite."

1881-83 Bailey Willis, Assistant Geologist for Northern Pacific Railroad explored for mineral resources, and investigated the geology of the west and northwest sides of the mountain. His work formed a basis for our geological knowledge of the area.

1883 A renowned German paleontologist, Professor von Zittel collected rocks at the mountain. They were later studied in Germany by K. Oebbeke of Munich, and written up in European scientific journals.

1895 Henry A. Sarvent made a comprehensive survey of the east side.

1897 Professor Edgar McClure lost his life during a descent after making a barometric determination of the height of Mount Rainier.

A U.S. Biological Survey party collected 180 fauna specimens, and accurately identified the limits of the life zones on the south side of the park.

1905 Professor Joseph N. LeConte of the University of California made the first study of the rate of flow of the Nisqually Glacier. This study was later expanded upon by park naturalist Floyd Schmoe and University of Washington Professor Henry C. Landes.

1910-13 U.S.G.S. under Mr. F.E. Matthes began work on an accurate topographic map of the park. The job was finished under C.H. Birdseye.

1913-21 Park ranger and botanist J. B. Flett studied park flora, and published *"Features of the Flora of Mount Rainier National Park."*

1919 A U.S. Biological Survey party, in conjunction with Washington State College and the Park Service, collected 172 bird and 363 mammal specimens.

1930-31 The City of Tacoma, USGS and the National Park Service united in a joint study on the lower Nisqually to determine rate of movement, thickness, and cubical content of the glacier.

1933 Professor James Slater of the College of Puget Sound did a study of amphibians of the area.

1934-39 E. A. Kitchin, a wildlife technician, published *"The Birds of Mount Rainier National Park."*

1935-36 The Park Service prepared a new forest map of the park. It replaced a work done in 1929 by C. Frank Brockman.

1936 Dr. Howard Coombs of the University of Washington published *"The Geology of Mount Rainier National Park."* He also collaborated with Professor G.E. Goodspeed of the U.W. in petrographic studies of rocks in the southeast section of the park.

1937-38 Dr. E.T. Bodenberg made the first moss study at the park.

1938 Walter Brown did a study on reptiles of the park.

1948-49 The Kautz Creek Flood launched a ten year investigation of soil formation and plant succession, a collaborative effort between park naturalists and the University of Washington College of Forestry.

1949 Botanist C. Frank Brockman published *"Flora of Mount Rainier National Park"* and Merlin K. Potts and Russell K. Grater wrote a book called *"Mammals of Mount Rainier National Park."*

Names - Specifically Rainier

The Scientific Names of various flora and fauna from Mount Rainier which bear the names of early scientists are:.

Dr. William Fraser Tolmie:

Tolmie Saxifrage (*Saxifraga tolmiei*)

Dr. Meredith Gairdner: (Gairdner's Woodpecker).

James J. Townsend, (who visited the Pacific Northwest in 1834):

(Townsend's Solitaire, Townsend's Warbler, Townsend's Mole)

Thomas Nuttall (who studied Natural History in the Northwest between 1834-36):

Nuttall Gilia (*Gilia nuttali*) a member of the phlox family

Cornus nuttalli (The Pacific Dogwood)

Edibles in the Park

Mount Rainier abounds with edibles. Naturally occurring foods at Mount Rainier are fish, berries, fungi including mushrooms, and a number of plants most people don't consider edible, but are. Among these are lichen, fiddle head ferns, (a delicacy which once ended up on the Space Needle menu), and nettles.

No food can be taken for commercial purposes, however food for one's own consumption may be taken in reasonable quantities. The park defines reasonable as one grocery bag per vehicle per week. Commercial collecting is prohibited.

There are six fish native to the Park: four species of trout (cutthroat, Rainier, Montana blackspotted, and brown trout), plus two charr (eastern brook trout and Dolly Varden) Lakes are no longer being stocked.

One park naturalist wrote that Mount Rainier has seven species of huckleberry (genus *Vaccinium*), of which six bear blue berries, and one, the whortleberry, (red huckleberry) is red. All huckleberries that are blue, may correctly be called blueberries. Delicious Cascade blueberries, (*Vaccinium delicious*) are the favorites of both the bears and the people. More frequently than many people know, they've picked them side by side. The berries were also a staple of the native Indians, who came to the mountains to pick and dry ample supplies to last them through the winter. These little delicacies also provide a feast for the eyes with their bronze-red autumn foliage. Other edible berries include Oregon grape, salal berries, blackberry and red and blue elderberries .

Mushrooms

Edible mushrooms are morels, chanterelles, oyster mushrooms, matsutake, hericium, and boletus. Matsutake mushrooms grow only in Japan and the Puget Sound area. They are highly prized by the Japanese-Americans who occasionally come to the mountain in 3-generation family groups to hunt for the elusive prize. A dramatic increase in mushroom harvesting occurred beginning in 1992. It is unknown why. Pickers are reminded that commercial harvesting is not allowed. Other types of vegetation such as beargrass, moss, and other forest plants have also been illegally harvested, and the pickers fined.

In Autumn, fall mushrooms pop up after the first rain. They provide good picking through October. There are poisonous mushrooms at Mount Rainier, so don't gamble with your life if you don't know your mushrooms.

Ferns

The forest floor of the Park abounds with the following luxuriant fern.

Genus	Species	Common Name
Family Polypodiaceae		
Adiantum	pedatum	northern maidenhair fern
Asplenium	trichomanes	maidenhair spleenwort
Asplenium	viride	green spleenwort
Athyrium	distentifolium	alpine lady-fern
Athyrium	filix-femina	lady fern
Blechnum	spicant	deer fern
Cheilanthes	gracillima	lace lip-fern
Cryptogramma	Crispa	rock-brake
Cystopteris	fragilis	brittle bladder-fern
Dryopteris	austriaca	mountain wood-fern
Dryopteris	cristata	crested shield-fern
Dryopteris	filix-mas	male fern
Gmnocarpium	dryopteris	oak-fern
Pityrogramma	triangularis	gold-fern
Polypodium	glycyrrhiza	licorice-fern
Polypodium	hesperium	polypody
Polystichum	andersonii	Anderson's swordfern
Polystichum	kruckebergii	Kruckeberg's swordfern
Polystichum	lonchitis	mountain holly-fern
Polystichum	munitum	swordfern
Pteridium	aquilinum	bracken fern
Thelypteris	nevadensis	sierra wood-fern
Woodsia	Oregana	woodsia

Rare and Strange

Probably the strangest edible is Umbilicaria or "rock tripe," an edible which grows on the summit among the hot rocks. It tastes like lettuce, but it's quite rare, so please don't sample it.

Those expert in "living off the land" (any land, not just this land), report there are a number of other edibles which would sustain one (but please do not try them), within the Park: -flowers, roots, fungi, bulbs, camas roots (which when baked, taste like sweet potatoes), leaves, bugs, etc. One which comes as a surprise is the bulb of the avalanche lily. Even though they're edible, please don't try these under any circumstances. Their true value is as a feast for the eyes.

Fungus

Roughly 200 species of fungus thrive in the moist decaying logs all over the forest floor.

The world's largest officially recorded tree fungus (Oxyprus nobilissimus) was found at Mount Rainier in 1946. The giant fungus measured 56 by 37 inches, and weighed more than 300 pounds. The non-edible, monster woody fungus specimen showed thirty-five annual growth layers. It was found growing at the base of a western hemlock in an old-growth forest. *(The Great Northwest Nature Factbook).*

Another Humungus Fungus Amongus

Until 1992 it was thought the "world's biggest *living* thing" was a 1,500-year old, 40-acre fungus in Michigan. That was before the discovery of a far, FAR larger organism thriving in our own Cascades. Washington's gargantuan fungus, an *Armillaria ostoyae,* covers 2-1/2 square miles, making it 40 times bigger. It would have been even more extensive, but loggers stunted its growth when they destroyed the stumps on which it thrives.

Our monster mushroom actually lives closer to Mount Adams than to Mount Rainier, but that's only because it hasn't yet crept over to discover that the west side of the mountains are actually cooler and wetter and more conducive to colossal growth. Perhaps it's just as well. We don't want to read about the fungus that ate Morton.

Mosses, Lichens and other Epiphytes

Old Professor Allen, who used to live outside the park had a collection of mosses which contained 147 specimens, and was conceded by botanists of the day to be the most extensive collection in the world. His mosses were gathered "in the grand forest of the Cascade range" and Mount Tahoma in the vicinity of his Nisqually Valley home and in the Paradise Valley. *(Tacoma News, 3/5/13).*

Over 100 species of moss still grow within the Park, with their habitat ranging from trees to talus slopes. One of the most fascinating is the pale green-grey "moss" which hangs from lowland firs and hemlocks which is in fact goatsbeard lichen. In reality, goatsbeard is not a moss, it is an epiphyte (air plant). This means it grows on a host tree, but extracts its sustenance from rainwater and passing airborne nutrients.

Nitrogen-fixing lichens are also common in old growth forests. Lichens (Alectoria fremontii), grow on alpine firs, but they do not harm them. They are extremely flammable, which is why they are frequently used as firestarters. Lichens (pronounced "likens") also grow on rocks and are the first form of plant life which appears on lava once it has cooled. They are a low form of plant life and are actually an alga and fungus living together symbiotically (benefitting each other). *(Nature Notes May-June 1939)*

Endemic Plants

At least three species of plant are endemic to Mount Rainier. They are

- Tauschia (formerly Hersperogenia) stricklandii
- Castilleja cryptantha, (no English name)
- Pedicularis rainierensis (Rainier lousewort)

Endangered Species

Castilleja cryptantha, found at Mt. Rainier, is a candidate to the Federal Endangered species list.

Environmental Threats (The Park's List)

The following is the park management's list of environmental "threats." By no means is there agreement that all these items are truly "threats." Some would say these are actually the administration's "wish list" (as in, - they wish these things would go away.)

- **Threats to air quality** are among the most serious problems facing the park. The park is downwind from the largest SO_2 source in the state. The four counties adjacent to the park emit 56% of the State's SO_2, and 21% of the NO_2. SO_2 emissions exceed SO_2 emissions from the entire state of Oregon. Air quality standards are not met in the area for ozone, CO, and particulates. Aquatic resources, soils, vegetation and dependent organisms are at risk.

- **Noise pollution.** Increased noise levels from vehicle traffic and aircraft overflights, air pollution from point and non-point sources outside the park already threaten park visibility and natural resources.

- **Land use adjacent to the park**. This includes timber harvesting over the past 100 years which has increased edge effects resulting in the decline of old growth and associated species, and altered habitat for species with large home ranges that utilize habitat both inside and outside the park (mountain goats, bears, mountain lions, etc.) Other impacts include degraded visibility and water quality from slash burns and windthrow.

Other "adjacent land use" items which *the park* considers threats are:

- Spillover recreational use from adjacent US Forest Service lands.

- introduction of exotic plants encroaching from adjacent lands.

- uncontrolled/undesirable fires resulting from fire outbreaks on adjacent lands.

- degradation of aquatic ecosystems from introduction of non-native fish species and urbanization.

• **Internal threats to park resources** include altered run-off and infiltration patterns caused by roads and parking lots; hazardous substance spills; air pollution from vehicle exhaust fumes, campfires, and building heating systems; water pollution from recreational use, including human wastes.

• **Introduction of exotic species:** non-native fish in naturally fishless lakes have dramatically altered these aquatic ecosystems (amphibians, invertebrates and certain plant populations). They also fear exotic plants brought in by visitors or through management activities are aggressive and capable of invading undisturbed natural areas causing disruptions to native plant communities.

• **Utilization of native materials from within the park,** such as management's use of gravel fill for trails or trees for bridge replacement; poached wildlife, fungii, berries, moss, and other plant gathering affect park ecosystems to some degree.

• **Human caused wildland fires** and suppression of naturally occurring wildfires remain threats to the integrity of park ecosystems.

Information from park resource management documents

Grazing

Beginning in the 1890's cattle and sheep grazed all over the mountains between the Yakima Valley and the eastern slopes of the Cascades. The cattlemen opposed establishing a national park, because they felt it might diminish their grazing lands. By 1899, wandering bands of sheep had already reached the high meadows of Yakima Park.

A 1923 Park Newsletter assured visitors that the sheep and cattle one might encounter in the back country were there legally. It pointed out that grazing was allowed in order to "utilize forage which would otherwise go to waste, and moreover, if not utilized would constitute a very real fire menace. This livestock is Washington owned, and helps to feed and clothe many of the State's citizens by furnishing beef, mutton, and wool - all important Washington products. The mountains may be enjoyed for camping and recreation, but it should be remembered that they are serving also a very real economic purpose by furnishing summer pasture for many thousands of sheep and cattle."

Grazing continued through World War I, and the Yakima Park flower fields, which once vied with those of Paradise for floral loveliness, never fully recovered.

Meadow Restoration

Each year dozens of Social trails in the Paradise meadows are stabilized, filled and partially planted or seeded. Sites damaged by human impact do not regenerate naturally. Accomplishing this ever-recurring task requires the efforts of many dedicated volunteers, both in growing and transplanting the seedlings.

Seventeen thousand native plants are produced in the park's greenhouse for use in the revegetation projects each year. Volunteers from the Washington Native Plant Society, led by long-time volunteer Mary Fries, have collected seeds for the project for the past twelve years. Staff and volunteer trail monitors also collect seeds. One volunteer spent several summers in the Tipsoo Lake area and collected most of the seeds used there. Others collected in the Sunrise area.

Also in 1994, a memorial donation was received which provided the funding for a new 1,800 ft^2. greenhouse to supplement the exisitng 270 ft^2. greenhouse.

Kings of the Forest: Trees

Forests cover two-thirds or about 200 square miles of the Park. Mount Rainier's twenty-seven species of trees are a study in contrasts. They range from towering giants to gnarled dwarfs. It isn't uncommon for Douglas fir, Western red cedar and Western hemlock (the valley/lower slope dwellers) to rise 200 feet or more in the air.

Douglas fir (*Pseudotsuga menziesii*). These big trees are among the world's tallest living plumbing systems. A 260-foot Douglas-fir may hold as much as 1,140 gallons, or 3.4 tons of water. Some of the largest Douglas firs in the park are in the Mowich River valley, and along the Ohanapecosh River.

The "Columbus Tree" was a large Douglas Fir over 750 years old, which was 3.4 miles inside the park, between the Nisqually entrance and Longmire.

In the 1920's there was a monumental record size fir tree about 3 miles down the road from the Ipsut entrance. Much discussion went on about how to best route the road around the tree, but while the talk went on, the man who owned the land went out one night and cut the tree down.

Alaska yellow cedar (*Chamaecyparis nootkatensis*). The "stinking cedar" has light bark, yellow green foliage and sparse branching. The upper Laughingwater Creek Trail has a lot of these old giants, but the biggest of all is about 1/2 mile below Ipsut Pass on the Wonderland Trail. For a while it was considered to be the largest one in the U.S. until a larger one was found on the Olympic Peninsula. The Alaska cedars in this cluster are over 1,200 years old.

The Yew tree (*Taxus brevifolia*), has been found to yield Taxol, a substance used to produce the only successful drug to date found to prove effective against ovarian cancer. Unfortunately, removing the bark kills the slow growing tree which even at 300 to 700 years old, may still only be up to 30 feet tall, and have a trunk diameter of only 5 to 10 inches. The Yew is found at Mount Rainier in the Humid Transitional zone.

Red Alder (*Alnus rubra*) , a pioneer plant which grows in abundance after a natural disturbance such as fire. A member of the birch family, red alder is characterized by its white trunk and deciduous habit. The white color is caused by an abundance of lichens, plants growing on the dark gray bark.

Trees of Mount Rainier

Pine Family (Pinaceae)

Western white pine   (*Pinus monticola*)

Whitebark pine   (*Pinus albicaulis*)

Lodgepole pine   (*Pinus contorta*)

Ponderosa pine   (*Pinus ponderosa*)

Engelmann spruce   (*Pinea engelmannii*)

Sitka spruce (*Pinea sitchensis*)

Western hemlock (*Tsuga heterophylla*)

Mountain Hemlock   (*Tsuga mertensiana*)

Douglas fir (*Pseudotsuga menziesii*)

Grand fir   (*Abies grandis*)

Pacific silver fir (*Abies amabilis*)

Noble fir   (*Abies procera*)

Subalpine fir (*Abies lasiocarpa*)

Cypress Family (Cupressaceae)

Western redcedar (*Thuja plicata*)

Alaska cedar (*Chamaecyparis nootkatensis*)

Yew Family (Taxaceae)

Western yew (*Taxus brevifolia*)

Willow Family (Salicaceae)

Scouler willow   (*Salix scouleriana*)

Pacific willow   (*Salis lasiandra*)

Black willow   (*Populus trichocarpa*)

Birch Family (Betulaceae)

Red alder   (*Alnus rubua*)

Dogwood Family (Cornaeae)

Pacific dogwood (*Cornus nuttallii*)

Maple Family (Aceraceae)

Bigleaf maple   (*Acer macrophyllum*)

Vine maple (*Acer circinatum*)

Douglas' maple   (*Acer glabrum var. douglasii*)

Rose Family (Rosaceae)

Wild crabapple   (*Pyrus fusca*)

Tree Zones and Life Zones

Picture driving north, from Puget Sound to the Arctic. The climate would grow colder and the vegetation would differ until you reached perpetual ice. This can be done in a brief trek by going to Mount Rainier. As you climb from the Sound to the mountain, the vegetation changes, and the temperature gets cooler. Were you to climb the mountain, you would reach the region of perpetual snow and ice, just like the Arctic.

The unit of measure used in describing the types of vegetation and wildlife at various altitudes are called life zones and there are four life zones within the park. An altitudinal difference of each 1,000 feet is the equivalent of a difference in latitude of about 300 miles. Thus the Humid Transitional Life Zone is the "Puget Sound zone." The Canadian Zone resembles Southern Canada in plant and animal life. The Hudsonian Zone resembles life in the latitude of Hudson's Bay, and the Arctic-Alpine Zone resembles the Arctic. These vary slightly with "micro-climates" and side of the mountain.

Humid Transition Life Zone (below 2,000 feet). This zone is dense old growth lowland forests composed of trees that tower 250 to 300 feet, and reach diameters of 80-100 inches at chest height. Trees here are Douglas fir, western hemlock, western red cedar, vine maple, alder, Pacific yew, and black cottonwood. Undergrowth plants are devil's club, vanilla leaf, salal, Oregon grape, huckleberry and blackberry. Wildlife here are black bear, black-tailed deer, beaver, hare, marmot, grouse and quail. This zone is found only in the southeast portion of the park, in the Stevens Canyon-Cowlitz River area.

Canadian Life Zone (2,000-3,500 feet). This comprises the most extensive forested zone at Mount Rainier National Park. Trees in this zone are Douglas Fir, Pacific silver fir, western white pine, noble fir, spruce, Alaska yellow cedar, and western hemlock. Undergrowth at these elevations is sparce, however it is at the upper end of this zone that some of the most magnificent flower meadows begin. Fauna is the same as in the Humid Transitional Zone.

Hudsonian Life Zone (3,500-6,000 feet). This zone is subdivided into two parts. At about the 4,500 foot level in the lower forest subzone, the Mountain Hemlock becomes the dominant tree in the forest. Other trees in this zone are Pacific Silver Fir, Subalpine Fir, white-bark pine and the Alaska Cedar. The upper (Parkland) subzone lies between 5,200-6,000 feet, is basically treeless. It has mostly flowering plants, alpine meadows, and Indian bear grass. Whistling marmot, mountain goat, least hare, grouse and ptarmigan make up the fauna.

Alpine Life Zone (above 6,000-8,000 feet). At Mount Rainier, timberline is above 6500 feet. Except for an occasional juniper or an arctic willow, no trees are to be found here, however mosses, grasses and sedges are plentiful. Mountain goats and Rainier white-tailed ptarmigan thrive at these altitudes.

Arctic Zone (above 8,000 feet) is just as the name implies, ice and snow.

Old Growth Forest

An old growth forest has four components: Large live trees at least 200 years old, multi-layered canopies, snags (standing dead trees) and down woody material (fallen, decaying trees). Within the Park boundaries, there are at least 91,139.478 acres of old growth forest at least 200 years old. In fact the vast majority of the forest within the park falls into the old growth category, with some stands estimated to be 1,000 years old.

Many people tend to revere old growth forest, and think of it as something permanent, that if "treated with kid gloves," the trees will live forever. This is simply not true. If the trees don't succumb to natural threats such as fire, insects or windthrow, the trees will eventually die of old age.

The Forest Hospital

It won't take much hiking through the forest to see the trees in various stages of their life cycle. This hospital contains both a nursery and a mortuary. Amid the millions of huge healthy robust trees, note too the dead and dying, the broken and the injured. Decaying trees are returned to soil by fungi, insects, and bacteria.

Included in this life cycle are "nurse logs," rotting logs with young trees growing on them. The decaying wood absorbs and retains water, which nourishes the seedlings and helps provide the nutrients they need to grow. Years later those seedlings will grow into a perfectly straight row of trees the length of the old nurse. Decaying stumps frequently serve the same role, and support young trees on their rotting tops. Their stepchildren are later recognized by "hollow roots" above the forest floor.

Snags (standing dead trees) are another important component of the forest, for they provide wildlife habitat.

For another fascinating forest phenomenon, when you come upon an uprooted giant take time to study the root system. It's amazing that such colossal trees can have such shallow roots. Yet not only do the small roots gather the water and nutrients from the earth necessary to sustain the tree, they anchor the giants (for centuries!) through drought, an occasional flood, tons of snowpack, and weather extremes ranging from roasting to sub-zero. Their vulnerability is wind!

The Secret of the Rings

Reading tree rings is the science of Dendrochronology. The rings tell a tree's age as well as a weather report of each year. Dark rings indicate summer wood, while light rings mean spring wood. A wide ring means lots of water and lots of growth. A narrow rings means a dry lean year. The only tree which may have more than one ring per year is the Alder, which occasionally gets two. The fluctuations of the glaciers have recorded less definitively the same information.

There are tree ring cross sections at Longmire and Ohanapecosh.

Yes, Logging

While it will come as a surprise to many, logging took place within the Park boundaries regularly up through the mid-50's. While to some, by today's standards cutting even one tree is one too many. Back then trees were regularly cut or removed because of blowdown, log jams, insect infestation, "dangerous" trees, boundary swaths, trail clearing, road right-of-ways, and avalanche damage. One 1944 report told of a protest by the Tacoma Chamber of Commerce, over the proposed logging of 304 acres by the Northern Pacific Railroad within Mount Rainier National Park.

Types of Forest

Forest	131,058.977 acres (GIS calc)
Old Growth Forest (200+ years old)	91,139.478 acres (GIS calc)
Subalpine	65,090.658 acres (GIS calc)
Alpine	25,227.922 acres (GIS calc)

Wildflowers

"Consider the lilies how they grow: they toil not, nor do they spin, but Solomon in all his glory was not arrayed as one of these." Luke 12:27

One early writer waxed poetic, and claimed there were 365 species of flowers, - one for every day of the year. The next book said there were over 700 species of flowering plants. The finest displays are at Paradise, Spray Park, Van Trump Park and Indian Henrys. John Muir wrote that the flower wreath of Rainier's Parks is incomparably greater than that of any other region he had known.

The first to bloom, the delicate avalanche lily, (Erythronium montanum), is in a rush to celebrate life, it earns its name by bursting through the receding snows, racing the melting snows uphill. The fragile lily blooms only once each five or six years, since the brief growing season is too short for the small bulb to absorb and store adequate energy. The lilies are soon followed by purple lupine, Indian paintbrush, columbine, phlox, beargrass and soon, forty species are in bloom. The very last beauty to bloom is the Mountain Bog Gentian.

Because of the high altitudes and extreme weather conditions under which some species must exist, many have shown unique adaptations as they struggle to survive. These range from restricted growth, using the same leaves year after year (instead of growing new ones), and putting their primary growth into roots instead of foliage.

Mount Rainier Flowers of the Sub-Alpine Meadows
White Section

Common Name	Scientific Name	Family
alumroot	*Heuchera spp.*	Saxifragaceae
beargrass	*Xerophyllum tenax*	Liliaceae
bog orchid	*Habernaria dilatata*	Orchidaceae
bramble; blackberry	*Rubus spp.*	Rosaceae
coltsfoot	*Petasites frigidus*	Compositae
cow parsnip	*Hercleum lanatum*	Umbelliferae
heather, white	*Cassiope mertensiana*	Ericaceae
hellebore, false	*Veratrum viride*	Liliaceae
huckleberry; blueberry	*Vaccinium spp.*	Ericaceae
lily, avalanche	*Erythornium montanum*	Liliaceae
marchmarigold	*Clatha biflora*	Ranunculaceae
meadow parsley	*Ligusticum grayi*	Umbelliferae
mountain ash	*Sorgus scopulina*	Rosaceae
mountain bisort; dock	*Polygonum bistortoides*	Polygonaceae
partridgefoot	*Luetkea pectinata*	Rosaceae
pearly-everlasting	*Anaphalis margaritacea*	Compositae
pedicularis, coiled beak	*Pedicularis contorta*	Scrophulariaceae
pedicularis, sickletop	*Pedicularis racemose*	Scrophulariaceae
rhododendron, white; Cascades azalea	*Rhododendrom albiflorum*	Ericaceae
sandwort	*Arenaeia spp.*	Caryophyllaceae
saxifrage, Tolmie	*Saxifraga tolmiei*	Saxifragaceae
saxifrage, yellowdot	*Saxifraga austromontana*	Saxifragaceae
springbeauty	*Claytonia lanceolata*	Portulacaceae
valerian, Sitka	*Valeriana sitchensis*	Valerianaceae
western anemone; pasqueflower	*Anemone occidentalis*	Ranunculaceae
yarrow	*Archillea millefolium*	Compositae

Yellow Section

arnica, broadleaf	*Arnica latifolia*	Compositae
buckwheat, wild	*Eriogonum spp.*	Polygonaceae
buttercup	*Ranunculus eschscholtzii*	Ranunculaeceae
cinquefoil	*Potentilla spp.*	Rosaceae
fleabane, gold	*Erigeron aureus*	Compositae
goldenrod, mountain	*Solidago spp.*	Compositae
groundsel; senecio;ragwort	*Senecio integerrimus*	Compositae
groundsel; arrowleaf	*Senecio traingularis*	Compositae
lily, glacier	*Erythronium grandiflorum*	Liliaceae
lomatium	*Lomatium spp.*	Umbelliferae
monkeyflower, common	*Mimulus guttatus*	Scrophulariaceae
monkeyflower, yellow	*Mimulus tilingii*	Scrophulariaceae
pedicularis, bracted	*Pedicularis bracteosa*	Scrophulariaceae
stonecrop; sedum		Sedum divergens
Crassulaceaeviolet, pioneer	*Viola glabella*	Violaceae
violet, pioneer	*Viola glabella*	Violaceae

373

Orange-yellow Section

Common Name	*Scientific Name*	*Family*
tigerlily, Columbia	*Lilium columbianum*	Liliaceae

Red Section

columbine	*Aquilegia formosa*	Ranunculaeceae
fireweed	*Epilobium angustifolium*	Primulaceae
heather, red	*Phyllodoce empetriformis*	Ericaceae
paintbrush, magenta	*Castilleja parviflora*	Scrophulariaceae
penstemon, cliff	*Penstemon rupicola*	Scrophulariaceae
spirea, rosy	*Spiraea densiflora*	Rosaceae
thistle	*Cirsium edule*	Compositae

Red-pink Section

Jeffrey shootingstar	*Dodecatheon jeffreyi*	Primulaceae
paintbrush, scarlet;	*Castilleja miniata*	Scrophulariaceae
pedicularis, birdsbeak	*Pedicularis ornithorhyncha*	Scrophulariaceae
pedicularis, elephanthead	*Pedicularis groenlandica*	Scrophulariaceae

Pink Section

monkeyflower, lewis	*Mimulus lewisii*	Scrophulariaceae
moss campion	*Silene acaulis*	Caryophyllaceae
phlox, spreading	*Phlox diffusa*	Polemoniaceae

Pink-purple Section

fireweed	*Epilobium angustifolium*	Primulaceae
phacelia, silky	*Phacelia sericea*	Polemoniaceae

Blue-purple Section

aster, alpine	*Aster alpigenus*	
aster, purple	*Aster ledophyllus*	Compositae
aster, tall leafybract	*Aster foliaceus*	Compositae
butterwort	*Pinguicula vulgaris*	Lentibulariaceae
daisy, mountain;fleabane	*Erigeron peregrinum*	Lenticulariaceae
speedwell, Cusick's	*Veronica cusickii*	Scrophulariaceae
violet, hook	*Viola adunca*	Violaceae
violet, marsh	*Viola palustris*	Violaceae

Blue Section

bluebell; harebell	*Campanula rotundifolia*	Campanulaceae
gentian	*Gentiana claycose*	Gentianaceae
Jacob's ladder	*Polemonium pulcherrimum*	Polemoniaceae
larkspur	*Delphinium spp.*	Ranunculaeceae
lupine	*Lupinus latifolius*	Leguminosae
lupine, subslpine	*Lupinus lepidus*	Leguminosae
Mertensia; merten's bluebells	*Mertensia paniculata*	Boraginaceae

Brown Section

fescue	*Festuca spp.*	Gramineae
sedge, black alpine	*Carex nigranicans*	Cyperaceae

Wildflowers of the Lower Forests

White section

Common Name	Scientific Name	Family
beargrass	*Xeroxphyllum tenax*	Liliaceae
bedstraw	*Galium triflorum*	Rubiaceae
bog-orchid	*Habernaria dilatata*	Orchidaceae
bunchberry dogwood	*Cornus canadensis*	Cornaceae
coltsfoot	*Petasites frigidus*	Compositae
cow parsnip	*Heracleum lanatum*	Umbelliferae
creeping raspberry	*Rubus lasiococcus*	Rosaceae
false solomon's seal	*Smilacina racemosa*	Liliaceae
foamflower	*Tiarella unifoliata*	Saxifragaceae
indianpipe	*Monotrapa uniflora*	Ericaceae
oxalis	*Oxalis oregana*	Oxalidaceae
ox-eye daisy	*Chrysanthemum leucanthemum*	Compositae
pathfinder	*Adenocaulon bicolor*	Compositae
pearly-everlasting	*Anaphalis margaritacea*	Compositae
queencup bead lily	*Clintonia uniflora*	Liliaceae
rattlesnake-plaintain	*Goodyera oblongifolia*	Orchidaceae
salal	*Gaultheria shallon*	Ericaceae
springbeauty	*Claytonia lanceolata*	Portulacaceae
starflower	*Trientalis latifolia*	Primulaceae
thimbleberry	*Rubus parviflorus*	Rosaceae
trailing rubus	*Rubus pedatus*	Rosaceae
trillium	*Trillium ovatum*	Liliaceae
vanillaleaf	*Achlys triphylla*	Berberidaceae

Yellow section

arrowleaf groundsel	*Senecio triangularis*	Compositae
monkeyflower	*Mimulus guttatus*	Scrophulariaceae
skunk cabbage	*Lysichitum americanum*	Araceae

Orange section

columbia tigerlily	*Lilium columbianum*	Liliaceae
salmonberry	*Rubus spectabilis*	Rosaceae

Red section

columbine	*Aquilegia formosa*	Ranunculaceae
coral root	*Corallorhiza spp.*	Orchidaceae
devils club	*Oplopanax horridum*	Araliaceae
penstemon	*Penstemon spp.*	Scrophulariaceae

Purplish-pink section

fireweed	*Epilobium angustifolium*	Primulaceae

Purplish-brown section

wild ginger	*Asarum caudatum*	Aristolochiaceae

Purplish-blue section

canada thistle	*Cirsium arvense*	Compositae
upine	*Lupinus latifolius*	Leguminosae
selfheal	*Prunella vulgaris*	Labiatae

1

Still true today

"Every one of these parks, great and small, is a garden filled knee-deep with fresh, lovely flowers of every hue, the most luxuriant and the most extravagantly beautiful of all the alpine gardens I ever beheld in all my mountain top wanderings." *(John Muir, Steep Trails, 1918)*

Practical Flower Conservation

"Unpicked flowers give unending enjoyment" wrote Floyd Schmoe in 1924. "You are only one of the many hundreds of thousands to whom these flowers belong. Those who come after you have as much right to the enjoyment of these God-given beauties as you have."

The Indians had a wise axiom, "do not pick the first plant you come to." We know now that the plant may be extending its range in that direction. Some plants in subalpine meadows bloom only once every several years. It takes years for them to recover after being walked on, which is why it imperative that hikers stay on established paved or rock-lined trails.

The excelsior you see in some meadows is repairing erosion damage. It protects seedlings, moderates ground temperatures and retains moisture. Eventually it disintegrates and turns to soil.

Fossils

No identifiable fossils were found in the Ohanapecosh Formation within the Park, but about 2,000 feet west of the boundary on the north side of the North Puyallup River, Dr. Roland W. Brown collected and identified the following fossils : *Sabal* sp., *Carya* sp. *Castanea* sp. *Chaetoptelea* sp. *Cercidiphyllum* sp., *Hydrangea* sp. *Platanus* sp. *Cinnamonmum* sp. *Laurus* sp. *Sassafras* sp. *Liquidambar* sp. According to Dr. Brown, this floral assemblage indicates a late Eocene Age.

D. W. Taylor identified a fossil mollusk from near Packwood. Additional fossil localities are in areas south and southwest of the Park. A fossil collection was taken from a tongue of coal-bearing arkose in the Ohanapecosh Formation on Summit Creek, about 2 miles southeast of the park. Dr. Brown dated the latter collection as being from the middle Eocene period.

In 1941, a well preserved lower jaw of the middle Oligocene to lower Miocene oreodont, *Eporeodon* was found about 1.5 miles north of the Tieton Reservoir Dam. *(Geology of MRNP, Wa., Professional paper 444)*

Two finds of fossil leaves and twigs was made in 1935 by Ranger Howard Coombs, however it was not noted where he found them.

In 1978 petrified wood was found on the Eagle Peak Trail. And in recent years, fossil leaf prints were found near the Ipsut Pass Trail. Just remember, if finding any fossils, it's against the law to remove them. Leave them in place, and notify a ranger of the find and the location.

Animals

Life in the Wild

For most people, seeing wildlife is the highlight of their park visit. A few minutes alone with a tiny chipmunk, brazen camp-robber or little masked-bandit raccoon can be a happy and exciting experience for a city dweller. But the diversity of creatures at the park ranges from tiny shrews to huge elk. At least 50 species of mammals are known to live within the park boundaries.

A 1924 count made by Naturalist Floyd Schmoe showed there were ten Elk, 350 deer, 250 goats, 200 bears, 300 coyote/bobcat/lynx, 15 timber wolves, 100 foxes, 30 cougar/mountain lions, 50 eagles (bald & golden) and 100 beavers. Some of those numbers have changed radically, with elk now numbering in the hundreds, and the last timber wolf seen at Crystal Mountain in the 1970's.

The National Park offers the best protection possible for the creatures and plants living within its confines. The shelter of the park provides safety from hunters, trappers, poachers, insecticides, herbicides, and nearly everything but an occasional encounter with a windshield or tire or bumper.

Black Bears (Ursus americanus)

Mount Rainier black bears (the only species in the park), top out at about three feet, shoulder height, and about six feet long. They weigh in at about 300 pounds, 120 of which is muscle. Yearlings weigh 60 to 120 pounds. They come in a variety of colors: - black, blue-black, gunmetal, brown, rusty cinnamon and smoky white. Whatever the body color, the muzzle is always medium brown. A litter may contain cubs of different colors.

It is estimated there are 30,000 bears in Washington state, with about 100 of those in MRNP. Bears are omnivores, which means they feed on both plant and animal material. Their natural food is carpenter ants, grubs, termites, berries, grasses, wood fiber, insects, eggs, nuts, fish, occasional meat and carrion, and fungi.

Cubs are born while the sow is still hibernating. Litters vary from one to three cubs. The female breeds only once every two years, and keeps her young in tow for nearly two years. She is fiercely protective and will attack if a human gets between herself and her cubs. When sows come out from hibernating, they will girdle young Douglas firs up to 10"diameter, in search of sap rising in the phloem.

Bears are primarily nocturnal, which is why they're often spotted making rounds to known food sources at night. Otherwise, backcountry bears are wary of humans, most encounters are purely accidental.

Because a bear's back legs are longer than the front, he prefers to escape uphill if startled. Thus in close encounters of the bear kind, you go downhill, because the bear will try to escape by going up. A bear running downhill can easily go tail over tincups and somersault down the hill.

The bears can be found anywhere in the park, usually below 6500 feet. Most of Mount Rainier's bears hibernate during the winter, although one may occasionally decide to "stay - up" and winter over in the low-lands.

Camouflaged Critters

Four species at the mountain have the unique distinction of changing the colors of their coats with the season changes. The ptarmigan, snowshoe hare (Lepus americanus cascadensis), weasel and ermine (or least weasel) wear white in winter, and brown in summer.

Hibernating Critters

Bats, Bears, chipmunks, jumping mice, marmots and squirrels all hibernate. Two other species, the skunk and the raccoon, enter into a state of dormancy, but not a true state of hibernation.

Coyotes (Canis latrans)

Coyote, are sometime called Prairie Wolves. (Canus) means "dog" and the coyote is indeed in the dog family. They're about the size of a collie, and similar in appearance, except for their brownish-grey color. Their paw print is a "maple leaf" shape. and their tracks meander. Coyotes are the most abundant of any predatory animal in the Park. Coyotes are frequently seen near "the goat overlook" below Longmire, also along Stevens Canyon Road and Box Canyon.

Deer (Cervidae)

Thanks to Walt Disney and Bambi, many people imagine deer as lovely docile animals that stand around meadows sniffing flowers while waiting to get their picture taken. Be forewarned: a deer can administer a hard enough kick to break the leg of the recipient. They kick to the side, not to the back, as might be imagined. In fact we found one old report of a doe at the park who knocked down a boy who was tormenting her, then jumped on him. They have also been known to drive off a cougar with their front hooves.

In the old days, people were continually making the mistake of bringing "abandoned" fawns in to the old rangers (They weren't abandoned. Fawns are taught to "freeze" when danger is near, and mother is never far away.) Once the young ones are touched by humans, the damage may be done, and mother will have nothing more to do with them, so the rangers then had no choice but to take them in. One such orphan was "Pete", a young male who was adopted by the Longmire community. Pete would come in a house and curl up in an easy chair if a door was left open. "Nancy" was another orphan who won the hearts of many old-time park families.

On the west side of Mount Rainier, the deer are Columbian black-tailed (Odocoileus hemionus columbianus). Those on the east side are Mule deer (Odocoileus hemionus hemionus). They have occasionally been known to interbreed. Both deer leave "dew prints" (split hoof prints). The antlers of deer grow at the rate of nearly an inch a day.

Elk (Cervus canadensis)

One morning the lady who owns the Wild Berry restaurant awoke to hear an ungodly clatter on her enclosed porch. She sprang from her bed to see what was the matter, only to find it was an elk who invited himself in to breakfast on her decorative Kale.

There are four sub-species of elk found in north America. Those found west of the Cascades from Oregon to British Columbia and on Vancouver Island are Roosevelt Elk.

They are the size of a horse, weighing 500-600 lbs. People tend to think all elk are only on the east side of Mount Rainier, but they're all over the park and far down into the foothills as far as Eatonville. Despite their size, they're agile and elusive, and can race through dense forest at a dead run. Their coloring is a rich reddish brown coat and a distinctive pale yellowish rump patch.

Aside from their size and strength, (even barbed wire doesn't phase an elk), an elk's antlers are particularly interesting. The antlers are solid dermal bone, primarily calcium and phosphorous, and are shed and re-grown annually. Growth is triggered by changing testosterone levels during the infertility period in the early spring. During the growth period, antlers are covered with velvet hair-like extensions of the skin. The velvet, through a network of fine blood vessels, carries the mineral salts and nourishment to the developing antlers.

A mature bull will grow a complete set of antlers in only 4 1/2 months. At an incredible rate of 1/2 inch per day, growth is completed around mid-July. Fully developed antlers are pure bone with a spongy bone interior. A mature bull's antlers can weigh 35-45 pounds. The size of the antlers are a combination of factors: age, heredity, and available nutrition on the bull's winter and summer ranges.

Shedding of antlers is the result of a rapid decrease in the testosterone levels in the blood after the fall mating season. This loosens the junction of the antlers at the pedicels.

Color of the antlers is a combination of hemoglobin residues left behind by the drying velvet, plus rubbing stains from the pitch and sap of trees acquired when a bull rids his new set of antlers of the dried velvet. Roosevelt elk antlers are generally smaller than those of the Yellowstone or Rocky Mountain elk.

Though elk were reported at the mountain much earlier, in 1924 "Frank & Frances" arrived from the Olympic Peninsula, as two young scared elk whose progeny were to populate Mt. Rainier for many years to come. *(Nature notes, 11/24)*.

North Side Elk Viewing Site

Those who want to get a close-up look at elk can do so at the new White River Elk Herd Viewing Site located about 30 miles east of Enumclaw. Here visitors can see some of the White River Elk Herd which numbers about 1,200 animals. Roughly 200 members of the herd stay in the lowlands year round.

Take Highway 410 about 25 miles east of Enumclaw to Forest Service Road 72. Follow the Forest Service Road for about 8 miles to the site. Drive slowly along the narrow gravel road, and watch for oncoming traffic.

Upon reaching the viewing area, walk quietly to the field, and scan the brush and trees for the elk. The animals are most active in the early morning and late afternoon/early evening. That's when they feed.

Winter Elk Feeding Stations

During the winter the large White Pass elk herd and a smaller herd of California bighorn sheep are fed at the Clemons feeding station in the 84,000 acre Oak Creek Wildlife Recreation Area. The feeding operation takes place daily at 1:30 p.m. from mid-November through late winter, off Highway 12, about 2 miles from the Highway 410 junction. The best viewing is in January and early February. Watch for animals on the road in the area. This is also a good place to see golden eagles, prairie falcons, various hawks, Lewis's woodpeckers, western tanagers, and other songbirds.

For a brochure or information, contact: Oak Creek Wildlife Area, Department of Wildlife, 23205 Highway 12, Naches, WA 98937, (509) 653-2390.

On the west side, just east of Elbe another large herd congregates to find natural feed between the Nisqually River and the lower foothills. Still another herd of 40-60 migrates to near Eatonville.

Fox (Vulpes cascadensis)

The little fox found at Mount Rainier is the Cascade Mountain red fox. Foxes used to be much more prevalent in the olden days than they are now. A 1937 Naturalist's Report noted several dens in the Paradise Valley. He noted one had four pups and the another had three. To help with identifying footprints, note that a fox walks in a straight line as opposed to the meandering of a coyote or dog.

Little Spotted Skunk

The little spotted skunk (Spilogale putorius) may not be popular, or plentiful, but will occasionally show up as roadkill around the park.

Marmots (Marmota caligata cascadensis)

All subalpine areas have large colonies of whistling marmots. Hoary marmots, the largest of the Park's rodents, can weigh as much as 18 pounds. They have an amusing morning ritual that's fun to watch. They go visiting from colony to colony, greeting other marmots by rubbing noses and cheeks (where there are scent glands), and touching mouths, giving the appearance of kissing. They have gotten a rise out of many a young female hiker who thought she was being whistled at. Little do the ladies know their secret admirer was a foot tall. Marmots hibernate.

Mountain Goats (Oreamnos americanus)

The only true Arctic Alpine Zone mammal in the park is the mountain goat. Even in winter, the nimble goats prefer life on the ridges, cliffs and other high points around the mountain. These shaggy cliff dwellers can perch on ledges too small to accommodate all four cloven feet. (However they also fall off of cliffs and snow cornices, and die!) Far from the park's 1924 count of 250 goats, the current goat population is estimated at about 450 animals. The best chance of seeing one would be to hike to Summerland, Panhandle Gap or Indian Bar.

The average billy weighs 200-250 pounds, and the average nanny 150-200 pounds. Their height is about 40 inches tall, and both males and females have short backward curving horns which are not shed. They range in bands of up to 40 or more. They are seldom found below 4000 feet, although the author's kids once found a lot of goat wool on trees and bushes in the woods behind Longmire.

Dr. Murray Johnson of Tacoma had graduate students up at the mountain for years doing studies on mice and mountain goats.

Goats also range out of the park now, and have been seen at High Hut above Ashford.

Mountain Lion (Felis concolor)

In the east they go by the name panther or catamount (cat of the mountains) and in the southwest they're red tigers or puma, but at Mount Rainier they're Northwestern cougars, or Mountain lions. These 4-legged power machines can carry off a full-grown cow or jump a 6' fence with a calf in its mouth. There were 1500 of them in Washington as of 1984.

There have been numerous cougar sightings in the last ten years, although a person may spend many summers at the mountain and never see a cougar. That doesn't mean a cougar has not seen him. Many a hiker has been shaken to find, if he has occasion to double back on the trail, fresh cougar tracks following him. They have been known to stalk humans for hours.

The sight of a full grown mountain lion can be an adrenalin rush of the first order. The average male is 7-8 feet long (from nose to tail), females average 6 feet long. They weigh between 150-200 lbs. In 1895, an Ashford man killed one on Tum Tum Mountain that measured 9 feet nose to tail. It's their characteristic l-o-o-o-ong round tail which sets them apart from other American cats. A grown lion varies in color from tan to grey to reddish brown but the tip of the tail is just about always black. They have typical cat family prints, 4 toes on front and rear, with front feet larger than rear. The tracks are 3" x 3". They regularly trot a 20 x 30 mile territory.

Their primary food is venison. C.A. Stoner, an old-time hunter, trapper and timber cruiser from Ashford, was a foremost authority on cougar. His studies showed that a cougar would kill at least one deer a week. One that he observed ate a full grown deer in three days, and the fourth day killed another. Stoner observed that they kill the deer by a bite on the neck behind the ears, and generally break the neck in a sudden twist. They do not strike down the animal with the fore paws as is sometimes thought. They feed by gutting the deer first, then eating the flesh, bones, and hide, but discarding the hair.

There have been countless sightings over the years within the park, but it's worth noting that there has been an increase in both the cougar populations in the Northwest, and in the attacks on humans in the last few years, but *no* attacks in the park. The most blatant attack was on Vancouver Island, when a cougar came in and attacked a young boy just a few feet from his father.

One hundred twenty have been tagged in the Greenwater area alone in recent years.

Raccoons (Procyon lotor)

Looking like little bandits, these black-masked nocturnal creatures are often seen in the trees, scurrying about in the evening, or using their paws like hands to wash their food. In the early days, raccoons had dinner routes around the Longmire residential area. If dinner wasn't waiting on the ranger's porches, they would rattle the screen door to protest the oversight. If they couldn't eat at home, and had to eat out, they all knew where to go: The National Park Inn. The candy counter was their favorite objective. They really are little bandits!

Rodents

Park critters classified as rodents are shrews, moles, voles, porcupines, conies (pikas), squirrels, rats, mice, beaver, chipmunks, gophers and marmots. The squirrels, mice, rats and chipmunks are world class scavengers and can empty an unattended pack in seconds.

Wood Rats (Neotoma cinerea occidentalis)

The most prevalent rat at Mount Rainier is the Western bushy-tailed wood rat, occasionally dancing on their hind legs. Actually they're jumping, not dancing, and this is part of their courtship ritual. The other rat is the Brown rat (Rattus norvegicus).

Species Formerly in the Park

Early ranger reports tell of animals that have not been sighted for decades:

Fisher	Martes pennanti (Erxleben)
Muskrat	Ondatra zibethica (Linnaeus)
Norway rat	Rattus norvegicus (Berkenhout)
River Otter	Lutra canadensis (Schreber)
Wolf	Canis lupus (Linnaeus
Wolverine	Gulo luscus (Linnaeus)

Animals Near, but not in, the Park

Myotis

    California myotis **Myotis californicus** (Audubon & Bachman)

    Little brown myotis   **Myotis lucifugus** (LeConte)

    Long-eared myotis   **Myotis evotis** (H. Allen)

Rabbit

    Eastern cottontail **Sylvilagus floridanus** (J.A. Allen)

Skunk

    Striped skunk   **Mephitis mephitis** (Schreber)

Squirrel

    Beechy ground squirrel   **Otospermophilus beecheyi** (Richardson)

The Fate of the Animals

Abandoned Animals

Resist the urge to pick up what appears to be orphans or abandoned animals and birds. The parents are probably just off foraging for food. It's natural to want to help the small creatures, but once a baby has been touched by humans, the parent will abandon it. Thus your 'help' may actually sentence the animal to life in a zoo or fenced game preserve. Animals raised by humans that get used to having their food provided for them, can seldom make it on their own in the wild.

Change of attitude toward animals

In 1912, the Park Superintendent paid hunters to kill and trap predators within the park. In 1914, rangers trapped two cougar, 2 wildcats, and 25 marten. Today the fine for doing that same thing would require mortgaging your house and probably jail time for killing animals in a National Park.

Apparently *all* animals in the park are protected. A couple years ago some backpackers stayed at the Paradise Inn a couple days prior to hitting the trail. The food in their packs attracted a mouse, which then proceeded to keep them up all night. Upon asking at the front desk for a mouse trap, they were told it's illegal to kill any and all wildlife in a National Park...even a mouse!

In February of 1925, five big cougars (one male, four females) were killed in three days in the vicinity of Ohanapecosh. The following year, 1926 Park records noted, "due to the trapping of predators by the government hunters of the US Biological Survey, only an occasional cougar was seen." Today that has changed, and there are numerous backcountry sightings.

Close Encounters of the Furry Kind

When encountering animals of any kind, keep your distance. They all hope for handouts, but do not feed them or attempt to touch them. They've never heard they're not supposed to bite the hand that feeds them.

Although it's a remote concern, keep in mind that in some areas, raccoons and skunks can carry rabies, although bats are the most common carrier.

Endangered Species

Endangered species protected by the federal Endangered Species Act residing within the Park are marbled murrelets and spotted owls. During the summer of 1994, nine adult and five juvenile spotted owls were observed in different areas of the park. Four spotted owl nest sites were found in 1994, at elevations between 3,200 and 4,600 feet. Marbled murrelets were observed in only a single location in the park in 1994.

Bull trout (Salvelinus confluentus) is a "candidate species" being considered for listing under the Federal Endangered Species Act.

Feeding the Animals

Do not feed, approach, or try to pet any animal. View them from a safe distance. Remember all animals at the park are wild, and your actions could cause injury to them, yourself or other park visitors. Feeding a baby animal may cause the mother to abandon it, or may cause it to not learn how to forage on its own. Persons feeding wildlife can be fined $100. *(CFR 36:2.2).*

Poaching/Encroaching

With a plethora of logging roads and Forest Service roads coming right up to the Park boundaries, some less than ethical hunters take advantage of the easy accessibility to use the Park as a private hunting preserve. In years past, cat hunting with hounds caused most of the problems. Today an insidious type of bear hunting called "bear baiting" is now being practiced. The hunter feeds the bear over a period of time by depositing large stashes of food until the bear learns there will always be food waiting at a certain spot. Some hunters even go so far as to install a timing/recording device to monitor the bear's feeding habits. Then as if going on a business appointment, the hunter can show up at the appointed time, kill the bear and be on his way without wasting a lot of time.

Some, while technically not setting foot in the Park to do their dirty work, do it within feet of the boundary. With neither the Park nor the State Wildlife Department having sufficient personnel to patrol the boundary at all hours, there are but two other options.

One proposal the Park Service wants, would be a buffer, perhaps ten miles wide, all the way around the Park, where no hunting would ever be permitted. This is their solution to protecting most meandering Park animals. Such a sanctuary would require the approval of the state legislature, the governor and the Department of Natural Resources.

A second, and more rapid solution, is turn in known poachers and rule breakers. The Poacher Hotline number is 1-800-562-5626.

Some recent examples of incidents at the Park are:

In the northern part of the Park, three elk, two cows and a bull, were shot and gutted on the West Fork of the White River. The poachers were caught, and rangers seized the elk, several firearms and a four-wheel vehicle, which later (unfortunately) was returned.

Three hunters' hounds ran a cougar into the Park and treed it. The hunters made no effort to retrieve their dogs. The ranger who investigated was unable to call off the hounds, so he (legally) killed them.

On the north side of the Park, six poachers were given $500 fines, lost their rifles, and were restricted from entering the Park for a specified period of time. Poachers are not all gunmen. Poaching archers have also been apprehended.

Several years ago, a contingent of social dropouts actually constructed buildings of sorts of the eastern edge of the Park, where they proceeded to "live off the land."

Other Mount Rainier Creatures

Amphibians

There are seven species of salamanders and newts, five species of frogs (tree, Cascade, red-legged, spotted and tailed, and one toad (Bufo boreas). The Tailed frog (Ascaphous truii) lives in fast streams. The tadpoles have a suction cup on their chin to help them stay put. Occasionally Western skinks are seen on the east side.

Newts Family		
Salamandridae	Northern rough-skinned newt	Tarichagranulosagranulosa
Salamander Family	Brown or Northwest Salamander	Ambystoma gracile gracile
Ambystomatidae	Long-toed Salamander	Ambystoma macrodactylum
	Pacific Giant Salamander	Dicammptodon ensatus
Lungless Salamander Family		
Plethodontidae	Western Red-backed Salamanader	Plethodon vehiculum
	Van Dyke's Salamander	Plethodon vandykei
	Ensatina	Ensatina eschscholtzi oregonensis
Tailed Frog Family	Tailed Frog	Ascaphus truei
Ascaphidae		
Toad Family	Western Toad	Budo boreas boreas
Bufonidae		
Treefrog Family	Pacific Treefrog	Hyla regilla
Hylidae		

Frog Family	Northern Red-legged Frog	Rana aurora aurora
Ranidae	Cascade Frog	Rana cascadae
	Red-legged frog	Rana aurora

Reptiles

Lizard Family	Northern Alligator Lizard	Elgaria coeruleaus or
Anguidas		Gerrhonotus coeruleus
Boa Family	Northern Rubber Boa	Charina bottae
Boidae		
Garter Snake Family	Northern Garter Snake	Thamnophis ordinoides
Colubridae	Puget Sound Garter Snake	Thamnophis elegans
		nigrescens
	Valley Garter Snake	Thamnophis sirtalis fitichi

Bugs

One problem which hasn't changed at the mountain is the large hungry bug population. In 1929, a party of four men were assigned to the task of draining all small ponds, and oiling all bodies of water that couldn't be drained. In later years, investigation was done into planting varieties of fish known to feed on mosquito larvae. Neither plan had much success.

Butterflies

Three of the most common butterflies at the mountain are from the same family (the Nymphalidae) or Brush Footed butterflies. These flittering brown and yellow butterflies are so named because their front legs are so small they're useless for walking. The most attractive of the three is the Mountain Silver Spot (Argynnis). The bright markings on the underside of its wings accounts for its common name.

Similar in coloring is the Fritillary (Brenthis), but it does not have the silver spots. The American Tortoise-shell (Vanessa) is recognized by the dark chocolate, almost black, color of the underwings which becomes visible as the butterfly folds them up upon alighting.

Also prevalent are the small delicate Common Blue (Lycoena). The bright blue color catches the eye of the observer, but when it alights on a flower, and folds its wings, it shows that the underwings are white, not blue.

One interesting thing about these, is that the adult butterflies may sip the nectar from a variety of flowers, the larvae or catterpillars feed on but one or just a few plants. For instance, the Tortoise-shell has a particular liking for nettle leaves, and the Fritillary feed at night on the leaves of the violet. -*Rainier National Park News*

Butterflies have been seen at the summit.

Salmon, Trout and Charrs - Family Salmonidae

Trout

Cutthroat trout	*Salmo clarki*
Brown trout	*Salmo trutta*
Rainbow trout	*Salmo gairdneri*

Charrs

Brook trout	*Salvelinus fontinalis*
Dolly Varden	*Salvelinus malma*

Fish in Formerly Stocked Lakes

Mowich Lake used to be the "hatchery" where fingerlings were raised to stock all the other lakes in the park. From there the young fish were taken in 5 gallon cans by backpackers or horseback to the other lakes. (The sloshing in the cans kept the dissolved oxygen level up.) Unfortunately stocking of lakes was discontinued in 1972. Some of the descendents are still around however, but not for much longer. Up until the 50's there used to be another fish hatchery at the confluence of the White River and Silver Creek maintained to supply over a million fish annually (brook, rainbow and black spotted trout) to the Park and the adjacent National Forest. Native fish were not found in Mount Rainier's high lakes, but did occur in Park streams and rivers. Of the 97 ponds and lakes with a surface area of 1 acre and greater, 44 were stocked with trout. 37 still contain naturally reproducing trout populations. The stocked fish have been established in the Park waters for so long, that today it would be difficult to evaluate the effects of introduced species on the population of native species.

Fish are a key link in the food chain of the entire park, and with an increase in fish comes an increase in bald eagles, bears and other predators.

Bye Bye, Fish

Until recently "the primary goal for recreational fishing in national parks has been to provide the recreational angler with a quality fishing experience while preserving the natural aquatic ecosystems. "Catch and release" fishing was encouraged as a means of allowing fishermen the thrill of the sport, while allowing the fish to live and multiply.

Mount Rainier's fish are now the most endangered species in the park, since it was decided that they are to be eliminated. Why? Because concerned over a theoretical worldwide decline in amphibians, and after determining that an occasional Mount Rainier fish eats an occasional Mount Rainier salamander for lunch, the decision was made by the park's Resource Specialists that the best way to increase the amphibian population is by killing the fish.

The fish from one lake (Harry Lake) were the first to go. They were gill netted in 1994. The next fish slated to be killed are in Hidden Lake (in the White River watershed), Upper Palisades Lake in the Huckleberry watershed, and

Bench Lake in the Cowlitz watershed. The next areas will be "chummed" to attract the fish. Underwater light traps will be used to capture young fish.

These fish have managed to survive and multiply even though the lakes haven't been stocked since 1972. They have survived their lakes being ice covered all but 4 to 6 months a year, and they have survived bears who fish, but they can't survive bureaucratic logic.

Fortunately for the fish, this killing program won't be carried out without funding. The program's sponsors are hoping to get money ($99,925) to purge the rest of the lakes from the Mount Rainier, Olympic and North Cascades Fund. *(MRNP Project Statement N-17, N-008).* (The Park Service will fund the "public relations" portion of the cost, however.) Many who feel the MRONC Fund has a higher purpose are disappointed to see it used for such a controversial (and unwanted by the public) project.

Further, even though part of the park's justification is because the fish are not native, they also are targeting stream fish. Inlet and outlet streams will be electrofished to remove all fish. *(same report as above).*

There may not be many fish at stake, but there are a lot of fishermen who care about them, and this promises to be an interesting battle to watch.

Also IN the Lakes

A 1973 study of the biotic relationships of Mowich Lake by Gary Lee Larson which was published in Archiv fur Hydrobiolgie found that smaller invertebrates consisted of 8 species of Rotifera. These are microscopic fresh water animals which feed on bacteria, algae, and small bits of organic matter. In their mouths, which are surrounded by fine hairs, the hairs beat in a manner to resemble a tiny pair of revolving wheels, thus the name "rotifer".

There was also one crustacean. Crayfish are abundant in Mowich Lake. Plankton populations were at their maximum between early October and mid-November.

A 1935 report said the bottom of Crescent Lake, near Windy Gap, was covered with "periwinkles."

Pests

Yellowjackets like dry forest duff, usually along forest trails, for their nests. These winged tormentors can be found anywhere around the Park. They're scavengers (meateaters), which is why they like to take on a nice juicy human occasionally. Worse yet, their stinger doesn't come out, and they can sting repeatedly. They're especially bad in August and September.

Yellowjackets figure prominently in Mount Rainier history.

In 1894 when James Longmire and a friend were returning to Longmire from Paradise, their pack horses were spooked when stung by yellowjackets. After getting back to Longmire, the men decided to go back up and get rid of the pests. They got rid of a lot more than they expected. The fire they set got out of hand, and soon the whole ridge was ablaze. The silver snags left from the conflagration became known as the silver forest, and twenty years later, many of the timbers were used to build Paradise Inn.

There are two kinds of ticks at Mount Rainier: wood ticks, which are about 1/4" across, and pinhead size Deer ticks. These tiny time-bombs can carry Lyme Disease, a nasty malady which can cause arthritis, meningitis, neurological problems and/or cardiac arrest. Symptoms can occur between a few weeks to a year after the bite. While not all ticks carry the disease, more cases are being reported in Washington each year. No known cases have been contracted at Mount Rainier, but reported cases are getting closer to the Park every summer.

Reptiles

Three species of garter snake and one rubber boa (Charina bottae) live at Mount Rainier. All are harmless. The boa can be up to 30 inches long, and even though it is the Northwest's most primitive snake, it can swim, burrow, and climb trees. It kills its prey by suffocating it, then swallowing it whole. When attacked, it coils as if to strike but the bobbing "head" is really its tail. The real head is safely hidden under its body.

Alligator lizards (Gerhantus Coverulis principis) are the only lizard in the park. Contrary to their menacing name, they are slow and non-threatening. They lose their tail when something grabs it, then regenerate the cartilage.

Lizard Family Anguidas	Northern Alligator Lizard	*Elgaria coeria or* *Gerrhonotus coeruleus* *principis*
Boa Family Boidae	Northern Rubber Boa	*Charina bottae*
Garter Snake Family Columbridae	Northern Garter Snake	*Thamnophis ordinoides*
	Puget Sound Garter Snake	*Thamnophis elegans* *nigrescens*
	Valley Garter Snake	*Thamnophis sirtalis* *fitichi*

Downstream Wildlife Preserves

Nature Center at Snake Lake

A 54-acre wooded wildlife preserve with park and nature trails which are open daily. No admission charge. Interpretive center, with wetlands displays open weekdays. South 19th and Tyler Street, Tacoma, WA 98405 (206) 591-6439

Northwest Trek Wildlife Park

If the animals weren't out the day you visited the mountain, you can see them any day at Northwest Trek. Six miles Northwest of Eatonville on SR 161, this 635-acre open-air wildlife sanctuary is devoted exclusively to animals native to the Northwest. (Elk, moose, deer, lynx, mountain goats, bobcats, mountain lions, river otters, raccoons and several others.)

A narrated 5-1/2 mile, hour-long electric tram ride allows people to see the wild animals roam free in their natural habitat. The woodsy-compatible architecture includes overlooks from which to see bears and wolves in native settings. The Cheney Interpretive Center features hands-on educational displays. The Visitor Center also houses a gift shop, cafe, and the Forest Theater. There are also 5 miles of nature trails including a paved section for wheelchairs and strollers.

This marvelous park is owned by Metropolitan Park District of Tacoma It was bequeathed by (pediatrician) Dr. David and Connie Hellyer. The park is open daily from mid-February through October; Friday through Sunday and selected holidays the rest of the year. The trams leave hourly beginning at 11 a.m.

Northwest Trek Wildlife Park, 11610 Trek Drive East, Eatonville, WA 98328 (360) 832-6117; Recorded information: (800) 433-TREK.

Nisqually Wildlife Refuge

This 2,817 acre Wildlife Refuge and Wildlife Recreation Area is one of the largest deltas in the state. The tall marsh grass among the many sloughs and branches of the Nisqually provides ideal cover for the many nesting birds which winter over and pass through the area. Each spring and summer, the area comes alive with nesting songbirds, mallards, great blue herons, belted kingfishers, killdeers, quail, swallows, teals, and pied-billed grebes. In the fall and spring, the migratory birds, the ducks, sandpipers, gulls and terns, pass through. Those who winter over here are mallards and pintails. There are over 300 species of birds and wildlife who find a protected habitat at the Refuge.

Interestingly, both the origin and the terminus of the Nisqually river are within sight of each other. From the glacier, you can see the Sound, and vice versa.

This appealing complex (dress warm and take the kids!) includes an observation deck, photo blinds, seven miles of walking trails and an interpretive trail with exhibits. There are environmental education exhibits for families and school groups in the Twin Barns Educational Center. ($ Admission).

Bordered on the north by the Nisqually River, Interstate-5 marks the southern boundary. Another significant aspect of this area is that it was the site of a Hudson's Bay trading post. It was also here that Territorial Governor Isaac I Stevens signed the 1855 Medicine Creek Treaty with several of the local Indian tribes. Disputes over fishing rights granted by that treaty are still not resolved to anyone's satisfaction. The "Treaty Tree", a lone Douglas fir under which stood beside the creek where the treaty was signed was damaged by the construction of Interstate 5, and had to be removed.

Nisqually National Wildlife Reserve Complex, Brown Farm Road, Olympia, WA 98506. Exit #114 off I-5. (360) 753-9467.

Wolf Haven

Wolf Haven, International is a unique organization with several worthy objectives. Their mission is working for wolf conservation through protection of the remaining wild wolves and their habitat, re-establishing wolves in their historic ranges, providing a sanctuary for captive wolves (including an 'Adopt-A-Wolf' package) and a public education program about wolves.

Wolf Ecology classes ($45 per person) are held Saturdays where participants get the opportunity to watch the wolves up close, learn how they communicate using body language, study their family structure, learn about their role as predators, learn the history of wolves in the Northwest, and hear about current wolf management programs.

In an effort to locate wolves, they conduct "howling brigades." Working in teams late at night, usually east of Mount Rainier, surveyors systematically "howl" every mile or so, then await a response. (There have been some, in the Bumping Lake area.)

If you would like to learn to howl like a wolf and take part Howl-in, contact Dr. Paul Joslin at (360) 264-4695. Students can get college credit through an arrangement with the Wildlands Studies Unit at San Francisco State University. Wolf Haven International, 3111 Offut Lake Road, Tenino, WA 98589.

Sanctuary Hours: May through Sept. 10 a.m. to 5 p.m. (last tour begins at 4 p.m.)Howl-Ins Friday and Saturday Evenings 7 p.m. to 9:30 p.m. (Gates open 6:30 p.m.) Adults $6 each, children aged 5-12 $3 each.

Mount Rainier Mammals

Bats and Myotis (Order Chiroptera)
  Bats

Big brown bat	**Eptesicus fescus** (Palisot de Beauvois)
Hoary bat	**Lasiurus cinereus** (Palisot de Beauvois)
Lump-nosed bat	**Plecotus townsendii** Cooper
Silver-haired bat	**Lasionycteris noctivagans** (Le Conte)
Hairy-winged myotis	**Myotis volans** (H. Allen)
Little brown myotis	**Myotis lucifugus**
Yuma myotis	**Myotis yumanensis** (H. Allen)

Carnivores (Order Carnivora)

  Bear

Black bear	**Urus americanus** Pallas

  Bobcat

Bobcat	**Lynx rufus** (Schreber)

  Coyote

Coyote	**Canis Latrans** Say

  Ermine

Ermine	**Mustela erminea** Linnaeus

  Fox

Red fox	**Vulpes fulva** (Desmarest)

  Marten

Pine Marten	**Martes americana** (Turton)

  Mink

Mink	**Mustela vison** Schreber

  Mountain Lion

Mountain Lion	**Felis concolor** (Linnaeus)

  Raccoon

Raccoon	**Procyon lotor** (Linnaeus)

  Skunk

Spotted skunk	**Spilogale putorius** (Linnaeus)
Striped skunk	**Mephitis hudsonica**

  Weasel

Long-tailed weasel	**Mustela frenata** Lichtenstein
Short tailed (Ermine) weasel (also called the Least weasel)	
	Mustela erminea

Moles (Order Insectivora)
  Moles

Coast mole	**Scapanus oraius** True
Townsend mole	**Scapanus townsendii** (Bachman)
Shrew-mole	**Neurotrichus gibbsii** (Baird)

Rabbits and Pika (Order Lagomorpha)

Pika	**Ochotona princeps** (Richardson)
Snowshoe hare	**Lepus americanus** Erxleben

Rodents (Order Rodentia)
  Beaver

Beaver	**Castor canadensis** Kuhn
Mountain beaver	**Apolodontia rufa** (Rafinesque)

    Chipmunks

Townsend chipmunk	**Eutamias townsendii** (Bachman)
Yellow-pine chipmunk	**Eutamias amoenus** (J. A. Allen)

  Gopher

Northern pocket gopher	**Thomomys talpoides** (Richardson)

Marmot
      Cascade hoary marmot   **Marmota caligata** (Eschscholtz)

Mice
      Gapper red-backed mouse   **Clethrionomys gapperi** (Vigors)
      Long-tailed meadow mouse   **Erethizon longicaudus** (Merriam)
      Pacific jumping mouse   **Zapus trinotatus** Rhodes
      White-footed deer mouse   **Peromyscus manicualatus** (Wagner)

Porcupine
      Porcupine   **Erethrizon dorsatum** (Linnaeus)

Rat
      Western Bushy-tailed woodrat   **Neotoma cinerea** (Ord)

Squirrels
      Cascades golden-mantled ground squirrel
            Callospermophilus saturatus (Rhodes)
      Northern flying squirrel   **Glaucomys sabrinus** (Shaw)
      Douglas squirrel, chickaree   **Tamiasciurus douglasii** (Bachman)

Voles
      Heather vole   **Phenacomys Intermedius** Merriam
      Oregon vole/Oregon meadow mouse
            Microtus oregoni (Bachman)
      Water vole/water rat   **Microtus richardsoni** (DeKay)
      Townsend vole/Townsend meadow mouse
            Microtus townsendii (Bachman)

Shrews (Order Insectivora)
   Shrews
      Dusky shrew   **Sorex obscurus** Merriam
      Marsh shrew   **Sorex bendirii** Merriam
      Masked shrew   **Sorex cinereus** Kerr
      Trowbridge shrew   **Sorex trowbridgii** Baird
      Vagrant shrew   **Sorex vagrans** Baird

Deer, Elk and Mountain Goat (Order Artiodactyla)
   Deer
      Black tail deer   **Odocoileus hemionus columbianus**
      Mule deer   **Odocoilcus hemionus hemionus**
   Elk
      Canadian (Roosevelt) Elk   **Cervus Canadensis** (Erxleben)
   Goat
      Mountain goat   **Oreamnos americanus** (Blainville)

Birds

There are 147 species of birds within the Park. The favorites are probably the Clark's Nutcracker, Thrushes, Kinglets, Chickadees, Nuthatches, Ptarmigan, grouse, finches, grosbeaks, gray Jays, Steller's Jays Mountain bluebirds and eagles.

Golden eagles (Aquila chrysaotos) are plentiful in the park. In fact if you do much hiking to some of the high country with its accompanying bird's-eye views, you'll feel like an eagle yourself. Look for eagles at Sunrise, Stevens Canyon, Paradise, the Colonnades and Crystal Mountain. They also skim along river courses looking for fish. Bald eagles (Haliacctus leucocephalus leucocephalus) are occasionally seen in the Park too. They're the Northwest's largest bird of prey, standing 3 feet tall, weighing 16 pounds, and having a wingspan of 6 to 8 feet.

The ptarmigan is an Arctic Grouse which rarely flies, even for a short distance. Found on slopes above timber line, the Rainier white tailed ptarmigan changes plumage according to season. From winter white, to spotted, barred or mottled, the ptarmigan ranges between 6,000 to 8,000 feet elevation, camoflaged from most detection.

A few birds have even made it to the summit. A Pine siskin was found dead on the summit, as was a curlew. Hummingbirds occasionally buzz climbers high on the glaciers of the mountain. A seagull was found in the "bird room" of the summit ice caves in 1970.

Surprisingly, even with the number of species birds in the Park, few are so-called song birds. Thrushes, although numerous, are rarely heard; meadowlarks are rare and warblers stay only briefly. Most of the lyrical birds are the little winter wren, the water ouzel, chickadees, song sparrows, kinglets and juncos.

Listen for God's sense of humor while hiking. The olive-sided flycatcher has a compelling call: "Oh SEE me."

Owls

Owls have infra-red sensors, just perfect for night flight. One ranger wrote a report of a large horned own which came at him with extended talons, and missed his Stetson by inches. (It was probably a great horned owl. They're not shy of people.) Another ranger wrote of not being able to make it back to Longmire by nightfall, and as he hurried through the woods in the dark, a pygmy owl practiced strafing runs by repeatedly coming at him and pushing his hat down over his eyes. Even more bizarre, years ago, a screech owl zoomed in and sat on A. E. Kitchen's pipe as he lay in his sleeping bag.

If you can't tell owls by sight, listen for a sound clue. The great horned owl generally gives six or eight "hoos." Other Mount Rainier 'hooting' owls are the barred and the northern spotted owl. The barred owl's call sometimes sound like "who-cook-for-you?" The spotted owl hoot is a distinctive series of three or four "hoos," which sound somewhat like a small dog barking.

The latest data indicates there is a total population of 14 spotted owls which inhabit the park. Spotted owls stand about a foot high and have a wingspan of 19 inches. They have no ear tufts. They have white spots on dark brown upper parts, and white under parts spotted with brown.

Contrary to what has been said about them having to live in old growth forest, apparently they don't all have to. We found one report of an old timer who discovered a pair of adults and two young ones living in the alders and vine maples near Ohanapecosh. He killed the oldest bird, and its stomach contained the remains of a flying squirrel.

Mount Rainier's forests are full of an owl's favorite food, mice, wood rats, and flying squirrels. The forests themselves are ideal habitats - they're old growth and filled with broken trees and old snags that provide ideal nesting spots.

Owls in the Park are:

Great horned owl	Bubo virginianus lagophonus
California pigmy owl	Glacidium gnoma californicum
Spotted owl	Strix occidentalis occidentalis
Saw- whet	Cryptoglax acadica acadica
Kennicott screech owl	Otus asio kennicottii
Long eared owl	(very rarely seen)

The Birds of Mount Rainier National Park

1. Great blue heron (V)
2. Mallard (V)
3. Pintail (V)
4. Barrow's goldeneye (R)
5. Harlequin duck (R)
6. Common merganser (R)
7. Goshawk (R)
8. Cooper's hawk (R)
9. Red-tailed hawk (R)
10. Swainson's hawk (R)
11. Golden hawk (R)
12. Bald eagle (V)
13. Marsh Hawk (V)
14. Sparrow hawk (R)
15. Blue grouse (R)
16. Ruffed grouse (R)
17. White-tailed ptarmigan (R)
18. Killdeer (V)
19. Spotted sandpiper (R)
20. Solitary sandpiper (V)
21. California gull (V)
22. Band-tailed pigeon (R)
23. Screech owl (R)
24. Great horned owl (R)
25. Pygmy owl (R)
26. Northern spotted owl (R)
27. Common nighthawk (R)
28. Black swift (R)
29. Vaux's swift (R)
30. Rufous hummingbird (V)
31. Allen's hummingbird (V)
32. Calliope hummingbird (R)
33. Belted kingfisher (R)
34. Red-shafted flicker (R)
35. Pileated woodpecker (R)
36. Lewis' woodpecker (R)
37. Yellow-bellied sapsucker (R)
38. Hairy woodpecker (R)
39. Downy woodpecker (R)
40. "Red-breasted" sapsucker (R)
41. Northern 3-toed woodpecker (R)
42. Traill's flycatcher (R)
43. Western flycatcher (R)
44. Olive-sided flycatcher (R)
45. Horned lark (R)
46. Violet-green swallow (R)
47. Tree swallow (R)
48. Gray jay (R)
49. Steller's jay (R)
50. Black-billed magpie
51. Common raven (R)
52. Common crow (V)
53. Clark's nutcracker (R)
54. Mountain chickadee (R)
55. Chestnut-backed chickadee (R)
56. White -breasted nuthatch (R)
57. Red-breasted nuthatch (R)
58. Brown creeper (R)
59. Dipper (R)
60. Winter wren (R)
61. Robin (R)
62. Varied thrush (R)
63. Hermit thrush (R)
64. Swainson's thrush (R)
65. Mountain bluebird (R)
66. Townsend's solitaire (R)
67. Golden-crowned kingle (R)
68. Water pipit (R)
69. Cedar waxwing (R)
70. Warbling vireo (R)
71. Yellow Warbler (R)
72. Myrtle warbler (R)
73. Townsend's warbler (R)
74. MacGillivray's warbler (R)
75. Wilson's warbler (R)
76. Redwinged blackbird (R)
77. Brewer's blackbird (R)
78. Western tanager (R)
79. Evening grosbeak (R)
80. Cassin's finch (R)
81. Pine grosbeak (R)
82. Gray-crowned rosy finch (R)
83. Pine siskin (R)
84. Red crossbill (R)
85. Oregon junco (R)
86. Chipping sparrow (R)
87. White crowned sparrow (R)
88. Fox sparrow (R)
89. Lincoln's sparrow (R)
90. Song sparrow (R)

The Future of the Park

Happy Birthday, Big Girl

We don't know her age, but we do know March 2, 1999 will be her 100th anniversary as a National Park. It promises to be a blast, though not volcanic, we hope!

What would be some fun birthday events? Put on your thinking caps, and send your ideas to Superintendent Briggle.

Here's one for starters. For several years, a popular feature at the Sunrise Visitor Center, was a display of original Mount Rainier art. On display (for about two months) were the best oil paintings, watercolors, photographs, sketches, and any other creative renditions of the Big Beauty that Northwest artists and photographers could come up with. Visitors particularly appreciated the display on days the mountain wasn't out, and the renderings had to substitute for the real thing.

What's your best idea?

Long Range Plan

The plan which will determine the "who, what, when, where, why and how" of the park for the next fifteen to twenty years is now in the making. The plan, called the "General Management Plan" contains many elements which will directly affect the way the public accesses and has use of the various park facilities and components. Items under discussion for inclusion are:

► defining a new purpose of the park (shifting from "use and enjoyment" to "protection for future generations").

► limiting and regulating day hikers by mandating day hike permits

► controlling the number of visitors entering at the gates

► more control over adjacent wilderness areas

►"orderly growth of gateway communities" and land management plans for surrounding public and private land owners.

► provide a transit system instead of private vehicles within the park.

► Instigating a winter use fee.

► plus other proposals such as closing the Mowich Lake Road at the Park boundary, closing access via Forest Service roads, and a variety of other items.

The plan is being coordinated by the Park Service's Denver office, although final approval of the plan rests with Superintendent Briggle.

Public input meetings were held in Seattle, Tacoma, Morton, Enumclaw, Yakima and Eatonville in November, 1994, however they were poorly attended (87 people total at all 6 locations) and considering the importance of the final plan, much more public input is needed. To be notified of future meetings or developments, contact Friends of Mount Rainier (next page), and/or Eric Walkinshaw at the park (c/o MRNP, Longmire, WA 98397.)

Friends of Mount Rainier

Friends of Mount Rainier is a new organization organized to promote the *responsible use*, by the public, of Mount Rainier National Park, in accord with the establishing legislation of March 2, 1899, which dedicated and set apart Mount Rainier National Park as a public park "for the benefit and enjoyment of the people."

Why is such an organization needed? Because of the handful of other Mount Rainier-oriented organizations that there are, the others have different agendas, primarily environmental and/or political. No one is looking out for the interests of those who believe that public has a right to (responsibly) *use* the park. We define "use", as any lawful and legitimate activity which would bring about benefit and enjoyment to park visitors without damaging the resources. That includes everything from camping, hiking and climbing, to picnicking, photography, fishing, cross-country skiing, and any of the other multitude of ways people can enjoy and partake in the many wonderful recreational, educational, scientific and spiritual experiences the mountain has to offer.

We want to be sure that the public will be well informed and represented when any plans which will affect use of the park are under consideration. This includes any further road closures, trail closures, removal of historic buildings, restriction of private vehicles, killing the fish, and limiting of backcountry use.

Such changes are currently under consideration in the park's proposed General Management Plan. This plan will affect the public's use of the park for the next two decades, and we feel it is imperative that the decisions be made not just by a handful of unaffected distant park personnel from Denver, or Washington, D.C., or local park professionals (however well intentioned they may be), but who will move on to other parks, or to retire to live elsewhere in the country, and leave us with an inaccessible or severely use-restricted park.

We're the opposite of "NIMBY's" (the **N**ot **I**n **M**y **B**ack **Y**ard folks) who don't want things in their "backyard". We *love* having Mount Rainier in our backyard, and we want a say in what goes on there if it's going to affect us or restrict our use, and the "benefit and enjoyment" congress intended for the public to have.

While we all care deeply about the environment and protecting the natural resources for future generations, we will leave those battles to the organizations already ably representing those interests. Our specialty will be to focus on and represent the public's right of *responsible* use of the park *now* in our lifetime.

If you want to receive a year's quarterly newsletter, and be notified of any meetings or hearings which are concerned with public use, please send $12 to:

Friends of Mount Rainier
Post Office Box 92
Issaquah, WA 98027
400

Enabling Legislation, Act of March 2, 1899

5. Mount Rainier National Park

An Act To set aside a portion of certain lands in the State of Washington, now known as the " Pacific Forest Reserve," as a public park to be known as " Mount Rainier National Park," approved March 2, 1899 (30 Stat. 993)

Be it enacted by the Senate and House of Representatives of the United States of America in Congress assembled, That all those certain tracts, pieces, or parcels Mount Rainier of land lying and being in the State of Washington, and Wash., established. within the boundaries particularly described as follows, lished. to wit: Beginning at a point three miles east of the. northeast corner of township numbered seventeen north, of range six east of the Willamette meridian; thence south through the central parts of townships numbered Location. seventeen, sixteen, and fifteen north, of range seven east of the Willamette meridian, eighteen miles more or less, subject to the proper easterly or westerly offsets, to a point three miles east of the northeast corner of township numbered fourteen north, of range six east of the Willamette meridian; thence east on the township line between townships numbered fourteen and fifteen north, eighteen miles more or less to a point three miles west of the northeast corner of township fourteen north, of range ten east of the Willamette meridian; thence northerly, subject to the proper easterly or westerly offsets. eighteen miles more or less, to a point three miles west of the northeast corner of township numbered seventeen north, of range ten east of the Willamette meridian (but in locating said easterly boundary, wherever the summit of the Cascade Mountains is sharply and well defined, the

101

said line shall follow the said summit, where the said
summit line bears west of the easterly line as herein
determined); thence westerly along the township line between said townships numbered seventeen and eighteen
to the place of beginning, the same being a portion of
the lands which were reserved from entry or settlement
Vol. 27, p. 1063. and set aside as a public reservation by proclamation of
the President on the twentieth day of February, in the
year of our Lord eighteen hundred and ninety-three, and
of the Independence of the United States the one hundred
and seventeenth, are hereby dedicated and set apart as a
public park, to be known and designated as the " Mount
Rainier National Park," for the benefit and enjoyment
of the people; and all persons who shall locate or settle
upon or occupy the same, or any part thereof, except as
hereafter provided, shall be considered trespassers and be
removed therefrom. (U.S.C., title 16, sec. 91.)

Secretary of the Interior to make regulations, etc.   SEC. 2. That said public park shall be under the exclusive control of the Secretary of the Interior, whose duty
it shall be to make and publish, as soon as practicable,
such rules and regulations as he may deem necessary or
proper for the care and management of the same. Such
regulations shall provide for the preservation from injury or spoliation of all timber, mineral deposits, natural
curiosities, or wonders within said park, and their reten-
Leases; disposition of funds. (Amended by 39 Stat. 535, as amended. See pp. 9–12.) tion in their natural condition. The Secretary may, in
his discretion, grant parcels of ground at such places in
said park as shall require the erection of buildings for
the accommodation of visitors; all of the proceeds of said
leases, and all other revenues that may be derived from
any source connected with said park, to be expended
under his direction in the management of the same and
the construction of roads and bridle paths therein. And
through the lands of the Pacific Forest Reserve adjoining
Rights of way to park granted through Pacific Forest Reserve. said park rights of way are hereby granted, under such
restrictions and regulations as the Secretary of the In-
terior may establish, to any railway or tramway company
or companies, through the lands of said Pacific Forest
Reserve, and also into said park hereby created, for the
purpose of building, constructing, and operating a railway, constructing and operating a railway or tramway
line or lines, through said lands, also into said park.[1]
Protection of fish and game. Trespassers. He shall provide against the wanton destruction of the
fish and game found within said park, and against their
capture or destruction for the purposes of merchandise
or profit. He shall also cause all persons trespassing upon
the same after the passage of this act to be removed
therefrom, and generally shall be authorized to take all
such measures as shall be necessary to fully carry out the
objects and purposes of this act. (U.S.C., title 16,
sec. 92.)

[1] Repealed, so far as relates to lands within Mount Rainier National park, by 46 Stat. 1044.   See p. 109.

SEC. 3. That upon execution and filing with the Secre- Grant of land to tary of the Interior, by the Northern Pacific Railroad Northern Pacific railroad in ex-Company, of proper deed releasing and conveying to the change for land United States the lands in the reservation hereby created, relinquished. also the lands in the Pacific Forest Reserve which have been heretofore granted by the United States to said company, whether surveyed or unsurveyed, and which lie opposite said company's constructed road, said company is hereby authorized to select an equal quantity of non-mineral public lands, so classified as nonmineral at the time of actual Government survey, which has been or shall be made, of the United States not reserved and to which no adverse right or claim shall have attached or have been initiated at the time of the making of such selection, lying within any State into or through which the railroad of said Northern Pacific Railroad Company runs, to the extent of the lands so relinquished and re-leased to the United States: *Provided*, That any settlers *Proviso.* Lieu lands to on lands in said national park may relinquish their rights settlers. thereto and take other public lands in lieu thereof, to the same extent and under the same limitations and condi-tions as are provided by law for forest reserves and national parks. (U.S.C., title 16, sec. 93.)

SEC. 4. That upon the filing by the said railroad com- Patent. pany at the local land office of the land district in which any tract of land selected and the payment of the fees prescribed by law in analogous cases, and the approval of the Secretary of the Interior, he shall cause to be exe-cuted, in due form of law, and deliver to said company a patent of the United States conveying to it the lands so selected. In case the tract so selected shall at the time of selection be unsurveyed, the list filed by the company at Description in selection list of the local land office shall describe such tract in such man- unsurveyed land, ner as to designate the same with a reasonable degree of etc. certainty; and within the period of three months after the lands including such tract shall have been surveyed and the plats thereof filed by said local land office, a new selection list shall be filed by said company, describing such tract according to such survey; and in case such tract, as originally selected and described in the list filed in the local land office, shall not precisely conform with the lines of the official survey, the said company shall be permitted to describe such tract anew, so as to secure such conformity.

SEC. 5. That the mineral-land laws of the United States Mineral land laws extended are hereby extended to the lands lying within the said to park. (Amended by 35 reserve and said park. Stat. 365. See p. 107.)

Act of Legislature of Washington, approved March 16, 1901, ceding to the United States exclusive jurisdiction over Mount Rainier National Park in the State of Washington. (Laws of Wash-ington, 1901, p. 192)

Exclusive jurisdiction shall be, and the same is hereby. ceded to the United States over and within all the territory which is now or may hereafter be included in that tract of land in the State of Washington set aside for the purposes of a national park and known as " Rainier National Park," saving, however, to the said State the right to serve civil or criminal process within the limits of the aforesaid park in suits or prosecutions for or on account of rights acquired, obligations incurred, or crimes committed in said State, but outside of said park, and saving further to the said State the right to tax persons and corporations, their franchises and property, on the lands included in said park: *Provided, however,* That jurisdiction shall not vest until the United States, through the proper officer, notifies the governor of this State that they assume police or military jurisdiction over said park.

An Act To accept the cession by the State of Washington of exclusive jurisdiction over the lands embraced within the Mount Rainier National Park, and for other purposes, approved June 30, 1916 (39 Stat. 243)

Mount Rainier National Park, Wash. Sole jurisdiction over, ceded by Washington to United States. State process, etc.

Be it enacted by the Senate and House of Representatives of the United States of America in Congress assembled, That the provisions of the act of the legislature of the State of Washington, approved March sixteenth, nineteen hundred and one, ceding to the United States exclusive jurisdiction over the territory embraced within the Mount Rainier National Park, are hereby accepted and sole and exclusive jurisdiction is hereby assumed by the United States over such territory, saving, however, to the said State the right to serve civil or criminal process within the limits of the aforesaid park in suits or prosecution for or on account of rights acquired, obligations incurred, or crimes committed in said State but outside of said park, and saving further to the said State the right to tax persons and corporations, their franchises and property, on the lands included in said park. All the laws applicable to places under the sole and exclusive jurisdiction of the United States shall have force and effect in said park. All fugitives from justice taking refuge in said park shall be subject to the same laws as refugees from justice found in the State of Washington. (U.S.C., title 16, sec. 95.)

Jurisdiction of Washington western district. SEC. 2. That said park shall constitute a part of the United States judicial district for the western district of Washington, and the district court of the United States in and for said district shall have jurisdiction of all offenses committed within said boundaries. (U.S.C., title 16, sec. 96.)

Punishment under Washington laws. SEC. 3. That if any offense shall be committed in the Mount Rainier National Park, which offense is not prohibited or the punishment for which is not specifically provided for by any law of the United States, the offender shall be subject to the same punishment as the laws of the State of Washington in force at the time of the commission of the offense may provide for a like

offense in said State; and no subsequent repeal of any
such law of the State of Washington shall affect any
prosecution for said offense committed within said park.
(U.S.C., title 16, sec. 97.)

SEC. 4. That all hunting or the killing, wounding, or Hunting, fishing,
etc., prohibited.
capturing at any time of any wild bird or animal, except
dangerous animals when it is necessary to prevent them
from destroying human lives or inflicting personal injury, is prohibited within the limits of said park; nor
shall any fish be taken out of the waters of the park in
any other way than by hook and line, and then only at
such seasons and in such times and manner as may be
directed by the Secretary of the Interior. That the Sec- Regulations, etc.
retary of the Interior shall make and publish such rules
and regulations as he may deem necessary and proper for
the management and care of the park and for the protection of the property therein, especially for the preservation from injury or spoliation of all timber, mineral
deposits other than those legally located prior to the passage of the Act of May twenty-seventh, nineteen hundred Vol. 35, p. 365.
See p. 107.
and eight (Thirty-fifth Statutes, page three hundred and
sixty-five), natural curiosities, or wonderful objects
within said park, and for the protection of the animals
and birds in the park from capture or destruction, and to
prevent their being frightened or driven from the park;
and he shall make rules and regulations governing the
taking of fish from the streams or lakes in the park.
Possession within said park of the dead bodies, or any Evidence of
violations.
part thereof, of any wild bird or animal shall be prima
facie evidence that the person or persons having the same
are guilty of violating this Act. Any person or persons, Punishment for
violations.
or stage or express company, or railway company, who
knows or has reason to believe that they were taken or
killed contrary to the provisions of this Act and who
receives for transportation any of said animals, birds, or
fish so killed, caught, or taken, or who shall violate any
of the other provisions of this Act or any rule or regula-
tion that may be promulgated by the Secretary of the
Interior with reference to the management and care of
the park or for the protection of the property therein,
for the preservation from injury or spoliation of timber,
mineral deposits other than those legally located prior to
the passage of the Act of May twenty-seventh, nineteen Vol. 35, p. 365.
See p. 107.
hundred and eight (Thirty-fifth Statutes, page three hundred and sixty-five), natural curiosities, or wonderful
objects within said park, or for the protection of the animals, birds, or fish in the park, or who shall within said
park commit any damage, injury, or spoliation to or upon
any building, fence, hedge, gate, guidepost, tree, wood,
underwood, timber, garden, crops, vegetables, plants,
land, springs, mineral deposits other than those legally
located prior to the passage of the Act of May twenty-
seventh, nineteen hundred and eight (Thirty-fifth Stat-

utes, page three hundred and sixty-five), natural curiosities, or other matter or thing growing or being thereon or situated therein, shall be deemed guilty of a misdemeanor and shall be subject to a fine of not more than $500 or imprisonment not exceeding six months, or both, and be adjudged to pay all costs of the proceedings. (U.S.C., title 16, sec. 98.)

Forfeiture of guns, traps, etc.

SEC. 5. That all guns, traps, teams, horses, or means of transportation of every nature or description used by any person or persons within said park limits when engaged in killing, trapping, ensnaring, or capturing such wild beasts, birds, or animals shall be forfeited to the United States and may be seized by the officers in said park and held pending the prosecution of any person or persons arrested under charge of violating the provisions of this Act, and upon conviction under this Act of such person or persons using said guns, traps, teams, horses, or other means of transportation, such forfeiture shall be adjudicated as a penalty in addition to the other punishment provided in this Act. Such forfeited property shall be disposed of and accounted for by and under the authority of the Secretary of the Interior. (U.S.C., title 16, sec. 99.)

SEC. 6. That the United States District Court for the Western District of Washington shall appoint a commissioner who shall reside in the park and who shall have jurisdiction to hear and act upon all complaints made of any violations of law or of the rules and regulations made by the Secretary of the Interior for the government of the park and for the protection of the animals, birds, and fish, and objects of interest therein, and for other purposes authorized by this Act.

Commissioner. Appointment, authority, etc.

Judicial powers in violations of rules, etc

Such commissioner shall have power, upon sworn information, to issue process in the name of the United States for the arrest of any person charged with the commission of any misdemeanor, or charged with a violation of the rules and regulations, or with a violation of any of the provisions of this Act prescribed for the government of said park and for the protection of the animals, birds, and fish in said park, and to try the person so charged, and, if found guilty, to impose punishment and to adjudge the forfeiture prescribed.

Appeals.

In all cases of conviction an appeal shall lie from the judgment of said commissioner to the United States District Court for the Western District of Washington, and the United States district court in said district shall prescribe the rules of procedure and practice for said commissioner in the trial of cases and for appeal to said United States district court. (U.S.C., title 16, sec. 100.)

Procedure in criminal cases.

SEC. 7. That any such commissioner shall also have power to issue process as hereinbefore provided for the arrest of any person charged with the commission within said boundaries of any criminal offense not covered by the provisions of section four of this Act to hear the evidence introduced, and if he is of opinion that probable cause is shown for holding the person so charged for trial shall cause such person to be safely conveyed to a secure place of confinement within the jurisdiction of the United States District Court for the Western District of Washington, and certify a transcript of the record of his proceedings and the testimony in the case to said court, which court shall have jurisdiction of the case: *Provided*, That the said commissioner shall grant bail in all cases bailable under the laws of the United States or of said State. (U.S.C., title 16, sec. 101.) *Proviso. Bail.*

SEC. 8. That all process issued by the commissioner shall be directed to the marshal of the United States for the western district of Washington, but nothing herein contained shall be so construed as to prevent the arrest by any officer or employee of the Government or any person employed by the United States in the policing of said reservation within said boundaries without process of any person taken in the act of violating the law or this Act or the regulations prescribed by said Secretary as aforesaid. (U.S.C., title 16, sec. 102.) *Service of process.*

SEC. 9. That the commissioner provided for in this Act shall be paid an annual salary of $1,500, payable quarterly: *Provided*, That the said commissioner shall reside within the exterior boundaries of said Mount Rainer National Park, at a place to be designated by the court making such appointment: *And provided further*, That all fees, costs, and expenses collected by the commissioner shall be disposed of as provided in section eleven of this Act. (U.S.C., title 16, sec. 103.) *Salary.[2] Proviso. Residence. Disposal of fees.*

SEC. 10. That all fees, costs, and expenses arising in cases under this Act and properly chargeable to the United States shall be certified, approved, and paid as are like fees, costs, and expenses in the courts of the United States. (U.S.C., title 16, sec. 105.) *United States fees, etc.*

SEC. 11. That all fines and costs imposed and collected shall be deposited by said commissioner of the United States, or the marshal of the United States collecting the same, with the clerk of the United States District Court for the Western District of Washington. (U.S.C., title 16, sec. 104.) *Deposit of fines and costs.*

SEC. 12. That the Secretary of the Interior shall notify, in writing, the governor of the State of Washington of the passage and approval of this Act. *Acceptance of cession.*

Excerpt from "An Act Making appropriations for sundry civil expenses of the Government for the fiscal year ending June 30, 1909, and for other purposes," approved May 27, 1908 (35 Stat. 365)[3]

The location of mining claims under the mineral land laws of the United States is prohibited within the area *Mount Rainier National Park, Wash.*

---

[2] Salary of United States commissioner amended by current Appropriation Acts.
[3] Amends section 5, 30 Stat. 993. See p. 103.

Mining locations prohibited.
Proviso.
Prior rights not affected.

of the Mount Rainier National Park, in the State of Washington: *Provided, however,* That this provision shall not affect existing rights heretofore acquired in good faith under the mineral land laws of the United States to any mining location or locations in said Mount Rainier National Park. (U.S.C., title 16, sec. 94.)

Mount Rainier National Park. Acceptance of donated lands, etc.
(Repealed by 46 Stat. 1028, but subject matter covered by U.S.C., title 16, sec. 6, 41 Stat. 917. See p. 13.)

Excerpt from "An Act Making appropriations for sundry civil expenses of the Government for the fiscal year ending June 30, 1918, and for other purposes," approved June 12, 1917 (40 Stat. 152)

The Secretary of the Interior is authorized to accept patented lands or rights of way over patented lands in the Mount Rainier National Park that may be donated for park purposes. (U.S.C., title 16, sec. 106.)

An Act To revise the boundary of the Mount Rainier National Park in the State of Washington, and for other purposes, approved May 28, 1926 (44 Stat. 668)

Mount Rainier National Park, Wash. Boundary modified. Description.

Be it enacted by the Senate and House of Representatives of the United States of America in Congress assembled, That the boundary of the Mount Rainier National Park is hereby changed so as to read as follows: Beginning at park boundary monument numbered 1, established on the east line of section 4, township 17 north, range 7 east, Willamette meridian, by a survey of the boundaries of Mount Rainier National Park, Washington, by the General Land Office, plat dated April 17, 1909; thence southerly along the present west park boundary line as established by said survey, being the midtownship line of range 7 east, to its intersection with the south bank of Nisqually River; thence easterly along said bank to its intersection with the present south park boundary line at a point east of park boundary monument numbered 28, as established by said survey, being the township line between townships 14 and 15 north; thence easterly along said south park boundary line to the southeast corner of the present park boundary; thence northerly along the present east park boundary line to park boundary monument numbered 59 as established by said survey, being the midtownship line of range 10 east; thence due north to the south bank of White River; thence northeasterly along said bank to a point due east of park boundary monument numbered 67; thence due west to said monument numbered 67; thence westerly along the present north park boundary line, as established by said survey, being the township line between townships 17 and 18 north, to its intersection with the north bank of Carbon River; thence westerly along said bank to a point due north of park boundary monument numbered 1; thence due south to place of beginning; and all of those lands lying within the boundary above described are hereby included in and made a part of the Mount Rainier National Park; and all of those lands of the present Mount Rainier National Park excluded from the park are hereby included in and made a part of the Rainier National Forest, subject to all national forest laws and regulations. (U.S.C., 6th supp., title 16, sec. 107.) Excluded lands added to Rainier National Forest.

SEC. 2. That the provisions of the Act of March 2, 1899, entitled, "An Act to set aside a portion of certain lands in the State of Washington, now known as the Pacific Forest Reserve,' as a public park, to be known as the ' Mount Rainier National Park,' " the Act of June 10, 1916, entitled "An Act to accept the cession by the State of Washington of exclusive jurisdiction over the lands embraced within the Mount Rainier National Park, and for other purposes," the Act of August 25, 1916, entitled "An Act to establish a national park service, and for other purposes," and all Acts supplementary to and amendatory of said Acts are made applicable to and extended over the lands hereby added to the park: *Provided*, That the provisions of the Act of June 10, 1920, entitled "An Act to create a Federal power commission; to provide for the improvement of navigation; the development of water power; the use of the public lands in relation thereto; and to repeal section 18 of the River and Harbor Appropriation Act, approved August 8, 1917, and for other purposes," shall not apply to or extend over such lands. (U.S.C., 6th supp., title 16, sec. 108.) Laws extended to. Vol. 30, p. 993. See p. 101.
Vol. 39, p. 243. See p. 104.
Vol. 39, p. 535. See p. 9.
Proviso.
Federal Power Act not applicable.
Vol. 41, p. 1063.

Excerpt from "An Act To provide for uniform administration of the national parks by the United States Department of the Interior, and for other purposes," approved January 26, 1931 (46 Stat. 1044)

The provisions of the Act of March 2, 1899 (30 Stat. 993), granting rights of way, under such restrictions and regulations as the Secretary of the Interior may establish, to any railway or tramway company or companies for the purpose of building, constructing, and operating a railway, constructing and operating a railway or tramway line or lines, so far as the same relate to lands within the Mount Rainier National Park, Washington, are hereby repealed: *Provided, however*, That nothing herein shall be construed so as to prohibit the Secretary of the Interior from authorizing the use of land in said park under contract, permit, lease, or otherwise, for the establishment and operation thereon of a tramway or cable line, or lines, for the accommodation or convenience of visitors and others. (U.S.C., 6th supp., title 16, sec. 92a.) Grants of rights of way, repealed. Within Mount Rainier, Wash. Vol. 30, p. 993, repealed. See p. 101.
Proviso. Exception.

An Act To extend the south and east boundaries of the Mount Rainier National Park, in the State of Washington, and for other purposes, approved January 31, 1931 (46 Stat. 1047)

Be it enacted by the Senate and House of Representatives of the United States of America in Congress assembled, That the tract of land within the following-described boundaries be, and the same is hereby, excluded Mount Rainier National Park, Wash. Lands added to.

from the Rainier National Forest and is hereby added to and made a part of the Mount Rainier National Park, in the State of Washington:

Description. Beginning at a point on the present east boundary of Mount Rainier National Park one and one quarter miles southerly from the northeast corner of the said park as fixed by the Act of May 28, 1926 (44 Stat. 668); thence extending east to the summit of the hydrographic divide between Silver Creek and White River; thence along the summit of Crystal Mountain to the summit of the Cascade Mountains; thence southerly along the summit of the Cascade Mountains to a point in section 20, township 15 north, range 11 east, Willamette meridian, whence flow the waters of Bumping River to the east and Carlton and Cougar Creeks to the south and west; thence southwesterly along the summit of the divide between Carlton Creek and the waters flowing into the main fork of Ohanapecosh River to the quarter section line of section 9, township 14 north, range 10 east, Willamette meridian; thence westerly along the quarter section line of sections 9, 8, and 7 to the west boundary of said township; thence due west to the right or west bank of Muddy Fork of the Cowlitz River; thence northerly along the right bank of said Muddy Fork to a point exactly due east of post numbered 34 on the south boundary of Mount Rainier National Park as surveyed in 1908; thence due west to said post numbered 34; thence along the boundary of said park as surveyed in 1908 to post numbered 35; thence easterly along the south boundary of said national park as surveyed in 1908 to the southeast corner thereof; thence northerly along the east boundary of said national park as surveyed in 1908 to post numbered 59; thence along the east boundary of said park as revised by the Act of May 28, 1928, supra, northerly to the point of beginning. (U.S.C., 6th supp., title 16, sec. 109.)

Regulations applicable to additions. SEC. 2. All laws applicable to and in force within the Mount Rainier National Park as of the date hereof, and all regulations issued pursuant thereto, are hereby made applicable to and extended over the land added to the said park by this Act: *Provided*, That no fee or charge shall be made by the United States for the use of any roads in said park built or maintained exclusively by the State of Washington. (U.S.C., 6th supp., title 16, sec. 110.)

Proviso. Free roadways.

17. Mount Rainier National Park

**An Act Authorizing the Secretary of the Interior to acquire on
behalf of the United States Government all property and
facilities of the Rainier National Park Company, approved September 21, 1950 (64 Stat. 895)**

Be it enacted by the Senate and House of Representatives of the United States of America in Congress assembled, That the Secretary of the Interior is hereby authorized, in his discretion and under such terms and conditions as he may deem proper, to acquire on behalf of the United States, at a price considered by him to be reasonable, all of the property and facilities of the Rainier National Park Company within the Mount Rainier National Park used for the purpose of furnishing accommodations and conveniences to the public visiting said park, excluding, however, such facilities of the company as are used in furnishing transportation for the said park. Rainier National Park Company. Acquisition of property by Interior Department.

SEC. 2. There is hereby authorized to be appropriated, out of any money in the Treasury not otherwise appropriated, such sum or sums as may be necessary to carry out the provisions of this Act. Appropriation authorized.

**An Act To authorize the Secretary of the Interior to provide a
headquarters site for Mount Rainier National Park in the
general vicinity of Ashford, Washington, and for other purposes, approved June 27, 1960 (74 Stat. 219)**

Be it enacted by the Senate and House of Representatives of the United States of America in Congress assembled, That, in order to apply the present headquarters site in Mount Rainier National Park to public use for which it is more suitable and to provide a headquarters for the park, the Secretary of the Interior is authorized to provide a park headquarters in the general vicinity of Ashford, Washington, and for such purpose to acquire in this vicinity, by such means as he may deem to be in the public interest, not more than three hundred acres of land, or interest therein. (16 U.S.C. § 110a [Supp. II].) Mount Rainier National Park. Headquarters site.

SEC. 2. The headquarters site provided pursuant to this Act shall constitute a part of Mount Rainier National Park and be administered in accordance with the laws applicable thereto. (16 U.S.C. § 110b [Supp. II].)

151

Legislative Brief

An Act to set aside a portion of certain lands in the State of Washington now known as the "Pacific Forest Reserve," as a public park to be known as "Mount Rainier National Park, " approved March 2, 1899 (30 Stat. 993).

Act of Legislature of Washington, approved March 16, 1901, ceding to the United States exclusive jurisdiction over Mount Rainier National Park in the State of Washington (Laws of Washington, 1901, p. 192).

An Act to accept the cession by the State of Washington of exclusive jurisdiction over the lands embraced within the Mount Rainier National Park, and for other purposes, approved June 30, 1916 (39 Stat. 243).

Excerpt from "An Act Making appropriations for sundry civil expenses of the Government for the fiscal year ending June 30, 1909, and for other purposes," approved May 27, 1908 (35 Stat 365). Amends Sec. 5, Stat 993.)

Excerpt from "An Act Making appropriations for sundry civil expenses of the Government for the fiscal year ending June 30, 1918, and for other purposes," approved June 12, 1917 (40 Stat. 152).

An Act To revise the boundary of the Mount Rainier National Park in the State of Washington, and for other purposes, approved May 28, 1926 (44 Stat. 668).

Excerpt from "An Act To provide for uniform administration of the national parks by the United States Department of the Interior, and for other purposes," approved January 26, 1931 (46 Stat. 1044).

An Act To extend the south and east boundaries of the Mount Rainier National Park, in the State of Washington, and for other purposes, approved January 31, 1931 (46 Stat. 1047).

An Act Authorizing the Secretary of the Interior to acquire on behalf of the United States Government all property and facilities of the Rainier National Park Company, approved September 21, 1950 (64 Stat. 895).

An Act to authorize the Secretary of the Interior to provide a headquarters site for Mount Rainier National Park in the general vicinity of Ashford, Washington, and for other purposes, approved June 27, 1960 (74 Stat. 219).

BIBLIOGRAPHY

A. H. Denman, *The Name of Mt. Tacoma*, Rotary, Lions and Kiwanis Clubs of Tacoma, 1924

A Heritage of Fishing: The National Park Service Recreational Fisheries Program, 1993

American Alpine Journal, Vol 2., #3, 1935 p. 320

Anderson, Louise Koehler, *Orting Valley Yesterday and Today Including McMillin and Alderton.* Ms Guided Adventures, Heritage Quest, July 1987

Bates, Malcolm, *Cascade Voices, Conversations with Washington Mountaineers,* Cloudcap, 1993

Bonney, W.P., *History of Pierce County*, 3 Volumes, Pioneer Historical Publishing Co., 1927

Bridges, Woodrow, *Scooting Skyward*, Smith Kinney Co., Tacoma, 1912

Brockman, C. Frank, The *Sun is Shining at Panorama Point.*

Brockman, C. Frank, *The Story of Mt. Rainier National Park,* 1940

Crandell, D.R. and Mullineaux, D.R., *Volcanic Hazards at Mount Rainier*, Geological Survey Bulletin 1238 (1967)

Crandell, D.R., *the Geological Story of Mount Rainier,* Geological Survey Bulletin 1292 (1969).

Decker, Robert W & Barbara B, *Mountains of Fire*, Cambridge University Press, 1991

Driedger, Carolyn. *A Visitor's Guide to Mount Rainier Glaciers.* PNW Nat'l Parks & Forests Assoc. 1986.

Decisions of the United States Geographic Board - Mount Rainier National Park, WA No. 29 - June 30, 1932

Federal Writers' Project, The New Washington, A Guide to the Evergreen State, Portland, OR, 1950

Fiske, R.S., Hopson, C.A., and Waters, A.C., *Geology of Mt. Rainier National Park, Washington,* U.S. (1963); Geological Survey, Professional Paper No. 444.

Gates, Charles M., *Readings in Pacific Northwest History Washington 1790-1895,* Pub. by University Bookstore, Seattle, 1941

Grater, Russell K., *Grater's Guide to Mt. Rainier National Park*, Binsford & Mort, Portland, 1948

Gustafson, Carl E., *Wapiti Populations in and adjacent to MRNP.* Archaeological and Ethnographic Evidence, Dec. 1983, Washington State University. Gustafson, Carl E., Wapiti Populations in and adjacent to MRNP. Archaeological and Ethnographic Evidence, Dec. 1983, Washington State University.

Haines, Aubrey, *Mountain Fever, Historic Quests of Mount Rainier*, Oregon Historical Soc. 1962

Halliday, Wm.R. & Anderson, Jr., Chas. H., *The Paradise Ice Caves,* 1972

Harper's Weekly, Jan 13, 1894 XXXVIII, 35-8

Harris, Steven L., *Fire Mountains of the West: The Cascade and Mono Lake Volcanoes.* Mountain Press Publishing Co., 1988

Harris, Stephen. *Fire and Ice: The Cascade Volcanoes.* Seattle: The Mountaineers and Pacific Search Press, 1980.

Hazard, Joseph T., *The Glacier Playfields of Mount Rainier National Park,* Western Pub. Co.,1920

Hitchman, Robert, *Place Names of Washington,* Washington Historical Society, 1985

Ingraham, E.S., *Pacific Forest Reserve*

Kirk, Ruth, *Exploring Mount Rainier,* 1968

Lakes of Washington, Volumes 1 & 2. Washington Dept. of Mines. 1947

Lenggenhager, Werner, *Historical Markers and Monuments of the State of Washington*

Meany, Edmund S., *Mt. Rainier, a Record of Exploration* (1916) 325 pp., illustrated Mt. Rainier, Seattle, 1895.

Meany, Edmund S., *Origin of Washington geographic names,* Seattle, University of Washington, 1923

Molenaar, Dee, *The Challenge of Rainier.* Mountaineers, Seattle, 1979

Nadeau, Gene. *Highway to Paradise: A Pictorial History of the Roadway to Mount Rainier.* Valley Press, Puyallup, 1983.

Nature Notes, National Park Society, Mount Rainier National Park, vols #6, #11

Northwest Parks & Wildlife Magazine, Igloos, January, 1994

Outdoors Magazine, Recreational Recycling, April 1992

Phillips, James W., *Washington State Place Names,* UW Press, Seattle, 1971

Prater, Gene, *The Mount Rainier Cloud Cap, Summit Magazine,* May 1966

Reese, Gary Fuller, *Origins of Pierce County Place Names,* published for the Friends of the Tacoma Public Library, R & M Press, Tacoma, WA 1989

Schmoe, F. C., *Our Greatest Mountain. A Handbook for Mount Rainier National Park,* G.P. Putnam's Sons, NY, 366 p. ill., 1925

Sparkman, LaVonne M., *The trees were so thick there was Nowhere to look but up! Early Settlers of Morton and Mineral Washington,* 1989, A Maverick Publication

Sparkman, LaVonne M., *From homestead to Lakebed. Kosmos: The Town that Drowned,* 1994, Maverick Publications

Taylor, Walter P., *Mammals and Birds of Mount Rainier National Park,* Dept. of the Interior, 1927

The Encyclopedia of Information on Mount Rainier National Park, 1932

The Mountaineer, Fifty Golden Years of Mountaineering, 1906-1956, Seattle Mountaineers.

The Mountaineer, (1948, 1949, 1950, 1951, 1952, 1953, 1954, 1955, 1958, 1959, 1960)

The New Washington, A Guide to the Evergreen State, Federal Writers' Project, Washington State Historical Society, Binsford & Mort, 1941

The NSS Bulletin, Journal of Caves and Karst Studies, Volume 56, Dec. 1994, Number 2, Pub. by The National Speleological Society

Thurston County Place Names, Thurston Co. Historical Commission, Olympia, WA., Nov. 1992

Tilden, Freeman, The National Parks, Alfred A. Knopf, NY, 1986

Tolbert, Caroline L., *History of Mount Rainier National Park,* Lowman & Hanford, Seattle, WA 1933

Washington State Place Names, UW Press, Seattle, James W. Phillips, 1971

Watson, Emmett, *Seattle Times* column September 27, 1992

Williams, John. *The Mountain That Was "God." New* York & London: G. P. Putnam's Sons, 1911

Wootan, Judy, *The Life and Times of Copper Creek,* pub by Lorene Co, 1993

Wood, Charles, *Volcanoes or North America, United States and Canada,* Cambridge University Press 1990, 350 pages.

MOUNTAIN DIRECTORY
Useful Phone Numbers on the Road to Mount Rainier
(Outside the Park)

Emergency

Police, Fire, Medical	911
Aircraft Accidents	(206) 431-2000
Drunk Driving Hotline	(800)22DRUNK
Forest Fire Reports Only	(800) 562-6010
Lewis County Sheriff	(800) 562-5620
National Weather Service	(206) 526-6087
Pierce County Sheriff's Department	(800) 562-9800
Poison Center (24-hour service)	(800) 542-6319
Poaching Hotline	(800) 562-5626
Washington State Patrol	911
Washington State Patrol (Lewis County)	(800) 383-7805
WSP Road Information	(360) 593-2157

National Park Service

System Support Office (former Pacific Northwest Regional Office)	
909 - 1st Avenue, Seattle, WA 98104-1060	(206) 220-4000
Recreation information	(206) 553-0170

National Weather Service Forecast	(360) 526-6087

Mount Rainier National Park (Park Headquarters),

Tahoma Woods, Star Route, Ashford 98304	(360) 569-2211
Ranger Station Extensions (* = summers only)	
Carbon River	*249
Longmire	275
Nisqually (entrance)	274
Ohanapecosh	238
Paradise	272/209
Paradise Visitor Center	277
Sunrise	*244
White River	*239

Outside Trail Systems

Avalanche Forecast	(360) 526-6677
Outdoor Recreation Info Center - 915 2nd Ave., Seattle	(206) 220-7450

Forest Service

Pacific Northwest Regional Office (Portland)	(503) 326-2877
Gifford Pinchot National Forest, Vancouver, WA 98668	(360) 750-5001
Mt. Baker-Snoqualmie National Firest, Mountlake Terrace	(206) 775-9702
National Camping Reservation Service - Gifford Pinchot	(800) 280-2267
National Camping Reservation Service - Other	(800) 280-2267
Naches Ranger District, Naches, WA 98937	(509) 653-2205
Randle Ranger District, Randle WA 98377	(360) 497-7565
Packwood Ranger District, Packwood, WA 98361	(360) 494-5515

Forest Service offices, continued...
Oak Creek Habitat Management Area,
    16601 Highway 12, Naches, Wa 98937   (509) 653-2390
Wenatchee National Forest, Wenatchee 98801   (509) 662-4335
Whitewater Hotline (April - November)   (206) 526-8530

Federation Forest State Park - Hwy. 410, E. of Enumclaw   (360) 663-2207
Mt. Tahoma Trails
Ashford   (360) 569-2451

Washington State Department of Fish and Wildlife
Director's Office
    600 Capitol Way N, GJ-11, Olympia, WA 98501   (360) 902-2250

Nisqually Indians
Council, Yelm 459-6780
Delta Association, Olympia   (360) 357-3792
Land Trust, Yelm   (360) 923-1808
Nature Center, Olympia   (360) 456-0890
Wildlife Refuge, Olympia   (360) 753-9467

Public Services
Cash Machines
Ashford Valley Grocery (BP)   (360) 569-2560
Blanton's Market - downtown Packwood   (360) 494-6101
Key Bank, Eatonville
Prairie Security Bank, Eatonville

Doctors
Dr. Thomas Van Eaton (Eatonville)   (360) 832-6106
Graham Medical Clinic (Graham)   (206) 847-9166
Randle Clinic (Randle)   (360) 497-3333

Dentist
Dr. Stephen Cossalman (Eatonville)   (360) 832-6102

Hospitals
Good Samaratin (Puyallup)   (206) 848-6661
Morton General Hospital   (360) 496-5112

Pharmacies
Eatonville   (360) 832-3121
Morton   (360) 496-5902
Packwood - Tatoosh Pharmacy   (360) 494-6666

RV Repair Parts
Packwood True Value, Packwood   (360) 494-2131

Shuttle Van Service
Rainier Overland Transportation Co.   (360) 569-0851

Towing
Bill's Towing (Yelm)	(360) 458-5963
El Camino Auto Center	(360) 832-3248
Fred's Towing Service (Enumclaw)	(800) 201-3100
Olin Johnson (Eatonville)	(360) 832-4524

Fuel

From Nisqually Entrance
Ashford Valley Grocery (BP)	(360) 569-2560
Elbe Mall (Chevron)	(360) 569-2772
Milltown (Eatonville)	(360) 832-4279

From Southeast (Ohanapecosh Entrance)
Cougar & Val's Packwood BP, Packwood	(360) 494-5167
Randle One-Stop, Randle	(360) 497-3261

Northeast Side (White River Entrance)
Greenwater General Store & Station, (E. of Enumclaw)	(360) 663-2357
Trout Lodge Chevron, Highway 12, Naches	(509) 672-2219
Eagle Rock Resort, Chinook Pass	(509) 658-2905

Lodging In the Park

Mount Rainier Guest Services
Paradise Inn and The Inn at Longmire	(360) 569-2275

Lodging Near the Park

Lodging Southwest Side (Nisqually Entrance)
Alexander's Manor, Ashford	(360) 569-2300
Alexander's Country Inn, Ashford	(800) 654-7615
Bob's Mt. Rainier Cabins, Ashford	(360) 569-0843
Cabin at the Berry, Ashford	(360) 569-2628
Eagle's Nest Motel, Alder	(360) 569-2533
Evergreen Motel, Morton	(360) 496-5407
Gateway Inn, Ashford	(360) 569-2506
Hershey Homestead Lodging, Ashford	(360) 569-2789
Hobo Inn, Elbe	(360) 569-2505
LaGrand Motel, LaGrand	(360) 832-6643
Medici Motel, Randle	(800) 697-7750
Milltown Village Motel, Eatonville	(360) 832-3200
Mount Haven, Ashford	(360) 569-2594
Mountain Village Inn, Ashford	(360) 569-2517
Nisqually Lodge, Ashford	(360) 569-8804
Rainier Country Cabins, Ashford (Lodging/Housekeeping)	(360) 569-2355
Rainier Overland Lodge, Ashford	(360) 569-0851
Seasons Motel, Morton	(360) 496-6835
Tanwax Lake Resort, Eatonville	(360) 879-5533
The Cabinette	(360) 569-2954
The Getaway Motel, Elbe	(360) 569-2663
Wild Berry Cabins, Ashford	(360) 569-2628

Lodging Northwest and Northeast Sides (White River Entrance)

Alta Crystal Resort near Greenwater	(360) 663-2500
Crystal Mountain Resort, Crystal Mountain	(360) 663-2265
Double K Mountain Ranch, Goose Prairie	no phone
(write: Double K Mountain Ranch, Goose Prairie, WA 98929)	
Mountain View Inn, Buckley	(800) 582-4111
Whistlin' Jack Lodge, Naches	(509) 658-2433

Lodging Southeast Side (Ohanapecosh Entrance)

Chateau Inn, Packwood	(360) 494-9224
Cowlitz River Lodge, Packwood	(360) 494-4444
Mountain View Lodge and Motel, Packwood	(360) 494-5555
Packwood Hotel, Packwood	(360) 494-5431
Packwood Inn, Packwood	(360) 494-5500
Peters Inn, Packwood	(360) 494-4000
Royal Inn Motel, Packwood	(360) 494-2191
Tatoosh Motel, Packwood	(360) 494-9226
White Pass Village Inn, White Pass	(509) 672-3131
Woodland Motel, Packwood	(360) 494-6766

Bed & Breakfasts

Alexander's Manor, Ashford	(360) 569-2300
Ashford Mansion B & B, Ashford	(360) 569-2739
Betty's Bed & Breakfast Yelm	(360) 458-3883
The Botzer House, Mossyrock	(360) 983-3792
Growly Bear Bed & Breakfast, Ashford	(360) 569-2339
The Hershey Homestead, Ashford	(360) 569-2897
Jasmer's Guest House, Ashford	(360) 569-2682
Log Cabin, Yelm	(360) 458-4385
Mill Village RV Park, Eatonville	(360) 832-4279
Mountain Meadows Inn B & B, Ashford	(360) 569-2788
Mount Rainier Country Cabins, Ashford	(360) 569-2355
Old Mill House Bed & Breakfast, Eatonville	(360) 832-6506
Patty's Bed & Breakfast, Eatonville	(360) 832-3124
Porter House B&B, 3155 Porter Street, Enumclaw	(360) 825-7671
Salish Mansion, Yelm	(360) 458-7741
St. Helens Manor House, Morton	(360) 498-5243
The Cabin at the Berry, Ashford	(360) 569-2628
The Wild Mint, Ashford	(360) 569-2235

Convention Centers (Group Facilities)

Alta Crystal Resort, Greenwater	(360) 663-2500
Mounthaven Cabins, Ashford	(360) 569-2594
The Lodge at Mt. Rainier, Ashford	(360) 569-2312
Tatoosh Meadows, Packwood	(800) 294-2311

Cottages - Rustic

John Sparrow, Ashford	(360) 569-2954
Mounthaven Cabins, Ashford	(360) 569-2594
Rainier Country Cabins, Ashford	(360) 569-2355

Cottages (Rustic) continued...

Rainier Overland, Ashford	(360) 569-0851
Tatoosh Meadows, Packwood	(800) 294-2311
The Lodge at Mt. Rainier, Ashford	(360) 569-2312
Wellspring Spa, Ashford	(360) 569-2514
Whittaker's Bunkhouse, Ashford	(360) 569-2439

RV Parks & Campgrounds

Ashford Valley Grocery/RV Park/gas/propane	(360) 569-2560
Eagle's Nest Motel, Eatonville, RV hookups	(360) 569-2533
Gateway Inn, Ashford, RV hookups/groceries	(360) 569-2506
Harmony Good Sam RV Park, Mayfield Lake, fishing	(360) 983-3804
Maple Grove Park, Randle, RV hookups, fishing, golf	(360) 497-2741
Milltown Center, Eatonville, RV hookups	(360) 832-4279
Mounthaven, Ashford, 20 full-utility hookups	(360) 569-2594
NACO West Rainier RV Park, Randle, hookups/groceries	(360) 494-7975
Packwood RV Park, Packwood, RV hookups, fishing	(360) 494-5145
Roy's Motel and RV, Morton	(360) 496-5000
The Meadows Campground, Randle	(800) 697-7750
Twelve West, 35 RV/campsites w/full utilities, Rimrock	(509) 248-2276

Mountaineering Supplies (enroute to the Mountain)

Sweet Peaks Mountaineering 38104 SR 706E, Ashford	(360) 569-2339
Elbe Mall Mini Mart, Elbe	(360) 569-2772
Coast to Coast, Morton	(360) 496-6444
Crystal Mountain Sport Shop, Crystal Mountain	(360) 663-2239
Growly Bear, Ashford	(360) 569-2720
Optimum Energy, Yelm	(360) 458-4602
Packwood True Value, Packwood	(360) 494-2131
Randle One Stop, (fishing supplies) Randle	(360) 497-3261
The Outback, Yelm	(360) 458-4618
The Survival Center, McKenna	(360) 458-4333
White Pass Sports Hut, Packwood	(360) 494-7321

Firewood

Carl Rotter, Eatonville	(360) 832-6465

Laundromats

Highlander Tavern & Laundromat, Ashford	(360) 569-2953
Milltown Center Laundromat, Eatonville	(360) 832-4279
Maple Grove Park, Randle	(360) 497-2741
Mounthaven RV Park, Ashford	(360) 569-2594
Packwood RV Park, Packwood	(360) 494-5145

Public Showers

Highlander Tavern & Laundromat, Ashford	(360) 569-2953
Milltown Center Laundromat, Eatonville	(360) 832-4279
Packwood RV Park, Packwood	(360) 494-5145
Henry M. Jackson Visitor Center - Paradise	no telephone

Food

Bakeries

Sweet Peaks Mountaineering 38104 SR 706E, Ashford   (360) 569-2339
Black Diamond Bakery, 32805 Railroad Av, Blk Diamond (360) 886-2741

Berry Pies

Copper Creek Restaurant, Ashford	(360) 569-2326
Gateway Inn, Ashford	(360) 569-2506
Sweet Peaks Bakery, Ashford	(360) 569-2720
Wild Berry Restaurant, Ashford	(360) 569-2628

Berries - Wild Blackberries

Carl Rotter, Eatonville   (360) 832-6465

Delicatessens

Baumgartner's, 1008 E. Roosevelt, Enumclaw   (360) 825-1067

Desserts & Sweets

Alpenstock, Greenwater	(360) 663-2445
Ambrosia, Packwood	(360) 494-4422
Rainier Overland Restaurant, Ashford	(360) 569-0851
Sweet Peaks, Ashford	(360) 569-2720
Whittaker's Bunk House, Ashford	(360) 569-2439

Espresso Shops

Ambrosia, Packwood	(360) 494-4422
The Gold Bar, Yelm	(360) 458-6368
Ma and Pa Ruckers, Packwood	(360) 494-2651
The Smiling Cow, Eatonville	(360) 832-7269
2nd Street Java, Morton	(360) 496-5235
Whittaker's Bunkhouse, Ashford	(360) 569-2439

Groceries

Ashford - The Country Store	(360) 569-2373
Ashford Valley Grocery	(360) 569-2560
Buckley	
Eatonville - Plaza Family Grocery	(360) 832-6151
Eatonville - Eatonville Market	(360) 832-4551
Enumclaw - Safeway	(360) 825-5023
Elbe Mini Mall	(360) 569-2772
Glenoma - Gene and Barb's Groceries	(360) 497-5225
Glenoma - Redmon's Glenoma	(360) 498-5240
Morton - Reeds Sentry	(360) 496-5021
Packwood - Blantons Market	(360) 494-6101
Randle - Fischer Shopping Center	(360) 497-5355
White Pass	(509) 453-8731

Restaurants

Aaron's Ark, Eatonville	(360) 832-6633
Adams & St. Helens, Randle	(360) 497-5556

Restaurants (continued)...

Adventures Restaurant, Morton	(360) 496-6660
Alexanders, Ashford	(360) 569-2300
Arnold's Country Inn, Yelm	(360) 458-3977
Big Bottom Bar and Grill, Randle	(360) 497-9982
Chateau Inn, Packwood	(360) 494-9294
Club Cafe, Packwood	(360) 494-5977
Cody Cafe, Main Street, Morton	(360) 496-5787
Copper Creek Restaurant, Ashford	(360) 569-2326
Crystal Cookhouse and Saloon at Crystal Mountain	(360) 663-2265
Crystal Mountain Summit House Restaurant	(360) 663-2265
Culinary Chameleon, Yelm	(360) 458-4071
Gateway Inn, Ashford	(360) 569-2506
Irish Rose Cafe, Mossyrock	(360) 983-3636
Joeys, Rainier	(360) 446-2525
Lake Mayfield Restaurant and Gifts, Silver Creek	(360) 985-2584
Ma & Pa Ruckers, Packwood	(360) 494-2651
McKenna Y, McKenna	(360) 458-5050
Mount Rainier Railroad Dining Co., Elbe	(360) 569-2505
Packwood Pizza, Packwood	(360) 494-4900
Peters Inn, Packwood	(360) 494-4000
Rainier Overland Restaurant, Ashford	(360) 569-0851
Road House Inn, Morton	(360) 496-5029
Tall Timber Restaurant, Randle	(360) 497-2991
Twelve West , Rimrock	(509) 248-2276
Victorias, Eatonville	(360) 832-4033
Village Inn, White Pass	(509) 672-3131
Whistlin' Jack, Naches	(509) 658-2433
White Pass Summit House Restaurant	(509) 672-3111
Wild Berry, Ashford	(360) 569-2628

Gift Shops/Souvenirs

Alpine Gallery, Ashford	(360) 569-2754
Blue Star, Ashford	(360) 569-2968
Cimino's, Eatonville	(360) 832-3273
Crystal Mountain Sport Shop, Crystal Mountain	(360) 663-2239
Gateway Inn, Ashford	(360) 569-2506
Little Tahoma Gallery, Ashford	(360) 569-2885
Mains Mountain Center - Morton	(360) 496-5823
Midici Gifts - Randle	(360) 497-7700
Mount Rainier Guest Services - Longmire	(360) 569-2411
Mount Rainier Guest Services - Paradise	(360) 569-2413
Mount Rainier Guest Services - Sunrise	(360) 663-2574
Mains' Mountain Center, Morton	(360) 496-5823
Packwood Toys, Packwood	(360) 494-5633
Painter's Art Gallery, Ashford	(360) 569-2644
Paul Chalk's Mountainscapes, 252nd & Meridian, Graham	(206) 847-7722
Shapes of Clay, Graham	(206) 847-6454
Our Mountain Ways, Packwood	(360) 985-2233
Rainier Country Originals, Ashford	(360) 569-2737

Gift Shops/Souvenirs (continued)...
Sweetbriar Hollow, Randle   (360) 497-3535
Treasures by Diane, Ashford   (360) 569-0843
Wapiti Woolies, Greenwater   (800) 766-5617
Whistlin' Jack, Naches   (509) 658-2433

Horseback Riding
Alta Crystal, Greenwater   (360) 663-2500
Crystal Mountain Corral, Crystal Mountain   (360) 663-2589
Indian Creek Corral, White Pass   (509) 925-2062
EZ Times Horse Rentals, Elbe   (360) 569-2449
Pierce County Chapter-Back Country Horsemen
    4314 - 350th St. E., Eatonville, WA 98328
Sahara Creek Horse Camp, Ashford

Llama Rentals
Llama Tree Ranch, Ashford & Packwood   (360) 491-5262
Mt. Son Llama Expeditions, Orting   (360)893-LAMA

Pack Mule Drivers
Jane Burnell, Ashford   (360) 569-2675

Steam Train
Scenic Rides - Mount Rainier Scenic Railroad   (360) 569-2588
The Cascadian Dinner Train   (360) 569-2588

Film Developing - 1 Hour Processing
Speedy 1-hour Photo, Spanaway   (206) 537-0538

Index

winter access, 292
winter road travel, 293
Winthrop, Theodore, 26, 116
Winthrop Glacier, 45, 116,
146, 309
Wolf Bauer, 29, 251
Wolf Haven, 391
wolves, 382, 391
Wonder Road, 285
Wonderland Trail, 105, 149,
155, 160, 261, 273, 335
Wonderland Trail guide
book, 274
wood alphabet, 11
world's highest lake, 232
world's tallest Christmas tree,
16
World War II, 27, 289
World War II Memorial, 141
World Wide Web, 314
worst climbing accident, 248
WPA (Works Project
Administration), 31
Wright Memorial, 141

Y

Yakima Park, 68
year round staff, 83
yellowjackets, 388
Yelm Prairie, 4
Yelm Trail, 4
youngest climbers, 237

Z

zip codes, 109
Zug, Engineer. John, 6

Photo by Charles H. Anderson, Jr.

Mount Rainier Merchandise

VIDEOS

Mount Rainier:
The Wonderland Trail
If you've ever done or thought of doing the Big Trail, this video shows what it's like. Great to relive the trip. $24.95

The Fire Below Us
by Michael Lieneau, a Mt. St. Helens survivor. To see what it's like to be in a mudflow, get this film! This is far and away the BEST film out of the St. Helens blast. $24.95

Mt. St. Helens,
Behind the Dome
This video takes you behind the lava dome and into the mysterious world of the ice caves forming there. You see inside the caves. $24.95

CAPS, CAPS, CAPS

choice of two styles,
canvas and poly,
and choice of two slogans:

(1) I'd rather be in Paradise at Mount Rainier or

(2) When I'm at Mount Rainier I'm in Paradise

Colors available:
poly hats come in 7 colors: red, royal blue, navy, Kelly green, all white, black and gray   poly caps $9.95
                    both styles adjustable - one size fits all
canvas hat colors are: natural color crown with blue bill/blue button or red bill/ red button   canvas caps $11.95

MAPS

MOLENAAR MAP

Acclaimed as the most accurate artistic portrayal of the mountain. An oblique view, incredibly detailed. This is one every Mount Rainier fan should own. Get it rolled if you want to frame it.

$6.50 folded/$8.50 rolled

EARTHWALK MAP

5-color *waterproof* topographic map that's a must if you intend to hike at the mountain. It's our favorite and we recommend it highly.

$6.95

NEW!! A FOOTHILLS MAP

What a find! A new map of the Elbe/ Tahoma State Forests put out by the Washington State Department of Natural Resources. Shows every logging road & every trail plus trailheads, campgrounds and huts. Includes Elbe Hills ORV Trail System, Sahara Creek/Nicholson Horse Trail System and Mount Tahoma Ski Trails. A must for recreationalists.

$2.25

MOUNT RAINIER BANDANA
An accurate topo map screened onto 22 x 22 100% cotton. Great to use as headband, pot holder, BIG hankie, sling for elves
$8.25

MOUNT RAINIER IN RELIEF

**Three-dimensional map
of Mount Rainier**
All the information of a flat map, plus a
scale model of the mountain and terrain
accurately and realistically reproduced on
durable vinyl. Available framed or
unframed. The framed map comes with a
rich two-tone matte, precut for keepsake
photos and/or postcards set in a solid oak
frame. Size 21-1/2" x 18"

Olympic National Park map also available (size of Olympic map is 25" x 27")
price of Olympic map is the same as Rainier
Framed map $35.00   Unframed map $13.00

Model Mount Rainier
Mount Rainier Affectionados will
love this precise minature stone-like
topographic model of the mountain.
Perfect for your desk or mountain
exhibit.

$36.00

**Want a Fantasy Mount Rainier Experience
right where you are?**

Toss a bottle of Tahoma Pure Glacier Water in
the freezer till ice crystals form, pour it in a metal
Sierra cup, put on some clammy wet clothes, go
outside and stand in front of a fan. Close your
eyes, and Voila!
Of course you could always drink it chilled
from a champagne glass, but we're simulating
Mount Rainier here.
Tahoma Pure Glacier Water
by the 1 liter bottle $1.59
(write for case price)
(Shipping $1.00 *extra* for single bottle,
Sorry, but the stuff weighs like water.)

WONDERLAND STUFF

WONDERLAND T's
All T-shirts are 50/50 heavtweight poly cotton blend.
Adult sizes S:(34-36) Medium (38-40) Large 42-44 XL (46-48)
All art in full color.   Shirts $19.95

WONDERLAND TRAIL PATCH
Celebrate your accomplishment with this beautiful patch for your pack or jacket. These are only sold to those who have completed the trail.

$12.95

CERTIFICATE OF COMPLETION
A beautiful full-color certificate personalized with your name and the highlights of your trip. They're laminated, suitable for framing. Your name in foil.
$12.95

BOOKS, BOOKS, BOOKS

MURDER ON THE MOUNT
(Mount Rainier, that is!)
If you love (1) Mount Rainier and (2) a good murder mystery, this is a book for you! Written by Sandy Dengler, author of 65 books and wife of Bill Dengler, Chief of Interpretation at MRNP, the descriptions of the points around the mountain where the story takes place are so vivid you'll picture every detail!

$8.95

DISCOVERING THE WONDERS OF THE WONDERLAND TRAIL
Whether you want to do the trail all at once or do it piecemeal, this is THE ultimate trail guide. It tells everything you need to know to do the trip as safely and easily as possible. Buy it as soon as you start your planning.
$12.95

THE BIG FACT BOOK ABOUT MOUNT RAINIER
Need a spare copy of this book for your favorite Mount Rainier fan? We'll be glad to autograph it   **$17.95**

And what's *your* best Mount Rainier Story?

In the course of researching this book, I unearthed many wonderful, incredible, hair-raising, tragic, and hilarious happenings (not all in the same story, of course). While most were too long for inclusion in this book, I tucked them all in the computer, and am already at work on that project. It will be a book of the untold, little known or seldom told tales of Mount Rainier, entitled, *If the Mountain Could Talk,* and will contain the human history of the mountain.

If you have any interesting stories about the mountain, or if your ancestors or acquaintances did, or if you have any great photos or historical memorabilia, please drop me a line. If you want to be notified when the book is out, let me know that too.

Thanks, Bette

FUN STUFF

Luminous Star Finder

Star buffs and students can master the constellations and the zodiac with this glow-in-the-dark best seller

$5.95 each or
Set of 10 Star Finders $49.95

Seasonal Star Chart Guide
A comprehensive guide with the charts of the sky printed in 4 colors for easy location and identification of the visible stars. Includes directions and position tables for locating planets. The star finder printed on the cover with luminous ink makes the guide ideal for outdoor nightime use

$15.00

CELESTIAL STAR GLOBE

Demonstrates the relationships of earth, stars, planets, and galaxies. A three dimensional star finder for learning names, shapes and locations of the constellations. Shows constellations, stars to 5th magnitude, major nebulae, bright star clusters and Milky Way. Includes earth globe, moveable sun, chrome meridian ring and horizontal mounting and Study Guide. 12" in diameter

$134.95

Send order to:

Dunamis House
P. O. Box 321
Issaquah, WA 98027

Name_____

Telephone (_____)_____

Address_____

City_____State____ Zip_____

Quantity	Item	Color/size	Price	Total

Check which card

☐ **VISA** (13-16 Numbers) ☐ **MasterCard** (16 Numbers) ☐ **AMERICAN EXPRESS** Card (15 Numbers)

| 1 | 2 | 3 | 4 | 5 | 6 | 7 | 8 | 9 | 10 | 11 | 12 | 13 | 14 | 15 | 16 |

EXPIRATION DATE:

Bank Name on Card _____

Cardholder's Signature Required _____

Subtotal _____

WA. tax 8.5% _____

Shipping _____

Total _____

Do you want your books autographed? ☐ yes ☐ no

Shipping: Up to $15.00 = $2.50; $16. - $25.00 = $4.00; $26- $99 = $5.50;
$100 or more, shipping FREE

Larry Filley photo

The author many moons ago on a 1964 climb of Castle and Pinnacle